Flower E
from the
Witch's Garden

"An exceptionally talented man, whose words are as beautiful as the flowers he explores, Nicholas Pearson has now created a must-have book for anyone interested in spirituality, magick, and the subtle use of plants. Profound and engaging, this book is a worthy and important addition to any flower essence library."

CANDICE COVINGTON, AUTHOR OF
ESSENTIAL OILS IN SPIRITUAL PRACTICE

"*Flower Essences from the Witch's Garden* is one of the most extensive compendiums on flower essences that I have ever read. Not only is there an in-depth exploration of a whopping 100 essences, but Nicholas also shares his extensive knowledge of the magick of essences that includes discussions of plant spirits, devas, the alchemy of essences, and so much more. If you read only one book on flower essences, look no further, because *Flower Essences from the Witch's Garden* has it all."

PAM MONTGOMERY, AUTHOR OF *PLANT SPIRIT HEALING*

"This book offers an important resource to the world of flower essences and fills a unique niche for students of this healing modality. Nicholas provides empowering tools for creating our own garden magick and getting to know familiar plant allies in a new and dynamic way. Weaving inspiration and practical guidance, this is a book you will not only benefit from along your personal healing journey but will also enjoy savoring to the last page. A treasured reference in my library for years to come!"

EMILY RUFF, EXECUTIVE DIRECTOR OF
THE SAGE MOUNTAIN BOTANICAL SANCTUARY

"An enchanting combination of medicine and magick. From describing the humble origins of flower essences to sharing practical guidance, magickal formulas, and personal insight, this book will enlighten both the beginner and those that are already enjoying the transformational effects of flower essences. The flower essence directory is an indispensable resource."

"An in-depth and detailed book about co-creating at the devic level. Through this magickal work, Pearson practically and intuitively connects us to the energetic medicine of flower essences, which first and foremost treat the spirit. He reminds us that we are a world in need of spiritual medicine."

"When I think of the term *witch,* I think of its etymology—wit (to know; wisdom)—and the feminine-style knowing that comes from deep listening. For those of us whose mission is to forge paths for scientific and mainstream accessibility of clinical flower essence therapy, *Flower Essences from the Witch's Garden* reminds us, in rich detail, to keep our wit aligned with the spiritually animated world of the plant kingdom, or, dare I say, queendom."

"Nicholas Pearson has given us a lucid and balanced explanation of flower essences. He is careful to define the terminology in a clear way. His focus on developing a context for flower essence use within magickal and ritual contexts fits perfectly with the subtle and metaphysical reality of essences."

"Nicholas Pearson performs the rare magick of creating an accessible guidebook to working with the plant world in a way that feels thoroughly modern. This book shows us a world in which natural science and natural magick work hand in hand to craft an informed spiritual path that is overflowing with wonder."

Flower Essences
from the
Witch's Garden

Plant Spirits in Magickal Herbalism

Nicholas Pearson

Destiny Books
Rochester, Vermont

Destiny Books
One Park Street
Rochester, Vermont 05767
www.DestinyBooks.com

Destiny Books is a division of Inner Traditions International

Text stock is SFI certified

*Note to the reader: This book is intended as an informational guide. The remedies,
approaches, and techniques described herein are meant to supplement, and not to be a
substitute for, professional medical care or treatment. They should not be used to treat
a serious ailment without prior consultation with a qualified health care professional.*

Cataloging-in-Publication Data for this title is available from the Library of Congress

ISBN 978-1-64411-300-4 (print)
ISBN 978-1-64411-301-1 (ebook)

Printed and bound in the United States by Lake Book Manufacturing, Inc.
The text stock is SFI certified. The Sustainable Forestry Initiative® program
promotes sustainable forest management.

10 9 8 7 6 5 4 3 2 1

Text design and layout by Virginia Scott Bowman
This book was typeset in Garamond premier Pro with Bookman Press used as the
display typeface
Illustrations by Steven Thomas Walsh

To send correspondence to the author of this book, mail a first-class letter to the
author c/o Inner Traditions • Bear & Company, One Park Street, Rochester, VT
05767, and we will forward the communication, or contact the author directly at
www.theluminouspearl.com.

＊
　★

This book is dedicated to my grandmother Phyllis Pearson.
We spent countless hours together tending her garden, where
she taught me to appreciate plants of all kinds.
Even today, the intoxicating aroma of gardenia and
orange blossom and the delicate taste of honeysuckle evoke
sweet memories of my precious time with her.
I learned that all flowers hold their own beauty,
that each one has value, from the striking purple hue
of tibouchina to the orange-and-blue fan presented by
the bird of paradise. I will always treasure our visits to
Menninger Park, a modest but verdant oasis in
my hometown of Stuart, Florida, that overflows with
flowering trees draped in mantles of gold and pink.
Thank you, Nana, for sharing with me your love of flowers
and teaching me that tending the garden brings
blossoms of beauty and yields fruits of magick.

Contents

EXPERIENCING THE WITCH'S GARDEN

Rituals and Techniques

Foreword

Flower essences, like any true medicine, simply make you more yourself. They restore your proper balance, yes, but more importantly they make you more of your true self. The vibrational nature of an essence reveals many of the unseen and unacknowledged patterns within us. As they are brought to the surface, at first we seek to reject them, because we want to believe they are not of our true nature: *The remedy made me feel that way. The essence triggered me. I wouldn't normally say or do that. It wasn't really me.* It's akin to "the devil made me do it," seeking to shift the blame to another. But an essence can't make you do something you wouldn't do. An essence can't make you not responsible for your words and actions. Like a torch, an essence can reveal in the darkness, illuminating. But it can only reveal what is already there to be seen. And like a flame, given time, it can burn away what no longer serves our true nature, like stripping dross from precious metal.

Essences allow us to make tremendous leaps in our evolution. They dissolve, break down, and otherwise transmute unnecessary patterns, creating shifts in consciousness. When we recognize the patterns in need of healing, we can transform them. Otherwise they lurk just beneath the surface, hiding from our conscious gaze, hoping to escape like a monster beneath the bed or hiding in the closet. By removing the unwanted patterns, essences make the space in our life, in our bodies, and in our consciousness to welcome more fully our true self into every thought, word, and deed.

I know my own journey into the world of flower essence healing began with a medical diagnosis in the early stages of liver disease. A metaphysically oriented friend, a covenmate in my first coven of Witches, suggested a local healer who used flower essences. As Nicholas mentions, many people confuse flower essences with essential oils, though they are two very different types of medicine. I knew potions and spells and how to blend essential oils, but I didn't know anything about flower essences at the time. The healer suggested a blend of the flower essences from herbs that healed and nourished the liver—dandelion, milk thistle, yellow dock, and a few others. He explained more deeply how the liver corresponds to anger and the herbs that heal the liver yield essences that heal the vibration of anger, thereby healing the liver. Having studied Hermetics and knowing the principle of correspondence, "as above, so below; as within, so without," this made magickal sense to me. I understood the chain of health and disease as our thoughts create feelings; feelings create sensations; and sensations contribute to our overall health and well-being. For the Witch, thoughts are things, and they have a powerful effect on our reality.

Three days later I found myself expressing my anger at the most inopportune time, feeling taken advantage of by a new employer. Where previously I would have just smiled and went along, I refused, quite forcefully. I quit on the spot, but it was for the best. I wouldn't have described myself as an angry person, but as a gay man who grew up in a very Catholic environment, I had a lot of repressed feelings. I just didn't realize how much. This episode illuminated a pattern: when my boundaries or trust were violated, I would go along with it under the guise of being "nice" or "spiritual." But I went to the healer to say the essence didn't work because I hadn't been that angry before, but I was now. But he seemed delighted by my anger. Revealing my anger so that it could be healed was only the first stage, he said, and I soon began to understand the true nature and power of this healing modality. After a year of intense healing, resulting in a healthy liver, I began a journey to become a certified flower essence consultant, and I created a line of essences and added this potent piece of healing to my repertoire of Reiki, crystals, shamanism, astrology, and tarot.

The community of flower essence practitioners was deeply versed in the metaphysics of the New Age rather than Witchcraft. Along with Reiki practitioners (a common thread among most of us), I found light workers, Theosophists, and students of the Merkaba, the Flower of Life, and *The Urantia Book*. At the time I thought I was leaving my Witchcraft, though I still kept celebrating the seasons and the full moon. My desire to be a better healer led to deeper study into the essences and then medicinal herbalism. The traditional medicines of Asia, India, and America got me curious about the Greek and then medieval healing traditions, which brought me back to alchemy, occultism, and, yes, where I began, Witchcraft. By the time I circled back, I realized it was all magick. Everything I learned was part of an overarching wisdom tradition of humanity that is, ultimately, devoted to healing and evolution.

At the time, few Witches worked with flower essences, and those who did straddled the line in explaining the power of essences. One side was more medicinal, couching descriptions of the essences and their effects in scientific—and what some would consider to be pseudoscientific—terminology, speaking of vibration, life force, and quantum entanglement. The other side was the magickal, invoking magickal virtues and plant spirit medicine, speaking of allies and devas. The truth is both and neither. The truth is the paradox of mystery. Healing is one of the great mysteries, along with birth, love, death, and rebirth.

So imagine my delight to see, more than twenty years later, the unapologetic *Flower Essences from the Witch's Garden* spring forth and so deftly and comprehensively handle the two sides of essences—medicine and magick. While we separate them today, at one point all medicine was magickal and much of our magick, particularly plant magick, had its roots in medicine. While there will always be separation in a secular society, as we grow, we must also find those points of union where that shared root of magick and medicine can be recognized and honored. Herbalism and in particular flower essences are one of those places. And here, in this book, Nicholas Pearson shares his formulary of potions for blending flower essences and a grimoire of essence-based spells, while simultaneously revealing in depth the characters and patterns of the flowers themselves, showing an underlying animist at heart, seeking allies in the world of the plant spirits.

It is my hope that this book will be another bridge between the occult traditions rooted in antiquity and the new traditions pioneering a New Age, both of which are forms of magick, though they are often misunderstood by each other. One accuses the other of being too dark; the other accuses the first of being too fluffy and light. Both are true and neither are true, another mysterious paradox, as it all depends upon the practitioners. Like Witchcraft, many of these essences will put you in touch with your own darkness, and the darkness of the world. If you deny something, if you reject it, it will never heal. You must integrate. And like Witches and the deities of Witchcraft themselves, these essences bear light into the dark places, revealing our wounds and the tenderness and sensitivity often at the root of our wounds. They can bring a joy, a lightness, and a laughter that is so necessary for true healing. Through the flowers, through taking and making essences, and casting our spells with them, we learn to awaken and play with the healing childlike heart within us all.

Like a true essence, this book reveals more of Nicholas's true self, taking us deeper into his love of nature. In his previous books, particularly those focused on the mineral realm, Nicholas blends his geological lore with several streams of crystal wisdom, old and new, along with his own insights and experiences. In a day when many popular texts are only simple reiterations of other people's knowledge, the knowledge here is hard-won. Built upon a solid foundation of history, theory, and tradition, this book embodies the wisdom of a practitioner who lives nature and applies nature to his own evolution and healing. Nicholas brings heart and soul to it, but most importantly he brings his magick. He reiterates the age-old role of the Witch as healer and shows that Witches may not always conform to modern expectations. We are walkers between the worlds, often straddling the lines between the occult and the New Age, between the old and the new. We go where we are needed. We go where there is magick to be done. We go to help those on a healing path find their own magick.

At the time of this writing, and no doubt still when the book is released, the world is experiencing a tremendous amount of chaos, suffering, and change. Times are uncertain. On a daily basis we are processing shocks, trauma, grief, and anger. While these things have always been a part of the world, the age of modern technology keeps us in contact with the news in a seemingly never-ending cycle of updates, interweaving with our entertainment and community connections, making a break from it quite difficult. We want to know. We want to witness. We want to support and take action, but the enormity can be quite overwhelming. I can think of no better time for this book to be coming out. I can think of no greater need for the medicines from the Witch's garden than our need today to process our personal and collective emotions—which flower essences can help with. The Witch believes fervently in that principle of correspondence. Not only do we observe the connection between above and below, within and without, but when we make a corresponding change internally, it brings about change externally. This is the true secret of magick, of Witchcraft. While it can appear to be power over outside forces and even people, at its heart, it is power of yourself and the transformation that occurs to the world when many selves change. This is the Great Work of the magicians, of the alchemists, and yes, of the Witches.

It is my deep desire that this book, an extension of Nicholas's magick, helps you on your own healing path and that it helps you find and use the tools to reveal more of your own true self and, for those called to heal, no matter how you may see yourself or identify, the necessary tools to help others help themselves.

In Love, Will, and Wisdom,
Christopher Penczak
Salem, New Hampshire
January 2021

CHRISTOPHER PENCZAK is an award-winning author, teacher, and healing facilitator trained as an herbalist and flower essence consultant since 1999. He is the author of *The Plant Spirit Familiar*, *The Mighty Dead*, and *Buddha*,

Christ, Merlin. Cofounder of the Temple of Witchcraft tradition and nonprofit, as well as Copper Cauldron Publishing, Christopher's work focuses on the contributions of traditional and modern Witchcraft to the wisdom and healing traditions of the world, with a particular emphasis on our relationship with the ancestors and the plant spirits.

Acknowledgments

Each and every book is the effort of a community of people and a network of praxes and principles. My thanks go out to everyone along the way who has supported, inspired, and uplifted this project. I am forever grateful to my clients, students, classmates, and colleagues for holding space for my ideas, encouraging me to experiment, and being my first experimental guinea pigs with some of these techniques. A special shout-out goes to Ashley Leavy for being so supportive of me stepping outside my comfort zone.

I owe a mountain of gratitude to Rita Truax for introducing me to the Bach flower remedies and supplying me with countless bottles of personalized blends. Your generosity and love, not to mention the essences themselves, have forever touched my heart and spirit.

Thank you, Christopher Penczak, for planting a seed for using essences in magickal and alchemical ways, as well as for helping me rebuild the foundations of my magickal and spiritual practice. Thank you for the gift of your friendship and for sharing your wisdom so generously over the past few years.

I don't know if I can ever give Sue Lilly enough gratitude for her and Simon's contributions both to my practice and to essence practitioners around the world. Thank you for being a fabulous mentor and guide; your Green Man Essences Practitioner course offered invaluable tools and brought me additional confidence as a flower essence practitioner.

Many thanks to Emily Ruff for leading me to a clearer understanding of the Bach essences and for encouraging me to look for the patterns in those essences. I'll treasure the experience of your flower essence course, and I'm grateful that it helped our paths cross.

Much love and gratitude flows to Deborah Craydon. You are an inspiration and a visionary, and participating in your Floral Acupuncture course was life-changing. Thank you for teaching me so many valuable tools and techniques, and thank you for listening to my experiences with such an open heart and mind.

Thank you to Loey Colebeck of Mind Is Body Therapy for your inspiration and information that supported my understanding of the astrological underpinnings of the Bach flower remedies, which helped refine descriptions of zodiacal signatures in chapter 6. Loey's lucid and thoughtful teaching style and deep love for flower essences nudged me to dive even deeper into the mysteries of the green kingdom. Her Bach Flower Essences and Chinese Medicine class is also brilliant and recommended to all.

I also owe a debt of gratitude to Natalia Montes for introducing me to the healing and magick of the Patagonia Essences.

Many thanks go to the Temple of Witchcraft community for inspiring so much magick in my life, both within and beyond the Mystery School. Special thanks go to Christopher, Adam, and Steve for blazing the path and to all the members across the world who contribute to our community. Thank you in particular to Sam Belyea for sharing information about planetary signatures at this year's TempleFest, which helped me greatly with chapter 6.

Thank you, Karen Ainsworth and Dan Lupacchino, for drawing me to Chalice Well in Glastonbury. The retreat we held together contains a mystery and magick that I'll carry with me for the rest of my life. The flowers, trees, and plants of Chalice Well Gardens opened me to experience the green world in new ways, and the Chalice Well Essences invited me to fall in love with essences all over again. I'm so grateful to you both, and to everyone who participated in the retreat, for making it such a sacred and memorable experience. Special thanks to Jessica Smithson, whose flower-infused treats nourished us, body and soul, during the retreat; thank you also for sharing your wisdom and experiences with essences.

For the love of my life, Steven, there aren't sufficient words in any language to thank you for all that you do to support me. Thank you for your unconditional love, as well as for helping me move and organize hundreds of bottles filled with strange liquids during the research and writing of this book. Thank you for gracing these pages with your art once again. I love you so much, and I'm excited to see what our next chapter looks like.

The wonderful and talented team at Inner Traditions deserves gratitude and recognition for their impeccable work. Thank you for believing in this project and for helping me bring it to fruition. Special thanks go to my wonderful editor, Jamaica, for her guidance and insight in polishing the manuscript.

Most importantly, thank you to Mother Earth for all that she is and does. I am grateful for the magick and medicine that flowers bring to my life. Thank you to the plant spirits, devas, and guides of the plant kingdom and all of nature for working with me each step along the way.

Entering the Witch's Garden

Flowers have held a special place in cultures around the world and throughout history. Ancient cultures used them for healing and in ceremony. They took on special meaning during the Victorian era through the language of flowers, a sort of floral code used to send messages and convey feelings to those around you. Flowers are magickal, and they always have been. It's no surprise that flower essences, vibrational elixirs carrying the energy or soul patterning of flowers, invite healing and transformation on so many levels.

MY JOURNEY WITH FLOWER ESSENCES

My love for nature is no secret. I write and teach about the wonders of the mineral kingdom, and its beauty and healing virtues support me in some way each day. Before devoting my life to rocks, other kingdoms in nature held equal fascination for me. I have so many memories of studying flowers in the garden and marveling over sprouts breaking through the soil days after sowing seeds. My grandmother loved her garden and shared her joy in it with me, and my father also shared his fascination with the natural world with me at an early age. Together we planted herbs and roses, and we visited many a park where I could appreciate nature from a close vantage.

In my teen years I learned that plants have a long history of use outside the culinary and medicinal. Herb lore fascinated me as I delved into spirituality and magick. While my love of rock and stone was never overtaken by that of leaf and bloom, I learned to appreciate the plant kingdom for its mystical side. Around this same time I developed an anxiety and panic disorder. While it would be a few years before I received a formal diagnosis, I tried my hand at alleviating the sense of dread that incessantly gnawed through my happiness. That's when I found flower essences—or, rather, that's when they found me.

Shortly before I left for university, one of my dearest friends offered to mix a bottle of Bach flower essences for me. Rita was the owner of the local metaphysical store, and she was the first person to invite me to teach about crystals. I'd been visiting the shop for maybe five or six years by that point, and I suspect she had observed the initial signs of anxiety growing like a noxious weed. She pulled out her box containing dozens of dropper bottles and explained to me that the essences were rather like tuning forks for the mind and emotions—they helped us come back into a state of balance. She walked me through a series of questions, jotted down some notes, and proceeded to create a personalized blend of the Bach remedies for me.

That was close to seventeen years ago as of this writing. Flower essences have seen me through a lot of life's ups and downs. Although there have been brief periods when I hardly used them at all, they've never *not* been part of my life since I first encountered them. Essences are part of my healing toolbox, and they work seamlessly with crystal healing, Reiki, and allopathic medicine. Although I've gotten to know a lot of other lines of essences along the way, I still rely on Bach's remedies to this day. Rescue Remedy, a special blend of five flowers for emergency use, accompanies me everywhere I go. I'm grateful to report that my mental health has flourished, in part thanks to flower essences—among other important steps I take to cultivate a state of well-being.

Some years ago I began to explore the flowering plants in my home state of Florida. It's worth noting that the state is named for the Spanish word *florida,* meaning "flowered." There are always plants in bloom here. I began researching the magickal and medicinal uses of native plants but never got very far with that project. One day it occurred to me that I ought to make essences from them—and so I did, making essences from local wildflowers. Later, I rediscovered the joy and magick of essences during a fateful visit to Chalice Well in Glastonbury, England. My renewed interest in essences spurred me to apply myself to the practice of flower essence therapy, and I sought out training in a variety of schools.

THE MAGICK OF ESSENCES

There is something rather mysterious about flower essences. There are lots of theories and models for how they work, but the truth is that we cannot truly measure what makes them effective. In spite of that, they really do work. Studies, formal and informal alike, show that flower essences work better than a placebo in a variety of contexts. Flower essence therapy aims to bring balance to the psyche by flooding the mind and emotions with the positive virtues of flowers, thereby enabling the body, mind, and spirit to return to a state of balance. In most cases, flower essences catalyze deep healing at psychological and spiritual levels, though many people who take flower essences also experience the amelioration of physical symptoms.

Despite—or perhaps because of—the mystery of their workings, the inherent power of flower essences lends to their use beyond the healing arts. As I began to truly engage with and explore flower essences, I started using them in my own spiritual practice, taking them well beyond their traditional role in therapy. I meditated with them, used them to facilitate journeying and dreamwork, and combined them with other ingredients in spellcraft and ritual. I did this with an investigative spirit and an open heart. The essences themselves, and the consciousness of the plants that works through them, led the process. I found other practitioners using essences in magick and ritual, too, which validated my exploration and motivated me to continue.

Whether we use essences as medicine or magick, as therapy or thaumaturgy, they always bring balance to the mind and spirit, eventually grounding this balance into our bodies. Essences offer more radiant health and a deeper connection to the parallel worlds of nature and spirit. They remind us that our very lives are equally as mysterious as the mechanisms by which they work, and they offer us tools for embracing the mystery and magick of everyday life.

USING THIS BOOK

Flower essences are easy to make and even easier to use. In light of that, I've tried to make *Flower Essences from the Witch's Garden* as practical as possible. The book opens with a discussion of what essences are and how they work, followed by a brief survey of flower essence history in chapter 2. Chapters 3 and 4 guide you through my perspective on plant spirits; here you'll find some experiential techniques to help you better perceive and commune with the intelligence of the plant kingdom, as well as learn how the different classes of spirits manifest themselves in flower essences.

Chapter 5 focuses on how to make flower essences; it will introduce you to the equipment you'll need and walk you through a variety of methods for making essences. Chapter 6 offers advice for discerning how to use a particular essence. By examining the shape and color of the flowers, as well as other attributes of a plant, you can glean valuable insight into the nature and effects of the flower essence derived from it. Chapter 7 provides practical information for selecting and using flower essences within a therapeutic context.

The next section of the book is decidedly more magickal. Chapters 8 and 9 will introduce you to some nontraditional uses for flower essences. These techniques are rooted in magickal and ritual practice, and you'll find tips for using essences in incense and for dressing candles, as well as a formulary of flower essence recipes that cover a wide range of intentions. Chapter 10 bridges the topic of flower essences with alchemy, introducing a special formulation called a flower essence spagyric.

The last chapter of the book details the therapeutic and magickal uses of one hundred different essences. Most books on flower essences tend to center on a particular line of essences as well as the therapeutic ideals and techniques taught by a given essence maker or founder. I've decided to cover essences that can be purchased from a variety of sources or made in your own garden. Many of the essences are made from plants that are staples of magickal herbalism, though some are relative newcomers to the realms of magick and flower essences alike. Each entry includes the plant's Latin name, the classification of plant spirit, and the elemental and astrological correspondences associated with the plant. You'll find a brief list of the magickal uses for each essence, as well as the indications for using the essence therapeutically. The entries for each essence weave together folklore, history, and botanical information to paint a picture of what each essence offers.

If you have any difficulty finding flower essences, please be sure to consult the appendix, which includes descriptions of some of my favorite lines of essences. These lines represent some of the most trusted and intentionally made products on the market, but there are hundreds of others from which to choose.

However you have used essences in the past, I'm hoping that *Flower Essences from the Witch's Garden* will offer you something new. Should you already use essences as part of a healing practice, perhaps shining a light on their magickal uses will offer you new tools for your toolbox. Likewise, if you already have a love of magickal herbalism, flower essences can broaden the scope of your work and provide safe and effective ways to work with plants that are otherwise inaccessible or dangerous. My hope is that this book will inspire you to create more magick and healing in your life, no matter what your practice looks like. May the green heart of nature bring you healing and magick each day.

1
What Are Flower Essences?

The human psyche has always been attracted to the alluring beauty of the plant kingdom. Plants supply food, medicine, and raw materials for weaving, building, and so much more. The plant kingdom offers inspiration for the arts, and flowers take the crown as the most beautiful and inspiring aspect of the green world. The beauty and majesty of flowers, long praised by painters, poets, philosophers, mages, and healers, transcend the ordinariness of everyday life.

Among the myriad ways that we can connect with plants, flower essences, sometimes called flower remedies, display an astonishing potential for helping us attain health, happiness, and spiritual growth. These liquid preparations of plant spirit medicine arose in their modern form through the work of Dr. Edward Bach (1886–1936), who prepared his thirty-eight remedies in the British countryside in the early 1930s.* Bach, a medical doctor skilled in bacteriology and homeopathy, sought a new method of healing that could be used universally and with ease among the laity and health professionals alike. The fruit of his labor has inspired and healed millions of people around the world since that time.

Since then, essences have been made not only from flowers but also

---

*There is some debate about the correct pronunciation of the good doctor's surname. The dominant pronunciation in the United States and many other parts of the world is like that of the composer, rhyming with "rock." However, Bach's family came from Wales, and his surname was pronounced "batch" since his college days. Prior to that, it appears that his name was pronounced "baytch," such that it rhymed with the name of the letter *H* ("aitch" or "haitch").

from other botanical sources, such as leaves, seeds, barks, and roots, as well as other sources of healing energy in the natural world, like gemstones, shells, animals, astrological and seasonal events, special environments, and even sound and light. Flower essences and other vibrational remedies represent the pinnacle of integrative medicine and spiritual healing, and they are rapidly becoming one of the most popular methods for people to support their health and personal development.

DEFINING ESSENCES

Flower essences are dilute solutions containing the energy or spiritual pattern of a flower (or other substance or vibration). They are usually made from water, to which a preservative such as alcohol is added. They are subsequently potentized through one or more stages of dilution. Essences contain virtually nothing, if anything at all, of their parent substance; they work because of the information somehow held within the water itself.

Flower essence makers and practitioners use a variety of different models and metaphors to describe just what essences really are. Bach himself never used the expressions "flower essences" or "flower remedies," instead calling them "remedies from Nature," "herbal remedies," or simply "remedies." His teachings about the essential nature of these remedies are vague, apart from explaining the action of the remedies, which we'll examine a bit later in this chapter. As a result, people around the world have come up with many explanations for what the essences are.

Descriptions of essences and their actions generally fall into two camps: those that rely more on spiritual concepts and those that rely on scientific ones. The latter group seeks to legitimize flower essences by employing models that may or may not explain the exact mechanisms at work in flower essences and vibrational remedies. These descriptions tend to rely on theories of electromagnetism, the memory of water, and the principles outlined in homeopathy as a means of explaining what essences are and how they work.

One such definition of flower essences comes from essence producer and researcher Machaelle Small Wright. She tells us that essences are "water-based solutions holding electrical patterns derived from the different kingdoms and elements of nature."[1] Water has been shown to have a sort of memory in the way that its component molecules arrange themselves. It is able to retain a record or imprint of the substances and electromagnetic fields with which it comes into contact. Some proponents of flower essence therapy, myself among them, believe that this is how essences are made: a strong source of electromagnetic energy, such as sunlight, helps the water retain the imprint of the flowers or other substance to which it is exposed. When taken internally or otherwise used, essences transmit this electromagnetic message to our physical and spiritual bodies, thereby catalyzing the healing process through electromagnetic entrainment.

Those who take a more esoteric route to defining flower essences tend to define essences in more abstract terms. Flower essences are often described as containing the subtle "pattern" or "vibration" of a flower or other source; this energy is outside the scope of what science can currently measure or identify. Other practitioners hold the view that it is not merely a matter of subtle energies, but it is the consciousness or spirit of the plant that does the imprinting. When flower essences are made, the indwelling consciousness or essence of the plant interacts with the water and leaves behind a trace of itself in the process. This second school of thought leaves the door open to experiencing more than simply the remedial effects of an essence—it means that we can take the essences to commune with the spiritual consciousness of nature.

The view that essences are created by the spirit or consciousness of a plant in no way conflicts with an electromagnetic model for what essences are or how they work. Since many different layers, both subtle and gross, comprise reality as we know it, I find myself using both models to describe flower essences. An essence is the energy signature of a plant, environment, gem, or other focus that is held in water. Defining exactly what makes that imprint is challenging, as orthodox testing reveals nothing within the essence except for the water and preservative. Although no physical trace of the original substance remains, taking flower essences illustrates just how effective they are. Ultimately, the nature of flower essences is something that we cannot yet measure. As a result, our task is to surrender to the mystery of not knowing and to observe what essences are by the effects they have on our bodies, minds, and spirits.

What Flower Essences Are Not

When I mention flower essences in conversation, someone almost invariably thinks I'm talking about essential oils. Sometimes essences are conflated with tinctures, homeopathic remedies, or other forms of plant medicine, too. While flower essences may share some superficial qualities with all of these substances (essential oils, herbal medicine, and homeopathic remedies), they are in a category all their own. To better understand what flower essences are, let's take a look at several things they are not.

Flower essences are most often conflated with essential oils; after all, they are both called "essences" and derive from botanical sources. The similarities end there, though. Flower essences are highly dilute solutions carrying the *energetic* signature of a flower, while essential oils are concentrated volatile oils that are usually steam-distilled or extracted by solvent from plants. They have strong aromas, whereas flower essences only smell like the preservative used in bottling. Essential oils are employed in aromatherapy, and they have applications that work predominantly on the body, followed by the mental-emotional level of your makeup. Flower essences work predominantly at the spiritual and mental-emotional levels, rather than working directly on the physical body. Essences and essential oils can be used together with ease.

Many people compare flower essences, and especially Dr. Bach's system of thirty-eight remedies, to homeopathic remedies. The Bach flower remedies have even been registered as homeopathic medicines in some countries and were included in the eighth edition of the *Homeopathic Pharmacopoeia of the United States* as such. When I first encountered the Bach remedies, they were described to me as homeopathic remedies, and they do indeed share several characteristics with them. These similarities include potentization, dilution, and the lack of parent substance in dosage bottles. Bach himself, as you'll learn in chapter 2, was a practicing homeopath and first introduced his new herbal remedies to practitioners of homeopathy in England. However, there are several key differences between flower essences and homeopathic medicines.

To begin, flower essences do not undergo the rigorous process of serial dilution and potentization that homeopathic medicines do. While essences are indeed dilute, different levels of dilution are not used to produce different clinical results, as is done with homeopathic remedies. In addition, flower essences do not work in exactly the same manner as homeopathic cures. While both aim to treat the whole person, homeopathy follows the law of similars in treating conditions with substances that might otherwise produce similar symptoms, whereas flower essences seek balance by negating and integrating polarities. Even though it is true that both flower essences and homeopathic medicines are highly dilute and energetic in nature, the mother tinctures of flower essences contain no traceable ingredients, while the mother tinctures of homeopathic remedies do include traceable ingredients. Thus, their effects are said to be qualitative rather than quantitative in nature. Flower essences and homeopathy can be used together, so long as the practitioner has a requisite understanding of homeopathy.

Flower essences are frequently assumed to be a sort of herbal remedy or tincture. Some of the terminology that has historically been used to describe essences supports this assumption, such as *mother tincture* and even Bach's designation of his essences as herbal remedies. However, herbalism employs herbs predominantly for their biochemical activity; medicinally active compounds are extracted from plant matter by tincture, decoction, infusion, or poultice. Flower essences have no chemical activity at all, and with the exception of a few essences made by boiling fresh flowers, the mother tincture offers no chemical trace of the plant. Essences are traditionally made only from freshly harvested flowers, while conventional herbal remedies can be made from virtually any part of the plant. Herbalism tends to address imbalances of the body, although there is a blossoming movement to address disease holistically, leading many herbalists to work with plant spirit medicine, flower essences, and other forms of healing to lead their clients to well-being in body, mind, and spirit.

Unlike essential oils, homeopathic preparations, herbal remedies, and even allopathic medicine, flower essences have no side effects. You cannot take too much of an essence, and taking the wrong one is likely to have no effect at all, rather than leading to an undesirable outcome. Flower essences are gentle, vibrational medicines that work at the soul level to introduce balance inside and out.

A Note on Nomenclature

The general trend today favors the term *essence* over *remedy,* as the latter has a medical connotation. The use of the word *remedy* is also regulated by many governments as a means of protecting the integrity of conventional medical practices and establishments. Since a burgeoning number of essences are being made from things other than flowers, many people have started to use terms such as *vibrational essence/remedy.* Other essence makers and users have coined other names for the essences they make, sell, and use.

In general, the word *remedy* implies that the solution fixes, heals, or otherwise adjusts something that is out of balance or diseased. Thus, a remedy is on some level only intended to address a negative state. The word *essence* connotes that the essential nature of a flower is somehow held within the water; it doesn't imply a level of activity aimed only at negative states of being. Some lines of essences are instead known as *flower elixirs,* or *flower enhancers,* as they are intended to enhance certain fundamental soul qualities in those who take them.

Throughout this book you'll find several of these terms used interchangeably. I tend to follow in the footsteps of my teachers, who prefer the word *essence* as it avoids sounding too medical and also illustrates that the essences themselves can do more than simply eradicate a negative state of being. I often use the term *flower remedy* when discussing Bach's system of healing, as the Bach flower remedies are permitted this designation out of historic association. Occasionally I'll use the terms *vibrational remedy* or *vibrational essence* to discuss those essences made from something other than flowers themselves.

HOW ESSENCES WORK

There is a lot of mystery involved in the making of flower essences, and not a lot of peer-reviewed research—though some promising studies have been published. Generally speaking, in describing the way essences work, most practitioners use language that is congruent with the nature of the essences themselves. In other words, you generally find that essences are described with either a more spiritual or a more scientific model.

Flower essences and other vibrational remedies work on the subtle levels of your being to initiate change and cultivate well-being. They are sometimes described as tuning forks for the emotional state, gently bringing your psyche into balance by demonstrating a more balanced emotional vibration. Dr. Edward Bach described the actions of his remedies as raising one's consciousness or vibration, thereby lifting the mind, body, and spirit out of the level at which disease operates. In his essay *Ye Suffer from Yourselves,* he wrote:

> The action of these remedies is to raise our vibrations and open up our channels for the reception of our Spiritual Self, to flood our natures with the particular virtue we need, and wash out from us the fault which is causing harm. They are able, like beautiful music, or any gloriously uplifting thing which gives us inspiration, to raise our very natures, and bring us nearer to our souls: and by that very act, to bring us peace, and relieve our sufferings.
>
> They cure, not by attacking disease, but by flooding our bodies with the beautiful vibrations of our Higher Nature, in the presence of which disease melts as snow in the sunshine.[2]

Bach also stated that each flower corresponds to a particular quality and that the remedy prepared from the flower strengthens that quality or virtue complementary to some negative state within us, such that the personality can transcend whatever negative state it is experiencing. Bach championed the idea that true healing takes place at the psychological and spiritual levels and that imbalances at these levels precede—

and may cause—physical illness. Taking the right essence or blend of essences can therefore initiate healing at the subtle levels that leads to radiant physical health, too.

One might be tempted to believe that flower essences are short-cuts to well-being, that they do our work for us. According to Patricia Kaminski, flower essence therapist and cofounder of the Flower Essence Society, this is most definitely not the case. She writes, "Each flower essence stimulates a positive virtue or quality [that] is inherent in our souls. The flower essences do not do our inner work for us, rather they catalyse our consciousness and capacity for self-reflection. The goal of flower essence therapy is that we become responsible for our soul life. By developing ever greater positivity and self-awareness, we deepen our capacity for human love."[3]

What Are Essence Vibrations?

What exactly are these vibrations that uplift us and dissolve disease? Some describe them as the soul patterning of the flowers, others as a form of light—either the literal sort, which exists on the electromagnetic spectrum, or a spiritual light that is still imprinted on the water that becomes a flower essence. The color, geometric pattern, and other signatures of the flower resonate with or amplify specific energies and soul qualities. Thus, when faced with a psychological or spiritual pattern that we would like to be free of, we can take an essence made from a flower that resonates with the complementary quality or state of being.

Those practitioners who use an electromagnetic model for what essences are and how they work depend on the role of energy in the physical and subtle anatomy to describe what flower essences do. Again turning to the work of Machaelle Small Wright, we find a model wherein each essence "balances, stabilizes and repairs the body's electric circuits in two ways: (1) They address weakened or damaged circuits in targeted areas of the body that have been hit by illness or injury, and (2) they also provide the needed balancing for specific mechanical functions and properties that are contained in and are part of biological electrical circuits no matter where the circuits located in the body."[4]

This assertion that flower essences work through some sort of electrical charge depends on two things: the nature of water itself, which is capable of holding a small electrical charge (probably measured at the picowatt level), and that the added preservative, such as alcohol, acts to hold the electric charge within the water.[5] Even those who use a more esoteric description of how and why flower essences work point to water as the vehicle for the healing that these elixirs offer.

The Mystery of Water

Water is the cornerstone of life on our planet, and since antiquity it has been regarded as precious for its spiritual qualities, too. Water cleanses, renews, and restores, and it also holds the keys to life, memory, and wisdom. To understand the magick and mystery of water, a short overview of the science of this sacred substance is necessary.

I'm sure you already know the chemical formula for water: H_2O. Two hydrogen molecules attach themselves to an oxygen molecule as a result of covalent bonds, wherein the adjoining molecules share electrons. Water is unusual among substances for a number of reasons. It is liquid at room temperature, and it is at its densest just a few degrees above freezing. If we take a tour of the periodic table, any of oxygen's neighboring elements form gases when bonded with hydrogen—many of them harmful or poisonous in the wrong quantity.[6] Water is the anomaly.

Thanks to their covalent bonds, water molecules are strongly polar. This means that although their net charge is neutral, the separate parts of a water molecule exhibit either a positive charge (in the case of the hydrogen components) or a negative one (oxygen). Accordingly, water molecules act somewhat like magnets. The polar nature of its molecules is part of what makes water the universal solvent, as it enables water to dissolve a wide range of compounds, particularly ions. The polar charges of individual water molecules also predispose them to a sort of weak bond, called a hydrogen bond, with each other. These hydrogen bonds form when water molecules cluster or otherwise organize themselves, with opposite poles attracting one another.

The way in which water molecules arrange themselves can be loosely grouped into the categories of *structured water* and *bulk water*.

Bulk water is what we usually find coming through our pipes and in bottles. Structured water, on the other hand, exists in a state called a liquid crystal mesophase: a state between liquidity and crystallinity that exhibits at least some of the organization and repeating structure unique to crystal forms. The actual shapes and patterns created by water molecules in this organized state vary greatly, and this is in part owed to the fact that water molecules do not have a consistent shape. The angle of the covalent bonds is highly variable, ranging from 104.27 to 108.29 degrees, and this angle can be altered when water is exposed to electromagnetic energy.[7] This means that water exists in many states and that its molecules arrange themselves into many different semicrystalline patterns.

Structured water is naturally occurring, and every cell in your body contains examples of it. Structured water can also be created or influenced by its environment. The father of liquid crystal research, Marcel Vogel, demonstrated in his laboratory at IBM that bulk water could be transformed into structured water via prayer, drumming, meditation, breathwork, and crystals. Other scientists have shown that human beings emit an electromagnetic field strong enough to alter the atomic bonds of water. Note, though, that since water is easily influenced by its environment, some sort of preservative must be added to maintain the liquid crystal mesophase and therefore preserve the information encoded in the water geometrically.

A deluge of evidence flowing from labs around the world illustrates that water's ability to organize itself actually demonstrates its ability to remember a substance, energy field, or phenomenon. This "memory of water" was first described by Jacques Benveniste in 1988. While his work was discredited by some, it has also been reproduced by many others. Perhaps this variability is in part due to water's response to the experimenters and their states of consciousness.

New experiments continue to support the idea that water has a memory, and this memory is the mechanism that allows flower essences, vibrational remedies, and homeopathic medicines to function. These substances are not active biochemically, as there is an insufficient amount (if any at all) of the original material present in them to initiate a chemical response in the body. Instead, they are information therapies: the information contained within the water is the factor that invites healing and transformation.

Consider that the human body is mostly water—approximately 60 percent water by volume (more when we are very young, and less as we age). But what happens when we factor just how small water molecules are in comparison with the organic compounds from which we are made? If we tally up the number of each different kind of molecule in the body, we can see the proportion of water in our body. Water molecules constitute approximately 99 percent of the human body by molecular count. In a healthy state, each one of them must be part of a liquid crystal mesophase—that is, all the water in the human body ought to be structured water. Essences may work by contributing more structured water to the body, thereby entraining or teaching our bodies to organize themselves in a similar fashion. Thus, essences can pass along the information they carry to the body, mind, and spirit.

The information carried by water works similarly to a hologram. A single drop of structured water, when added to a larger container of bulk water, can serve as a seed crystal, a sort of nucleating point around which the molecules in the container can arrange themselves. Thus, one drop of an essence contains the blueprint for the effects of the essence as a whole, which is encoded geometrically via the water molecule's patterns, and this information is imprinted by the spirit or consciousness of the plant (more on plant spirits in chapter 3). It is often said by essence practitioners that taking a couple of drops is just as effective as drinking an entire bottle, which reminds me of the way that a fragment of a hologram contains the information for producing the entire image.

The process of making flower essences is a bit like taking a photo with a film camera, except instead of capturing the image of a flower, you are capturing the imprint of its soul or spirit. In a camera, light travels through the lens and aperture and makes an imprint on the film. With flower essences, the camera is the glass bowl, and the film is the water. Light is the vehicle that drives the entire process; it is the energy required to hold the imprint on the water itself. Light and consciousness are forms of pure energy, and water remembers and organizes itself in response to these energy sources, much in the way that film responds to the energy of light to retain an image.

Water is a marvel, and our scientific understanding of it continues to unfold. But our modern-day knowledge only underscores what the ancient inhabitants of our planet already knew: water is sacred, miraculous, and magickal. Exploring the scientific models of how essences are made does not detract from the sheer mystery and magick inherent in water, and it is water's spiritual virtues that truly make it so healing.

WITCHES AND FLOWER ESSENCES: ESSENCE AS POTION

In spite of widening overlap between holistic practitioners and witches (and other magickal people), there are a lot of people who may be surprised to hear that flower essences have a place in magickal practice. Although essences have become increasingly more mainstream (you can find Rescue Remedy at virtually any drugstore or pharmacy), they still retain a mysterious and spiritual element.

Flower essences and other vibrational remedies were born out of holistic medicine. The realm of medicine and healing has long been occupied by a diverse group of people. Among those working in the healing arts you'll find conventionally trained doctors and other medical professionals, as well as indigenous healers, midwives, bodyworkers, herbalists, energy healers, faith healers, and many more. Throughout the ages, science and medicine have intersected with religion, occultism, and spirituality in many different ways. Dr. Edward Bach's own desire to heal transcended merely addressing the physical body, and he found that the healing virtues of flowers worked at the psychological and spiritual levels, much in the same way that complementary, alternative, and integrative medicine may be rooted in spiritual practice.

Flower essence therapy shares many elements with the occult traditions of herbalism and alchemy. Witches and healers across many cultures and ages have long worked with the spirits or consciousness of plants, and flower essences are imprinted by that very same spiritual force. Essences are a spiritual distillation of the plant spirits' medicine.

As potions, they not only facilitate healing but also can be used as a direct connection to the consciousness of the plant kingdom and as *materia magica*—the ingredients used in spellcraft, in ceremony, and for other magickal purposes—in spells and rituals.

Flower essences are indeed magickal, because magick is medicine for the soul. Essences are infused with the life force, healing virtues, and consciousness of the plant kingdom. They offer safe, economical, and environmentally friendly ways to connect with plant spirits and add their blessings and powers to your magickal practice. Witches have long been healers, spirit workers, and co-creators with the plant kingdom; flower essences are tools for achieving all these goals—and more.

2

A History of
Flower Essences

Although flower essences as we know them today are a relatively recent innovation, they exist on a continuum of practices that stretch back to the beginning of human history. Plants were the very first medicines, and Dr. Edward Bach's discovery of the healing virtues of the flowers from the British countryside in the 1930s is just one way in which the curative powers of the plant kingdom have been harnessed.

Most retellings of flower essence history focus on Bach, drawing connections between his work and that of the great homeopaths, physicians, alchemists, and healers who came before him in the annals of Europe's history of medicine. Rather than starting in the Middle Ages and working forward, as most of those retellings do, let's begin our story much earlier by imagining the beginnings of medicine and tracing a common thread to today's traditions of flower essence therapy, alchemy, and magickal herbalism.

BOTANICAL WISDOM
IN THE ANCIENT WORLD

For our earliest ancestors, plants were indispensable—just as they are today. Plants provided food, medicine, and raw material for clothing, shelter, and tools. Plants were also important parts of religious and spiritual practice. Although we may not be able to clearly reconstruct the earliest religions in their entirety, archaeological evidence highlights many ways in which plants factored into early humans' conception of and relationship to the spirit world and divinity.

Ancient peoples across the planet observed nature to learn the secret teachings of the green kingdom. Over time, our ancestors learned to build intricate and meaningful relationships with plants by learning directly from them. In the modern world, anthropologists and ethnobotanists are seemingly shocked to discover that indigenous healers do not learn about the uses of plants by trial and error; instead, the spirits of the plants themselves instruct the healers about their uses.

The most ancient of medicines may have been more spiritual than material in nature. Healers, shamans, and herbalists cultivated profound relationships with plant spirits, invoking those spirits when they prepared plant medicines. In this way, making medicine was more than just the extraction of beneficial compounds that correct chemical, mechanical, or other imbalances in the physical body—it was an act of cooperating with nature to produce true healing by realigning with the cosmos, within and without. These medicines were, at least in part, vibrational in nature, not unlike the flower essences we know and love today. Thus, it was not merely the phytochemicals but also the essential nature or vital energy of the plants and their indwelling consciousness that allowed the botanical preparations to effect healing.

This relational and observational approach to medicine continued well into the period when history began to be recorded. The ancient Greeks formulated a system of science and natural history founded on the direct, empirical experience of nature. These ancient philosophers observed plants, creatures, stones, and other elements in nature and looked for the deeper meanings, messages, and patterns at work. In this way, science and medicine became intertwined with philosophy, religion, and magick.

The Greeks viewed the essential nature of plants through the complementary lenses of science, medicine, and magick all at once. There exists a Greek word that encompasses the diverse and overlapping uses for plants: *pharmakeia*. We derive our modern words *pharmacy* and *pharmaceutical* from this ancient root. *Pharmakeia* means three things at once: medicine, magick, and poison. Plants served all three purposes, for they could be employed for baneful or curative purposes and for mundane or spiritual ones, as needed. Pharmakeia became the practice of the healers, witches, and poisoners of the ancient world. Physicians and cunning folk, European practitioners of folk medicine and magick alike, would carry on the lineage of the *pharmakeute,* or "knower of herbs."

In a similar fashion, the Romans had the Latin word *veneficia* to describe both magick and poison. It shares a root with our word *venom.* The word *veneficia* is also sometimes linked to Venus in folk etymology; Venus is not merely the goddess of love, she is sometimes depicted as the queen of witches and the celestial goddess from whom all magick flows. From the footsteps of Venus sprang flowers and healing herbs, legend tells us, and her devotees recorded the secret uses of these plants.

Botanical wisdom from the ancient world blurs the lines between medicine, magick, science, and philosophy. The same plants could be used to kill or cure, contingent upon the dose. Over time healers developed many ways to work with plants, some predicated on the active effects of the chemistry of plants, others purely spiritual or symbolic in nature. Whether relying on chemical or vibrational effects, healers still typically relied on the spirits of the plants themselves to drive or improve the efficacy of their plant medicines.

THE MIDDLE AGES AND THE INFLUENCE OF ALCHEMY

The magick and medicine of the plant kingdom continued to play an important role during the medieval period. We can see our first glimpse of proto-flower essences emerging in Europe during the Middle Ages, largely thanks to the importance given to dew as celestial moisture imbued with healing virtues. Dew was considered to be the condensation of the soul of the cosmos that appeared out of the expanse of the starry sky, carrying heavenly forces with it. Dew was holy and sacred, and alchemists, magicians, and healers collected it by laying out cloths outdoors and wringing the moisture from them the following morning.

One of the most celebrated medicinal texts from the medieval period was written by Hildegard von Bingen (1098–1179), a German abbess of the Benedictine order. She was a brilliant writer, composer, and philosopher and a visionary mystic who was later canonized as a saint. Hildegard wrote extensively about the curative powers of plants and stones, and she is also considered the founder of scientific natural history in Germany. Her writings record the use of dew for healing several different ailments, although whether she practiced this herself is subject to debate.[1]

Among medieval alchemists, the best known today is Paracelsus (1493–1541). Born Philippus Aureolus Theophrastus Bombastus von Hohenheim in present-day Switzerland, Paracelsus trained as a physician and became a gifted healer and surgeon. He was taught by his father, Wilhelm, "to observe nature directly and learn by personal experience, rather than from books, authorities, and dogmas."[2] He put forward many ideas that survive into modern medicine and is credited as the father of toxicology. Paracelsus synthesized empirical, folk traditions of medicine with the classical, academic teachings of his era, fusing them with his own complex spiritual observations to create a holistic model of healing.

In addition to his many contributions to science, medicine, and alchemy, Paracelsus used the morning dew from flowers in the production of his medicines, spagyrics, and other elixirs. One of his medicinal preparations involved placing the bright yellow flowers of broom (possibly *Cytisus benehoavensis*) in water and preserving the resulting liquid in schnapps; the remedy was used in the winter months to uplift emotions and maintain energy.[3] Modern flower essence producers and practitioners often connect the art of making essences with the alchemical principles put forward by Paracelsus, and my own experience of making essences aligns with the alchemical, mystical nature of the essence-making process.

ESSENCES BEFORE BACH

There is some anecdotal evidence that flower essences, or essence-like preparations, existed before Bach began his research. Many age-old indigenous traditions, for example, make use of flower essences. Ian White, founder of Australian Bush Flower Essences, and Marion Leigh, creator of Findhorn Flower Essences, both mention the Aboriginal people of Australia making flower essences,[4] though I'd imagine these floral medicines were not entirely like those of Dr. Bach. Similarly, Emily Ruff of the Florida School of Holistic Living shared in a workshop I participated in that she learned of treatments used by indigenous people of Central America that rely on the physical and spiritual qualities inherent in flowers, which reminded her of modern flower essence therapy. I've also read of some Ayurvedic remedies that are made by simply soaking fresh flowers in water for a few hours. These simple remedies cannot contain much in the way of phytochemicals and thus are likely to have more in common with vibrational remedies than chemical ones.

There are also some modern examples of essences in use shortly before Bach. In his book *Orchid Essence Healing,* flower essence maker Don Dennis recounts the family history of Dr. Judy Griffin, founder of Petite Fleur Essences, which is based in Texas. Griffin's family immigrated to the United States from Italy. Her earliest childhood memories are of her mother, Flamina di Torrice, soaking roses in a crystal bowl under the sun and drinking the resulting essence. Flamina had learned the process from her own mother, who made essences in the family's hometown of Salerno: "A rose would be packed in some snow, and the melt-water would be given to people in the local village. They had learnt this technique from their mother Carmella Monzo, who was Judy's great-grandmother. Carmella would have been making her snow-rose essences in the Salerno area in the mid 1800s."[5]

Dennis describes another vignette of essence making that preceded Bach in the Carpathian Alps. Maximillian Ottowitz, grandfather to one of Dennis's friends and fellow flower essence therapists, made flower essences after studying the works of Paracelsus. Ottowitz lived from 1884 to 1969, and his granddaughter discovered his experiments with essences after reading his journals. Dennis writes, "Max would not keep the essences for any length of time, and usually they were made for a person on that day."[6]

Perhaps the most salient and immediate predecessor of Bach's experiments with flowers was Dr. Robert Cooper, a homeopath and herbalist who developed his own remedies from the flowers of various medicinal plants. Cooper called them "arborvital remedies," and he produced them by collecting a single specimen of the inflorescence, bottling it in spirits of wine, and exposing the bottle to direct sunlight for twenty minutes to produce a potentized remedy.[7] The similarity between Cooper's method and Bach's method are undeniable. Cooper's son was a close friend of Dr. Bach, and he very likely introduced the two accomplished homeopaths. However, Cooper used his arborvital remedies to directly treat disease, rather than the mind and emotions, unlike Bach.

EDWARD BACH, FATHER OF FLOWER ESSENCES

Edward Bach was born on September 24, 1886, in Moseley, a suburb of Birmingham, England, just three miles to the south of the city itself. He was a delicate child, fraught with ill health in his youth—a theme that would return later in life. From an early age, Bach had a profound love of the natural world. The suffering of anything—plant, tree, or creature—aroused in him a desire to help and heal others, and he aspired to become a doctor. After leaving school at the age of sixteen, he worked in his father's brass foundry from 1903 to 1906 to set aside money for medical school. During this period he considered joining the seminary, as he saw Christ as the Great Healer. Ultimately, though, he decided to pursue schooling in medicine as a means of helping a greater number of people.

Bach obtained many degrees during his medical training. In 1912 he earned the conjoint diploma of MRCS and LRCP (Membership of the Royal College of Surgeons and Licentiate of the Royal College of Physicians), and the following year he was conferred Bachelor of Medicine and Bachelor of Surgery degrees from the University College Hospital Medical School in London. These degrees are equivalent to an MD in the United States and granted him the necessary credentials to practice medicine. In 1914 he also received his Diploma of Public Health from the University of Cambridge.

Early in his medical career, Bach made a name for himself as a brilliant pathologist, immunologist, and bacteriologist. He studied the relationship between intestinal toxemia and a variety of illnesses, eventually creating seven vaccines from the bacteria he analyzed.

During these years of studying and practicing medicine, Bach observed that patients presenting the same symptoms did not respond to the same treatment in the same manner. As a result, he began to question the treatment of disease with specific remedies for specific illnesses. Bach eventually concluded that patients with similar personalities or temperaments tended to respond in a similar fashion, thus prompting him to use treatments that were tailored to the psychological profile of patients, rather than merely the physical symptoms they exhibited.

Dr. Bach took a new position with the Royal London Homeopathic Hospital in 1919, wherein he would study the work of Samuel Hahnemann, founder of homeopathy. One of his greatest takeaways was Hahnemann's concept of treating the patient rather than the illness. The vitalistic and holistic models of homeopathic medicine were aligned with Bach's observations about disease. He believed that illness was the result of disharmony between the body or mind/personality and the soul and that physical disease was ultimately a manifestation of negative states within the mind and emotions. Similar ideas were espoused by forerunners of modern medicine, including Hippocrates and Paracelsus, and research into the relationship between mental affect and physical health continues to demonstrate these ideas today.[8]

Turning to Nature

As Bach explored homeopathy, one of his reservations was that so much of the medicine of his time, both allopathic and homeopathic, was derived from poisons and agents of disease, such as poisonous metals and minerals and vaccines derived from pathogenic bacteria and viruses. His wish was to find substitutes made from healing plants filled with beneficent virtues that uplift the spirit. In time he would leave behind his lucrative practice—as well as his wife and children—to seek these alternative remedies in the field and forest.

Bach arrived in the Welsh countryside and set about finding plants filled with the healing virtues he required. He initially experimented with remedies prepared from the seeds of flowering plants prepared more or less via traditional homeopathic processes. Although he had success with this, he was still seeking a method of making remedies that could be prepared and used by everyone. Eventually, he found that morning dew collected from the flowers after having been potentized by the morning sun conveyed the healing qualities of the plants. However, collecting dew in this fashion was tedious and produced very little of the remedies. Thus, in the summer of 1930 he created the sunlight method for potentizing his remedies, floating flowers atop fresh spring water in a clear glass bowl in direct sunlight.

Bach initially developed a system of healing based on twelve basic personality types, each one with a corresponding flower essence. He published his findings in a small book called *The Twelve Healers,* which went through several editions as he added more remedies to his repertoire. By 1936 he had a collection of thirty-eight remedies, made mostly from plants in the British countryside. In choosing which plants to make remedies from, he relied largely on his intuition, with corroboration from the successful treatment of patients with the essences.

After the publication of his final edition of *The Twelve Healers and Other Remedies,* Bach's health began to fail. With his time waning, he trained others in the methods of preparing and using the remedies. Bach passed in his sleep on the night of November 27, 1936.

Bach's Inspiration

Bach certainly drew upon his medical background and clinical observations when embarking on the journey that ended with his flower essences, but it is increasingly apparent that something altogether mystical took place during his experiments with them. His books, lectures, and correspondence hint that astrology, alchemy, and intuition were important parts of his work with the remedies, even if he did not make that fact widely known.

Bach was strongly influenced by the teachings of Hahnemann, as evidenced by his work in homeopathy. He cited the work of both Hahnemann and Paracelsus in a speech he gave in February 1931 to an audience of homeopaths (the speech was later published as *Ye Suffer from Yourselves*). In this address, Bach described the work of these two figures as bringing "a light to humanity in the darkness of materialism" and shared that both men "knew that if our spiritual and mental aspects were in harmony, illness could not exist."[9] Bach aspired to draw upon the Paracelsian and Hahnemannian models in a manner that would lead medicine and humanity to further advancements.

Bach's writings also indicate his connection to esoteric orders and occult teachings. He is known to have built relationships with Romany people then in Cromer, Norfolk, England; with these friends he exchanged ideas about herbal remedies, natural cures, and perhaps other topics. Bach was also a Freemason, and he delivered a lecture about his remedies at a Masonic lodge in 1936, presumably because the spiritual nature of the remedies would appeal to the order. It has even been suggested that the twelve remedies he first produced were meant to be prescribed according to one's natal chart—likely according to the sign in which the moon appears. Bach himself wrote that the personalities represented by these twelve plants "are indicated to us by the moon according to which sign of the Zodiac she is in at birth."[10]

Bach surely considered his work to be alchemical and mystical in nature, and we can see it in his description of his process for making the remedies: "Let it be noticed that the four elements are involved: the earth to nurture the plant; the air from which it feeds; the sun or fire to enable it to impart its power; and water to collect and to be enriched with its beneficent magnetic healing."[11] These same four elements are familiar to many of the world's magickal and spiritual traditions, and this elemental description of essences illustrates how potent they are for curative and magickal uses alike.

Bach's work was deeply spiritual, as he felt that all illness was caused by disparity between the soul and the personality. His remedies were meant to eliminate this inner conflict such that any person could better express the fundamental light of their soul. Thus, flower essences are spiritual medicine; they treat the spirit first and foremost, and that has laid the foundation for further study and experimentation with their use in healing, alchemy, and magick.

THE EVOLUTION
OF FLOWER ESSENCE THERAPY

Bach's remedies continued to be made by his successors, Nora Weeks and Victor Bullen, who worked from his former center of operations at Mt. Vernon in Sotwell, England. Bach's vision had been that the remedies could be made by anyone so long as they were made with care from the correct plants, and it appears that there were practitioners who undertook that work. Nevertheless, the primary source for Bach's remedies remains Nelsons Homeopathic Pharmacy. Bach supplied mother tinctures of his essences to Nelsons in the 1930s, and the Bach Centre at Mt. Vernon continues to produce remedies for the pharmacy today. A number of other essence producers maintain the good doctor's legacy by producing high-quality remedies made from the same thirty-eight sources identified by Bach.

Proponents of Bach's work maintain that flower essence therapy, or at the very least the system Bach taught, is a closed and complete system unto itself. No further essences are required. I do find that Bach's thirty-eight remedies more or less cover the full range of human emotion, especially when they are combined into personalized blends.

Bach's remedies were the only extant flower essences until Arthur Bailey produced a line of essences in Yorkshire in 1967. Bailey came from a rigorous scientific background and had a profound love of nature, not unlike Dr. Bach. He developed over a hundred essences before his passing in 2008, including his own line of Bach's thirty-eight remedies. In the 1970s essence making would spread to North America, as Lila Devi developed her own line of twenty essences, originally called Master's Flower Essences, now known as Spirit-in-Nature Essences. Devi's essences are made from the blossoms of fruits and vegetables and were inspired by Paramhansa Yogananda's teachings about the vibrational qualities of foods. Richard Katz and Patricia Kaminski also developed a line of essences made from Californian flowers; they would go on to found Flower Essence Services and the Flower Essence Society to further the study and use of essences.

In the ensuing decades, hundreds, if not thousands, of essence producers have flourished in all parts of the globe. Essences have been produced by many different methods, not only from flowers but also from other botanical ingredients such as fruit, seeds, leaves, roots, and bark. Vibrational essences are also made from gemstones, seashells, environments, astrological events, lunar phases, colored light, sound, channeled energies, and so much more. Therapeutic applications have evolved far beyond Bach's simple instructions, although following his example still offers profound results.

Today practitioners can choose from innumerable essences from many lines. Training is accessible in person, online, and via correspondence courses. Professional organizations have been formed to protect the integrity of flower essence therapy and further its acceptance in more conventional settings, such as alongside health care. The use of flower essences continues to adapt, evolve, and refine in myriad ways.

THE RISE OF ESSENCES IN MAGICKAL PRACTICE

The past few decades have seen the use of flower essences reaching further than merely prescribing essences according to the emotional and mental state of a client. Divinatory techniques, like pendulum dowsing, meditation, and communication with plant spirits have become standard tools in the flower essence practitioner's toolbox. Essences are sprayed and diffused in rooms and outdoor spaces, given as offerings to the land and nature, and blended together with intention during auspicious lunar phases and astrological events. They are used for boosting psychic ability, conferring protection, and manifesting abundance. In short, flower essences have entered the realm of magick and ritual, even if most practitioners do not consider themselves witches or magicians.

Among witches, pagans, and occultists who are searching for new ways to work with plant spirit medicine, we see a growing trend toward using essences as materia magica in spell and ritual. In fact, many people are turning to flower essences as a safer way to work with the witching herbs—baneful plants like mandrake and belladonna—that are otherwise hazardous if mishandled. In light of this surge of interest in flower essences, I'm finding that magickal people are discovering new uses for flower essences far beyond the therapeutic context described by Bach and his successors.

Essences are excellent tools for magick because they contain the pattern or imprint of the spirits of the plants themselves. They are a direct link to the spirit world and consciousness of the plant kingdom, and they are allies in the spiritual arts. Essences can be added to potions, incense, and offerings, or they can be taken as a means of facilitating the inner changes—shifts in consciousness—that magick requires. The burgeoning interest in essences among magickal people is perhaps a collective remembering of the ancient botanical wisdom that the first priestesses, magicians, and shamans used.

To better understand why essences are so magickally potent, the following chapter will explore the world of spirits, particularly the spirits of plants.

3
Devas, Plant Spirits, and Green Familiars

The biggest overlap between flower essence therapy and magickal herbalism hinges on the nature of the spirit world. The occultist and essence practitioner alike depend on more than the mere materiality of the plant kingdom. Flower essences themselves contain little if any actual plant matter; they are a *vibrational* remedy. So where exactly does this vibration come from? Most practitioners of flower essence therapy point to the intelligence of the plant, a sort of spiritual force that is the guardian consciousness of the plant itself. This is the same force, the very essence of the plant, that the green witch calls upon in plant magic, too. To truly appreciate what the classical witch, alchemist, conjure doctor, shaman, and flower essence maker have in common, we must explore the animating intelligence of the green world.

THE NATURE OF SPIRITS AND THE SPIRITS OF NATURE

That we live in an enspirited world is an immutable fact to most people across the planet. Contrary to the materialism espoused by the rational, scientific models adopted in our relatively recent history, the default for humankind has been an animistic model of the world. Though it is sometimes regarded, quite unfairly, as a primitive or unsophisticated philosophy, I think there is something rather eloquent about the simplicity of animism, itself a belief that the material world is filled with or guided by immaterial forces. In short, every rock, tree, and creature has a spirit of some sort that animates it.

This idea of animating force or spirit is a near-universal phenomenon; what differs from culture to culture and era to era are the names and roles of these spirit-beings. A materialist worldview presents the world as an objective series of phenomena bound by precise laws that govern reality, many of which are not fully understood. Materialism constricts and limits; what we see is what we get. With a materialist orientation, we might view the natural world as consisting of living and nonliving resources waiting to be taken and exploited. Animism, however, allows for myriad possibilities. It enables us to consider that we are not the only enspirited beings, and that we are neither the masters nor the stewards of nature. Instead, when we view nature as full of intelligences, we develop an awareness of humankind as an intrinsic part of nature, not separate or above nature.

So what exactly is a spirit? *Spirit* might mean the animating principle or vital force that is responsible for life (in other words, the soul). It might also convey the meaning of some sort of supernatural, nonphysical entity (like a ghost or the Holy Spirit). We might talk about *spirit* in terms of the essential presence or ambience of place and object. The word *spirit* might also denote mood, temper, or attitude ("in high spirits"), or it might indicate the prevailing tendency or intent ("spirit of the law").* The spirits involved in essence making are in one way or another linked to all of these concepts. They animate the plants, but they are also nonphysical beings not bound solely to the body of a plant. Essences affect our own spirits by influencing our moods and attitudes, perhaps even guiding our intrinsic tendencies.

If the idea of spirits is alien to you, stop for a moment to remember a time when you visited some special place in nature, perhaps a forest, mountain, or cave, or an impressive building, like a skyscraper, temple,

---

*We can't forget about the other type of spirit that is vital to making essences: alcohol. Without distilled spirits, or a suitable replacement, we'd never be able to preserve the imprint of the plant spirits and devas in the essences, thereby allowing us to work with the plant spirits in a practical way. Talk about an intermediary spirit!

or cathedral. How did it make you feel? Calm, inspired, small? In these instances the essence of the place has impressed upon you some ineffable quality that exists only there. This is the spirit of place, the conscious presence or vital force that dwells therein; it is often referred to as the *genius loci*. Sensing these spirits of the landscape is part of the human experience; it's something shared by all people, distant ancestors and close kin alike.

I can remember my first time sensing the indwelling spirit of nature. It was a childhood trip to my favorite Florida beach with a barrier reef, now sadly diminsihed by development and eroded by the battery of hurricanes. By some accounts, my grandparents had taught me to swim by the time I could walk, if not sooner, and I took to the water like a fish. I was snorkeling and scuba diving before I started school. Eventually the time came when I was finally old enough to venture out unaccompanied into the water beyond the reef at high tide. On one of those summertime trips to the beach with my grandparents, I swam out past the shallow reef and dove under the choppy waves to the sandy ocean floor. I was overcome with stillness and wonder as I observed this world apart from my own. The reef was so close to the dry land that I called home, and yet it was somehow so foreign to reality as I knew it. There, moving all around me, was life that could be perceived only when you left the ordinary behind. I think that strange mix of stillness and busyness, familiar and unfamiliar, opened my perception to see just beyond what I'd been conditioned to see, and I felt the spirit of everything around me, enfolding me just as the water did.

Spirits are everywhere in all things. In a sense, all spirits are nature spirits, because everything ultimately comes from nature, though sometimes only very, very indirectly. There is a spirit in every blade of grass and grain of sand. But there is also a spirit in your home and your car, in your kettle and your wind chimes. There are spirits unconnected to material things; they move all around us, unfettered by cumbersome bodies. Our ancestors are spirits, as are our gods. Spirits can be large or small, overseeing processes both great and seemingly insignificant. These spirits hold the blueprints for everything in the manifest and unmanifest worlds. They are the stewards of all things with form, seen and unseen.

Devas, Angels, or Spirits?

The literature about flower essences often uses terms like *deva, angel, oversoul,* or even simply *consciousness* to describe the spirits of the green world. Although they are sometimes used interchangeably, each of these terms may describe a different level of a plant's spirit. Let's explore some of them in greater depth.

The word *deva* means "shining one" in Sanskrit; originally it was the title given to all supernatural beings, gods and spirits alike, in the earliest Vedic sources. Etymologically, *deva* is related to words like *divine* and *deus* (Latin for "god"). Later uses for the word *deva* relate it to lesser orders of divine beings, and by the time the word was adopted into Buddhism it took on the meaning of an order of spirit-beings with a parallel evolution to our own. In the nineteenth century, the Theosophical movement adopted the word to mean any spiritual force in nature. Eventually it came to take on the meaning of the archetypal, universal intelligences responsible for the creation and maintenance of the forms we see in nature; in other words, they are a bit like the group soul or oversoul of a particular species. The idea of deva-as-oversoul was cemented by the founders of the Findhorn community, who communed with the spirits of nature in Findhorn, Scotland, to produce an uncanny garden in an unlikely place. With the help of the devas, the founders of Findhorn, Eileen and Peter Caddy and Dorothy Maclean, were able to grow enormous vegetables and herbs in the barren, sandy soil in a caravan park. Devas are often equated with angels, and some of the literature from Dorothy Maclean names these archetypal beings as angels.

My understanding is that devas are the architects of all forms that we can experience. The idea of form is not limited to physicality as subtle and energetic forms also require blueprints. Devas are the higher intelligences of the natural world. (Again, remember that even man-made objects have form and are ultimately derived from nature and therefore must have devas.) Devas function as a sort of oversoul or overlighting consciousness of the things we see and experience, and there are often several levels of devic consciousness, much as there are several levels to our own. These beings hold the blueprint or the pattern for everything that comes into existence; implementation of the instructions held in the blueprint is carried out by other spirits, such as elementals and nature spirits. Sue and Simon Lilly, prolific authors on the subjects of crystal healing and flower essence therapy, describe devas as containers that hold the shapes of their contents; though the vessels (devas) are not made of the same substance as their contents (form), they inform or enfold the matter and energy within.[1]

Spirits exist at many levels of organization, from the *anima mundi* (world soul) or planetary logos to the oversoul of entire genera down to the devas of individual species. Other spirits, like elementals and nature spirits, also inhabit the landscape. They maintain each part of nature, from the tiniest speck of dust to the mightiest mountain. Other spirits merely inhabit those features of the landscape.

When you commune with the spirit of an ancient oak, you might actually be communing with several spirits at once. There is the oversoul, or overlighting deva, of all oaks, as well as the devas of the landscape in which that particular oak resides. These spirit-beings hold the blueprints for the oak and its environs (we will see later that trees in particular are in some ways inseparable from and responsible for the spiritual and material well-being of their environments). There are also the worker spirits—the elementals responsible for the ingredients and the nature spirits who put them together—that carry out the devic blueprints in order to manifest and maintain the tree. Then there is the indwelling soul, or essence, of the individual tree, for it has its own individual identity and nature. For simplicity's sake, we will simply call this the *plant spirit* or the *soul*. Ancient and powerful trees are also the residence for many other spirits, like the spirits of the organisms who make their homes in the trees (birds, fungi, insects, et cetera) and other discarnate spirits who also dwell therein. In a sense, the essential spiritual nature of the oak is composed of all these things.

We might visualize these spirits in a sort of chain or branching diagram to understand their relationships and functions. To the spirits, however, there is no order of importance linked to their magnitude, no vertical hierarchy that determines worth. Each of the smaller devic entities is a cell or organ within the body of the larger ones. Every plant spirit and deva is part and parcel of the oversouls that guide and govern

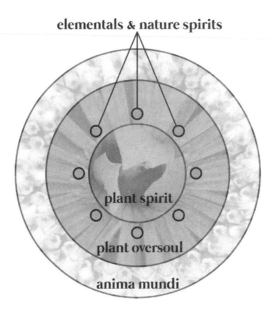

Venn diagram of devas

them, and these overlighting devas constitute part of the world soul, the anima mundi. Each of the larger devic forces is consciously aware of every cell within its body and is in constant communion with every deva, nature spirit, and elemental. Likewise, every tiny cell in the body of the world soul, or planetary logos, contains the seed of the whole. In this way, devic consciousness is holographic; even the smallest part contains the blueprint for the entire devic order. For this reason, when we make an essence of a particular flower—no matter where we are in the world—we are tapping in to the oversoul for the species with which we are co-creating.

Each deva or spirit is important in the grand scheme of things, and you'll work with many types of spirits or devas as you create flower essences. In addition to the devas of the plants, there is also the deva of water to consider, as well as the devas of your bowls, shears, funnels, and bottles. The solar and lunar devas also play their parts, as do the devas of the land. Your own spirit interacts with these other spirits (consciously or not) as you undertake the steps to produce essences, so it is vital to be mindful of your psychological and spiritual state of being as you work.

Anima Mundi

The anima mundi is the deva or spirit of the world. A spirit this large is often deified and personified, hence our expressions "Mother Nature" and "Mother Earth." Some spiritual traditions identify the anima mundi with specific gods or masters. The Theosophical writings of Alice Bailey defined this overlighting presence of the planet as "a great deva lord," and she described how each plane of existence, from the densest and most physical to the subtlest and most rarefied, has its own deva lord.[2]

Whether we view the planetary deva as personified or abstract, the soul of the world permeates and nourishes every part and particle of Earth. It is the matrix that maintains the reality of everything we experience—physical and nonphysical alike—here on our home planet. The planetary logos is both the architect of the world and the sum total of all the spirits that are responsible for directing each individuated aspect of our world. You could think of it as the fabric of consciousness out of which everything we know and hold dear is woven. This worldwide deva is, in turn, woven out of the light of the solar system, the galaxy, and the cosmos as a whole. Each level is a cell in the body of the next highest order, and each level has its own architect or demiurge.

The nature of the anima mundi is the nature of light itself. Some esoteric traditions maintain that the world soul is Phosphoros or Lucifer, the Light-Bearer (a far cry from the figure depicted by mainstream religious traditions). Others hold that the soul or regent of Earth is Sanat Kumara, a Luciferian figure originally recognized in Hinduism. For pre-Christian peoples the world over, the soul of the world was almost invariably personified as the Great Goddess, Mother Earth herself. Within the texts of the Chaldean Oracles, philosophical and spiritual writings known to the Greek Neoplatonists of the third to sixth century CE, the role of anima mundi was assigned to Hekate, who would later take on the role of the goddess of magick and the night. She is also the keeper of the poison garden and an important figure in connecting to the spirits of the green world.

However we view the soul of the world, this is the divine devic level that maintains the order of all the systems of our planet. Ultimately, the anima mundi or planetary logos is responsible for the health of every species, ecosystem, and biome on Earth, even if only at the highest level. This means that when we interact with the spirit of place and the souls of individual plants in the act of making essences, we are co-creating with part and parcel of the anima mundi, whether or not we are conscious of it.

Oversoul

In most of the metaphysical literature that I have encountered, the term *deva* is used to mean the oversoul or overlighting consciousness of a particular mineral, organism, or other form. There are devas for every variety of rock and mineral, as well as for every species of plant, fungus, and animal. Since devas are responsible for all things that have form, chairs, automobiles, and skyscrapers have devas, too, just like daisies, manatees, and hawks. Since this is a book on flower essences, we will focus on the devas most relevant to the process of making essences.

The deva of a given plant is the steward for that species or cultivar. It draws up the blueprints for that plant, complete with all the idealized instructions for the inception and growth of the plant. Devas guide the plant from seed to sprout to flower and fruit; they are the guiding light that provides every opportunity for each plant to flourish. Devas are sometimes described as the angels or angelic stewards for a species; this terminology is likely a vestige of older occult traditions that maintained that angels were the demiurges or creators of the universe, each one in charge of a separate part of creation.

Devas work on a universal, rather than individual, level, functioning as a sort of group soul or oversoul for a species or cultivar. For this reason, they are sometimes called the "overlighting" spirit or deva of a plant (or stone, creature, et cetera). There is but one oversoul for all the potatoes of the world; the same goes for each plant or flower we can dream of. The deva that I contact when producing an essence of elderflower here in central Florida is the same deva that you'll contact when you're working with elderflower, whether you live in my neighborhood or on the other side of the world—provided, of course, that you're working with the same species of the plant. Although we will connect to the same oversoul, the personalities of individual plants will be informed by other spirits less universal in nature; they are the nature spirits, land spirits, and plant spirits that we will discuss in greater detail a little later.

When we make flower essences, it is important to acknowledge and invoke the deva of each plant, as it is the deva that is ultimately responsible for imprinting the energy of the plant upon the water. By connecting to the deva, we ensure that our essences receive an unadulterated and idealized pattern. Since the devic kingdom is holographic in nature, all it takes is one or more flowers to awaken the devic blueprint for the entire species of a plant. The whole is contained in each part. Don't forget that it's not merely the deva of the flower you've chosen that is involved in the act of making an essence. The devas of the sun, of water, and of the bowl are also part of the energetic dialogue taking place. If you take the time to connect with the oversoul or architect of each of these components in your essence making, you can bypass any imperfections or deviations from the blueprint that might be expressed on an individual level here in the material plane, thereby ensuring a radiant and powerful flower essence.

Genius Loci, Elementals, Nature Spirits, and Plant Spirits

Terms like *elemental* and *nature spirit* mean a lot of different things to a lot of different people. Part of the challenge that faces us when we try to define the ineffable, intangible forces that animate the universe is that we have to simplify these concepts enough to communicate them to others.* They exist in myriad forms and functions, ranging from the consciousness of the land itself to anchors for a particular elemental energy such as earth, air, fire, or water. Truthfully, each environment is the result of a confluence of spirits,

---

*It is often hard to find absolute agreement among all the people who use these and related terms; please bear that in mind if my use of them differs from what these words mean to you. Please also pardon my use of words such as *larger* and *smaller* to describe these spirits. Although they do not literally differ in size, there is no easy way to portray their relative scopes without using some sort of relative descriptors.

a veritable ecosystem on the subtle plains that maintains the material environment. I'll refer to these categories of spirits as *nature spirits,* which will include the spirits of place, elementals, plant spirits, and other spirit-beings found in nature.

The first class of nature spirits function very much as devas but work on the local level. They are the land spirits, known in folklore from around the world by many different names. The land spirit of a particular place—the genius loci, or "spirit of place"—is the container in which all the constituents of the land are incubated. Although rightfully classed as a sort of oversoul or overlighting deva, the genius loci is, like its name implies, localized. It can only be contacted where it dwells.

Next come the orders of elementals and nature spirits. Devas draft the blueprints, elementals supply the raw materials, and nature spirits build the forms. Elementals are guardians of the archetypal alchemical forces referred to as fire, water, air, and earth, as well as the elusive but all-pervading quintessence. All things that exist in the material plane are composed of all the elements, though the proportions of each element will differ from one object or organism to the next. Nature spirits execute the instructions from the deva, using the raw energy and materials offered by the elemental realm to bring forms into manifestation. No part is more or less important than any other; an architect's plans mean nothing if no one supplies the lumber and concrete or puts the plans into action.

Marko Pogačnik describes his understanding of the difference between nature spirits and devas in his book *Nature Spirits & Elemental Beings* after having a conversation with the deva of fennel.

> First of all [the fennel deva] explained that it was not her task to oversee the development of each individual plant. The nature spirits of the earth element would take care of this. . . . I asked the deva to convey her function in pictures. She proceeded to put the picture of a plant into my consciousness. A plant can only thrive when it is sprinkled with rain from the clouds and is illuminated by beams of sunlight. The effect of raindrops on plants is equivalent to the

impulses of the fairies of place [i.e., nature spirits*] on the landscape which they oversee. In contrast, the rays of the sun are symbolic of the connection an angel [i.e., deva] maintains with each plant species and its cosmic blueprint. The angel radiates the blueprint through its unique pattern of vibrations.[3]

From the image that Pogačnik received from the fennel deva, we recognize that the deva is like the sun. The same sun shines on all plants; in this way there is one deva who designs and guides every fennel plant. However, it takes more than just sunshine for that fennel to thrive. Localized environmental factors, like raindrops, must also be present. These raindrops symbolize the nature spirits and elementals that maintain plants. Devas work on the universal level, but nature spirits and elementals work on the local level. (See the illustration on the following page.)

Additionally, there are the individuated spirits, souls, or personalities embodied in any given plant specimen. Though we might simply call them *plant spirits,* we must be mindful that the term is a bit vague, as it also describes the other levels of consciousness. Devas are plant spirits that work on a higher, more universal scale, and elementals and nature spirits are plant spirits in some ways, too. Ultimately, when we make flower essences or otherwise connect to the spirits of the green world, we are in communion with every order of these spirits.

If you acquaint yourself with the flower essence market, you'll soon notice that different essence makers provide strikingly different descriptions of essences made from the same flower. How can this be so if the same deva is responsible for imprinting the water with the plant's vibration? Put simply, other spirits participate in the making of each flower essence, not least of all those of the human makers themselves. The genius loci, elementals, nature spirits, and other plant spirits will have different personalities, purposes, and abilities in different

---

*Note that while Pogačnik uses the term *fairy* to describe nature spirits and elementals, the fairy folk as known in traditional folklore, folk religion, and magickal practice are a different order of being altogether. They can and often do act as stewards of the land and preside over particular plants and places, but they are not nature spirits in the popular sense.

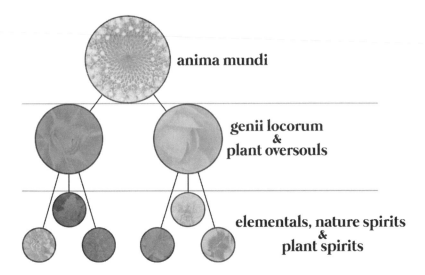

anima mundi

genii locorum
&
plant oversouls

elementals, nature spirits
&
plant spirits

A hierarchy of spirits. The first level illustrates the planetary deva
or logos. The intermediate level represents the oversouls or
overlighting devas. The lower level represents the smaller spirits that
act upon the blueprints provided by the oversoul, including
plant spirits, elementals, and nature spirits.

places. The other point to contemplate is that humans do their best to translate the ineffable mystery of the spiritual world into terms we can all understand, but there is always something lost in translation. Whether you make your own essences or use commercially prepared essences, remember that a multitude of beings co-created the essences in your toolbox.

WORKING WITH THE SPIRITS OF PLANTS

Understanding, even observing, that there is an ecosystem of spirits all around us is only the first step in working with them. In some ways getting to know spirits is a bit like meeting people; you can't just watch them from a distance and then expect them to become friends and allies. At some point an introduction is made and you start a conversation, which may eventually lead to a cooperative relationship of one sort or another. Spirit work is not so different in this regard.

One of the hallmarks of magickal traditions is the connection to the spirit world. Whether we look to the Yakut people of Siberia or the ceremonial magicians of medieval Europe, magick involves spirits. In fact, an old definition for a witch is "someone who keeps familiar spirits." Plant spirits have been depicted alongside witches and magicians for centuries, if not longer, and they hold a special place in the spirit ecology of the magickal arts.

Although many practitioners might not realize it, any time we use some dried leaf or bits of bark and root or a few precious drops of essential oil for magickal purposes, the power is coming from the plant spirit itself. And while the plant material of course contains energy, just like anything else in our universe, the real driver for our magickal work is drawn from a consciousness beyond that material form.

Folk magick, in particular, has preserved this notion, especially in practices such as conjure and rootwork. In these instances the practitioner is not merely relying on the innate power of plant material; rather, they are *conjuring the spirit of the plant*. This is why it is traditional to charge, enchant (meaning to "sing to"), or otherwise recite your intentions aloud in many forms of magickal herbalism. The "charging" of magickal ingredients is not like charging a battery, for we are not imbuing the plants with some external power. Instead, the word *charge* assumes the alternate meaning of "imposing a task or responsibility." In charging our herbs, we are not merely announcing our intentions to the universe so much as we are entering into relationship with the plant spirits and requesting their assistance in specific matters.

All work with plants is supported by engaging with plant spirits—not just magick. Traditional healers and herbalists, particularly those from indigenous cultures, don't merely prescribe a tincture, decoction, or poultice because they've observed a cause-and-effect relationship between sickness and cure. Instead, they've invariably learned from the spirits of the plants themselves, or perhaps learned from the experience of another who has communed with the souls of the green world. Even today this trend continues among those herbalists, homeopaths, and flower essence practitioners who tune in to the energies of their plant medicines intuitively.

Plants as Totems and Familiars

People of many backgrounds have become familiar with the concepts of familiars and totem spirits, though there continues to be disagreement and controversy over the use of both terms. Today, a totem is generally regarded as some sort of personal ally in the spirit world. Totemic spirits are usually visualized as the spirits of animals, and they were originally considered to be representative of a tribe, clan, or family. The word *totem* is derived from the Ojibwe word *doodem* or *nindoodem,* which describes the animal, plant, or other element of nature that is emblematic of the group.

Although the terminology arises from Native American roots, the belief in totemic spirits is practically universal, found in cultures around the globe. Totems act as intermediaries with the spirit world and tutelary spirits who offer instruction and guidance in matters both sacred and mundane. Various groups of people around the world have adopted animal and plant spirits as tokens of tribe and individual alike, and these totemic spirit allies are sometimes even described as the ancestor or origin of a clan or family line.

Today we see a much more individual focus on totems in metaphysical circles, one in which people discover and work with their own personal spiritual allies or "spirit animals," as they're called in pop culture. With regard to that development, there has been understandable pushback from indigenous people and champions of social justice. It is important to distinguish traditional belief and practice from modern variants that are not necessarily rooted in indigenous teachings. Another criticism of totemism comes from the academic arena, for some anthropologists criticize attempts to categorize all forms of totemism under one umbrella.

Modern practitioners of totemism often define the spirits they work with in similar terms as devas or oversouls. For example, in her book *Plant and Fungus Totems,* Lupa describes a totem as "a spiritual being that embodies the qualities of a given species of animal, plant, fungus, etc. . . . The totem is a being of spirit, meaning, and connection that watches over those physical beings of its species."[4] Thus, when we work with the totemic energies of mandrake or lavender, we aren't merely connecting to the spirits of individual plants; we are connecting to the archetype or oversoul of those plants. This overlighting force speaks to the collective consciousness of each representation of its species in the physical world, and it points toward the concept of a collective spirit ally of the tribe or family that we see in some indigenous circles.

Truly totemic spirits are more than just the deva or oversoul of a type of plant or animal. Many layers of meaning and function comprise a totem: the history and characteristics of the species, its relationships with other species and the environment, and its relationship with humans (including mythology and folklore). Thus, totems are inherently relational. There is another term that describes a spirit that works in such a relational manner: *familiar.*

The familiar spirit is a concept recorded as far back as biblical eras, perhaps most famously in the story of the Witch of Endor in I Samuel 28:3–25. In this passage, King Saul calls upon the witch to consult her familiar spirit for divinatory purposes. Although the magick she performs is necromantic in nature, as it calls upon the spirits of the deceased, the tale of the Witch of Endor illustrates how ancient the relationship between witches and spirits truly is. Later reports of witchcraft, such as trial records from the Inquisition and the witch hunts of western Europe, often describe the relationships between witches and the spirit world. The familiar spirit was sometimes said to have been given to the witch by the devil himself as a reward for her loyalty. The familiar became both intermediary and a source of the witch's power.

I like to think that this image is a corruption of the ecstatic, shamanistic practices of European indigenous practices, in which the familiar spirit is gained through some sort of initiatic experience. Perhaps the image of the devil granting the familiar is conflated with the personification of nature—the anima mundi or world soul—bestowing upon the practitioner a particular guide and guardian in the spirit world. Even as the concept of the biblical familiar took on animal form in the medieval and early modern periods, this link to the natural world likely points toward the nature-based and shamanistic practices of European witches.[5]

The familiar spirit was described as some sort of demon or imp in most records of European witch trials. While often depicted in animal form, familiars were said to have the power to shape-shift, turn invisible, and become incorporeal. Jacob Grimm's *Teutonic Mythology* also presents a long list, taken from sixteenth- and seventeenth-century witch trial records, of familiars named after plants.[6] This practice overlaps with contemporaneous stories of fairies and elves named after plants and flowers. It stands to reason that the familiar spirits of witches and other magick-makers would not be limited to the animal realm; they were likely the spirits of a wide range of natural and preternatural phenomena.

Many shamans and similar practitioners around the world receive a familiar spirit during their initiatory trials. This spirit is often an ancestor, a deity, or the spirit of some natural phenomenon (animal, plant, mountain, et cetera). It functions, rather like the familiar of the witch, as a tutelary spirit who instructs the practitioner, an intermediary and guide for the spirit world, and in some cases as a part of or extension of the practitioner's own soul.

The evidence is clear that plant spirits have served the roles of totem and familiar throughout history. For today's herbalists, flower essence therapists, and practitioners of the magickal arts, plant spirits are important allies in the work that we do. Connecting to the spirits of the green world allows us a more intimate experience with plant medicine. They help us forge a stronger relationship to the land itself and all who dwell there—animal, vegetable, and mineral alike. Plant spirits deepen our spiritual practice by challenging us to find ways to communicate nonverbally, and spending time in communion with them better attunes us to the rhythms and tides of nature. Plant spirit familiars guide and instruct us in using their healing and magickal qualities. Evoking the consciousness of plants is a necessary step in making flower essences, too; you'll find that your most potent essences tend to come from plants whose spirits you have taken the time to get to know.

Meeting Plant Spirits

While not everyone may be predisposed to working with plant spirits in a totemic sense or as familiar spirits, everyone can commune with the spirits of nature. You may already be in touch with the spirits of the plants in your landscape, or you may just be starting to think of everything in nature being enspirited. Either way, meeting plant spirits is a relatively simple process. The simplest version looks like this: go into nature, sit with a plant, open your heart, and wait.

There is no single formula for meeting a plant spirit that works universally. However, it tends to be easiest to meet one in its natural setting, or at the very least in a cultivated area where the plant grows. The goal is to be as close to the physical body of the plant as you can. From there, you can state your intention to start a relationship with the plant spirit and observe the plant in detail. Silly as it may sound, I like to introduce myself to the plant when trying to make contact with its spirit—I find that it is important to have good manners when meeting new allies, even if they aren't people. The goal here is to be open to meeting the plant's spirit; you can't force it to show up any more than you can force a new acquaintance to become your best friend. Try the following simple plant spirit attunement exercise to help you make contact with plant spirits.

☽ Plant Spirit Attunement

Choose the plant with whom you wish to commune, whether wild or cultivated. Plants in the wild are often more palpable for those just beginning to attune to the green world, but use any plant that you feel drawn to. Make yourself comfortable and close your eyes. Spend a few moments breathing in and out; allow all the tension to dissolve from your body, mind, and spirit. Once you are properly relaxed, you may choose to cast a circle around you (see page 170) or simply proceed without one.

State your intention, silently or aloud, to connect with the consciousness of your chosen plant. Ask the plant and its spirit(s) or deva(s) to join you and share its wisdom. If you feel guided, you may open your eyes and gaze upon the plant, or you may look within to see the plant with your inner vision. Remain open and unattached while waiting for the plant spirit to make contact.

Once you sense the presence of the plant spirit, allow it to take the lead. The spirit may appear to you as an anthropomorphic being, a swirling mass of light, or an oversized version of the plant; it may also appear in any number of other guises. Sometimes, rather than seeing a plant spirit, I just sense that it is there. If it feels appropriate, you can introduce yourself. Plant spirits do not generally communicate in words. They are usually somewhat wild and untamed, but the impressions and feelings they evoke might be translated into words by your mind.

Note how you feel in the presence of the plant spirit. Take inventory of the sensations that arise in your body and where they are. Notice any emotions or thoughts that flow through you that seem unusual or atypical. Pay attention to the small details and the meanderings of your mind; these are all clues to the nature of the plant spirit.

If the plant spirit seems amenable, you can ask questions. Answers may or may not come in words and sentences. Instead, you might receive images, feelings, or other sensory impressions that can be interpreted by your conscious mind. Ask about the spiritual qualities the plant offers, as well as its use as a flower essence, herbal medicine, and magickal ally. Ask the plant about how you can best partner with it and what it expects from you (and be sure to follow through on these requests after the meditation).

When you are finished with your plant spirit attunement, thank the spirit for sharing its time and wisdom with you. Take a few deep breaths and return your awareness to the space around you. I like to ground myself by touching the earth beneath me and visualizing any excess energy discharging into the ground. After you've returned to normal consciousness, open your eyes and record your experience.

Plants act out the universal drama of life, death, and rebirth with each season and cycle. Watching that transformation unfold can deepen our relationship to the spirits of the green kingdom. Indeed, one of the best ways to get to know a particular plant spirit is through observation of the life cycle of the plant. As I write this, I'm looking out onto the developing garden that my partner and I have planted in our new home. Although most of the plants will provide food, like tomatoes and strawberries, some, like lavender and datura, were chosen because of the magickal relationships I have with their plant spirits. The lonely datura sprout in our garden began from a seed that was given to me by my friend Justin, and seeing it transform from a small speck to a leafy plant has been a magickal process.

Some plant spirits evade our grasp when we attempt to initiate communication via the method outlined above. In most cases the resistance is our own, not that of the plant spirits. In these instances, a visualization practice, like the Seed-to-Flower Meditation below, can keep our conscious mind occupied in a way that still allows for communing with the essence of the plant.

Before you begin, observe the plant in the wild (if possible), and take note of every part of it, from the leaf shape and distribution to the size and shape of the stem. If the plant has flowers, fruit, or seed, study them closely, too. Alternatively, research the plant in books or on the internet. Make notes of its life cycle and try to commit the images of the plant to memory so you can recall them in your visualization practice. If all else fails, picture what you think the life cycle of the plant might resemble, with the intention that the spirit of the plant guides and inspires your imagery. I have done this with several plants I did not know well only to find out later that the seeds and sprouts I pictured in my meditation were startlingly accurate. A sincere heart can open doors to plant spirit attunement in myriad ways.

The following exercise can be adapted to accommodate all varieties of plants, including those without flowers or those that reproduce asexually.

☽ Seed-to-Flower Meditation ⋯⋯★⋯⋯⋯★⋯

Find a quiet place to meditate, preferably in nature and near to the plant you've chosen for the meditation. If this is not possible, consider taking a couple drops of the essence or diffusing or spraying it in your space. You might also hold a part of the plant, such a twig or leaf or blossom. When you are settled into your space, close your eyes and ground and center as needed.

On the screen of your mind, visualize the seed of the plant in sharp detail, inspecting it from every angle. Picture the seed being planted in the fertile earth and receiving the necessary nutrients and water to initiate the plant's growth. See the first sprout emerging from its slumber as roots begin to dig into the earth below. Allow the seed to give way to the newborn plant as it continues to develop before your eyes. With as much detail as you can conjure, allow the life cycle to continue before your eyes. Allow the plant to reach a mature size, at which point it prepares itself to seed the next generation of plants. Watch as the seasons shift, signaling different modes of the plant's growth and development. Eventually flowers (or other reproductive parts) emerge, and the embryos within are fertilized. Watch as the flowers drop their petals and wither away, leaving behind the growing fruit or seed. Picture the seeds dispersing as the plant's spirit prepares the next generation of life to sprout.

Try to put as much detail into your visualization as you can muster. Take your time with each step of the plant's life, so you can really marvel in its majesty and wisdom. Feel the changes in the energy and personality of the plant as it moves from one stage to the next. Compare the feeling of the seed with that of the sapling. Investigate how the energy of the plant transforms as it grows older, paying special attention to its flowers. If you are working with a perennial plant, you can witness the birth and dispersal of seed infinitely, but if you have chosen an annual, consider watching the plant fade away after it sends forth the seeds.

After you have gotten comfortable with the meditation as described above, try repeating it with this variation: *imagine you are the seed.* Feel yourself shrouded in the darkness of the soil. Sense the emergent need to sprout grow so strong that you can remain within the seed no longer. Dig your roots into the earth below while your first leaves rise heavenward. Feel the body of your plant-self grow stronger and bigger with the passing of days. Feel the movement of energy and nutrients through your body, and sense the exchange of gases in your leaves. Note the way your energy changes when buds appear and blossoms emerge from them. Where does your energy go with the changing of the seasons and the transformation of your green body? As the fruit ripens, you can feel its weight tugging at its stem. Finally, move your consciousness into the seeds and experience their dispersal. Try "planting" yourself while you meditate beside a plant that you'd like to get to know better; becoming one of its kind in meditation may facilitate deeper and clearer communication.

Attuning to the spirits of plants takes time and practice. They do not always come when called, and some can be so elusive that months will go by without contact. Intent matters quite a bit, as does the motivation behind it. Spirits can generally sense your sincerity and authenticity, so do your best to show up in the right frame of mind.

Also remember that the key to all good relationships—and not just relationships with spirits—is *reciprocity*. Don't just show up and make demands; learn to listen to the plant's needs, too.

If you've never experienced a plant spirit you might be wondering what they look like. My experience with spirits is that their appearance is not fixed; many kinds of discarnate intelligences take on forms that have meaning to the person communing with them. Angels are a good example of this. Traditional biblical lore describes angels as fearsome beings of flame and eyes and wings. Today, the same angels appear to most people as beautiful, anthropomorphic beings. Our personal, psychological filters translate the energy of spirits into symbols and words that make sense to us personally. That being said, there are some trends that many practitioners experience.

Plant spirits often appear to me as ethereal, oversized versions of the plant I am working with, though in other instances they are merely swirling masses of color and light, spiritual forces in constant motion. For me, the spirits of individual plants tend to appear smaller than the oversouls or devas of plant species. Some people experience plant spirits that are more human in design, but this has never been the case for me. In fact, many times I don't have any particular image of the plant spirits in mind—I merely sense their presence.

Similar rules apply for communicating with plant spirits. Their language is unlike our own in every way, and that means that I do not usually hear their voices as words. The messages come to me in feelings and impressions, and sometimes as symbols; my mind translates these experiences into words that are more useful. Rarely, I'll hear an oversoul or deva speak outright, but this isn't always the case. Ultimately, however plant spirits show up for you, the important bit is that they've shown up at all.

What can you do to meet those spirits whose plants grow nowhere near you? Maybe you'd like to meet the spirit of the sakura (Japanese flowering cherry) but you live in the desert, or you'd love to connect to rainbow kelp but live on a mountain. With practice, hopefully gained by communing with the spirits already in your environment, you can learn to connect with plants in faraway lands. You can study the characteristics of a plant, find images of it online and in books, and invoke its spirit through the same exercises described above. Another easy way to facilitate contact with plant spirits is by taking their flower essences.

Plant Spirits and Flower Essences

Flower essences can be a remarkable tool for exploring relationships with the spirits of the plant kingdom. When we make an essence, the spirits of the plants work together to imprint their vibration on the water. I mentioned in chapter 1 that essences work holographically, meaning that every drop of an essence contains the whole of the information or imprint of the plant spirit. Thus, taking one or more drops of a flower essence instantly offers the virtues offered by a particular plant spirit.

Using a flower essence directly and immediately attunes us to the energy of a plant spirit, thereby facilitating contact with the spirit itself. We need only place a few drops in our mouth or on our body to feel closer to that spirit. Doing so right before meditation, ritual, or other spiritual work helps us maintain a clearer connection to our plant spirit allies and can expedite the process of finding and bonding with a green familiar.

Essences allow us to call upon the healing and guidance offered by our plant spirit familiars. The unique relationship we have with a plant spirit familiar provides a special kind of soul medicine that goes above and beyond the textbook indications for a given essence. Because of the intimate relationship that we build with that plant, its essence will often work outside of its normal therapeutic indications, with the potential for profound healing and magick. For example, if you have an intimate relationship with trillium, it might be the essence you turn to when you are fearful or uncertain or just plain burned out. This isn't because trillium is particularly useful in these arenas; rather, it's because you've built a reciprocal relationship with the plant spirit of trillium, and it is willing to help you beyond its documented effects.

A simple method for communing with plant spirits is to take their essences intentionally. The key word here is *intentionally*. Some people, particularly those who are very sensitive to subtle energy and have cultivated relationships with spirits and guides, may be readily aware of the presence of a plant spirit when taking flower essences throughout the day. The rest of us, however, are likely to need a little help with establishing that connection.

There are many approaches for using essences to commune with plant spirits. You might enter meditation and take the essence when you feel you have adequately left behind your normal consciousness. You might create a sacred space and invite the spirit to visit, or perhaps you might take the essence while going deep into trance for a shamanic journey with the plant spirit. My favorite method is one that I learned from Christopher Penczak, presented in a slightly adapted form below.

☽ Invoking Plant Spirits with Essences

Start by selecting the essence with which you'd like to work and find a quiet space where you won't be disturbed. Relax your body, mind, and spirit. After all the tension has dissolved, ground and center yourself. You might imagine roots growing from the base of your spine and/or the soles of your feet deep into Mother Earth, or perhaps you'll simply become aware of the weight of your body in your seat as it is held downward by the gentle tug of gravity. Allow any excess or disharmonious energy to dissipate as you become more fully grounded.

When you are ready to connect with the plant spirit, hold the essence bottle in your hands and call to the plant spirit, silently or aloud. You might say something like "Spirit of chamomile, I call to you. Please join me in this space and share your wisdom with me." Spend a moment or two in silence as you allow the invitation to ring out into the ether. Next, make an offering of breath to the plant spirit; the carbon dioxide in your out-breath is a suitable gift for plant spirits, but it must be free of expectations, attachments, or strong thoughts in order to maintain the energetic integrity of your essence. It might be helpful to state your intention, such as by saying, "Gentle spirit of chamomile, I give you this breath as my offering." Breathe in deeply, visualizing not only air but also light or life force filling your lungs. Exhale slowly, directing your breath to the spirit via the dropper bottle. I like to hold the bottle to my heart for a few moments, waiting to feel the presence of the plant spirit before proceeding.

Finally, when you are ready to commune directly with the plant spirit, take a few drops of the essence as a sacrament. The plant spirit may appear in your mind's eye, or you may simply feel its presence in your space or within your heart. From here, you can choose to have a conversation with the plant spirit or simply share in its energy. You can ask questions of it or request healing for yourself or a loved one. I like to invite the plant spirit to share anything it would like to with me when I'm first getting to know it. Often I'll try this before reading too much about the therapeutic uses of its essence, and later I will find that the information I received or the energy I experienced corroborates the details given in the literature about the plant.

When you are ready to complete your meditation, thank the plant spirit for its time, wisdom, and energy. I like to hold the essence bottle to my heart again as I thank the spirit. When you sense that its presence has left, take several deep, centering breaths and ground again as needed. Open your eyes and return to ordinary consciousness when you are ready.

Making Offerings

Every relationship requires a balance of give and take. I do believe that the plant kingdom is usually more than willing to sacrifice flower, leaf, bark, and root for the benefit of other beings. Plants usually exhibit a remarkable ability to regenerate, such that respectful harvesting can be maintained on an ongoing basis. However, relationships are by their very nature meant to be reciprocal.

Whether we are looking to meet the spirit of the plant in meditation or to harvest pieces of its body for making essences, medicine, or magick, it is helpful to learn to listen to and respect the needs of the denizens of the green world—both embodied plants and plant spirits. This means learning that plant spirits have their own autonomy; they do not always come when called nor volunteer their bodies for our work. When we work with plant spirits, we build a better alliance through the practice of making offerings. This establishes a reciprocal relationship with the green world. Simple offerings might include fresh, clean water and breath. Our own in-breath carries oxygen thanks to the plants and other photosynthetic organisms that exhale oxygen into the atmosphere. We can direct our out-breath, which carries the carbon dioxide necessary for photosynthesis, to plants as an offering, too.

Cultivated plants can be given offerings of compost, fertilizer, food and beverage, crystals and gemstones, dried plant matter, smoke, and other gifts. Wild plants may also be willing to receive such offerings, but always exercise caution. A smoke offering might appear to be a blessing unless you accidentally start a wildfire. Similarly, gifts of food, drink, or water might be okay in some areas but could upset the delicate balance of other ecosystems; I've read of water offerings causing tree roots to rot in more arid soils. Know that offerings of food or drink are likely to be taken by animals, so only leave behind offerings that are safe for them to consume. When all else fails, leave small offerings of compostable, natural items, or give your time, appreciation, and energy to the plant spirits.

My favorite offerings to give the plants are essences. A few drops can be added to a vessel of pure water and poured onto the ground, a plant, or any other meaningful place. Giving essences as offerings is a way to show that you aren't using plant medicine solely for your own benefit. Instead, by sharing essences with plants and the land, you are offering healing to the larger ecosystem. Spirits dwell within a deeply interconnected system, and giving spirit medicine back to this network is a wonderful way to ingratiate yourself among the many spirits that comprise this system. You can select essences that are indicated for issues playing out in the environment, or you can use essences that are generally good for the spirits of nature, such as lilac and foxglove. I love to give plants offerings of essences made from the same plant, such as giving a few drops of rosemary essence to the rosemary plant growing in our garden.

No matter what offerings you decide to employ, know that giving back is the best way to establish trust with the spirits of the green.

4

Balms, Banes, and Tree Spirits

Plant spirits come in a variety of forms on many levels of existence, as illustrated in chapter 3. When we make contact with plant spirits, we are essentially inviting their consciousness to impart teaching, healing, and transformation on one level or another. However, not all plants work toward the same ends or use the same mechanisms for those purposes. Loosely speaking, it is possible to group plants and their spirits by their temperament and the manner in which they work. The system I use for categorizing and understanding the nature of plant spirits was taught to me by my friend and mentor Christopher Penczak, and it is outlined in detail in his book *The Plant Spirit Familiar*. Christopher calls it the "three kin," for it is a threefold classification consisting of balms, banes, and trees.

Balms are the healing herbs. Their spirits are generally affable, bright, and a delight to know. Balms provide food and medicine for body and soul. *Banes* are plants with an adversarial nature, particularly those of a poisonous persuasion. Banes are initiators; they guard the threshold between worlds and help us face the toxic patterns in our own lives. *Trees* are the teacher spirits of the plant kingdom. Trees mediate between the worlds, with their verticality aligning and bridging heaven, earth, and the underworld. Each category of plants and the spirits thereof offer a unique brand of healing and wisdom. Thus, essences made from the plants of one category differ in effect from those of the other two.

Interestingly, I find that these three branches (pardon the botanical pun) of plant spirits correlate to the three meanings of *pharmakeia,* the Greek word denoting medicine, magick, and poison all as one, as we learned in chapter 2. In a literal sense, all three categories of plant spirits may be used for magick, medicine, or poison according to the properties of the individual plants. However, there is a poetic connection to explore, too. Balms, the healing herbs, most readily relate to the medicinal aspect of pharmakeia, as they are the most accessible medicines of the plant world. Balms nourish and heal the body, mind, and spirit. Baneful plants are usually poisons in a literal sense, and they are used to fight fire with fire—their spirits help us overcome the poisonous thoughts we imbibe each day. Trees are the high priests and priestesses of the plant kingdom, and they therefore represent the magickal aspect of pharmakeia. Like the magus, sorcerer, and shaman, the tree stands at the threshold between worlds.

It is worth noting that not every plant neatly fits into one of the three categories. Perhaps a plant has an herbaceous stem and therefore is not a tree, but it is neither particularly medicinal nor poisonous. Others may span more than one category; yew, for example, is notoriously baneful but is also a mighty and ancient species of tree. While the threefold classification system is a helpful model for interacting with plant spirits, it is not an absolute truth that depicts the work and wisdom of each and every plant spirit in nature. I've made an effort to classify the plants in the directory of essences (see chapter 11) as accurately as possible according to the nature of the plant spirit and the effects of the essences themselves.

The main reason for learning to identify and work with the three kin is to help the practitioner build a better relationship with the green world. As you get to know various plant spirits, you can build a team of helpers that can assist your healing or magickal practice. Balms can instruct you in ways to nourish and bless. Banes will guide you into the realm of shadow. Tree spirits align you with the bigger picture and offer profound grounding and wisdom. My experience is that anyone seeking a relationship with plant spirit allies can forge relationships with a representative of each of the three kin as their primary plant spirit familiars.

BACH'S THREEFOLD CLASSIFICATION

Before exploring the three kin, I'd like to set the stage for understanding them better. The classification of plants as balms, banes, or trees is not the first threefold system to be applied to the making of flower essences. Dr. Edward Bach had his own method of classifying plants for his work. His mission was to develop a form of medicine that could be administered by laypeople and practitioners alike, and safety was one his highest priorities. Bach sought to find his remedies among plants as he thought the animal and mineral kingdoms to be inappropriate for a number of reasons (although essence producers today co-create their essences with minerals and animals in safe and humane manners). Bach divided plants into the following three categories:

★ Primitive plants
★ Food-producing plants
★ Healing plants[1]

Bach considered the first category of plants to be below the spiritual level of humankind. It consisted of seaweed, cacti, parasitic plants, and orchids, as well as the baneful herbs and other dangerous plants. His belief was that these plants would lower the vibrations of the human body. He ranked the second category, food-producing plants, on par with humankind; they were unable to lift the vibrations or consciousness any further. The third grouping, the healing plants, were those that possessed the qualities necessary to raise consciousness and displace the true cause of disease.

In some ways, these three categories correspond with the three kin: baneful plants comprise a wide sector of the primitives, balms are synonymous with healing plants, and it could be argued that many important sources of food are derived from trees—though many other kinds of plants are also important sources of food. Some of Bach's remedies appear to contradict his categories, however, as he considered all of his remedies to be produced from plants belonging to the third category: healing plants. For example, crab apple, sweet chestnut, cherry plum, vine (grape), and olive are all important sources of food, and even acorns from oak and rose hips from wild rose are still eaten today. Clematis, on the other hand, also known as old man's beard and traveller's joy, is a baneful herb that can cause severe abdominal pain and irritation of the skin and gastrointestinal tract; the scent of the foliage can even cause the eyes and nose to water profusely.[2] Similarly, star-of-Bethlehem straddles the divide between medicinal and toxic, as it contains compounds that are known to kill livestock and humans alike. Both white and red chestnut (*Aesculus hippocastanum* and *Aesculus carnea*)* contain toxic compounds in their seeds, suggesting that they display at least some of the qualities of the primitive plants outlined by Bach. Furthermore, Bach describes the healing plants as those whose medicine has been forgotten—his intention was to reclaim their curative powers through his new system of healing. Yet there are flowering plants in his system that appear to have no known medicinal uses in history, such as water violet (*Hottonia palustris*). This threefold division of plants was clearly more subjective than literal.

Bach produced thirty-eight remedies, and they can be categorized thusly with fifteen balms, twenty trees, two banefuls, and one environmental essence. (See the table on the following pages.)

While it is not possible to know exactly what parameters Dr. Bach used to define his three categories of plants, nor precisely how and why he chose the plants for his remedies, we can see that he had a relatively specific goal in mind, which required a narrower scope of flowers than many modern-day practitioners feel necessary. While Bach's system of flower essences is complete in its own right as a healing modality, it does not always adequately address the consciousness of the plants. By merely observing the wide array of essences available today, made from plants that span all three of Dr. Bach's plant categories, we can surmise that there are adequate healing qualities to be found in every type of plant. It is the overall action or mechanism of healing that differs from

---

*Some of Dr. Bach's nomenclature differs from the common names in use today. *Aesculus hippocastanum* is better known as horse chestnut, and *Aesculus carnea* is typically called red horse chestnut. I've retained Bach's names whenever discussing his remedies.

one group to the next, and it appears that Bach mostly found the mechanisms of balms and trees to be most compatible with the vision he held for his remedies. Even though Dr. Bach asserted that flower essences should be made only from those divinely enriched healing herbs, today we can enjoy essences made from balms, banes, and trees alike.

CLASSIFICATION OF BACH REMEDIES

BALM ESSENCES	TREE ESSENCES*	BANEFUL ESSENCES	ENVIRONMENTAL ESSENCE
Agrimony (Agrimonia eupatoria)	Aspen (Populus tremulus)	Clematis (Clematis vitalba)	Rock water†
Centaury (Centaurium erythraea)	Beech (Fagus sylvatica)	Star-of-Bethlehem (Ornithogalum umbellatum)	
Cerato (Cerato willmottiana)	Cherry plum (Prunus cerasifera)		
Chicory (Chicorium intybus)	Chestnut bud (Aesculus hippocastanum)		
Gentian (Gentiana amarella)	Crab apple (Malus sylvestris)		
Honeysuckle (Lonicera caprifolium)	Elm (Ulmus procera)		
Impatiens (Impatiens glandulifera)	Gorse (Ulex europaeus)		

*Of the plants in this list, gorse, heather, and vine (that is, grapevine) are not usually labeled trees in the botanical sense, but they do share a lot of spiritual qualities with trees, and they are included in the Green Man Tree Flower Essences line from the U.K. and in the books on tree essences written by Sue and Simon Lilly. They are also represented in the medieval ogham, or "tree alphabet," used to write the Irish language and were at least anecdotally considered to be trees by the people who used the alphabet.

†Authorities on the Bach system disagree about the classification of the rock water remedy. Purists maintain that since it is made simply of solarized spring water, it cannot be considered a true environmental essence. However, I think that if Bach were using the terminology available today, he might see the close parallel between rock water and other environmental essences.

BALM ESSENCES	TREE ESSENCES	BANEFUL ESSENCES	ENVIRONMENTAL ESSENCE
Mimulus (*Mimulus guttatus*)	Heather (*Calluna vulgaris*)		
Mustard (*Sinapsis arvensis*)	Holly (*Ilex aquifolium*)		
Rock rose (*Helianthemum nummularium*)	Hornbeam (*Carpinus betulus*)		
Scleranthus (*Scleranthus annuus*)	Larch (*Larix decidua*)		
Vervain (*Verbena officinalis*)	Oak (*Quercus robur*)		
Water violet (*Hottonia palustris*)	Olive (*Olea europea*)		
Wild oat (*Bromus ramosus*)	Pine (*Pinus sylvestris*)		
Wild rose (*Rosa canina*)	Red chestnut (*Aesculus carnea*)		
	Sweet chestnut (*Castanea sativa*)		
	Walnut (*Juglans regia*)		
	White chestnut (*Aesculus hippocastanum*)		
	Vine (*Vitis vinifera*)		
	Willow (*Salix alba* var. *vitellina*)		

BALMS, THE HEALING HERBS

Balms are the traditional medicines used around the world, the healing herbs of both garden and glen. They are revered and employed by healers, doctors, magicians, and laypeople. While any kind of plant can be used for medicinal purposes, balms are specifically those plant spirits that are relatively benign. They are humble, friendly, and often quite nutritious. Balms do not need to carry the warnings of banes—which, despite their potential medicinal benefits, must be used with great care. Bach specifically described his healing herbs as offering no severe reactions; their actions are gentle and sure.[3]

Balms carry phytochemicals that act as medicines for the bodies of humans and animals alike. The exact cause or meaning for these chemical constituents is not always well understood. Why should plants produce chemicals that are so nutritious or therapeutic for other organisms? These compounds are usually not of any direct benefit to the plants themselves. Unlike banes, who may weaponize their phytochemicals to prevent animals from eating their leaves or roots, balms appear to invite being eaten. Natural selection surely plays a role in the making of medicines. Creatures great and small help medicinal plants spread far and wide with or without the conscious intention to do so, and this process has probably favored those plants with stronger medicines just as much as it has benefited those plants with the most fragrant flowers and sweetest fruit. The result creates a plant that does more than encourage other organisms to eat it; when consumed, it heals them as well.

Balms seemingly *want* to serve others. They are the helper spirits of the plant kingdom; they are genuinely invested in the health and wellness of other beings. Sometimes their medicine is aimed not at humans or animals but at other plants or the environment itself.[4] Balms are the plants with the most widely known lore and legends. They feature not only in medicine but also in magick and cuisine. Even those that have fallen out of use medicinally are still ensouled by powerful spirits. These plant spirits are generally considered active and bright; their magickal and medicinal properties enhance the flow of life force.[5] Their powerful medicines knit together wounds of the body and soul alike, and they offer their healing without expectation or caveat.

Balms are often used in magick to draw in a positive energy or outcome; they are the plants of magickal blessings. They nourish us with loving, healing energies and help manifest prosperity, peace, love, joy, and comfort. By strengthening and healing us, many balms also fortify our natural defenses. They can support our resolve to release and let go of old scenarios just as easily as they can draw in new ones. Their spirits are naturally inclined toward helping with the healing arts, and befriending a balm plant spirit might enhance our healing gifts and boost our ability to diagnose and treat a wide range of imbalances.

Bach considered the truly healing herbs to have powers that were somehow divinely enriched. Across his many publications he describes the healing herbs as having been placed in nature by Divine Providence or by God for the express purpose of offering solace and salvation to humankind, thereby pointing toward plants with a higher calling. Balms are those plants that he describes as "beneficent and of a very high order."[6] They are those plants that seek to raise our consciousness and enhance our well-being of body, mind, and spirit.

Balms are widespread throughout the plant kingdom. They include accessible and obvious medicines, like mints, sage, angelica, yarrow, passionflower, and rosemary. St. John's wort, mugwort, and rose are all balms. Even some plants that seemingly put up great defenses, like nettle, are balms because they heal much more greatly than they harm. Balms are cultivated far and wide, though they also grow wild—often in the hedges and borders long associated with the witching herbs. Those weedy and liminal balms illustrate the overlap between witch and healer and the intersection of magick and medicine.

Balms as Essences

Healing herbs were Dr. Bach's focus when he set out to create his remedies. He was interested in neither poisonous plants nor food crops, as he felt that they did not offer the healing potential that balms did. Nora Weeks, Bach's close colleague and biographer, tells us that the medicinal herbs (i.e., the balms) that "contained true healing power were of a different order and few in number. Many plants possessed medicinal properties which soothed and relieved the sufferings of the human body, . . . but the true *healing* plants held a greater power than this."[7]

As flower essences, balms tend toward actions of restoration, repair, and nourishment. According to Dr. Bach, they "help us preserve our personality."[8] Rather than working directly on the agents of illness or attacking the patterns of psychological or spiritual imbalance, balms seek to bring us back into a state of harmony by means of tapping in to higher consciousness. Recalling Bach's own description from chapter 1 (see page 12), "They cure, not by attacking disease, but by flooding our bodies with the beautiful vibrations of our Higher Nature, in the presence of which disease melts as snow in the sunshine."[9]

Balms tend to make the safest, gentlest, and surest flower essences. Their actions work on the soul to lift our consciousness when the weight of the world otherwise drags us down. Balms are many and varied, generally accounting for those essences that are made from plants that are neither treelike nor particularly baneful. Thus, balms exhibit a wide range of effects and influences when we take them. Generally speaking, they help the burdens of worry, fear, grief, and oversensitivity to abate, and they restore hope and energy when circumstances are bleak or draining. The essences made from balms, especially those widely known for being medicinal plants, tend to be the most nourishing of flower essences.

BANES, THE PLANTS
OF POISON AND POWER

Banes are the plants that carry an element of danger. Sometimes they are thorny or prickly, defying our wishes to peacefully harvest them; other times they bear invisible toxins in lieu of visible weapons, making them poisonous or even psychoactive. Baneful plants are those that have historically been connected to malefic magick and witchcraft; they are said to have grown in the devil's garden and were used for the most evil intentions, like cursing and killing. That dark shroud of lore and legend has obscured their beneficent virtues. For example, many poisonous plants contain compounds that, when used sparingly and cautiously, initiate profound healing in the body. Since many banes are outright deadly, working with them as flower essences and vibrational remedies offers the safest means for communing with their spirits and receiving their healing virtues.

Spiritually, the poisonous and adversarial nature of banes leads us to the realm of the shadow self. The overculture's preoccupation with the goodness of nature and its tendency to ignore nature's uncomfortable, dangerous, or toxic aspects creates an imbalance. Fear of danger and discomfort—if not fear of power altogether—has contributed to a collective state in which humans are ill equipped for genuine spiritual experience. When dark and destructive actions upset the status quo, we flounder. Rather than allowing inner poisons to overtake us, we must learn to confront the shadow and make peace with what we find there if we are ever to have true healing and spiritual growth. Baneful plants are catalysts for this work. Christopher Penczak describes them as the "dark twins of the balms."[10]

Baneful plants are magick and power embodied in the plant kingdom. Ancient literature allies poisonous plants with Hekate, the goddess of magick and witchcraft, as well as with sorceresses and witches of many cultures. Poison has long represented the transmission of occult knowledge and the acquisition of power. Daniel Schulke, author and occult herbalist with an expertise in baneful plants, writes, "Poison is a glyph for magical power itself: complex, concentrated, liberated in the hands of the elect, and disastrous in the hands of the fool. Its very nature is transmutative, changing all it touches, the maker and breaker of laws, policies, and epidemiological systems."[11]

Many psychoactive baneful plants are considered "power plants," including cannabis, datura, peyote, and ayahuasca. Indigenous people journey with these sacred, baneful medicines to acquire spiritual power, especially during initiatory rites. Banes are also connected to the will of the gods, as they have the power to both kill and cure. They are often linked to themes of fate, karma, and death and rebirth. This makes them powerful initiatory tools that catalyze deep spiritual growth and profound healing.

Most of the plants of poison and power are associated with liminal spaces. They grow at the edge of the civilized world, and they help us cross the threshold between this world and the beyond. Baneful plants are linked to the underworld and the ancestors because of their obvious connections to death. However, banes are also symbolic of another sort of death: the death of one state of being and rebirth into the next. In other words, banes are the initiators of the plant kingdom; they are midwives on the soul's journey.

Baneful plants are the gatekeepers between realms. We can use them to journey within as well to leave behind the limits of ordinary consciousness. In both a chemical and metaphysical sense, banes remove life force. Many of these plants are psychoactive in some way when ingested, and they have been used in the infamous witches' salves and flying ointments of lore and legend. Their dangerous alkaloids can facilitate otherworldly travels of an entheogenic or hallucinatory nature when used in nonlethal doses. Their spiritual medicine, however, helps open the threshold of the mind and expands the consciousness. Many baneful plants cause unpleasant side effects, like vomiting and diarrhea, literally causing the body to purge itself. Energetically, banes purge us of the most deadly poisons of all: the toxic beliefs, ideas, and behaviors held in the mind and heart. This deep and powerful cleansing prepares us for initiatory experiences.

In magick, baneful plants help us contend with darkness and danger. They may be potent wards against evil and misfortune, or they may be used to banish malefic influences from our lives. Historically, these plants have also been used for cursing and hexing. Today, banes are employed in a wide array of magickal uses, from stopping gossip to easing disputes. Most baneful plants can be used in magick and ritual aimed at spirit communication, as well as for spirit flight and astral travel.

Some of the plants that I've chosen to categorize as baneful are not the traditional poisons or shamanic power plants. Some are close relatives, like potato and tomato—the wrong parts of which are rather unpleasant to consume, being milder versions of their more potent relatives. Some are unassuming but otherwise toxic plants, like snowdrops.

Some banes, like enchanter's nightshade and parsley, aren't especially toxic but have a long association with magick and witchcraft, and they have taken on baneful qualities from long histories of being used alongside more poisonous plants. Cannabis, a plant praised for its medicine, is regarded as a baneful spirit rather than a balm, not because it is toxic, but because of its consciousness-altering qualities.

Banes as Essences

When I was a fledgling witch, I read about poisonous plants with a certain degree of incredulity. It was hard to imagine why anyone would want to place themselves at risk by using baneful herbs in magick. Although I now realize that, with a little caution, many of the witching herbs are reasonably safe to handle, I remain respectful and wary of poisonous plants with which I don't have any experience. Thankfully, when the banes are properly made into flower essences, none of their physical toxicity is transferred to the finished product. Flower essences are the safest methods for working with otherwise dangerous plants.

Traditional lore aside, why go out of our way to make essences from poisonous plants? In short, toxic plants are the best tools for addressing toxic energies. To understand the mechanism behind this concept, we can revisit Paracelsus's teachings: the difference between poison and panacea is a matter of dose. Thus, working with baneful flower essences in many ways follows the principles of homeopathy, as we are using the law of similars (like cures like). Baneful flower essences are vital tools for exploring, releasing, and transcending toxic patterns. They can be used to eliminate harmful thought patterns, break negative habits, and remove toxic people and situations from our lives.

I learned early on in my magickal practice that one of the primary reasons for working with baneful herbs, apart from tradition, is their speed. Discusssing the magick of poisonous plants in her book *To Stir a Magick Cauldron,* witch and author Silver Ravenwolf notes that most of these plants produce measurable results within a few short days, if not mere hours, when used in magick and ritual. For example, Ravenwolf says that lily of the valley produces *immediate* results, and monkshood takes effect within several hours.[12] Comparatively, nontoxic plants generally have a slower response time. Flower essences made from poisonous plants also tend to offer noticeable changes in much shorter times, too. Generally speaking, I've found that the relative toxicity or psychoactivity of baneful plants directly correlates to their potency as flower essences. In other words, highly toxic plants like belladonna, hemlock, and monkshood typically produce much more intense effects as flower essences than significantly less toxic plants like snowdrop and clematis.

Many baneful plants bear the five-petaled blossoms that signify a doorway of sorts, and their essences help the soul leave the body, thereby facilitating astral travel and other spiritual journeys, such as into the underworld. They can be used singly or in blends designed to assist in journeys, like the flying essence blends discussed in chapter 9. Baneful essences are especially adept at aiding in the transmission of occult knowledge and personal gnosis. These essences enable us to better reach the state of nonordinary reality, the state of consciousness in which shamanic and magickal endeavors take place. Baneful essences therefore boost psychic skills and enhance intuition.

Baneful essences are attuned to deaths and endings. They bring solace and resolution to painful and toxic patterns that have played out in our inner or outer world. In fact, the most famous group of baneful plants, the Solanaceae family, derives its name from the Latin *solare,* meaning "to soothe." Baneful essences help us put our fears, worries, and destructive beliefs or behaviors to rest. Because of their innate affinity for the shadow self, plants of poison and power create essences that help us examine and transform what we find buried in the subconscious mind. They help us find greater balance by providing darkness and decay as counterpoints to light and birth. Thus, baneful essences help us complete and release cycles and seasons that no longer serve us.

Many baneful plants are associated with Venus in astrological herbalism. Their flowers have seductive scents and five petals, both signifying the planet of love and romance. The stark contrast between seduction and poison makes many of these baneful essences ideal tools for healing trauma related to sex and romance. Baneful essences can help us move on after toxic relationships, reclaim our sexual sovereignty, and boost our self-esteem.

As mentioned earlier, Dr. Bach avoided baneful plants in the preparation of his flower essences, considering them to be "primitive plants." In his career in homeopathy, he had worked with the products of illness and contagion, as well as poisonous plants, minerals, and metals, to initiate the healing process. Afterward, Bach felt compelled to seek healing agents that supported wellness by flooding the body, mind, and spirit with positive qualities, rather than using poisons and agents of disease to combat the negative conditions at play in disease states. He also encouraged laypeople to make their own remedies from the plants, and he likely avoided highly toxic plants so as to ensure safe results across the board.

Bach described these primitive plants as "lowering the vibrations" of the body, rendering it unfit for the habitation of the soul.[13] This may well be a tongue-in-cheek way to describe the biological effects of consuming poisonous plants, for they can, in the wrong dose, cause death. But while Bach's system of flower essences draws extensively from the virtues of the healing balms and the tree teachers, baneful plants also offer a depth of healing. The quality that Bach describes as "lowering the vibrations" perfectly corresponds to one of the common paths of power exhibited by baneful plants: they help our consciousness descend into the lower worlds—into the deep subconscious and unconscious and into the realm of shadow and shade. While the healing plants or balms flood the system with light, banes invite us to explore the aspects of the self riddled with darkness; they help us discover where we are most deeply wounded. This underworld journey is in itself an initiatory experience.

However you choose to work with baneful flower essences, do so in moderation. Making essences from toxic plants requires caution and common sense; they can also be purchased from trusted essence makers. Overall, baneful essences offer more profound and immediate results than balms or trees do. Thus, consider using them in smaller doses and with less frequency. I usually take only one or two drops of the more potent baneful essences, and sometimes only once per day. Taking a small dose before bed is an ideal way to allow the baneful plant spirit to guide and enhance your dreamtime journeys. When combining banes with other essences, it is helpful to use essences that are more stabilizing, protective, and nourishing, rather than those that act more as catalysts or purgatives, or that are themselves banes—especially for sensitive people.

TREES, THE WISDOMKEEPERS

Trees once covered much, if not most, of the Earth's landmasses in the forgotten days of our planet's history. Massive and ancient forests were the primordial dwelling place of our earliest ancestors. Those trees offered shelter, food, and medicine—though they also hid danger and mystery in the depths of their green hearts. For this reason, trees have been sacred since prehistory, and they feature in the religions and folklore of virtually every culture on Earth. The ancient Canaanites worshipped wooden posts carved from trees as emissaries of the goddess Asherah. The Celts and their clergy, the druids, gathered in sacred groves; even the word *druid* is purportedly derived from the Celtic root word for "oak." Trees continue to feature in cultural and spiritual celebrations the world over, from the Christmas tree and Yule log to the sakura (Japanese flowering cherry) that is celebrated in *hanami,* the tradition of flower viewing.

Tree spirits are the elders of the plant kingdom; they are the wisdomkeepers and storytellers of the green world. The most common motif of the sacred tree is the World Tree, or Tree of Life; it is the *axis mundi,* the celestial pole around which all of Creation dances and turns. Found in the cosmologies of the Maya, Norse, Egyptians, Zoroastrians, Babylonians, and countless shamanic people, the World Tree spans the three worlds. Its branches reach heavenward, growing upward into the abode of the gods. Its trunk is the cosmic pillar that anchors the material realm in which we live, the meeting place of the four directions. Its roots dig deep into the underworld; this chthonic plane is the abode of our ancestors and the world of spirits. In various myths, the World Tree has been depicted as an ash, oak, kapok, and countless other trees.

Sue and Simon Lilly, flower essence experts and makers of Green Man Tree Essences, posit that trees are the creators and maintainers of

The World Tree spans the three archetypal levels of reality: heaven, Earth, and the underworld.

our reality.[14] They base this concept on two fundamental understandings: that mature trees play a vital, life-sustaining role in physically maintaining the well-being of the planet as a whole, and that the nature of a tree extends beyond its mere physical form. Trees maintain the stability of the climate and atmosphere, as well as protecting local environments by regulating numerous factors, such as water and soil. In fact, the Lillys tell us, trees are among the oldest, largest, and most stable life-forms on Earth.[15]

Author and shamanic practitioner Ross Heaven tells us that trees were sacred to the ancient Celts as transformers, both practically and spiritually. The Celts understood trees to be, among other things, transformers of toxins, purifying their environment. Indeed, as modern science has since shown, trees are carbon sinks, meaning they absorb more carbon than they release, thereby lowering the net amount of carbon dioxide in the atmosphere. Trees also purify on an energetic level, offering outlets to the ouranic and chthonic worlds to discharge negativity and harm. The Celts also saw trees as transformers of the human spirit, providing healing, guidance, and wisdom, and as transformers of worlds, offering doorways to other realms through their role as the axis mundi. And in the Celtic spiritual tradition, trees were said to be transformers of the soul, serving as psychopomps that lead the soul from one plane to the next between incarnations.[16]

Christopher Penczak describes trees as the "ministers of the plant world" and the "priestesses and priests mediating the energy between the heavens, Earth and underworld, and between the world of green and the world of flesh and blood."[17] (Humans share this role with trees, at least in part, as evidenced by the vertical orientation of our own inner axis: the spine.) Trees are the wisdomkeepers and storytellers, too, for the rings of growth within their wood record the history of their region. Trees, especially large and lush ones, tend to command attention and evoke a sense of kinship. Even people who aren't students of the green mysteries often find themselves attracted to or comforted by trees, for trees are the mediators between the kingdoms of plant and animal. They minister to their plant, animal, and human kin alike by holding space and sharing the wisdom of the ages stored within.

Some plant spirits function in the same manner as tree treachers, even though they are not trees in a botanical sense. Shrubs like gorse may lack the singular trunk of a true tree but share a sense of verticality and the ability to stand out in the landscape. Other examples include the mighty saguaro cactus and bamboo; their verticality and commanding presence align us in the same way as proper trees. Grapevine is another plant example; it has a tough, woody stem that climbs upward along a tree or another support to create a vertical axis as it reaches the canopy. Other plants work so closely with the realm of the tree spirits that they are virtually inseparable from it, such as mistletoe and Spanish moss, and they help bridge tree spirit consciousness with that of other kinds of plant spirits.

Trees as Essences

Essences made from trees are profoundly healing, as they immediately ground and align us, offering the balance we need to weather the ups and downs of life. They help us stabilize our spiritual progress and teach us to set the right pace for long-term growth and evolution. Just as trees encase their own trunks in a protective layer of bark, they confer qualities of protection, defense, and safety to us via their essences.

We can learn a lot about the mechanism of flower essences made from trees by examining Dr. Bach's system. He grouped his flower essences into seven categories, each one representing a certain family of moods and emotions. Of those categories, two have a predominance of trees: the remedies for despondency and despair, where seven out of eight remedies are trees, and the remedies for fear, in which three of five essences are trees. Flower essences made from trees thus seem predisposed to transforming or displacing fear, panic, despair, and gloom.

In the group of seven essences that Dr. Bach categorized as remedies for insufficient interest in the present, three are also trees. Tree spirits are powerful allies for grounding and learning to be more aware of our current scenario. Trees function as anchors for the landscape and as centers of community in the natural world. As essences, tree spirits similarly act to ground and center larger patterns. In addition to our personal healing, tree essences can work effectively for treating conditions with their roots in generational karma, the group consciousness of communities and nations, and planetwide wounds. Trees offer shelter and resources to a variety of organisms, and essences made from them typically promote understanding of interdependence and community. Each of these healing themes is enhanced by or built on the foundation of being present and aware.

Tree flower essences display a wide range of uses, and there are entire lines of essences dedicated solely to trees. Trees' bark is protective, their roots grounding, and their branches expansive; we can receive the blessings of each of these qualities when we take tree essences. Flower essences made from trees invite us to become more attuned to the kingdoms of nature, as tree spirits themselves are, among the three kin, the most closely tied to the spirits of the land. Tree essences help us integrate the wisdom of nature and may evoke memories of the distant past, both in this life and beyond. As wisdomkeepers and storytellers, trees invite us to really listen to the messages of nature and of the spirit world. Tree essence practitioner and author Daniel Tigner summarizes the virtues of tree essences beautifully: "In a wider sense tree essences are about deepening our awareness of nature, loosening self-contained boundaries that feed our illusion of being separate. Heightening this understanding of relatedness is fundamentally healing as is allowing ourselves to be nourished by the qualities of a particular tree."[18]

As stabilizing and protective remedies, tree flower essences are excellent adjuncts to the work of balms and banes. They keep us anchored in the present moment so we can better experience the therapeutic effects of the other essences, too. Tree essences also seem to unlock our innate awareness of the bigger picture, revealing how we fit into the story in any situation—often by helping us rewrite the self-centered narrative we tell ourselves.

While balms and banes also promote magickal fluency in their own ways, tree essences help us attune to the upper and lower worlds simultaneously to improve our magick, meditation, and other spiritual endeavors. Tree essences can help us transform into the high priests and priestesses we are meant to be by claiming our sovereignty and wisdom and using them to co-create a more magickal world.

YOUR PLANT SPIRIT ALLIES

The natural outgrowth of learning about the specific natures of the three kin is to develop working relationships with plant spirits that can help you on your journey through the green world. In addition to using their flower essences, you can make contact with the spirits of the plants themselves to enhance your therapeutic and magickal work. Over time, you'll cultivate a veritable garden of plant spirit allies, but there are often three primary familiars that will come to the fore: one balm, one bane, and one tree.

Throughout this chapter we've explored the general themes that pertain to the three kin and looked at the context for their use in flower essence therapy and in magick. While generalizations can be made for each of these categories, each and every plant spirit will have its own mission and purpose. In light of this, there is no substitute for getting to know the individual plant spirits that show up for you on your journey. Building authentic relationships with them can accelerate your path and make you a more sensitive therapist and more capable magician.

The remainder of this chapter is dedicated to helping you meet your personal familiars or totems among the three kin. Generally, most people will find one representative from each of these three classes of plant spirits that is willing to act in the role of the familiar spirit or totemic ally. Working with the plant allies that appear to you in these meditations will help you deepen your relationship with the green world. These allies may offer personalized insight and teachings to facilitate your growth with flower essences, acting as your own tutelary spirits and guides in their respective domains. While it isn't necessary to obtain an essence from your personal bane, balm, and tree, you will find that taking their essences singly or in combination will catalyze the work you do with them.

One of the requisite meditations to facilitate journeying with plant spirits is visiting the World Tree. Similar journeys to the World Tree are used in many spiritual practices and magickal orders as a means of accessing the underworld, the upperworld, or other planes of reality. A journey to the World Tree can be a meditation unto itself, too, as it offers an opportunity to attune to and align with the axis mundi, as well as tap in to the soul of the world for healing and learning. In my very first experience of the World Tree in meditation, it appeared to me as an ancient magnolia with leaves bigger than beach towels and blossoms so large I could have taken a bath in them. You might experience the World Tree differently; most people encounter it as a single species, commonly oak or ash, though perhaps it will be a species of tree with personal significance.

Over the years I have come to experience the World Tree in myriad forms, but in the most commonly recurring image it is a fusion of different trees. The bark is a jumble of different textures and colors, and leaves, needles, fruit, and flowers of innumerable variety hang from every branch. I like to use the image of this fantastical tree because it is simultaneously every tree and no tree at all; it is the sort of paradox that we expect to find in our travels into the spirit realm. This will be the image used in the following meditation.

☽ Visiting the World Tree

Begin by making yourself comfortable in a space where you will not be disturbed. Breathe deeply and comfortably, allowing each out-breath and in-breath to unwind any tension held in your body, mind, and spirit. Take a few moments to still your mind and allow the troubles of the day to float away.

On the screen of your mind, visualize the distant outline of a mighty tree. With each breath, the tree draws nearer. The World Tree is as tall as a skyscraper, with a trunk so wide that even walking around it seems a long journey. It has branches and boughs draped with the leaves and needles of every tree on Earth. Some hold fruit, others cones or flowers. The bark is a patchwork quilt of textures and colors. Enormous mushrooms grow like a spiral staircase around the mighty trunk that leads to the heavens, while the roots form archways and tunnels into the underworld. When it is nearly close enough to reach out and touch, imagine yourself stepping through the screen of your mind and walking up to the mighty tree.

Approach the tree with reverence and respect, and you will be met in kind. If you need alignment, healing, or grounding, reach out and embrace the trunk or sit with your spine against it. You might also just choose to spend time basking in the holiness of the World Tree, passively attuning to its mysteries; conversely, you might introduce yourself to the spirit of the World Tree and await a reply from its consciousness.

On your first visit to the World Tree, do not try to ascend to the heavens or climb down into the roots. Merely allow yourself to feel its presence here in the middle world. When you have finished your meditation, step back through the screen of your mind and allow the image of the World Tree to drift away into the distance. Take several deep, cleansing breaths to ensure that you are grounded and centered before opening your eyes.

After you get comfortable visiting the World Tree, you can prepare to return to it many times and access the realms above, below, and within it. The next three meditations will take you through the process of revisiting the World Tree as a means of accessing three sacred gardens. The first is filled with balms, the second with banes, and the third a forest of trees.

☽ Journey to the Medicine Garden

Begin as before, making yourself comfortable in a place free from distractions. Breathe deeply and comfortably, allowing each out-breath and in-breath to unwind any tension held in your body, mind, and spirit. Take a few moments to still your mind and allow the troubles of the day to float away.

On the screen of your mind, visualize the distant outline of the World Tree, allowing it to draw closer with each breath. When it is nearby, picture yourself stepping through the screen of your mind and approach the World Tree.

Hold your intention to visit the garden of medicine to meet your balm spirit ally. Your attention is drawn to the mushrooms that spiral around the World Tree, and they beckon you to climb up the trunk of the mighty tree. You find the climb to be effortless, as if you are being drawn forward and upward by a celestial force. As you reach the crown of the tree, you find yourself in the world above. A path leads from the branches through a lush landscape in the sky. Rolling hills give way to reveal a garden of healing herbs, one that shines with celestial light. You feel the welcoming atmosphere of the garden and saunter through its ornately carved gates.

The herbs are arranged in orderly rows along a winding path that leads to the center of the garden. Mint, sage, rosemary, lemon balm, and other aromatic herbs release their heavenly scents as you pass by them. Rose, jasmine, and honeysuckle are replete with blooms, and ponds sport the lively blossoms of lotus and water lily. Lavender and other medicines are arranged in beautiful displays throughout the garden. As you near the heart of the garden, you see a lone plant or figure awaiting your approach. This is your totemic balm, the healing herb that seeks to forge a relationship with you as a personal guide and ally in the green world.

This plant spirit may appear to you as the plant or else in an anthropomorphic or abstract form. Introduce yourself, and if you do not recognize it, ask the plant spirit to identify itself. Allow it to share its healing wisdom with you while you spend time together in the garden. If it has appeared to you in a form that can move around, your plant spirit ally might guide you on a walk through the garden as it instructs you in the ways of the healing herbs. It might invite you to pluck some blooms to make a flower essence, or perhaps it will ask you to get to know the plants in the garden through other means. If appropriate, you may ask questions and seek advice from your ally. Do not forget to ask how you can help your plant spirit ally, too, for all relationships are reciprocal.

When your conversation draws to a close, thank your balm spirit ally. The plant spirit might offer you a token to carry with you, such as a leaf, flower, seed, or fruit. Tuck this item away safely and bid the spirit farewell. Make your way out of the garden and back to the crown of the World Tree. Allow the upper world to fade from view as you descend along the staircase of fungi that encircles the trunk of the World Tree. Once you reach the ground, spend a few moments communing with the World Tree to ensure that you are grounded and centered.

When you are ready, step back through the screen of your mind and allow the mighty tree to fade into the distance. Take several deep breaths and open your eyes. Write down your experiences so you may review them later.

☽ Journey to Hekate's Garden

Begin as before, making yourself comfortable in a place free from distractions. Breathe deeply and comfortably, allowing each out-breath and in-breath to unwind any tension held in your body, mind, and spirit. Take a few moments to still your mind and allow the troubles of the day to float away.

On the screen of your mind, visualize the distant outline of the World Tree, allowing it to draw closer with each breath. When it is nearby, picture yourself stepping through the screen of your mind and approach the World Tree.

Search among the roots of the World Tree for an opening that leads into the underworld. If you do not see one, silently request that the World Tree reveal it to you. After locating this portal to the realms below, state your intention to journey to Hekate's garden, filled with the plants of poison and power. Step in to the tunnel among the World Tree's roots and make your descent in to the underworld. As you venture downward, the path twists and bends and spirals upon itself. An eerie blue-green light seems to shine from the stones and earth lining the walls of the path. As you reach the bottom of the tunnel, the path levels out and reveals a world of endless night.

You follow the path forward until you arrive at a crossroad. One of the ways will be marked with a sign pointing you to Hekate's garden. Follow the path in that direction, and you will discover a mighty walled garden with a wrought iron gate. The entrance is crowned by a three-faced statue of Hekate, and torches light the way into the interior of the baneful garden. Before you step forward, ask for permission to enter the garden, and ask for guidance in finding your personal guide among the baneful plants.

Explore the garden and get to know its contents. The plants here are feral and untamed; this garden is not as orderly as the medicine garden from the previous exercise. You'll find mandrakes, datura, monkshood, hemlock, henbane, belladonna, and other classic witching herbs. Ancient yews cast more shade on already darkened areas, while hedges of blackthorn line the perimeter of the garden. Mushrooms dot the landscape, and psychoactive vines like morning glory and ayahuasca climb both tree and trellis. Some plants found there, like mugwort, garlic, and parsley, may not be poisonous but have special connections to the queen of witches and to magick itself.

In the wild heart of Hekate's garden, you'll find a place where three paths intersect. The light of several torches dances among the shadows. In the center of this crossroad, you'll find your totemic bane. It may appear to you as the plant itself, in an anthropomorphic form, or as swirling light. If you do not recognize the baneful plant, ask it to reveal its identity to you. Introduce yourself and thank the bane for meeting with you. Ask any questions or listen to whatever wisdom it has to share. You might sit on a bench near the path or, if it appears to you in a mobile form, wander together through the garden. Allow your plant spirit ally to share anything that it deems appropriate.

When your meditation draws to a close, thank your baneful plant spirit ally for appearing to you in Hekate's garden. It might give you a token to carry with you, such as a leaf, berry, seed, or blossom. Tuck this item away safely and bid the spirit farewell. Exit the garden and retrace your path back into the tunnel leading to the World Tree. Climb up into the middle world, following the path until you pass through the portal among the roots of the World Tree. Spend a few moments communing with the World Tree to ensure that you are grounded and centered, if needed.

When you are ready, step back through the screen of your mind, allow the mighty tree to drift away, and return to the room. Take several deep breaths and open your eyes. Be sure to record your experience of meeting your baneful plant spirit ally.

☽ Journey to the Forest of Wisdom

Begin as before, making yourself comfortable in a place free from distractions. Breathe deeply and comfortably, allowing each out-breath and in-breath to unwind any tension held in your body, mind, and spirit. Take a few moments to still your mind and allow the troubles of the day to float away.

On the screen of your mind, visualize the distant outline of the World Tree, allowing it to draw closer with each breath. When it is nearby, picture yourself stepping through the screen of your mind and approach the World Tree.

Announce your intention to seek the forest of wisdom as you stand beside the World Tree. Circle around the tree's immense trunk, looking for some sort of gap or opening in the bark. As you wander, you see a glimmer of light shining through a cleft in the bark. Knock three times on the tree near this cleft, and a doorway swings open, leading you into the heart of the World Tree. Step onto the path within the tree and follow it inward, journeying into an impossibly large inner world. The path leads straight ahead, and the light is neutral and ambient. Soon plants begin to appear along the path. Small shrubs and saplings line the way, but the farther you go, the larger the trees become.

The path ends at a stone archway at the edge of an infinite expanse of forest. The forest is lit by a strange and ceaseless twilight, and a barely discernible path meanders through it, branching and twisting its way around the trees. You follow the path. The trees here are breathtakingly varied. Familiar trees like oak, ash, and birch are met by exotic trees from faraway lands, like magnolia and cacao. As you explore the forest, you find that different areas are experiencing different seasons: spring, summer, fall, winter. There are trees bearing fruit, like apple, cherry, and pomegranate, and ancient sentinels of the forest, like yew and redwood. Trees of every stature can be found growing in the forest of wisdom.

As you trace the labyrinthine path through the forest, you find a clearing ahead of you. In the center of that glade stands a lone tree: your tree teacher spirit. It might appear to you alone or alongside an anthropomorphic or abstract representation of its spirit. Approach your tree teacher with reverence, and introduce yourself as you draw near. If you are unable to recognize it, ask the tree to identify itself. As with the previous meditations, the tree spirit may walk with you through the forest if it is able. Allow the tree spirit to share its wisdom with you. While spending time with this plant spirit ally, you notice your own spine standing straighter; the tree helps you better connect to the sky above, the soil below, and the world around you. Ask any questions that feel appropriate.

When it is time to return home, thank your tree spirit teacher. The spirit might offer you a gift of bark, twig, leaf, or some other piece of itself. Tuck this item away safely and bid the spirit farewell. Then return the way you came. If you find it hard to find the way back, ask for guidance; the forest of wisdom will usher you back through the stone arch and onto the straight path back to the doorway in the bark of the World Tree. Once you have left the inner world behind, the portal closes. Thank the World Tree for allowing you to find the forest within its heart. Then spend a few moments communing with the World Tree to to ensure that you are grounded and centered.

When you are ready, step back through the screen of your mind and allow the image of the World Tree to dissipate. Take several deep breaths before opening your eyes and returning to ordinary consciousness. Record your experiences from the journey to the forest of wisdom.

Although you need only visit each of these gardens a single time to meet your plant spirit allies, I encourage you to repeat these meditations often. It is a simple and easy way to build relationships with your three kin spirits and to learn more about their teachings. Once you've discovered your personal triad of plant spirit familiars, you can take the flower essences that correspond with them before reenacting these journeys as a means of making better contact with them.

Over time you may meet new plant spirit allies. These spirits may take the place of others you've worked with, or they may join your team for short- or long-term stages of your spiritual journey.

Personal Power Blend

One of the most powerful ways of using flower essences for personal development and for building magickal power is to make a blend of your three primary plant spirit allies. By combining the essences of your personal balm, bane, and tree allies, you create a sort of customized panacea for your spiritual journey. I call this a *personal power blend*. Your personal power blend is akin to a magickal remedy or a constitutional essence that works to heal and empower you at the core level. By engaging with your three primary plant spirit allies in the form of a personalized blend of flower essences, you can internalize the work that you do with them.

You can make your personal power blend just like any other combination of flower essences. If you are unsure of which essences to include, you can dowse or use any of the essence selection techniques described in chapter 7. Ideally, use essences that you have made yourself, if it is possible. My first personal power blend—combining the essences of my three primary plant spirit allies, which were lemon balm (*Melissa officinalis*), pokeweed (*Phytolacca americana*), and southern magnolia (*Magnolia grandiflora*)—contained only two homemade essences, as I didn't have access to lemon balm in bloom at that time. I generally use equal amounts of each of the three kin in my personal power blend—most often three drops of each.

Take your personal power blend as you would any other blend of essences. When you are first getting to know your plant spirit allies, you may find it helpful to take the personal power blend as often as possible. In time you'll find yourself able to conjure the benefits of the three kin without the aid of their essences. You might then take your personal power blend only when you need additional support or before engaging in ritual or meditation to connect with your allies. I also find the personal power blend helpful in times of emergency; the support my plant spirit allies offer is usually comparable to taking Dr. Bach's Rescue Remedy or other emergency support formulas.

Whether you are a flower essence practitioner, clinical herbalist, or witch, your practice can be enhanced and supported by partnering with the spirits of the green world. Getting to know your three primary plant spirit allies—bane, balm, and tree—helps you integrate the wisdom and healing benefits of the green world and enables you to be better attuned to the virtues of their essences.

5

Making Flower Essences

While you can buy flower essences from countless commercial producers, large and small, making your own is a powerful magickal and spiritual act. I used commercially prepared flower essences for more than a decade before I had even the slightest inclination to make my own.

I remember the day I made my first flower essence rather vividly. I wanted to work with wildflowers native to Florida, but the land I was searching was overrun by invasive and exotic species. The heat and frustration left me feeling defeated, and I was near to giving up. I thought I might have to either return home empty-handed or settle for a nonnative flower. Finally, I came upon a clearing full of sand blackberry in full bloom! Suddenly I was filled with the urge to take decisive action. Only later did I learn that blackberry essence is indicated for feelings of indecision or an inability to bring projects to fruition.

In time I came to make scores of essences from flowers that I found all through my home state of Florida, from native and introduced wildflowers, leaves, fungi, and roots. Throughout this chapter I'll discuss the methods for making and bottling essences so that you too can prepare your own.

GETTING STARTED

Every essence maker has their own personal protocol they use for making essences. I've made essences spontaneously with no preparation and no formality; I've also made essences with a full set of ritual regalia and tools. Each essence is unique, and I sometimes think the spirits of the plants and the land dictate exactly what the process of making a particular essence or vibrational remedy will look like. Nevertheless, there are some steps that are common to most, if not all, processes. Read through this section thoroughly to prepare for making your first essence, and be sure to have all the supplies at the ready.

Essence-Making Supplies

The most basic tools for making essences are clear glass bowls, scissors, a preservative, and storage containers. Ideally, a few other pieces of equipment facilitate the process of making essences. Here is a more complete list:

* Clear glass bowls, preferably unmarked
* Sharp scissors or pruning shears
* Funnels
* Coffee filters or cheesecloth
* High-quality water
* Preservative, such as alcohol, vinegar, or glycerin
* Glass jars or bottles
* Dropper bottles
* Labels and pens

I prefer to keep my essence-making supplies separate from their more mundane counterparts used in the kitchen. I keep my essence-making tools on a shelf together with other supplies I use for magickal and spiritual purposes.

It is imperative to sanitize everything that you use for making essences. Wash your tools with soap and water and then sanitize them with boiling water; you may do this by immersing them in or rinsing them with boiling water for a minimum of thirty seconds. I also spiritually cleanse and consecrate my tools and glassware before putting them to use to ensure that they are ready to hold the spiritual essence of the plant, rather than just being containers for water. I like to physically and spiritually clean and clear the space in which I'll be working, too, and I make sure that I can work undisturbed.

☽ Cleansing and Consecrating Your Tools

Many methods exist for cleansing and consecrating ritual tools. Different methods may be better suited to different practitioners and practices, so here are some starting points to inspire you to find the method that works best for you.

Popular cleansing methods include using smoke from sacred herbs, asperging with water, spraying cleansing essences, and visualization. You can burn plants such as sage, cedar, rosemary, rue, and juniper—as well as resins like copal and frankincense—to cleanse yourself, your space, and your tools. Water that you have charged with the intention to cleanse (usually with a pinch of blessed salt added to it) is also an effective agent of cleansing. A few sprays of cleansing flower essences—like sage, lemon, garlic, or crab apple—works wonders too. My favorite method for cleansing flower essence tools, though, is simply to visualize a brilliant white light or white flame engulfing the tools and transmuting any discordant or unneeded energies. I prefer this method since I like to keep my essence-making tools free from the energies of other plants, whether in essence or smoke form.

Consecration is the act of making something sacred or dedicating it to spiritual use. You may simply do this in prayer or with a short incantation. You may call upon any spirits, deities, or other forces that you typically work with and petition their aid in consecrating your ritual tools, asking that they ensure the tools will help you in producing your flower essences.

There are a few other supplies that may be helpful for making flower essences. I keep a *wildflower identification guide* for my region with my essence-making kit, and I also have a few books on native wildflowers in my home library for further research. It's helpful to know exactly what species you're using to make an essence—you wouldn't want to cut the blossoms of an endangered or protected species, and knowing whether or not the plant is toxic to handle is also important. When I cut flowers from plants, I use a *small plastic scoop* to catch the flowers and transfer them to my bowl full of water; I find this much easier than trying to hold scissors in one hand while balancing the bowl full of water in the other to catch the flowers as they fall. A small dish or plate may be useful for this, too. I prefer plastic or glass, as opposed to metal, because they are not conductive, so they protect the flowers from outside energies (namely me!) while I pick them. *Tongs or chopsticks* can come in handy when you need to remove foreign matter, small insects, or other materials from the bowl, but a twig from the same plant the essence is being made from will work well, too.

There are a couple more esoteric tools that can be used for enhancing the process of making essences. A *wand or crystal* may be used to direct energy from the plant to the bowl of water, cast a circle (see page 170), or otherwise help you direct energy during the act of making your essences. I also use a *copper pyramid* to energize my essences for at least twenty-four hours after making them. Copper pyramids are made from copper pipe or wire, and they are frequently employed to cleanse, charge, and otherwise enhance crystals and other ritual tools. Allowing the mother tinctures to rest inside a copper pyramid helps the energy of the flower essence imprint more permanently, inhibits the growth of microorganisms, and boosts the efficacy of the essence.

A Note about Water

Water is arguably the most important component in an essence, apart from the flowers themselves. The higher the quality of water you use, the better the resulting essence will be. The water should be free of chemical *and* vibrational contaminants. Pure spring water was Bach's choice for making his essences, and it continues to be the choice among many essence makers today. However, many people do not have access to fresh spring water, and bottled water contains contaminants from the plastic packaging. I use tap water that has been thoroughly filtered and allowed to stand for at least two hours, and I find that it works perfectly well for making essences.

You can use a number of techniques to spiritually prepare the water to become an essence. You could, for example, enhance the water with shungite, though bear in mind that a small amount of the shungite's energy will then carry over to the essence. To use shungite, simply place a small piece of natural shungite in the water for a couple of hours and remove it afterward. Another easy method is to add a drop or two of holy water or water from a sacred well or spring to your water. You can also perform a simple blessing or consecration of the water prior to using it for essences. Sometimes I merely sit with the water and ask the devas and elementals of water to help me prepare it for the task at hand.

Preparing Yourself

Whether or not you intend it, your state of mind will be the biggest outside influence on your essences. It is vital that you find the right balance of presence and detachment so you can perform your part appropriately, without interfering with the plant spirits, devas, and nature spirits responsible for the deeper work of producing essences. You might choose to cleanse yourself, such as with sacred smoke, a cleansing mist, or a visualization. It may also be helpful to ground and center yourself and spend a few moments in meditation so you can unplug from the mundane world long enough to make your essence.

Part of my preparation for making essences is shifting into a more meditative, prayerful state while I venture out to the flowers. From the moment I start packing supplies, I start to tune in to the subtle realms and make my silent prayers to the plant spirits and devas involved, even if I haven't decided on which flower to make yet. As I'll describe below, I always spend some time attuning to the plant before collecting flowers, and I ask permission before starting the actual act of making essences.

Some essence makers sit in communion with the essence while it potentizes or infuses. You might be drawn to observe the entire process, or perhaps you will stick around for just a bit and come back when it is time to collect your newly infused essence. When I make essences here in Florida, I generally don't stay to observe for the simple reason that I *can't*. The sun and heat can be unbearable for anyone, and I sunburn too easily. Instead, I spend a few minutes observing the essence at the beginning and end of the process; if the weather is particularly nice and shade is available, I'll stay longer. This is a wonderful opportunity to record observations about the plant as well as jot down any psychic or intuitive information that comes to you. If you converse with the plant spirit directly, you may want to record what you receive.

Simon Lilly of Green Man Tree Flower Essences offers a contrary point of view, suggesting that he finds it better to refrain from communing with the spirits of the plant and landscape. He writes, "I feel that the less I can be involved energetically, the better for the clarity and purity of the essence. The essence is, after all, of the plant, tree or whatever, not of me meditating, musing, daydreaming, chatting to or otherwise interacting with the plant. There is no way of avoiding some energy interaction, but I prefer to keep it to the minimum at the making stages."[1] Many essence makers follow similar guidelines and take great care to avoid allowing their energy to permeate the essences they produce. Others, like my teacher Christopher Penczak, see making essences as a cocreative act, and they handle the flowers directly and allow their energy to influence the essences. Personally, I prefer to avoid direct contact with the flowers I'm harvesting in an effort to reduce the amount of my own energy imparted to the finished essence. No matter how you approach it, your energy affects your essences, so be as intentional as you can during the entire process.

Choosing Flowers

There is a subtle art to choosing the right flowers for an essence. First and foremost, it is vital to work with flowers at the height of their blooming period. It is better to pick them a little too early rather than too late, as the life force of the flowers will wane once the blooms begin to wither. For most flowers, you'll want to pick them in the morning shortly after they open; this is when their energy is at its peak. For night-blooming flowers, you'll want to pick the flowers in the evening, when they open, and prepare the essence overnight. Other flowers, like passionflower (*Passiflora incarnata*), do not bloom according to a regular cycle, and you may have to wait until later in the day to gather enough open blooms to make an essence.

Dr. Bach recommended collecting flowers from as many plants of the species as possible. This prevents strain on any one plant, thereby being better for the environment, and it helps tap in to the archetypal, devic consciousness of the plant, rather than focusing on the individual spirit of a single plant. While it is possible to make an essence from any flower found anywhere, the most potent flower essences are usually made from wild plants, rather than cultivated ones. Nevertheless, many fine essences can be made in gardens so long as the plant spirits and devas are adequately involved, guided by the intention or focus of the maker.

Remember to pick flowers from places that are not contaminated by automobile exhaust and other chemicals. Harvest in places far from roads, with healthy greenery and an abundance of flowers, whenever possible.

ESSENCE-MAKING METHODS

The act of making flower essences is simple—almost deceptively so. You place flowers in a clear glass bowl atop pure water and leave them to soak under the sun. The process used today was pioneered by Edward Bach in May 1930, although indigenous healers around the world have used similar methods to make medicine and magick throughout time. Light and heat are the driving forces behind imprinting the water with the soul patterning of the flower, depending on the exact method used to make the essence. There are four main approaches:

* Sunlight method
* Moonlight or overnight method
* Boiling method
* Indirect and living methods

We'll discuss the merits of each approach below. No matter which one you use, it is important to remember that the key to successfully making a flower essence relies upon direct and express interaction with devas and plant spirits. Otherwise, all you are making is a weak herbal infusion.

Sunlight Method

By far the most popular method for making flower essences is the sunlight method, which aims to reproduce the vibrational qualities found in fresh dew. Simply place freshly cut flowers atop clean water in a clear glass bowl. Ideally, you will have cut the flowers relatively early in the morning, while the plants' life force is rising toward the blooms. Traditionally you'd use enough flowers to completely cover the surface of the water, though I've made and seen many essences prepared with fewer blooms. Once the flowers are floating on the water's surface, place the bowl in direct sunlight, as close as possible to the plants from which you harvested the flowers. Leave it to infuse for two to three hours. While making essences in Florida, where the sunshine is abundant, I've found that some essences are ready after only an hour or two. Essences made on cloudy days may require four to six hours.

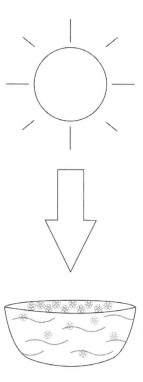

The sunlight method discovered by Dr. Bach simulates the vibrational qualities of fresh dew on flowers in the morning light.

How do you know when an essence is ready? You'll find that the inside of the bowl is usually coated with tiny bubbles. The water takes on a quality that is difficult to put into words; it just looks and feels more *alive,* sparkling and refracting light more brilliantly than before. When the essence is ready, strain thoroughly and bottle with a preservative, as described on pages 98 and 99.

If for some reason the essence didn't take—which can happen when you are distracted or don't take the time to connect to the plant spirits—the water in the bowl will seem dull and lack the profusion of pearly bubbles. When this happens to me, I give the cut flowers and the water back to the plants and thank them for allowing me to practice.

Solar essences work most readily on the outer expression of the personality, as well as on the emotions. They have a bright, strong energy that expresses the nature of the sun.

Moonlight and Overnight Methods

It is necessary to make essences from night-blooming flowers under the light of the moon and stars. Traditionally, the best timing to do this is under the full moon, but any overnight infusion—so long as you have the cooperation of the plant spirits—will yield a satisfactory flower essence.

Moonlight and overnight infusions have a decidedly more introspective quality. Though they may lack the dynamism of a solar essence, essences made at night can travel into the deep subconscious and work toward healing the shadow self. Lunar essences are also attuned to karmic patterns, and they can help transform and release the weight of the karma we carry.

The moon's phase and the sign through which it is traveling can affect the essence that you're making. You might choose to pick the flower and allow it to infuse when the phase and sign align with the intention or energy of the essence. If a plant doesn't bloom when the astrological timing is ideal, merely focus on the plant spirit itself rather than what is happening in the sky above.

Moonlight infusions are ideal for making essences from baneful plants. Not only does a nocturnal process match the energy and personality of many of the banes, but it also ensures a safer product. Sunlight infusions extract more compounds from plant matter thanks to the greater heat; overnight infusions will result in a essence that contains fewer compounds from the plant without losing any energetic potency.

The process for making an essence via lunar infusion is more or less identical to the solar infusion described earlier. You'll place the bowl of water with the freshly cut flowers under the light of the moon and stars to infuse. Usually, I leave them overnight and remove the flowers in the morning, but you may find that a couple of hours is sufficient time to infuse.

Boiling Method

Nearly half of the Bach flower remedies are produced via the boiling method. Dr. Bach felt that the amount of sunlight in early spring was insufficient for solar infusion of plants that bloomed then—especially in England, where he was working. He experimented with boiling the plant matter and found that this produced excellent results. Most of the essences he made this way came from trees, though Bach found a few herbaceous plants that also benefited from the boiling method. Thanks to the Florida climate (it is the Sunshine State, after all), I've never had to use this technique for making essences, but it can be effective.

To make essences via the boiling method, you'll need an enamel or stainless-steel saucepan with a tight-fitting lid. Collect enough flowers, leaves, and twigs* from the plant to fill three-quarters of the saucepan. Cover the vessel with its lid to prevent contaminants from falling in as you take the pan home. Add enough water to cover most of the plant matter and bring the pan to a boil, using a twig from the same plant to press the plant matter below the surface of the water. Let boil, uncovered, for thirty minutes, and then remove the pan from the heat.

---

*Dr. Bach used a fair amount of leaf and twig or stem for his essences made by the boiling method. Since this technique requires more plant matter than the solar method, you don't have to be so discriminating in what parts you cut, just as long as the pot contains a good proportion of flowers to the rest of the plant matter. It does not seem that Bach ever explained *why* he collected more than just the flowers for this method, so I have presented his technique above without any changes or commentary.

Let it cool outdoors, preferably under the sun and near to the host plant. Strain thoroughly—you'll probably need to filter it twice—and bottle with a preservative, as described on page 99.

It should go without saying that great care should be exercised if you choose to make essences with the boiling method. Since this process is actually a decoction, it extracts a large amount of phyto-chemicals from the plant matter. It is imperative that you use only nontoxic plants for producing an essence via the boiling method. Many commercial essence makers today avoid the boiling method so as to prevent flower essences from resembling traditional medicinal herbal remedies.

Indirect and Living Methods

You can also make essences using *indirect methods,* as they're known, to avoid direct contact between the water and the plant, which mini-mizes the risk when you're working with baneful plants. The most straightforward indirect method is akin to the indirect methods used for making crystal elixirs and gem waters. Fill a small cup or jar with freshly cut flowers, taking care not to squish them. Place this vessel inside a larger bowl, and fill the larger bowl with water. Ensure that the water level rises higher than as many of the cut flowers as possible without actually flowing into the small glass or jar. I like to spray the flowers in the smaller container with some fresh water to help them last a little longer while the essence infuses. The energy from the flowers will imprint on the water in the larger container without making direct contact.

Some producers practice what are called *living methods,* wherein they make essences without harvesting flowers from the plants, either to avoid damaging the plants or to work with flowers that are too high to reach or otherwise inaccessible. One such method is to set a bowl of water at the base of the plant and then delicately bend a stem or branch bearing one or more flowers down to the bowl, so that the flowers touch the surface of the water; you might have to weigh the stem down to keep it in place, taking care not to injure the plant. Another method is to pour water over the flowers and catch it in a bowl beneath the stem or branch, then leave the bowl in place at the base of the plant for as long as possible to imprint with the energy of the plant spirit.

If the flowers are too high to reach or otherwise inaccessible, you can use a wand or a crystal point to direct the energy of the flowers into the water from a distance. Some people employ this technique to make essences from Amazonian orchids that grow too high in the canopy of the rain forest to be harvested. If you're going to use a crystal, then before you do so, cleanse it and program it to carry the energy of the flowers into the water. When I have experimented with this method, I aim the point of the crystal at a flower and very slowly and intentionally draw a line of energy from the flower to my bowl of water. After repeating this several times, I either place the crystal in the water or set it beside the bowl with its base pointed in the general direction of the flower and its termination pointed at the water. I let the essence infuse for several hours and then check in on it intuitively (alternatively, you can muscle-test or dowse*) to see if it is ready. I find that if I do not properly maintain my clarity of intention and strength of will, essences prepared in this manner are more likely to imprint as environmental essences instead of flower essences.

You could try casting a circle (see page 170) around the plant and the bowl of water to better concentrate the effects of any of the indirect methods of making essences. Whatever method you choose, when the essence is ready, bottle it with a preservative, as described on page 99.

---

*Dowsing is a form of divination that uses a pendulum or another tool to answer questions or locate objects. A short description of dowsing appears in chapter 7, with instructions for dowsing to find the right essence. To apply this method to determining whether an essence is ready for bottling, you can hold the pendulum in your hand and ask a simple yes-or-no question, such as, "Is this essence ready?" The movement of the pendulum reveals either a yes or no—although that movement is often different for each dowser. Muscle testing for whether an essence is ready will follow similar procedures as outlined in chapter 7; mentally connect to the bowl of water and ask the same question: "Is this essence ready?" The response for your muscle testing will reveal a yes or no the same way as testing for the correct remedy for yourself or a client.

MAKING ESSENCES:
STEP-BY-STEP INSTRUCTIONS

While the boiling, indirect, and living methods are viable alternatives for producing flower essences, I still prefer the simplicity and efficacy of the sunlight and moonlight methods for making my own essences, and I use them whenever possible. Here, let's explore these two methods in greater detail.

In its simplest form, the ritual of making a flower essence consists of cutting flowers, floating them on the surface of a bowl of water, and leaving the bowl to infuse in sunlight or moonlight for as long as necessary. Each flower essence maker has their own approach, but several key themes are virtually universal.

1. Prepare Your Supplies
Gather whatever tools you'll need (see page 85), and sanitize anything that will come into contact with the plant matter or water.

2. Prepare Your Water
Make sure your water is pure, free of environmental and vibrational contaminants. If you like, you can perform a ritual to spiritually prepare your water to become an essence (see page 87). While spiritually preparing your water is an optional step, it greatly enhances the outcome of your essence-making endeavors.

3. Prepare Yourself
Perform a brief cleansing and move into a meditative, prayerful state. While I'm walking through green spaces on my way to an appropriate place make an essence, I work to stay in this meditative, prayerful state as best I can. I silently connect to the spirits of the land, the devas of all the plants in the area, and the overlighting devas of essences as a whole. I ask them for guidance, protection, support, and cooperation during the essence-making process.

4. Connect to the Plant Spirit

Once you've found the right flowers, spend time connecting to the plant, such as via the plant attunement exercise on page 47, and ask for permission to harvest its flowers. On the occasion when permission isn't granted, I usually try to find another flower to work with, but there have been times when I've merely turned around and headed home.

5. Cast a Circle

Once you have permission from the plant spirit, you can cast a circle, evoke deities, and call upon the plant spirit to be a conscious participant in the process (see exercise on page 53). While casting a circle is an optional step, I find that it helps in several ways. First, the circle serves as a spiritual container for the work, concentrating the energy of the plant spirit in the bowl of water. Second, the circle protects the essence from outside energies, and it even serves as a subtle deterrent to mundane interruptions and influences. Finally, I find that the energies are greatly magnified when I work with flowers, plant spirits, and other beings in an intentional, sacred manner.

Since I rarely stay on-site for the entirety of the infusion process, I'll cut a doorway in the circle after collecting the flowers and seal it behind me. I repeat the process when returning to finish the essence. Please see pages 170–72 for complete directions for casting a circle.

6. Harvest the Flowers

Now it's time to cut the flowers, as sensitively and decisively as possible, trying your best not to cause any extra injury to the plant while harvesting its blooms. Allow the plant to lead you in the process, staying as open as possible to see or sense which flowers have volunteered to be part of the flower essence. Set the flowers in your bowl of water, allowing them to float on the surface. Once you've collected enough flowers, set the bowl in a safe place near the stem or trunk of the plant where it will receive as much direct light as possible.

7. Seal in the Energy

This step, which you can take at the beginning of the infusion time or afterward, is simply a matter of setting intention: Set or state your intention that the water receive the soul patterning from the flowers or the blessings of the plant spirit, and that it *permanently* hold this energy. Some essence makers set their hands over the water and flowers and visualize the energy being locked in. Others (including myself) draw symbols over the water. Those symbols might include the lemniscate or figure eight, spirals, pentagrams, or others, like those found in the system of Reiki. I like to use an invoking pentagram (drawn from the top of the star to the lower left point and continuing on to the upper right point, tracing your way through all five points and back to the start) at the beginning of the process to open the flow of energy between the plant spirit and the water and a banishing pentagram (start at the lower left point and continue up to the top point, and then down the bottom right and continue through the rest of the star) at the end to seal in the energy. I usually do this with a special quartz wand that I reserve for this process, but I've also used a more traditional wand, an athame, and my fingers depending on what was available to me in the moment.

8. Allow the Flowers to Infuse

As noted earlier (see page 91), infusion usually requires two to three hours.

9. Filter and Bottle the Essence

After enough time has passed for the energy of the plant to lock into the water, experess your gratitude to all the spirits and beings you've worked with during the process. Line a funnel with a couple of coffee filters and pour the contents of the bowl through the funnel and into a sterilized bottle or jar. Once all the liquid has passed through, seal the container and label it immediately. I usually taste one of the spent flowers (as long as they are safe to consume), and I'll wring out the coffee filters so I can taste a couple drops of the mother essence. I like to observe how the mother makes me feel, without any judgment or expectation.

When you're ready, place the spent flowers at the base of the plant so they can decompose and return their nutrients to the earth. I also like to give the plant a small amount of the essence I've just made from it as a token of gratitude.

10. Thank the Plant Spirit
Before you go, offer a hearty and formal thank-you to the plant spirit, devoke any deities or spirits, and release the circle.

11. Add a Preservative to Your Essence
Head home immediately to add a preservative and properly bottle the essence you've just made.

BOTTLING ESSENCES

As soon as you return home, it will be necessary to add a preservative to the flower essence. The resulting liquid is called the *mother tincture.* The mother tincture is then greatly diluted to make *stock bottles* and even further diluted in *dosage bottles,* which are used for the administration of flower essences.

Preservatives
A preservative protects an essence against contamination by bacteria, mold, or other microorganisms. The preservative is also said to help the water maintain the imprint of the flower's consciousness; Don Dennis, founder of Living Tree Orchid Essences, suggests that alcohol—a primary preservative for flower essences—by nature acts to maintain an electric charge derived from the flowers, though it is likely measurable only at the picowatt level.[2]

Preservatives include:

* ★ Brandy
* ★ Vodka
* ★ Organic grape alcohol
* ★ Vegetable glycerin
* ★ Apple cider vinegar

* ★ White vinegar
* ★ Salt (only used in tandem with other preservatives)
* ★ Red shiso leaf infusion (usually stabilized with vinegar)

Brandy is the traditional preservative for flower essences, as it is made from the fruit of *vine* and aged in *oak* barrels—both plants belonging to Bach's system of flower essences. Some essence makers use a combination of water, alcohol, and vegetable glycerin to make stock bottles that contain less alcohol and taste sweeter. A handful of flower essence producers add a small amount of salt to their stock bottles, as this both enhances the work of the preservatives and is required by some governments to prevent essences from being labelled as alcoholic beverages. Red shiso leaf is preferred by some essence makers as an alternative to alcohol-based preservatives. Shiso is a member of the mint family, which has antimicrobial properties, and its leaves can be steeped in hot water or tinctured in vinegar to produce an effective preservative for flower essences.

When you're making your own essences, the choice of which preservative to use is largely personal, especially for mother tinctures. I've always preferred vodka, as it doesn't stain if I spill it and has less aroma and flavor than other preservatives, especially in a dosage bottle.

Mother Tinctures

Generally speaking, a mother tincture is roughly 50 percent essence and 50 percent preservative. For non-alcoholic preservatives, such as vinegar and glycerin, this ratio is always the same. However, there is a little wiggle room available when using alochol to preserve the mother tincture. The higher the proof of the alcohol you use as a preservative (that is, the more alcohol it contains), the less you need in the mother tincture. Extremely high-proof grape or grain alcohol, for example, might constitute only 30 to 40 percent of the total volume of a mother tincture, rather than the typical 50 percent. Avoid alcohol that is less than 80 proof; it won't be strong enough to effectively protect against microbial growth.

Once you have added preservative to an essence to create the mother tincture, I advise letting it rest for a day or more before you do any further work with it. When I make a mother tincture, I usually let it rest within a copper pyramid to stabilize and magnify its energy. Once the mother is stabilized, you can begin the process of successive dilution to make stock bottles and dosage bottles.

Stock and Dosage Bottles

Stock bottles (also known as concentrate bottles) are made by adding several drops of a mother tincture to a one-ounce dropper bottle filled with a preservative and water. The preservative usually makes up 30 to 50 percent of the bottle, though some essence producers use undiluted brandy or vinegar in their stock-level essences. Most flower and vibrational essences available commercially are stock bottles.

Although you can use essences directly from the stock bottle level, it is more effective and economical to dilute them further to make a dosage bottle. Dosage bottles (also known as treatment bottles) are made by adding two or more drops of a stock-level essence to a one-ounce dropper bottle filled with 25 percent preservative and 75 percent water (unless the preservative is glycerin, in which case the ratio is 50 percent glycerin and 50 percent water).

The exact dilution varies from one practitioner to another, as well as from one line of essences to the next. The Bach system suggests two drops of mother tincture per one-ounce stock bottle, and two drops of the stock bottle per one-ounce dosage bottle. The only exception is Rescue Remedy, which uses four drops of the stock bottle per dosage bottle. I tend to use somewhere between two and seven drops of a stock bottle when formulating a dosage bottle, and I usually allow my intuition to guide me. If you are using dropper bottles of any size smaller than one ounce, you can use the same number of drops of mother tincture without any change in the efficacy or quality of the stock bottle.

I've found very few references to a dilution greater than that of a standard dosage bottle. Some systems of essences make use of a *fine dosage,* wherein several drops of a dosage bottle are diluted in a one-ounce dropper bottle.[3] In addition, some flower essence producers have introduced an additional level of dilution and renamed the dilutions accordingly: mother tincture, daughter tincture (analogous to the stock

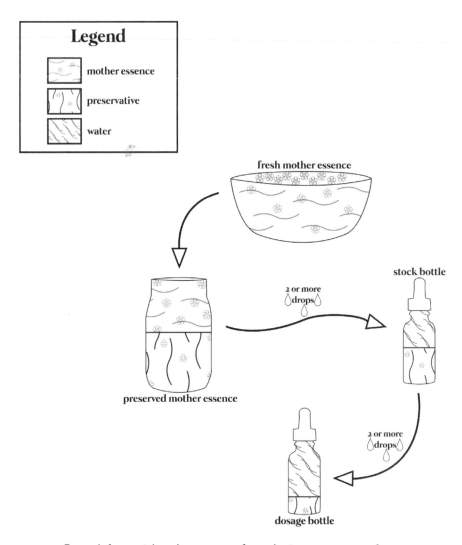

Legend

mother essence

preservative

water

fresh mother essence

stock bottle

2 or more
drops

preserved mother essence

2 or more
drops

dosage bottle

From left to right, the stages of producing an essence from
the mother tincture to the dosage bottle

bottle), stock bottle (analogous to the dosage bottle), and dosage bottle
(similar to the fine dosage). Rachel Singleton of LightBringer Essences
describes the effect of the additional level of dilution as appearing "to
lift, soften and lighten the effect of the final stock essence," and she
describes it as more energetically fluid and better able "to reach beyond
the physical and permeate right through to the spiritual."[4]

I myself rarely ever use the additional level of dilution with clients. I suggest the fine dosage dilution for the most sensitive of clients, or perhaps for addressing deeply rooted patterns, beliefs, or behaviors that lie well below one's conscious awareness. Fine dosage should be reserved only for very rare instances, and it may require several months of consistent treatment before effects are visible. I do not use fine dosage potency for magickal purposes, as I find it too subtle to give timely effects.

Avoiding Alcohol

If you are sensitive to or wish to abstain from alcohol, or if you are preparing essences for people who want to avoid it, note that stock bottles contain very little alcohol. Even the standard dosage of approximately four drops from a stock bottle prepared with 75 percent water and 25 percent brandy contains less alcohol than a ripe banana.[5] However, if someone who is sensitive to alcohol finds that the scent or taste of brandy, vodka, or other alcohol triggers them, it is best to preserve stock bottles and dosage bottles with glycerin or vinegar. Another method to reduce alcohol also exists: if essences preserved in alcohol are added to a cup of hot water or tea and left to stand for ten minutes or more, much of the alcohol will evaporate from the cup before consumption.

Dilution as Refinement

I found the notion of diluting essences to make them more effective difficult to process at first. Although I understood the premise of potentization, as spelled out and explored in depth in homeopathy, I wasn't quite ready to accept that my homemade essences and blends would be made more effective by being watered down. At best, I saw practitioners treat the remedies contained in stock bottles and dosage bottles as more or less equivalent; in other cases, I saw cues that seemed to suggest that store-bought stock bottles would be stronger than dosage bottles. For example, a minority of producers call stock bottles by their alternative name, *concentrate bottles,* which would seem to imply that they have a more concentrated and thus more powerful form of the remedy. Producers that sell both potencies often charge more for stock bottles than for dosage bottles, which also seems to send the psychological message that they are somehow stronger or more effective.

Seeking clarity for myself and confidence in my practice, I asked one of my flower essence teachers, Emily Ruff of the Florida School of Holistic Living, point-blank if there was any difference in the effects of these two dilutions. Emily shared the perspective that she had learned in her training with the Bach Centre at Mt. Vernon in Sotwell, England. Practitioners of the Bach system advise that dosage-level essences are stronger or more effective than that of stock-level essences, and this potency can most clearly be seen over long-term use. Another of my flower essence teachers, Christopher Penczak, has observed that stock-level essences have a greater resonance with the physical body, while dosage-level essences are more psychological and spiritual in nature.

For acute and emergency situations, use whatever is on hand, though stock-level dilution is typically considered to bring "more rapid and dynamic response," Rachel Singleton comments, thereby making them the best essence to turn to when we need "quick, efficient and rapidly stabilising" results.[6]

I reflected on this teaching, trying to find a way to understand the difference in potency when flower essences are more diluted. I found that it's helpful to think of dilution or potentization as *refining* the essence. It isn't so much about strength outright. Instead, the more refined an essence or blend is, the deeper its effects can travel. Imagine that the layers of your psyche are composed of mesh; as you move inward, each layer is finer than the ones that came before. Stock bottles are by their nature a little denser and therefore work more closely with our physical bodies, even though they are not biochemical in nature. A more dilute or refined essence can travel through the finest layers or filters in our consciousness, thereby penetrating the root causes and underlying themes of the patterns we look to heal.

The gradual refinement from mother tincture to stock bottle to dosage bottle provides a more effective end result, especially for long-term essence use. For acute and emergency situations, use whatever potency you have on hand; the energy of the essence will do its job either way, as these conditions tend to affect us closer to the surface layer of the psyche. The only exception I have found is in wearing essences, such as by programming a crystal or putting a few drops in a perfume bottle or other container; these uses require stock potencies for optimal results. For the magickal use of essences, I tend to stick with the stock-level concentration, as the essence will usually be diluted in some sort of carrier or otherwise used as a small part of a bigger working.

Storing Essences

Mother tinctures should be stored with a small amount of space between containers to maintain the integrity of their energy. Store them away from direct light, heat, electronics, and other sources of strong energy. I have some shelves dedicated to my mother tinctures, and I keep a small grid of four quartz crystals—one at each corner—on each shelf that holds the mothers.

I apply many of the same rules to storing my stock and dosage bottles. I have a couple of shelves dedicated to storing these essences away from light, heat, electronics, and so on to keep them free of energetic contamination. I also keep stock and dosage bottles of flower essences and vibrational remedies all over my office and home so they are in easy reach. Stock and dosage bottles are easier to replace than mother tinctures, so it is not necessary to exercise as much caution with them.

MAKING OTHER KINDS OF ESSENCES

There are a multitude of essences available on the market, and many of them are not made with flowers. Even Dr. Bach used more than just flowers in his system; chestnut bud and rock water are prime examples, and roughly half of the Bach flower essences are made via the boiling method, which includes twigs and leaves in addition to flowers. Today, you can find essences made from:

* ★ Leaves and buds
* ★ Roots

- ★ Seeds
- ★ Pollen
- ★ Fruit
- ★ Bark
- ★ Mushrooms and other fungi
- ★ Environments
- ★ Astrological transits
- ★ Animals
- ★ Sound
- ★ Color and light
- ★ Channeled energies

The sheer amount of options is astounding. The world has come a long way since Bach's first remedies, and we will continue to see new kinds of essences flourish. Although the primary focus of this book is on flower essences, a short description of leaf, root, seed, mushroom, and environmental essences is worthwhile, as they are relatively easy to make or purchase, and they are potent tools for both healing and magick.

Leaf Essences

Leaf essences generally come in two varieties: living leaves and young shoots (sometimes called spring leaf essences) and dead or dying leaves (autumn or falling leaf essences). There seem to be precious few of the former, although Canadian Forest Tree Essences produces a line of them. Falling leaf essences are more widely available. Some producers gather autumnal leaves sorted by color to provide a generalized autumn leaf essence, while others, such as Grant Lambert of Advanced Alchemy, offer falling leaf essences from individual species of trees. Leaf essences are generally made via the traditional sunlight method.

Generally speaking, spring leaf essences tend to work rather similarly to flower essences, though I've noted that some of them take much longer to produce lasting effects—up to three to five months, according to David Tigner of Canadian Forest Tree Essences.[7] Spring leaf essences usually exert a harmonizing and tonifying effect. Their energies are comparable to essences made from flowers of the same plant, but seem softer in their focus. They also tend to invite hope and remind us of our potential, like the budding leaves that promise to open. Falling leaf essences primarily assist us with letting go. They help us rebalance the ego, release fear and unwanted habits, and let go of personal trauma. Falling leaf essences have a much faster action than spring leaf essences, typically similar to or faster than flower essences; I often see them working within a few days. Magickally speaking, falling leaf essences attune us to the tides of the fall and winter seasons, and they can help us celebrate the passage of time.

Root Essences

Although root essences are scarce on the market, they can be easy enough to make on your own. The first plant to call me to make a root essence is one that I'd already used for a flower essence: Florida betony (*Stachys floridana*). Its delicious, tuberous roots resemble grubs, and after communing with the plant spirit I knew that I'd have to try my hand at making an essence from them. The primary mechanism of root essences, as you might imagine, is grounding. They tend to operate more on the lower chakras and help us integrate and anchor the positive changes catalyzed by other essences. Root essences also tend to focus their energy on the physical body more than the subtle bodies.[8] They work slowly, though they can hasten the effects of complementary flower or leaf essences when used conjunctly.

Make root essences via the traditional sunlight method. If a large plant or tree has exposed roots, you can also make the essence indirectly by placing the vessel of water on, near, or in the roots themselves. Be sure to have extra water on hand to rinse off roots before placing them in your bowl of water.

Seed Essences

Bach experimented with making remedies from the seeds of clematis before discovering the sunlight method for preparing flower essences. Today, seed essences are available from several makers. Seed essences focus on potential. Spiritually speaking, the seed is aligned with the element of spirit; it is the synthesis of the entire life cycle of its parent plant, and it contains the blueprint for another whole plant therein. Taking seed essences helps us become more aware of the blueprint contained within our spirits, thereby helping us grow and develop according to our soul's calling. Seeds tend to be enclosed in hard shells, and the young roots and leaves must break through; we can similarly have breakthrough moments when taking seed essences. These vibrational essences tend to highlight periods of dormancy, stillness, and death as a necessary part of life and rebirth.

Seed essences can be made in the same manner as traditional flower essences. I favor letting the seeds infuse in the water for a complete cycle of day and night, taking the essence through both darkness and light, which underscores the seed's journey from the underground darkness as its first leaves emerge into the light. Seed essences can be useful in magick related to healing, abundance, creativity, and new growth. They may also be used to celebrate the spring season and the blossoming of new life in nature.

Mushroom Essences

With the ever-increasing interest in mycology, it is no surprise that more essences are being produced from mushrooms and other fungi. Mushrooms are strange and somewhat uncanny to most of us. They are the fruiting bodies of an unseen community of organisms. Though they superficially resemble plants in some regards, mushrooms are more closely related to animals. Their essences have different actions than those of flowers. One of the pioneers of mushroom essences, herbalist and mycologist Robert Rogers, tells us that mushroom essences bring awareness to our shadow, and that they "represent the underbelly or underworld energy of the planet. Unlike flower essences, which are connected to the sun, bringing light into areas of darkness, fungi are lunar, dark, and mysterious."[9] Since they have a special affinity for darkness, mushroom essences are best made as lunar or overnight essences, and it may be necessary to use an indirect means of producing them to ensure that the resulting essence is safe to consume.

Mushroom and other fungus essences have a range of uses. Just as mushrooms are able to absorb heavy metals and other toxins from their environments, mushroom essences tend to remove toxic beliefs and behaviors that have accumulated over the course of our lives. They tap in to our most ancient and primordial memories, past-life experiences, and the programs impregnated on our psyche during early childhood. They help us get to the roots of these issues and provide the insight necessary to catalyze profound healing. Fungi are important for decomposition, and their essences can help us break down the beliefs that hold us back. Their association with decay also makes them potent allies for connecting to the underworld, the ancestors, and chthonic spirits of the land.

Environmental Essences

If the spirit of a plant can leave its imprint on water to create a healing elixir, it stands to reason that the genius loci, or the spirit of a place, can do the same. Although Dr. Bach's rock water essence is considered by many to be an environmental essence, the inception of environmental essences really began with the late Steve Johnson, founder of Alaskan Essences. After being intuitively guided to co-create his first environmental essence, Johnson went on to formulate an entire line of them, subsequently inspiring many essence makers to follow suit.

Environmental essences tend to sustain and nourish us from the most foundational level, just as the environment offers sustenance to each living being in it. Environmental essences are considered to be catalytic in nature, and they are ideal when strong cleansing energy is needed to bring vitality to someone who is not responding to other essences or healing modalities.[10] Environmental essences are excellent for clearing spaces and for bringing healing and nurturing energies to your home, office, or land.

Environmental essences can be made from more permanent features of the landscape, like forests, mountains, lakes, and glaciers, and from ephemeral events, such as storms, meteor showers, and the aurora borealis. Making them requires conscious and sensitive attunement to the landscape and the phenomena taking place there, as well as focused intent to connect to the spirit of place and direct that energy into the water. For witches, pagans, and occultists, environmental essences offer a means of attuning to the spirit of place when we are unable to travel to a sacred site to which we feel a strong connection. Conversely, making an environmental essence is a means of capturing and storing the experience of a place that is holy and magickal for us—whether it's an exotic, faraway location or in our backyard.

6

Deciphering the Language of Flowers

The doctrine of signatures, a system for interpreting the secret language of plants, is rooted in the idea that a principle of correspondence connects all things in creation. This correspondence starts at the most ethereal and cosmic levels and trickles down to the material, visible world. It is embodied in the occult axiom "As above, so below," and it underpins the idea that the macrocosm influences the microcosm, and vice versa.

While popularized by Paracelsus, the doctrine of signatures is an ancient practice—it precedes the formal name, which dates back to the first century CE—and has been used by indigenous healers since prehistory. It tells us that the color, shape, taste, scent, environment, and overall appearance of a plant are clues that indicate what sort of medicine, physical or spiritual, the plant provides. As an example, the shape of a leaf or flower might resemble that of the organ it best treats. The color red might indicate a medicine for the blood, while yellow signifies a medicine for the liver and bile. The hard shell of a walnut, with its meaty flesh inside, might signal to us that walnut is a medicine for the brain. More esoterically, certain plant gestures (their posture or bearing), colors, and textures might indicate a connection to the planet Mercury or to the elements of fire or water. Learning to read the doctrine of signatures provides a firm foundation for understanding the effects of flower essences, too.

DECODING THE
DOCTRINE OF SIGNATURES

Entire books have been written to discuss the interpretation of plant signatures, so a complete examination of the system is beyond the scope of this book.* However, it is helpful to learn the meanings of several key signatures that are important to the study of flower essences. The main themes that we'll explore here are the color, shape, and number of petals of the flowers. We will also briefly look at elemental and planetary signatures, and, finally, we'll examine the signatures and themes embodied by several botanical families as a whole.

Flower Color

Perhaps the first thing that we notice about a flower is its color. Color speaks to us on such a profound and personal level, and a plant's flowers tend to be the most vibrantly or interestingly colored parts. In light of this, we can understand a large part of a flower essence's effects based on the color of the flower it comes from.

Red

Flowers that bloom in shades of red resonate with the body and the world around us. Many essences made from red flowers relate to over-involvement with the material world as well as to themes of blood, power, and sex.[1] Essences of red flowers tend to be energizing and many center around fiery emotions, like anger. These essences can offer us the stamina required to heal long-standing trauma. Darker shades of red can be detoxifying and grounding and can counteract shame.

---

*I recommend three books for anyone wanting to learn more about the doctrine of signatures and plant gestures within the scope of flower essence therapy: *The Language of Plants,* by Julia Graves; *Flower Readings,* by Suzy Chiazzari; and *Bach Flower Remedies: Form & Function,* by Julian Barnard. Other important works on the doctrine of signatures include Christopher Penczak's *The Plant Spirit Familiar* and Sajah Popham's *Evolutionary Herbalism.*

Orange

Orange flowers are bringers of joy and rejuvenation. Their essences tend to promote healthy communication, especially within relationships, and focus on social integration.[2] Orange flowers produce essences that confront and transform themes related to embodiment and the use of our vital energy. They are expressive essences that can offer action and clarity when we are overly cerebral or mentally and spiritually depleted. Many orange flowers address the psychological underpinnings of disorders affecting the sex organs and sexuality as a whole.

Yellow

Yellow blooms are bright, expansive, and lightening. They offer an uplifting and stimulating effect, thereby counteracting gloom, despair, depression, and fear. They are also often very mentally focused; they sharpen and focus the mind and can improve language skills. They tend to help us examine the mental patterns we learn in early childhood and are subsequently reinforced later in life.[3] Yellow flowers may influence the solar plexus chakra and develop leadership skills; they promote empowerment and authority, helping our light shine to its fullest. Essences made from yellow flowers expand our consciousness and dispel negative energy, break up congestion, and address the cause of depressive states.[4] Some shades of golden yellow energize and open the heart chakra, which attests to the ability of yellow flowers to lift heavy emotions, such as depression.[5]

Green

You might at first assume green flowers to be a rarity—until you consider the inflorescences of trees, grasses, and other plants not known for their showy blooms. Most green-flowered plants are wind pollinated; their essences balance the emotions, especially when we are subject to mood swings. Green flower essences tend to attune us to the rhythms and cycles of nature, even helping us perceive and relate to the Earth as a living being.[6] Many of these essences also assist us in perceiving and communicating with the spirits of nature: devas, elementals, land spirits, and plant spirits. Green is the midway point between red and violet, and it has an overall balancing effect; essences of green flowers mitigate the tendency to stray toward extremes. Green flower essences also tend to work on the heart chakra, feeding and aligning it with the nourishing wisdom of Mother Nature.

Blue

Flowers that bloom in shades of blue carry the celestial gifts of hope and meaning. Like the expanse of the sky above, blue flowers can expand your perspective; essences of blue flowers also invite a sense of meaning and purpose. Overall, essences made from blue flowers are uplifting, calming, and spiritualizing; they help us see our place in the greater scheme of things. These essences bring comfort and teach us to communicate without aggression, while fostering a sense of trust. Blue flowers produce essences that tend to ease tension, enhance expression, and help us remember to breathe deeply.

Purple and Violet

Purple and violet flowers direct their gifts to the third eye or brow chakra. Their essences tend to clear obstacles to intuition, clairvoyance, and other psychic faculties. They also restore hope and help invite deeper and more refined spiritual progress. Many essences made from flowers ranging in shades of purple, lavender, and violet can also be helpful in treating an overdeveloped sense of spirituality that results in aloofness, as they bring spirituality and mental awareness into the realm of practicality.[7] Some purple flowers can also be helpful in resolving parent-child conflict and offer ease in our familial relationships.

White

Flowers with white petals are cleansing, protective, and restorative. Their essences tend to repair the energy field, energize the mind and spirit, and elevate consciousness. White light contains all other colors within it, and white flower essences usually affect us on many levels at once or have a variable effect depending on our needs when we take them. These essences are often clarifying to the mind and may be able to anesthetize or soften the background pain caused by trauma and bring solace to the soul. Many white flowers also alleviate grief and shock, and they may be helpful in contending with the dying process—both for the person leaving the physical plane and for those who are caring for them or affected by grief and loss.

Pink

Pink flowers bring a softening effect, making them helpful for easing the walls erected after trauma. Essences made from pink flowers usually work directly on the heart chakra, bringing emotional balance by nurturing us with divine love. Pink flowers can address issues related to love, romance, and intimacy. Their essences often work on issues related to sensitivity and tenderness.[8]

Magenta

Magenta is an important color in flower essence therapy. It lies opposite green on the color wheel, as it is produced from the overlap of red and violet. Green is the predominant color of the plant kingdom, and magenta brings a sense of dynamic balance to that greenness. By combining the qualities of red and violet, magenta brings spirituality into the material realm. Essences made from magenta flowers restore the etheric body, rejuvenate us when we feel most depleted, and offer deep healing to the Earth itself.[9] Magenta can also clear away old mental and emotional patterns rooted in fear, leading the mind into a state of wholeness.

Brown

Flowers displaying the color brown represent earthy and grounded states of being. Most flowers with a predominantly brown color help us accept impermanence and death, while also providing grounding and cleansing energies.[10] Brown flowers can also relate to karmic patterns and inherited beliefs.

Black

Black flowers are appreciably rare. Most flowers that appear black at first glance are merely very dark shades of another color, though some flowers have black(ish) centers or accents. Black is the color of the subconscious or unconscious mind, and flowers exhibiting shades of black often help us plumb the depths of consciousness. Most flowers containing traces of black result in essences that reflect the nature of the shadow self and reveal energy blockages; they are also helpful in treating dark, morose, and morbid moods. Essences of flowers sporting prominent black features often address our blind spots—those parts of life that we are unable to truly see.

Multicolored

Many flowers are multicolored, and interpretation of the influence of color in each one should be approached individually. Start with the predominant color, then work your way through the minor colors. Consider where the colors are in relation to one another. Is one within another, or below? What patterns emerge, such as spots, stripes, veins, or a mosaic? Record your overall impressions of the colors and patterns, and observe the effects of the essence in relation to flowers of solid colors. Over time, your personal understanding of the language of color will develop and refine.

Flower Petal Number

Number and form are primordial messengers of spiritual truth, and the number of petals and their overall shape provide important insight into the themes and energy of a flower's essence. Some plants bear flowers whose petals are arranged in many rows, offering multiples of the base numbers described below, while others may be innumerable or absent altogether. Most cultivated roses, for example, have many petals, but their fundamental geometry is based on the fivefold petals of the wild rose. Some flowers have parts that resemble petals, like sepals and bracts, and they can offer signatures similar to petal numbers, too.

No Petals

Flowers without petals tend to symbolize the inherent emptiness of the material world, almost as if recalling the famous line from the Heart Sutra: form is emptiness; emptiness is form. Reflecting on

Bach's essences produced from petalless flowers, Julian Barnard, flower essence producer and expert on the Bach remedies, writes that "the lack of petals suggests that something is missing from the emotional being. It correlates to a remedy state where there is a detached mentality, an indifferent or confused process of thinking about oneself, also a certain emotional dryness and lack of warmth."[11] In other words, the essences made from flowers without petals address detachment or a missing sense or quality in our emotional constitution. With flowers that have components resembling petals, such as sepals, bracts, and spathes, but lacking true petals, their essences tend to address the disparity between the appearance of something and its true nature or identity. Examples of flowers without petals found in the Bach system include clematis, scleranthus, and wild oat. Grasses typically lack petals, as do anemones, which instead have sepals easily mistaken for petals.*

One Petal

One-petaled flowers work on the level of the whole self; they offer healing in an undifferentiated way to the entire person, rather than working on a singular aspect of the personality, soul, or body. The oneness embodied in these flowers represents the ideas of the seed or point of origin of the soul; contained within that seed is the entire blueprint of the soul's potential, just as seeds contain the potential for the plant they shall become. One-petaled flowers focus on oneness and union, inspiring harmony among all parts of the body, mind, and self. Essences made from flowers with a single petal tend to activate the entirety of the light body, as the flowers themselves resemble the mandorla or aureole often depicted around holy figures in many of the world's spiritual traditions. Few flowers truly have a single petal, though arum flowers are enclosed by a single petallike hood called a spathe. Other blooms that appear to have a single petal actually have their petals fused together. Essences

---

*Flowers with structures that resemble petals will still exhibit the traits of the number they correspond to. For example, clematis has four sepals; it displays the qualities of flowers with no petals and of flowers with four petals, as its overall form shows a strong quality of fourfold symmetry.

from such flowers help fuse disparate ideas, emotions, or personalities into a cohesive whole.

Two Petals

Two-petaled flowers epitomize the concepts of duality, polarity, and complementary forces. With twoness comes the idea of sameness versus otherness, and essences made from two-petaled plants can help overcome an "us versus them" sort of mentality. These essences reconcile opposing forces and help balance polarities within us; the nature of twoness invites progress through reconciliation. Two is a number both divisive and conjunctive. Thus, two-petaled flowers can help us separate from behaviors or beliefs that no longer serve our highest good, while they can also help us adopt patterns that support our well-being and personal development. Two is also the number of choice, and flower essences made from two-petaled flowers might invite us to make better choices. Flowers with two petals often resemble a lemniscate (figure eight) or a pair of wings or lips. Their essences deepen inner vision and imagination, and they help the mind take flight. As a result, they tend to support the health of the third eye or brow chakra. These essences help us articulate our innermost thoughts. Few flowers have two petals, though dayflower (*Commelina communis*), bladderworts, and other examples exist. Members of the mint family have a bilateral symmetry that suggests an innate twoness in their essences (although most are actually made of five petals fused together).

Three Petals

Three-petaled flowers are emblems of movement and harmony. Numerologically, three is typically regarded as the number of change and transformation. Flowers with three petals help harmonize and integrate the body, mind, and spirit. Three is the number of union of opposites; it symbolizes the union of yin and yang, of the divine feminine and divine masculine. Three-petaled flowers often relate to sexuality, particularly female sexuality. Three is a number associated with manifestation, too, as the triangle is the first and simplest polygon. Essences derived from three-petaled flowers help us gain traction in the manifestation process and boost magickal fluency. Three symbolizes the beginning, middle, and end of every process in the universe. Essences embodying this threeness help us examine the trajectory of our healing and our spiritual progress, thereby highlighting where we stand in the way of success. Three-petaled flowers include trillium, spiderwort, and iris (which has three sepals that make it appear to be six-petaled).

Four Petals

Four-petaled flowers are grounding, stabilizing, and anchoring. These essences usually influence the root chakra, as they bolster personal strength, power, and life force. Fourness is centering, as the shape of four-petaled blossoms evokes the image of the compass. The square formed by four-petaled flowers represents the earth element; essences made from such flowers help spacy people become more grounded and embodied. Many four-petaled flowers produce highly protective essences, such as rue. Flowers with four petals (or petallike structures) include members of the mustard family (broccoli, cauliflower, kale, et cetera), poppies, and clematis—one of Dr. Bach's remedies.

Five Petals

Five-petaled flowers are among the most abundant and are generally the most therapeutically and magickally important. Five is a sacred number connected to the Goddess and the planet Venus, whose transit across the night sky traces an arc that resembles a five-petaled flower. The pentagon and pentagram express the golden ratio, the proportion of beauty and life itself. Five-petaled flowers thus signal the nature of life. The five petals symbolize the five appendages (head, arms, and legs) of the human body and therefore represent incarnation. I learned from Christopher Penczak that flowers with five petals represent doorways, and that they open the gates between worlds—the gates of spirit and of life. While many five-petaled flowers produce essences that are simply general tonics for the entire body and life processes, many others have more specialized functions. They can open the gate between life and death, ushering life force in one direction or another. Consider the fivefold petals of St. John's wort, which draws light and life into the body. On the other end of the spectrum, five-petaled belladonna and datura direct consciousness and the spirit outward and away from the body, such as by assisting astral travel. Such essences are often protective, as they can tightly seal the aura against intrusion. The rose may be the quintessential five-petaled flower, along with other members of its botanical family. Most nightshades also sport five petals, as do periwinkle, violet, and many others.

Six Petals

Six-petaled flowers tend to produce the most balancing and harmonizing essences. They capture the essence of both twoness and threeness and represent the highest order of balance and union. Essences made from six-petaled flowers bring together the higher mind with the earthly self; in magickal terms, they can be said to align the three souls. Flowers with six petals often resemble stars, and they can evoke a profound connection to the celestial realms. Six-petaled flowers assist with integrating new ideas, beliefs, and behaviors. Essences made from these flowers can help us integrate spiritual lessons and recover after shock. Popular flower essences made from six-petaled flowers include star-of-Bethlehem, daffodil, lilies, and many others.

Flower Position and Shape

There is a lot of information encoded in the shape and position of a plant's inflorescence. Flowers that hang downward link us to the ground beneath us. Blooms that gaze heavenward have an expansive quality to them, connecting us to higher consciousness. Those flowers that face outward horizontally often help us focus on being present, expressing ourself, and meeting challenges head-on. Those that form a single bloom on a stalk tend to speak toward individuality and self-identity; they may help people facing isolation. Flowers that cluster concentrate their energy into the head and mind.

Star-Shaped Flowers

Star-shaped flowers reinforce our innate connection with the cosmos. They ground and integrate higher ideas and energies, simultaneously lifting our consciousness to higher levels. Star-shaped flowers are helpful for deep spiritual imbalances, grief, and trauma. Their shape radiates outward in all directions from the center, which connotes a sense of openness that can dispel fear and prevent us from closing or hardening our heart after loss and shock. Star-shaped blooms are profoundly spiritual, and they help us follow our inner star. Five-pointed stars are doorways in occult practice, and flowers bearing this shape can assist with embodiment, astral travel, and invoking the divine.

Trumpet-Shaped Flowers

Trumpet-shaped flowers assist communication, expression, and projection. Those that point outward are best suited for communication with those around us. They inspire the confidence needed to express our feelings. Trumpet-shaped blossoms help us project our true will and will clarify our ideas for better and more effective communication in all that we do. Downward-pointing trumpets can initiate communication with the higher realms, as well as teaching us to listen more than we speak.

Cup-Shaped Flowers

Cup-shaped flowers form a receptacle for the soul. They speak of containment and often make very nurturing essences. Work with cup-shaped flowers to overcome feelings of rejection, lack of support, and longing for comfort. They also help heal imbalances associated with the inner feminine, as the cup or chalice is a traditional symbol for the Goddess. Cup-shaped blooms also treat physical pain that is rooted in emotional causes. They teach us to value the self so we can better appreciate and enjoy intimacy with others, helping us navigate situations involving being receptive and needing receptivity from those around us.

Bell-Shaped Flowers

Bell-shaped flowers can resemble trumpet- and cup-shaped blooms, except that they narrow toward their opening, or else they lack the taper of a trumpet. Like the trumpet, the bell shape evokes a sense of openness and expression, but the difference in taper balances expression with containment. These flowers address issues related to the physical body and the soul's relationship to it. Bell-shaped blooms signify moderation and healthy self-restraint. Since they often hang downward, they stimulate the flow of energy in this direction, often resulting in essences that are grounding and address imbalances of body and mind. Many bell-shaped flowers also reach deep down into the psyche to release blocks from childhood. They help release blocks that cut us off from our supply of life force.

Umbels

Umbels are flowers that cluster together, held aloft by stems of roughly equal length that emerge from a common point. Their closely grouped blooms relate to themes of group consciousness, individuality, and connection. Many plants bearing umbels (like members of Apiaceae, the carrot family) promote group harmony without loss of self-identity. They can also emphasize common connections in any situation, thereby helping us see the innate connections between people, places, and events. As a result, umbels often boost psychic activity. These flowers bring together separate ideas and people to work for the greater good, and many boast a connection to the spirit realm, especially angelic beings.

Spikes

Flowers grouped into spikes build confidence and self-awareness and offer overall upliftment. The strong vertical axis in flower spikes points heavenward, and such flowers tend to focus on the spirit and mind. They are strengthening, gently protective, and shed light on our life's path. Flower spikes may bring renewal, purification, and transformation, especially if their overall appearance is reminiscent of a candle or flame. By being held aloft, often above the rest of the plant, flower spikes help us rise above negative thinking. They are a soothing balm against self-criticism, neglect, and a relentless drive to perform or produce.

Drooping Flowers

Flowers that droop, such as the catkins found on some trees, teach sensitivity and flexibility and help overly self-reliant people relax and surrender. Any flower that hangs downward can signify a sense of being top-heavy; such flowers help us when we are caught in cycles of overthinking. They ground our mental state into our heart and body and balance thinking with acting. Essences made from these flowers encourage flexibility of mind and body; they can be helpful when we find ourselves clinging to rigid ideas and beliefs.

Leaf, Stem, Habitat, and Other Signatures

Clues to the nature of an essence can be found in all parts of the plant, not merely the flower itself. The overall gesture of a plant—that is, its carriage or bearing, or the manner in which it holds itself—can indicate the personality traits or mental states that it helps balance, as well as give an idea as to the magickal qualities of a plant. Does the plant have a strong vertical axis, like a pine tree or like foxglove's inflorescence? Such a plant tends to help us build our identity and strengthen our awareness and resolve. On the other hand, plants with a stronger horizontal inclination help us grow and expand, teaching us to move outside our comfort zone. You'll also find clues in the shape and number of a plant's leaves, as well as in its bark, roots, fruit, and seeds. Learn to read these clues in much the same manner as you would a flower's color, shape, and position.

Another cue to the nature of a flower essence can be found in a plant's medicinal uses or chemical makeup. While there is not always a direct correlation, there are frequently similarities in the medicinal qualities of a plant and its effect on the psyche as a flower essence. Even Bach himself explored these signatures; he described at least one of his earliest remedies as having roughly the same effects as its traditional medicinal preparations.[12] Although he later abandoned that remedy in favor of others, it shows that vibrational effects can resemble the medicinal action of some plants. For example, rosemary essence works on the mind and memory, which are two traditional uses for the rosemary plant in folk medicine. Similarly, the toxic nature of baneful plants can be used to break down negative beliefs and behaviors in the same way that the toxic compounds can break down healthy tissue in the body. It's helpful to study the traditional uses of plants to help round out your understanding of how essences work.

Elemental Signatures

The appearance and life cycle of a plant may also point toward the elemental correspondences that it embodies. The use of elemental signatures in herbalism is a long-standing tradition, especially for magickal practitioners. Many magickally minded practitioners rely on the system originating in ancient Greece, which recognizes four elements: earth, air, fire, and water. Bear in mind that a plant may exhibit features that correspond to a variety of elements, but usually one or two elements will dominate its overall energetic signature.

Earth

In plants, the earth element tends to be expressed as dense, broad, woody structures, such as wide leaves, dense growth, and broad stems or trunks. The roots of a plant are naturally associated with the element of earth, for they literally anchor the plant into the ground. Flowers, fruit, or branches that droop downward sometimes represent earth, too. Colors that correspond to the earth element include red, brown, and green. The earth signature in plants speaks to themes of structure, grounding, stability, and physicality. Plants with a strong earth signature may have a greater impact on the physical, rather than the mental or emotional, level of our makeup. Flower essences made from these plants often inspire renewal and help rebuild wellness from the ground up. Earthy essences also help us feel more grounded and better embodied. In magick, the earth element often represents healing, abundance, and manifestation, in addition to matters of home and family.

Air

Plants with an air signature often exhibit feathery, hairy, or dissected leaves or petals, as well as tufts of stamens and other fluffy structures. The appearance of space between the separate parts connotes the qualities of the air element, as this permits air to flow through the plant. The leaves of a plant generally represent air because they are the primary site of transpiration, or the exchange of gases. Many airy plants are also aromatic; their volatile oils are carried on the air itself. Wind-pollinated plants, like grasses and trees, as well as plants with seeds carried great distances by the winds also resonate with the air element. The colors white and yellow may represent elemental air. Essences made from air-element flowers are calming and clarifying; many of them relax the nerves and quiet the mind. Air is a drying element, and it can help us get some clarity and objectivity by "drying out" the water of the emotions. Air is the breath of life itself, and it is the medium through which we express ourselves via speech. Essences with an air signature can improve communication and stimulate the imagination.

Water

Plants with a water signature often have moist, watery, vascular structures and high water content, or they may grow in or near the water itself. When broken, they tend to ooze sap, latex, or mucilage, and their general appearance is delicate and flowing. Some water-element plants have specialized structures to capture and hold water. Blue and purple flowers and silvery leaves are generally a sign of a water connection. Overall, the stems and trunks of plants are associated with the water element, as they contain the vascular structures that transport water throughout the plant. Flower essences that strongly resonate with the element of water tend to be cleansing and invite movement. They often treat trauma, especially by bringing life and movement to atrophied emotions and balancing overactive ones. Water-element essences may also help us examine our relationships, and they invoke ancestral wisdom to deepen our healing and magick.

Fire

The fire element is usually represented by warm, spicy aromas, thorns and spines, and flowers that resemble the sun. Bright shades of red, orange, and yellow also point toward a connection to fire. Fiery plants might seem dangerous or combative, with spines, irritants, and harsh aromas. Plants with a fire signature are stimulating and transformative; they energize and revitalize us from the very core. Fire-element essences kindle the flame of creativity and help us drive forward. Fire is related to the processes of digestion and metabolism, and essences made from fire-element flowers can energetically help us better digest our thoughts, feelings, and experiences. These essences can warm up cold, aloof dispositions and ignite willpower. Fire is often engaged magickally for protection, sex, and power.

Planetary Signatures

According to the classical system of planetary influences, which has long been used in folk and medical traditions, each planet and luminary (as the sun and moon are not truly planets but are often regarded as such in astrology) projects cosmic principles, healing energy, and magickal themes through the plants, stones, metals, and animals to which it corresponds. Planetary signatures in plants are clues to the therapeutic effects of flower essences and help us connect to the power and wisdom of the stars for our magickal practice. Note that different parts of a plant may exhibit different planetary signatures, resulting in correspondences that are layered and unique to each plant.

Sun

The sun is represented by shades of gold and yellow. Flowers with petals that radiate from a round center, like sunflowers and daisies, are perfect emblems of a solar signature. Plants that make the skin photosensitive also resonate strongly with the sun. Essences with a solar signature are warming and vitalizing. They offer a radiant energy that inspires success and strengthens our sense of identity. In flower essence therapy, flowers with a solar signature lessen irritation and help us get hold of heated emotions.

Moon

Flowers connected to the moon are traditionally white, and most night-blooming plants have at least some lunar correspondence. Silvery leaves, moist sap or mucilage, and white latex are all lunar signatures, too. Lunar flowers are gently calming and sedating, and they cool the temper. They also generally open the doorway to intuition, and they can help attune us to the rhythms and tides of life and magick.

Mercury

Plants with a Mercury signature are usually airy and aromatic; think of the mint family when considering Mercurial energy. Mercury can point toward stimulating plants, like coffee and tea, as well as those that readily spread and propagate via rhizomes. These plants can quickly travel through a garden, underlining the association among Mercury, travel, and movement. Mercurial essences work principally on the mind, and they often invite quick thinking and movement.

Venus

Venus, the planet of love and beauty, resonates with five-petaled flowers, as well as petals in shades of pink, red, and pastel colors. Plants with a Venusian signature usually have showy flowers, and their petals or leaves are soft and supple. Venus also rules sweet, luscious scents, like that of rose. Medicinally, Venusian plants are often related to the health of the reproductive system, and as essences they may help with issues surrounding love, intimacy, and sexuality.

Mars

Plants with a Mars signature are well defended, often adorned with spines, thorns, or prickles. Erect plant stems are Martian in nature, for they resemble both phallus and spear, and they indicate direction of growth, just as the god Mars directs armies. Martian scents and tastes are often aggressive and intensely hot, like cayenne. Flower essences related to Mars can be used for triage; they help us recover from events that wound and traumatize us so we can mobilize again. Mars essences are also decisive, inspire action, and can be used to confer protection, strength, and the tenacity to face confrontation and conflict head-on.

Jupiter

As the largest of planets, Jupiter encodes itself in the plant kingdom as large, broad plants, as well as in the color gold and crown-like shapes. Edible fruits, nuts, and all things rich and fatty are Jovian in nature. Essences made from Jovian flowers strengthen and nourish us; they help us expand our influence into the world and crown us as the sovereign of our life. These essences lift the spirit and cultivate faith; working with them helps us leave behind self-imposed limitations and work toward our goals.

Saturn

Saturnian plants are liminal beings. They live life at the edge, in borders, ruins, hedgerows, graveyards, and roadsides. They are stiff and rigid and quite often bitter and astringent—or even toxic, as Saturn also rules over most poisons. Many Saturnian flowers are white, with five or six petals. Saturnian essences invite order and structure, and they may be useful in releasing and banishing influences from the psyche. Saturn is the lord of karma, so flower essences under Saturn's rule may reveal karmic patterns that are playing out in our lives. Saturn has an affinity for the bones, and its essences may affect us at the structural level, both literally and metaphorically.

Uranus

Uranus deals in stimulants, like caffeine. Uranian plants are usually unconventional or unusual in some way; they inspire imagination and help us break free from ingrained habits and restrictive social norms. Flowers essences that heighten awareness or focus on the nervous system may have an Uranian nature.

Neptune

Neptune is typically considered the mystic of the solar system, and it is linked to entheogenic and psychedelic plants, in addition to plants with a strong watery nature. Many of these plants evoke intense sensations of universal love when taken internally, and their flower essences can invite us to contemplate this transcendent love that holds the universe together. Neptunian flower essences are deeply stimulating to the psychic senses and may support trance work and the attainment of ecstatic states.

Pluto

The plants of Pluto are invariably associated with death, sex, and the underworld. As a result, many Plutonian plants are toxic. Pluto rules over the deadliest and most toxic of banes, especially those with sweet scents or tastes (not that it is ever advisable to taste them). Rich, sweet, and earthy spices also fall under the dominion of Pluto, as do delicious tubers and roots, for they grow in Pluto's underworld domain. Plutonian flower essences plumb the depths of the psyche and help reveal hidden patterns. They are catalytic in nature and help us grow and transform from the inside out.

Zodiacal Signatures

Just as the influence of the planets is coded into the signatures of plants, so, too, are the energies of the twelve signs of the zodiac. Each sign of the zodiac rules different aspects of the body, mind, and spirit, and there are clues in the appearance of plants that reveals which sign or signs they are connected to. There is often much over-lap between the zodiacal signature and the signature of a sign's rul-ing planet and element; you can refer to the discussion of planetary and elemental signatures beginning on page 124 to enrich your understanding of the characteristics associated with each sign of the zodiac. Modern flower essence therapists also assign essences to zodiac signs that exhibit the personality and character traits that the essences balance.

Aries

Aries, ruled by Mars, represents courage, ambition, drive, and leadership. Herbs of Aries tend to be fiery, dominant, and stimulating. Flower essences made from such plants generally balance qualities such as restlessness, impatience, intolerance, insensitivity, fear, low self-esteem, aimlessness, and feeling stuck.

Taurus

Taurus is ruled by the planet Venus and the element of earth. Taurean herbs are usually earthy and feminine, and they bring pleasure. Essences derived from the plants of Taurus balance stubbornness, pessimism, overindulgence, lethargy, resentment, blocks to both creativity and sen-suality, and difficulty giving or receiving love.

Gemini

Ruled by Mercury and the air element, Gemini is a sign of communication, adaptation, coordination, learning, and many other mental endeavors. Plants connected to Gemini are often airy, dry, and somewhat androgynous in nature. Working with flower essences made from these plants supports mental acuity, communication, memory, curiosity, and a quick wit. Gemini essences can also assuage fickleness, indicisiveness, poor concentration, feeling scattered, and close-mindedness.

Cancer

Cancer is a water sign ruled by the moon, and it is associated with themes of tenderness, family, boundaries, and empathy. Cancerian herbs are feminine and nurturing, and their essences balance states of emotional overwhelm, anxiety, insecurity, abandonment, and worry. These essences also help resolve issues related to family bonds (particularly mothers) as well as help us learn to better nurture ourselves.

Leo

Leo is ruled by the sun and the element of fire; it is connected to confidence, creativity, performance, courage, and justice. Leonine plants are masculine and expansive, and they evoke a sense of approval from within. Essences made from the plants of Leo can neutralize narcissism, short tempers, jealousy, vanity, pride, low self-esteem, lethargy, low passion, lack of courage, and pessimism.

Virgo

Virgo is attributed to the planet Mercury and the earth element. This sign symbolizes organization, analysis, service, and pragmatism. Herbs of Virgo have a sense of order and precision, and their essences alleviate restlessness, irritability, perfectionism, frugality, lack of discernment, and a tendency to be overcritical.

Libra

Libra is an air-element sign ruled by Venus. It is associated with balance, harmony, love, romance, and luxury. The herbs of Libra exhibit strong

Venusian qualities, and their essences address themes of indicisiveness, rapidly changing moods, confusion, lack of intimacy, isolation, strong need to be liked by others, and a sense of overall imbalance.

Scorpio

Scorpio is the sign ruled by Pluto and Mars, and it is connected to the water element. Scorpio represents the quest for personal truth, and it also symbolizes transformation, death, sex, and revelation. The herbs of Scorpio excite passion, and as essences they can relate to themes of trauma and survival. Scorpio essences also address themes of bitterness, control, revenge, secrecy, fear, and grief. Many poisonous plants are attributed to Scorpio, and they, like other plants of this sign, can initiate powerful transformation.

Sagittarius

Sagittarius is the sign of Jupiter and the element of fire. This sign tends toward all things philosophical, and it relates to learning, goal-planning, exploration, and freedom. Sagittarian herbs are outgoing and expansive, and their essences alleviate restlesness, boredom, bluntness, risk-taking, extravagance, and difficulty learning or teaching. Taking these essences inspires generosity, good humor, and the pursuit of wisdom.

Capricorn

Capricorn is ruled by Saturn and the earth element. Its nature is serious, disciplined, conservative, practical, and responsible. Capricornian plants are usually earthy and solid, and—thanks to their Saturnian nature—sometimes poisonous. Essences made from these plants balance pessimism, rigidity, austerity, self-denial, stubbornness, isolation, and a tendency to idealize and overemphasize tradition, career, and achievement.

Aquarius

Aquarius is an air-element sign ruled by Uranus and Saturn. It is the rebel of the zodiac, symbolizing revolution, innovation, idealism, and egalitarianism. Its plants often seem a little out of the ordinary, and their essences resolve patterns of aloofness, ungroundedness, impatience, and rebelliousness. Taking these essences can also alleviate feelings of rejection, erratic behavior, and a disconnect between the heart and the mind.

Pisces

Pisces is ruled by water and Neptune, and to a lesser extent Jupiter. This sign is viewed as adaptable, fluid, empathetic, and mystical. Piscean herbs are often quite watery in nature, and their essences help reduce confusion, escapism, martyrdom, impracticality, addiction, emotional burnout, and poor psychic or emotional boundaries. Essences made from Piscean plants also promote emotional clarity, compassion, and creativity, while facilitating mystical experiences.

BOTANICAL FAMILIES

Another layer to understanding the qualities of a flower essence is the signature of its botanical family as a whole. A plant's botanical family tends to define the bigger-picture action of its essence. Essences made from different plants within the same family will very likely exhibit similar mechanisms for their healing and magickal qualities, albeit expressed differently through the individual personalities of each species. It would require an entire book to devote adequate space to really understanding botanical families within flower essence practice, but there are some overarching qualities worth exploring within the context of this book. I've selected some sample families to examine the common traits and their meanings below.

Aster Family (Asteraceae)

Asteraceae, sometimes known as Compositae, is a diverse group of flowering plants. It is one of the two largest of all the botanical families, the other being the orchid family. The defining characteristic of the aster family is the composite flower heads. Although they might seem to be single flowers, each inflorescence is made up of many individual blossoms. The ray-like flowers around the perimeter of the head are strap-shaped, providing the fringe of petals familiar in plants like sunflowers, daisies, and asters. The center of the inflorescence is populated by disk florets, which bear five petals that are fused together.

The aster family is steeped in solar and stellar symbolism. Many members of Asteraceae open with the rising sun and close at sunset; others, like the sunflower, turn their inflorescence to follow the sun's path with each passing day. Even the daisy, so emblematic of this family, takes its name from "day's eye." These flowers express themes of awareness, wakefulness, and light. The solar nature of this flower family strengthens the sense of self and personality, as the sun is the predominant force behind our personality in astrology. Members of the aster family help us integrate all the different aspects of the self into our identity; they are adept at reconciling all the beliefs, patterns, and behaviors that we have inherited and learned throughout life. The solar energy of these plants also points toward a positive expression of masculine or yang forces within. Essences made from aster-family flowers promote integrity, strength, and resilience. They reflect solar themes magickally, too, and are helpful for spells for success, sovereignty, and power.

One of the key themes of essences made from the aster family is the balance between individuation and the whole. Asteraceae flower essences support the integration of all the different aspects of the self into a greater and more cohesive whole. Many flowers in this group are excellent healers after trauma because they can help us bring the fragments of our experience and identity back together again. Composite flowers also signal our roles in the cosmos; they can help us navigate life and make sense of our place in the order of the universe. They also help harmonize groups and allow us to maintain a sense of personal identity while still forging relationships to our communities. Think of these flowers as constellations—individual stars take on greater meaning when grouped together, and these groupings paint a picture that relays practical and spiritual information to us.

Many asters and their relatives bloom late in the year and have long-lasting flowers. As a result, their flowers help us accept the aging process with grace, reminding us that we can still radiate light and joy in our later years. Some essences made from this flower family enable us to better cope with death and the dying process. They help us grieve resiliently for those we have lost, and they can help us face the inevitability of our own passing with poise and acceptance. Examples of the aster family include the well-known daisy and sunflower, as well as calendula, dandelion, echinacea, mugwort, thistle, wormwood, and yarrow. Dr. Bach produced only one remedy belonging to Asteraceae: chicory.

Buttercup Family (Ranunculaceae)

Several important flower essences can be found in the buttercup family, Ranunculaceae. This botanical family is quite an ancient one, and extant species today still retain many ancestral, primitive characteristics; they are sometimes described as being like a window back in time. The flowers are highly variable and often typefied by having multiple pistils with hooked ends. Many of these plants are strongly toxic, and they are considered baneful plant spirits.

One of the key themes of the buttercup family is our relationship with the world around us. Members of the buttercup family tend to focus on materialism and our presence in the world. Clematis, one of only two baneful remedies in Dr. Bach's system, belongs to Ranunculaceae, and it is the remedy indicated for daydreamers and those focused on the future. It also helps us overcome feelings of faintness or of being far away. Another buttercup-family member, pulsatilla, or pasqueflower, similarly combats shyness, aloofness, and unclear boundaries. The hooked pistils of Ranunculaceae grab the consciousness, helping it stay more present. Essences made from these flowers help us deal with the present moment when we would rather get lost in daydreams or retreat away from the material.

Many of the buttercup family also address materialistic urges. Monkshood (aconite or wolfsbane), for example, teaches us to give up materialism and go within. It is the essence for the hermit or mystic, helping conquer the urges to be overly identified with the material so as to cultivate the primacy of the spirit. The bitter, acrid taste borne by most members of Ranunculaceae speaks to this relationship; these flowers tend to address feelings of resentment or bitterness over not having enough or denying ourselves pleasure. On the other end of the spectrum lies buttercup, an essence that teaches us to enjoy the richness of life; buttercup helps us find joy and fulfilment with the material and embodiment. Somewhere between the two we find larkspur (*Delphinium* spp.), whose essence inspires leadership and contagious enthusiasm. It helps us align our life with our spiritual ideals; it reconciles our material existence with our soul. Similarly, pulsatilla helps those who feel uncertain about their path, and it addresses fear and timidity that prevents us from taking risks to explore and manifest our life's path. Most members of this family can improve confidence and self-worth.

Ranunculaceae is an ancient family of plants, and it addresses ancient patterns. Anemone is a prime example, as it specifically addresses concerns that are long-standing. Its essence, as well as that of others in the buttercup family, tends to focus on the karmic level of our makeup. These ancient plants also resonate with the beliefs, ideas, thoughts, and values that we inherit. What do we inherit from our family or tribe, whether genetically and socially? Buttercup-family flower essences can help us reveal and address these patterns.

Carrot Family (Apiaceae)

The carrot family, sometimes referred to as the parsley family, is called Apiaceae or Umbelliferae. The members of this botanical group are usually herbaceous plants with hollow stems, strong taproots, and pinnate leaves. The inflorescence is a characteristic compound umbel: radiating groups of tiny flowers that branch outward from a single point at the end of a stalk, rather like an umbrella. Individual flowers have five petals, sepals, and stamens each. Many carrot-family members have white flowers and rich, spicy aromas.

One common element among all members of Apiaceae is their ability to stimulate the psychic senses. Essences made from Queen Ann's lace and angelica, for example, are often noted for strengthening the connection to the higher self and for opening the third-eye chakra. The hollow stems help clear blockages and enable us to become better conduits and vessels for spiritual information. The branching forms of the flowers symbolize the connections that the higher mind and spirit make.

Many essences made from Apiaceae flowers center around themes of sensitivity. Some, such as Queen Anne's lace, endow us with greater psychic sensitivity, whereas others, like dill, are indicated when we are oversensitive. The great clusters of flowers borne by Apiaceae members represent our ability to sensitize ourselves to those around us or to the psychic threads woven through existence, or they can symbolically fortify us when we feel too sensitive around groups or in other settings. Hollow stems are also a common feature among plants in the carrot family, which suggests that they help us be clear vessels and perfect conduits for psychic information to flow through.

The roots of its member plants also provide clues to the overall action of the family. According to Bach flower essence expert Julian Barnard, roots symbolize "physical connections, family relationships, and the past."[13] He points out that root systems that are vigorously attached to the soil represent continuity of life purpose, thereby bridging past and present with the future. Apiaceae plants are often noted for their deep, starchy taproots, which are storehouses of energy for the future. These essences nourish us for future growth, helping lay a foundation of self-care, spiritual practice, and practical action that keeps us moving forward. This can result in essences that teach us to rely on ourselves, and they can mitigate the tendency toward being a people pleaser. They teach the meaning of genuine connection and encourage reciprocal relationship.

Magickally speaking, many plants in the carrot family are associated with abundance and prosperity. These plants reproduce prolifically, as they tend to seed readily and abundantly. Most produce essences that are psychically stimulating, though they also offer protection against being too open. The powerful banes in this family are often phototoxic and attack the nervous system. Their essences open us to seeing the light in the darkness and help us enhance perception on every level. Examples of flowers in this botanical family include angelica, dill, hemlock, Queen Ann's lace (or wild carrot), and water hemlock. Many commercial flower essence producers offer a wide range of other essences from Apiaceae, too.

Mint Family (Lamiaceae)

The mint family, called Lamiaceae or Labatiae, displays square stems, simple and opposite leaves, and highly aromatic oils. The flowers of the mint family are deeply invaginated and have a pronounced bilateral symmetry. They have five petals, which are united or fused together, as are their five sepals. Mint flowers characteristically have two lobes pointed upward and three hanging downward. Mint plants can be aggressive growers, and they often propagate quite easily. They have a wide range of culinary and medicinal uses and are popular in the garden.

The mint family has a connection to the animal kingdom in that the deep invaginations in the flowers draw pollinators inward, while the warming aromatic oils in the leaves suggest a link to animals that can warm themselves and regulate their own temperature—mammals.[14] The heat sparked by mint's oils usually stimulates digestion, a process related to the alchemical element of fire. This contrasts with the square stems, as square shapes represent the earth element. Thus, the mints often unite bodily awareness (via the earth element) with spiritual consciousness (fire element).[15]

Members of the mint family tend to thrive in very wet or very dry conditions. Those that prefer wet and mucky soils are often used medicinally to treat conditions of moisture in the body. They also resonate with the watery nature of the emotional body, and their flower essences promote movement and flux when the emotional body is otherwise stagnant and heavy. They often can help us "digest" our emotions little by little, until we are better able to understand the scenario playing out in the present moment. Drier members of the mint family, like sage, offer better perspective by generating distance from our emotions as they arise. All mint essences stimulate the mind and may boost cognitive abilities. They also tend to strengthen healthy traits of the ego and the mind, and they tend to soothe the nerves; most members of the mint family grant clearheadedness and self-control.

The mint family has a very rhythmic structure, with pairs of leaves and stems growing from the central stem at regular intervals. The flowers show symmetry and are also produced in rhythmic intervals. Flower essences made from plants in the mint family support rhythmic breathing, thinking, and release of emotions. They work to prevent any single emotion or thought pattern from purging all at once. Medicinally, mints work on the digestive tract to restore its normal rhythm and balance.

The mint family has a wide range of uses in magick. Many members are cleansing, and they are often used for healing and peace. More traditional mints can be used to calm tempers as well as draw money. As essences, they can help shift our mind-set to create many of the same outcomes from the mental level.

There are countless flower essences made from members of Lamiaceae. Basil, lavender, lemon balm, peppermint, rosemary, and sage are examples found in this book. Bee balm, catnip, dead nettle, thyme, tulsi, and wood betony are just a few other examples.

Nightshade Family (Solanaceae)

The nightshades are often collectively referred to as the "witching herbs." Even the name *nightshade* conjures images of something dark, sinister, and inherently magickal. While many nightshades are powerful poisons, many others are important food crops. Nightshades are characterized by their five-petaled flowers, typically in shades of white, yellow, or blue. The petals are usually united or fused; the five stamens are often fused, too. The flowers tend to display radial symmetry. Though often star-shaped, the blooms may also resemble trumpets or may be reflexed, with petals that point backward.

Nightshades are famed for their toxicity. Even those that are cultivated as food crops, like tomato and potato, typically have toxic parts, though they may be much milder than plants like mandrake and belladonna. This family is often associated with taboos, like witchcraft and uncleanliness The scent of many nightshades is repulsive to some people; they smell somehow dirty or animal-like. Ingesting poisonous members of Solanaceae causes unpleasant reactions, like diarrhea and vomiting. All of this points to something primal and somewhat uncomfortable in the nightshade essences. They confront animal instincts and primordial fears. They may also help us deal with our psychic baggage—the things we are ashamed about, those parts of our psyche trapped in the deepest recesses of our mind. Magickally, the strong smells and toxins of night-shades have been considered apotropaic; they can ward off evil, just as they might be used for acts of malefic witchcraft.

While the five-petaled Rosaceae act as doorways into incarnation, nightshades, which also sport five petals, tend to open the gates to leaving the material plane. From a medicinal perspective, these baneful herbs were once used to induce sleep for the gravely ill or injured, sometimes as an aid to the dying process; too much of any of the more potent nightshades results in a person leaving this incarnation permanently. Magickally and vibrationally speaking, many nightshades are also associated with astral travel and shamanic journeys. They also help us move beyond our perception of the material plane. Nightshade poisons have a strong astral connection, and ingesting these plants produces sensations of flying, floating, and movement beyond the body. Taking nightshade essences can therefore assist in our nonphysical journeys.

Despite all the dark lore associated with the nightshade family, many of them have a lighthearted side, too. I've been told by more than one witch that mandrake is a joy to grow, and the essence is surprisingly gentle if used conscientiously. Several nightshades share Venusian qualities, and they produce very loving, if not occasionally intense, essences. In magick, nightshade essences can banish unwanted influences (especially those that arise from within) as well as help us journey beyond the confines of the body to make contact with spirits and guides. They are used in spells for drawing love, perhaps akin to their five-petaled analogs in the rose family. Examples of nightshade essences include angel's trumpet, belladonna, bittersweet nightshade, black nightshade, cayenne, datura, henbane, mandrake, potato, tobacco, and tomato. Several other common flower essences also belong to this botanical family, such as eggplant, petunia, and wild potato bush.

Rose Family (Rosaceae)

Rosaceae is easily one of the most important botanical families; many of its members are vital food crops, while many others produce potent medicines. Nearly all members of the rose family exhibit flowers with five petals and many stamens arranged in a spiraling whorl. The flowers tend to be showy, with pronounced radial symmetry. Many Rosaceae plants have serrated leaf margins, and many also have thorns or spines.

The rose is the quintessential flower symbolizing the Western mystery traditions, and its fivefold symmetry and symbolism can be translated to most other members of its family. In particular, the rose family awakens our perception of and relationship to the divine feminine, as well as to unconditional love. The juxtaposition of petals with thorns or spines, a trait shared by many members of Rosaceae, reminds us that we are able to learn through love or through pain. Essences made from rose-family plants tend to offer a reminder of our choice either to withhold love (spine) and subsequently experience pain, fear, or separation or to express love (petal) and subsequently create more beauty and harmony in the world. The five-petaled flowers relate to our embodiment and ability to create and shape the world around us, so Rosaceae plants teach us that love is an active expression of the heart; their essences help us make the decision to love rather than succumb to lower or disharmonious emotions.

Patricia Kaminski, cofounder of the Flower Essence Society and a flower essence practitioner, teacher, and producer, explains that essences made from this botanical family bring spiritual forces into fruitful manifestation on earth. She writes, "As soul medicines, the Rose Family plants anchor and sustain cosmic ideals within the human body and the body of the earth."[16] Rose-family essences thus lift the energy of a person or place via an infusion of universal love and a return to the cosmic blueprint meant to guide and inform the soul's progress. In her book *The Language of Plants,* Julia Graves describes the action of this botanical family as acting upon the relationship of the center to the periphery of our five limbs.[17] Many of these plants are used medicinally for the heart and circulatory system, thus moving blood from the heart (the center) into the head and limbs (the periphery). Vibrationally speaking, essences made from plants in the rose family help us embody the heart and unconditional love, bringing that sense of identity and awareness of love through the five limbs and into human incarnation. These essences help us overcome the roadblocks to being more fully embodied. Many have spines that can protect against or pierce through patterns of apathy or procrastination, as well as spur the psyche toward becoming more fully realized in the material world through our actions. The essences of this group of plants have effects that range from treating total disconnection from earthly matters (rose) to being aware of the true will but otherwise unable to manifest it (blackberry) to overcoming overawareness or hypersensitivity to the material world (crab apple). Magickally speaking, rose-family plants tend to express the Venusian qualities of love and beauty. Many are emissaries for the divine feminine and can help us build relationships to the Great Goddess in all her expressions.

Apart from the eponymous rose, other members of Rosaceae include agrimony, almond, apple, blackberry, blackthorn, cherry, cinquefoil, crab apple, hawthorn, lady's mantle, pear, plum, raspberry, rowan, and strawberry. Some genera and species of the rose family have a wide array of cultivars available. Many members of this botanical family are available as flower essences.

PUTTING IT ALL TOGETHER

The doctrine of signatures allows you to take a deeper look into the nature and function of a flower essence by examining the resonance between the plant and the universe. Start with your observations about a flower's color, petals, and shape. From there, expand your investigation to the nature of the plant as a whole: its stature, leaves, growth cycle, and environment. Look for clues about elemental and planetary signatures, too. Finally, consider the traits shared by other members of its botanical family; these will give you insight into the framework for how the essence works its magick and medicine.

The part of the process that I enjoy the most is finding connections between a plant's folklore, its medicinal uses, and the indications for its flower essence. Usually you can find a common thread weaving together all of these seemingly disparate pieces of plant spirit medicine. As a case study, let's examine henbane (*Hyoscyamus niger*) via the doctrine of signatures.

Henbane is one of the quintessential members of the nightshade family, Solanaceae. It is traditionally used in witches' flying ointments, and it was said to be a constituent in the incense burned at Delphi to help the oracle deliver her prophecy. It is often used in magick for banishing, protection, and communion with the dead, and it is said to have a deep relationship with the underworld.

Henbane's blooms exhibit five petals fused into a roughly trumpet-like shape. The flowers are a dirty yellowish color with purplish-black veins that lead to an even darker center. Yellow is sometimes connected to light and fire, but the dim, almost dusky quality of this shade of yellow reminds me of the last rays of sun before twilight. The black center of the flower clearly denotes a relationship to the shadow self, the unseen levels of reality, and themes of death and decay. The lines of purplish black seem to trace a pattern, like roads or rivers that lead deep into the dark center. Henbane flower essence is often connected to Hekate, who rules the crossroads and bears a torch into the darkness of the night and the underworld. The essence offers insight into the path we take; it helps us navigate our decisions in life to get a clearer sense of where we are headed. I find that the marbled veins on the petals remind me of a city map, similarly veined by streets. Henbane helps us read the roadmap of life, but ultimately it reminds us that there is always an unknown factor to which we must surrender, as those dark highways along its petals lead into the near-black center of the bloom.

With their five petals, the flowers of henbane connote a doorway or gateway of one sort or another. Since the plant has a long connection to the underworld and the flight to the witches' sabbat, it's no surprise that the essence facilitates astral travel and dreamtime journeys. Like other members of Solanaceae, it is connected to magick, spirit communication, and death. The trumpet shape of the flowers indicates the ability of this plant to enhance spiritual communication, and many flower essence practitioners use henbane essence to connect to ancestors and guides.

Henbane has an overtly Saturnian signature. The seedpods resemble teeth, which, like all bones, fall under Saturn's domain. It is highly toxic and prefers liminal spaces, both of which indicate Saturn again. As a Saturnian flower essence, henbane is helpful for revealing the karmic underpinnings of our pain, transforming family karma, and breaking generational curses.

The elemental signature of henbane is connected to both fire and water. The seedpods resemble round cauldrons, especially after the frills decay, and cauldrons contain water (or other liquids). The veiny patterns on the petals also resemble waterways, and the anthers are a shade of deep blue—another water signature. Water points to the deep subconscious as well as to the ancestral connections in this essence. The plant's fiery nature comes from the shades of yellow and red-black in the petals, as well as from the toothed leaf margins, which resemble wild flames. The plant has been linked to various gods of sun and fire throughout history. Fiery henbane essence affords protection, illumination, and defense against darkness.

Looking at the gesture of the plant as a whole, the flowers are borne on tall, erect stems with broad leaves that bear ragged, toothed margins. The plant has an intensity that helps our personal identity stand out against the backdrop of our inherited beliefs, behaviors, and values. It rises from the underground toward the heavens, bridging the upper, middle, and lower worlds to give us a better perspective, just as a city seen from above resembles the maplike pattern on henbane's petals.

CONCLUDING THOUGHTS

The art of deciphering the gestures and symbols of plants will help you understand the deeper levels at which a flower essence works. The first step is always observing the plant and communing with the spirit thereof. Following that, I like to take the essence and sit with my thoughts and feelings for a few minutes to half an hour; this step allows me to assess how the essence interacts with my mood and perception. When I'm working with an essence that does not have a textbook definition for its applications, I sit with the plant (or pictures of it in the absence of a live specimen) and I take into consideration the doctrine of signatures.

While there is no absolute rule or truth for any given signature, there are trends that emerge from decoding signatures and observing the effects of flower essences. The best way to build a vocabulary of plant signatures, symbols, and gestures is to get to know the essences in your toolbox. Take them and experience their medicine, while also consciously connecting to the plant spirits for advice and guidance. Finally, go out into nature or sit down with photos of the plants to map out their morphology, environment, and appearance. Taking a hands-on approach to unraveling the secret language of leaf, stalk, and petal will transform your practice in ways you've never dreamed.

7

Choosing and Using
Flower Essences

With thousands of commercially produced essences available to choose from, it's easy to amass a large collection. You can add your own homemade essences to your toolbox, too. Although you might make or purchase an essence for a particular situation, eventually you will need help discerning which essence, out of all the ones you have access to, is the best choice for a particular situation.

CHOOSING THE RIGHT ESSENCE

Choosing the right flower essence is an art that takes experience and sensitivity to develop. A variety of techniques have become popular in the flower essence community. Some are also used in other holistic practices, such as homeopathy and crystal healing. Each method carries its own advantages and disadvantages. Many people who work with flower essences employ different selection methods to meet the needs of different people and scenarios.

Familiarizing yourself with several, if not all, of the selection methods described below will enable you to be prepared for a variety of situations in which you'll use essences. Interview-style selection methods, such as logic and pattern matching, can put first-time flower essence clients at ease, while intuitive methods or communing directly with the plant spirits might be better suited for magick, meditation, and ritual. Ultimately, the way you select the right essences is up to you. Choose the selection method that best suits your needs and your practice.

There is no substitute for becoming acquainted with the essences in your toolbox one at a time. Developing a relationship and gathering firsthand experience with your essences enables you to be a more competent and sensitive therapist. Whether you make or use essences for your personal development or offer flower essences alongside a professional practice to help others, spend time with each of them so you can better know and understand them. Observe how they work for you, read about their effects, and look for the evidence of the miracles that essences can produce. This helps you select the best ones, no matter which selection method you employ.

What If It's Not the Right Essence?

Chances are good that you won't pick exactly the right essence every time. It can be hard to choose between similar essences, and not every situation presents a black-and-white distinction. So what happens if you pick the wrong one? Is there such a thing as a wrong essence?

Recalling the similarities between flower essence therapy and homeopathy, let's look at the homeopathic law of infinitesimals (or the law of infinitesimal dose), which states that minute doses of a substance can treat the symptoms it would cause at a larger dose. The key here is that the amount is *infinitesimally* small. At such a dilution, harmful side effects are not expected. In other words, if a remedy does not help, it does not harm, either. Flower essences are generally similar in their effects.

If you select a flower essence that absolutely doesn't apply to the situation, person, or goal in mind, then it very likely won't have any effects at all. This makes flower essences absolutely safe for all people. The worst thing that happens if you get it wrong is *nothing,* and the best-case scenario is that life improves.

In relatively few cases, some people experience a so-called healing crisis—that is, a strong reaction to treatment in which the condition worsens at first, but then quickly, almost abruptly, the reaction ends. A healing crisis generally reveals the severity of the underlying condition, rather than actually exacerbating it. An easy solution to it is to use one of the many emergency care formulas available, such as Bach's Rescue Remedy (also called Five Flower Formula by some makers), Soul Support from Alaskan Essences, or the Crisis-Desert Emergency Formula from Desert Alchemy. You can also blend the Witchy Rescue Remedy on page 196. Several doses of an emergency care formula can alleviate a healing crisis in short order.

Methods for Selection

There are a host of methods for choosing the right essences for the right situations. They range from a more conversational approach to hands-on techniques of dowsing and muscle testing. There are others that rely on spiritual skills, such as selecting essences intuitively or by communicating directly with the plant spirits. Each method has its own merits and disadvantages. The most common ones include:

* Logic and pattern matching
* Dowsing
* Applied kinesiology
* Client preference
* Intuition
* Communication with plant spirits

There is no single best approach to be used universally. Different practitioners, clients, and scenarios might require a different method for selecting essences. Let's take a deeper look at each of them.

Logic and Pattern Matching

I was first introduced to the Bach flower essences as a young adult by my friend Rita, who owned a local metaphysical store. She would sit down with me and we would chat about life. Occasionally she'd jot down a quick note or ask a thoughtful question. Before long, based on all the information she had gleaned from our conversation, she had narrowed down the appropriate essences for me. This is a prime example of the selection method that Sue Lilly refers to as logic and pattern matching in *The Essence Practitioner*.[1]

Logic and pattern matching may be simple and conversational, relying on a client's description of their life and emotions. It may also be more structured, like an interview or questionnaire; the Bach Centre in England even has a short quiz that you can take on your own or with an essence practitioner to narrow down which essences are the most appropriate for your situation. Many flower essence books have repertories (glossaries or directories of essences organized by the condition being treated) and cross-reference guides to help you select essences based on the presenting conditions or patterns.

This method is simple and can be used by everyone; it also feels familiar to clients, as it resembles the process of anamnesis—taking a patient case history—in traditional health care practices. Nevertheless, it relies heavily on the listening skills and interviewing prowess of the practitioner as well as the honesty and transparency of the client. In addition to the information a client relays verbally, practitioners should take note of nonverbal communication, like facial expression, posture, and body language.

Dowsing

Dowsing with a pendulum has become one of the mainstays for flower essence selection. By holding a pendulum and asking appropriate questions (usually yes-or-no questions), the practitioner receives guidance by interpreting the movement of the pendulum. The meaning of the pendulum's movement will differ from one practitioner to the next, so it is vital to experiment and verify the movements. Many flower essence authors and commercial producers offer charts that can be used with a pendulum to help with the selection process.

Dowsing can feel unfamiliar to newcomers, especially if they do not already have a background in metaphysical, spiritual, or occult practices. The art of dowsing can easily be influenced by the user, too; if you strongly desire a certain result, it's likely that you'll subconsciously cause the pendulum to move accordingly. In spite of this, dowsing is an excellent method because it can point to information that hasn't been verbalized by the client, and it doesn't rely on the practitioner's interview skills.

You can quickly narrow down the essences available even without a reference chart. Begin by asking your pendulum questions to help trim down the number of essences you're considering, such as "Is the appropriate essence in such-and-such line of essences?" or "Does the name of the essence begin with the letters A to F?" Once you've shortened the list of possible essences, it is much easier to go down the line and ask if each individual one in the group is the correct essence. With dowsing, it is important to double-check; always ask if the essence (or essences) you've selected is the correct one after you have picked it out.

For the magickal practitioner, dowsing is usually seen as a means of communicating with spirit allies and guides, as well as with the higher self. It may also be useful in selecting essences for magickal uses, especially if other methods of selection, such as logic and pattern matching, have resulted in too many options.

Applied Kinesiology

The term *applied kinesiology* refers to the practice of testing muscle resistance as an indication of health or sickness or to indicate the correct course of treatment. Originally taught as an adjunct to chiropractic medicine in the 1960s, applied kinesiology has been adopted by many practitioners of holistic and integrative medicine, and it has even been used by the metaphysical and occult circles as sort of dowsing technique, using the body and its muscles to obtain answers. Literature about flower essences refers to the use of muscle testing as early as the 1980s, and today many flower essence practitioners use applied kinesiology as part of their selection methods.

The commonest form of applied kinesiology requires two parties: the practitioner and the client. The client holds an arm outstretched at their side and is asked to resist as the practitioner presses against the arm. A baseline test determines the average resistance that the client can maintain. Following this, the practitioner asks the client various questions or has the client hold an essence, and the practitioner tests for resistance under these new conditions. If the resistance strengthens, the essence is determined to be applicable to the client's scenario; if the resistance weakens, the essence is not the correct one.

Applied kinesiology permits the practitioner to determine the correct essences even if they are not intimately familiar with the essences in their toolbox or if they are unable to ascertain the correct one from the client's anamnesis. One disadvantage of this technique is that it can be time-consuming to test individual essences, and the client's arm may tire before the end of the session, thereby resulting in inaccurate results.

Other methods that rely on the fingers exist, thus providing alternatives that can prevent muscle fatigue in the arms. The muscle-testing procedures using the fingers may also be used for self-testing, thereby allowing practitioners to select essences for themselves. One method requires you to form interlocking rings with the thumb and forefinger of each hand. You contemplate an essence or a yes-or-no question and then quickly (but not too forcefully) tug your hands away from one another. If your linked fingers hold and your hands do not separate, the answer is positive. If the links break and your hands separate, the answer is no.

Another muscle-testing method has you form a circle with the thumb and small finger of your nondominant hand. Use the thumb and index finger of your dominant hand to make a pincer-like shape, and place this into the loop formed by the fingers of your other hand. Ask your question, and then try to maintain a closed loop with your nondominant hand while trying to pry the loop open by spreading the pincer-fingers of your dominant hand. If the loop remains closed, the answer is yes; if it breaks, the answer is no.

One of my favorite methods of muscle testing is called the body pendulum, and it allows a client to perform the test without the assistance of a practitioner (which also means that you can easily use it for yourself, too). Start by standing up straight, with your spine erect and your feet shoulder-width apart. Take a couple of deep, rhythmic breaths to ground and center yourself. Select an essence that you would like to test and hold it to your center of gravity, roughly level with your solar plexus. As yourself if this is the correct essence, and intend that your body's innate wisdom will reveal the answer. You will sense yourself leaning slightly forward or backward at this stage. Leaning forward into the essence is a positive response, while leaning backward away from the essence is a negative response.

I learned methods of muscle testing as part of my witchcraft and occult training, but I don't see too many practitioners using it as their default tool of divination. In spite of this, it can still be a helpful means of selecting essences for magickal use.

Client Preference

Occasionally a client will be able to simply tell you which essences they want to work with. The same holds true when we choose essences for ourselves; we may have a conscious or unconscious desire to connect to a particular plant. You can also ask the client about their favorite trees, flowers, culinary herbs, colors, and so on to highlight specific essences for them to choose from. Conversely, try asking about the plants or colors that they have an aversion to, as they often indicate plant spirits that hold profound healing for the client.

Allowing a client to express their preference can feel empowering to them as they continue their journey to wholeness with the essences. Client or practitioner preference can be applicable for magickal uses, too; sometimes we use specific materia magica largely because of the relationship we have with them. Even when a particular plant does not correspond with our working via logic and pattern matching, our preference for its energy can make it a useful ally.

Intuition

Learning to receive and trust intuitive and psychic information can elevate your work with flower essences to a new level. You might just have an inner image of a particular flower or bottle, or you may receive guidance in the form of symbols, words, or a gut feeling about using specific essences. Using psychic skills in discerning the correct essences for yourself and your clients can open new doors in your practice, as you are no longer limited to the information presented by the client. Many times I have been drawn to a relatively unfamiliar essence for myself or my clients, and upon reading about the essence we discover that it perfectly fits the situation at hand. Clients can also receive intuitive information about which essences are best for them, and I always do my best to incorporate their psychic impressions and intuitive feedback into flower essence blends.

One way to use your intuition for choosing flower essences is to hold your hand over the bottles of essences and "feel out" the energy, slowly moving your hand over each bottle in turn and seeing which one has the strongest draw. Sometimes you may feel a magnetic tug toward a particular bottle, while other times you might feel warmth, tingling, pulsing, or some other tangible sensation. Some people simply have an inner knowing that they are hovering over the correct essence, without any palpable sensations. This method works best for people who are sensitive to energy, although anyone can learn to perceive subtle energy with practice.

Many years ago I learned another method for using intuition from my best friend, Kat. She simply connects to her spiritual allies and guides and states, silently or aloud, "Show me white for 'yes' or black for 'no.'" Then she asks a yes-or-no question and waits to receive an image or symbol in her mind's eye. I use this method with flower essences, and it is effective and fast—I simply move my gaze down the line and receive an inner, visual answer for each essence in turn.

The main challenge with using intuitive or psychic feedback to select essences is that your conscious and subconscious thoughts will affect the outcome if you are not centered and detached from the outcome.

Nowadays many commercial essence makers offer cards, posters, and books with images of the plants to help you connect to the plants on a psychic level. Many companies even display images of the plants on their essence bottles, allowing you to present the bottles to your clients for input. Ask them which flower(s) they like and which they dislike. The flowers they feel an affinity toward represent the energies that may support their health and well-being, while the flowers they dislike could point to the energies or ideas that their subconscious or unconscious mind is avoiding.[2]

Another method for selecting essences intuitively is bibliomancy: Balance a book containing a directory of flower essences (like this one) on its spine and allow it to fall open, or flip through its pages with your eyes closed until you land on a page that *feels* right. Read about the first essence you see when you open your eyes. If practiced with focus and sincerity, bibliomancy can help you find just the essence to suit your situation.

Following intuitive and psychic guidance to chooseflower essences is a wonderful method for working with them magickally and ritually. I often picture the process as allowing the essence to step forward as a volunteer, rather than letting my ego do the picking. This method is most effective for meditation, shamanic journey, or spirit-led rituals.

Communication with Plant Spirits

I haven't seen much discussion in flower essence literature about choosing flower essences by communicating directly with the spirits of the plants themselves. You could perhaps see it as an extension or evolution of intuitively choosing essences, but spirit communication is a deeply shamanic and magickal process that requires the practitioner to check their ego and forge a relationship with the spirit world. It can be a life-changing skill to learn, as it opens the doors to regular feedback from your spirit allies and guardians.

Communication with plant spirits takes time to cultivate. It requires a solid foundation of regular meditation, plant attunements, offerings, and conscious and intentional work. It may present itself in meditation as an inner-world conversation between your consciousness and that of the plant. Some people may receive the communication audibly or in words, while others might experience a language of visual symbols or simply an inner knowing. You can also employ methods of dowsing, automatic writing, or other divinatory techniques to contact plant spirit allies for selecting flower essences.

Plant spirit communication can provide insight that you would not otherwise have access to during a flower essence consultation. Although this selection method is not strictly based on your familiarity with the therapeutic effects of flower essences, like logic and pattern matching is, it is still helpful to have had firsthand experience with the essences in order to have a good working relationship with the spirits of those essences. Having a regular spiritual practice, such as meditation, is helpful for authentic spirit communication, as it helps you detach from the expectations and judgments of your ego. This helps you filter out the mental noise and projections coming from your own mind so that you can better perceive the messages from the plants.

I don't have a set method or outline to recommend for plant spirit communication as a means of choosing flower essences. It is an organic process that depends on your personal relationship with the consciousness of the plant kingdom. My best advice is simply to find a sense of inner stillness and quietude and then call out to the plant spirits, asking them to give you guidance about which flower essences to choose. You may see or sense the spirit of a particular plant responding to you, indicating that you could use an essence made from that plant. Or perhaps one of your personal plant spirit allies (see chapter 3) may give you guidance or counsel about the appropriate essence or blend to use. However you receive your information, always be sure to express gratitude to the spirit(s) that assist you.

USING FLOWER ESSENCES

Once you've selected the appropriate essences, it is time to put them to work. Start by deciding whether you'll use them straight from the stock bottles or diluted (potentized) in a dosage bottle. The latter allows you to use essences more economically and gives you the opportunity to blend various essences for a custom combination. Using stock bottles is convenient, as it does not require you to dilute. Take care that when using stock bottles you do not touch the dropper to your mouth, skin, or other surface; otherwise you will contaminate the bottle.

Single Essences, Blends, and Sequential Processing

A single flower essence can be laser-like in its focus. Working with a single essence at a time allows you to more easily monitor its effects on your well-being. It also affords you a closer relationship with the associated plant spirit, thereby improving the results of your therapeutic and spiritual uses of the essence in the long run. For these reasons, when you're working with an essence that is new to you, it's best to use it on its own for several days or weeks.

A well-made blend offers a synergistic effect, yielding magnified results. When you're preparing a blend, "less is more" is good advice. My dear friend Rita, who first offered me flower essence blends, did not often exceed five or six of the Bach remedies in a dosage bottle. Dr. Bach himself began by using one remedy at a time, preferring to use single flower essences in sequence rather than as a combination. Eventually he decided to combine essences, twice using as many as nine in a single bottle—but this complexity seems to have been the exception rather than the rule for him.

I usually stick to four to six essences per dosage bottle. Too many essences can muddy the waters, rendering the therapy less effective. It's a bit like trying to read too many books at once; you get all the information, but it is hard to keep track of or retain it all.

Exceptional circumstances will necessitate exceptional blends, however. Your selection method may indicate a larger-than-average number of essences for some situations (and if that concerns you, you can always double-check the accuracy of your selection before you blend them). Some essence makers offer combination formulas with a dozen or more flower essences, and you might occasionally find yourself crafting a similarly complex blend.

I also strive to create blends that are energetically cohesive and organized around a central theme or goal. If you try to address too many unrelated conditions or goals with one blend, there is a chance that you cannot effectively heal or transform each of the patterns all at once. It is best to find the most urgent or most important theme that you are working on and formulate your flower essence blend around that theme.

When blending essences, use an equal number of drops of each stock essence, unless otherwise directed to do so. You might, for example, receive inner guidance to add more of a grounding essence for someone whose emotions are unusually volatile. You can also dowse to determine the appropriate number of drops of each stock essence to include in a personalized blend.

Instead of blending, some people prefer *sequential processing,* a method of administration that relies upon using a selection of essences in sequence, rather than as a combination.[3] You can use the same selection methods described in this chapter to determine the number of essences to use, which ones they are, and the ideal order to apply them. Though sequential processing can be used for any application method, it's usually done topically: Place a couple of drops of the first essence on your wrists and then rub your wrists together. Wait approximately one minute and proceed to the next essence in the sequence, repeating until each one has been administered. This is a potent technique that initiates a rapid response.

Dosage, Frequency, and Duration

The standard dosage for most single flower essences and blends is two to four drops, up to four times a day. Larger doses do not make flower essence therapy more effective. Frequency, rather than quantity, is the key factor; taking smaller doses around the clock is much more effective than just a couple large doses.

Some essences have different dosage guidelines. For example, mushroom essences are typically taken in smaller doses once or twice a day for maximum effect. The essences from Chalice Well Essences in Glastonbury, England, are meant to be taken seven drops at a time. Dr. Bach diluted two drops of a stock bottle in an average-size apothecary bottle (approximately 4 ounces) and recommended taking teaspoonfuls of the remedy throughout the day. David Dalton of Delta Gardens has specific dosage guidelines for his line of essences made from medicinal plants, having arrived at these from years of practical experience and observation. For example, for thistle he suggests using one drop of stock essence per one hundred drops of neutral solution, three to five times per day.[4]

Many practitioners dowse to determine the right dosage and frequency. Dowsing charts for use with flower essences can be found in many books and online, and you can easily make your own.

The duration of treatment depends on the issue at hand. Generally speaking, I recommend taking an essence or blend for at least two to four weeks for most conditions. Acute patterns can be treated for shorter amounts of time, whereas long-standing ones may require a much longer duration. After a couple of weeks of working with a particular essence or blend, it is a good idea to assess your progress and, as needed, adjust the blend, dosage, or frequency for the best results.

Some sensitive individuals may find flower essence therapy to be overstimulating. In these rare scenarios, use essences in smaller, less frequent doses. Baneful herbs in particular can elicit stronger effects than essences made from healing herbs or trees. It may be best for people who are extra-sensitive to subtle energy to take one drop at a time twice a day at first and gradually increase the frequency to three or four times per day.

Ways to Use Essences

Just as there is more than one way to select essences, there are several ways to use them. They include:

- ★ Oral use
- ★ Topical application
- ★ Inhalation
- ★ Sprays
- ★ Spreading essences through the aura
- ★ Using essences in the bath
- ★ Diffusing essences into the air
- ★ Wearing essences
- ★ Meditating with essences

Each method has its own merits and disadvantages, and learning how to use essences via several of these techniques allows you to maximize the benefits they bring to your life. Let's examine each method in greater depth.

Oral Use

Most people take essences orally, often directly from a dropper or spray bottle. Usually you place the drops under your tongue, as this assists the absorption of the essences. Some essence makers also offer pilules and pastilles for people who prefer not to carry a dropper bottle full of liquid.

Administering essences orally can feel instinctually medicinal. It can recall the experience of taking other medicines and sets the psychological stage by helping the subconscious mind *expect* healing to take place. One of the major downsides to oral administration can be the taste; in particular, many people find essences preserved with alcohol or vinegar unpleasant.

Still, for the majority of people, oral use is the most convenient. A small dropper bottle, such as a half-ounce size, can easily be carried in a pocket or purse to be on hand at all times. I seldom go anywhere without a bottle of Rescue Remedy, and I almost always have a personal blend of essences nearby to support me throughout the day.

Topical Application

Topical application is just as effective as—and possibly more effective than—internal use, but it often works best when the two methods are used in tandem. The skin is semipermeable and absorbs the essences quickly. External application enables you to direct essences into specific energetic points that augment their efficacy, such as chakras or acupuncture points. This method works well to direct the focus of the essence to the physical body, thereby addressing the mind-body connection and helping to resolve psychological and spiritual causes of physical symptoms. Topical application often works best when combined with oral use of flower essences.

Although you can squeeze a drop or two of an essence directly onto the skin, it's more effective to dilute the remedy first: Add several drops of each of the essences you'd like to use to a small container of clean water. Let the water stand for several minutes, then use a cotton ball, swab, towel, or tissue to dab or wipe the essence-infused water onto the target area. I like to apply a grounding and rejuvenating essence to the soles of my feet. Within minutes I feel more present and alert, as if I'd just awakened from a power nap.

You can also add essences to cosmetics, soap, shampoo, and similar products that are applied topically. When I was first introduced to Bach flower essences, I instinctively added them to everything I could: hand soap, dish soap, shampoo, body wash, and anywhere else I could reasonably hide a few drops. One of the key principles of using flower essences stresses the *frequency of use* rather than the *quantity*. Having dilute amounts in products that you use often helps flood your energy field—and consequently your mind and body—with the healing energies of flower essences. Today you can find many creams, lotions, and other body-care products that contain flower essences, often in combination with other botanical remedies, on the market.

Inhalation

Although flower essences have no smell of their own (apart from whatever aroma their preservatives might have), inhalation of flower essences can yield surprisingly quick therapeutic results. I'd never tried to inhale flower essence energy until I learned about this method from Sue Lilly. She suggests placing a few drops of the essence in the palms of your hands, rubbing them together, and cupping your hands around your nose. With a nice deep breath, you can breathe in the evaporating flower essence.[5]

Inhalation is easily the fastest way to introduce an essence to your body and energy field, and it requires only one or two drops to be effective. Bear in mind that some preservatives may have unpleasant aromas. This method is particularly good for flower essences that are blended with essential oils or other botanical products, including the flower essence spagyrics described in chapter 10.

Sprays

Flower essences can be added to an atomizer or spray bottle and spritzed over the aura or in a room or other environment. Many essence makers, large and small, offer sprays, often paired with compatible essential oils to add an element of aromatherapy. As with dropper bottles, you can make your own custom blends in spray bottles, too.

Sprays make for quick and easy essence application, and they are a hygienic way to share your essences with others. They are ideal for use in a group setting, and they can also be used to cleanse, clear, and uplift the space around you. Spraying an essence over your head invites it to affect your aura as a whole, and it will filter its way through the chakra system as it descends from crown to root.

Spreading Essences through the Aura

Another technique that I learned from Sue Lilly is spreading an essence through the aura.[6] Place a few drops of essences in your palms, rub your hands together, and then quickly sweep your hands through the air around your body. As your hands move, they disperse the essence into your aura, allowing for quick absorption into the subtle bodies. You can target specific chakras, meridians, and other areas with this technique.

Baths

It's no secret in my household how much I love to soak in the tub. Adding flower essences to the bathwater is one of my favorite ways to benefit from their energies. In the tub, you can absorb the essence through your skin from the water and through your lungs from the the steam.[7] Meanwhile, bathing with an essence distributes its energy immediately into your aura—much like misting does—and fills each of the subtle bodies with its healing power.

Advice on how to add essence to a bath varies. Gurudas, author of several books on herbalism and essence therapy, recommends four to seven drops of an essence in the bath, suggesting the number seven for enhancing the spiritual properties of the essences.[8] If using a single essence or a blend of essences, I generally use no fewer than seven drops; typically I aim for twelve drops, or perhaps the deliciously witchy number thirteen. If I am using several individual essences, I'll usually add equal amounts of each to the water. For flower essence spagyrics and other mixtures that contain more plant matter than mere flower essences, I usually use an entire dropperful. Flower essence pioneer Patricia Kaminski suggests using twenty to thirty drops of an essence in the bath and recommends stirring in the pattern of a lemniscate or figure eight.[9]

Ideally, soak in the tub for as long as it is comfortable; at least thirty minutes is advisable. It is best to be mindful and receptive, perhaps practicing some form of meditation, prayer, or mantra recitation while you are immersed. Some sources recommend avoiding soap or other ingredients in an essence-enhanced bath, but I've never found soap, bubble bath, salts, or other additives to take away from the efficacy of flower essences or other vibrational remedies.

Diffusing Essences

Flower essences can be diffused into your environment in several ways. Common to all methods is the central belief that the energy of the flower essence can be passively transmitted into your environment via the appropriate medium. The easiest method requires only a glass or crystal bowl filled with clean water. Add several drops of the essence to the bowl, then place the bowl in the room or area that you want to fill with the essence's energy. After several hours, the essence will have run its course, and you can dispose of the water or offer it to your garden.

In a similar fashion, you can use a clear quartz cluster to broadcast the essence into your space. Be sure to start with a freshly cleansed crystal—you can use cleansing essences such as onion, crab apple, sage, or cherry blossom to clear the stone. Close your eyes and connect to the crystal; invite it to participate by serving as the antenna for the essence. Next add your essences; you can sprinkle a few drops over the cluster or spray from a mister. The crystal will transmit the essence's energy for several days, after which it will require cleansing and reenergizing to ensure that it maintains the integrity of the essence.

For these two methods, the size of the carrier will affect the overall radius that the essence reaches. A larger bowl of water or bigger cluster of crystals results in a larger sphere of influence for the flower essence. Adding more drops of a flower essence will not drastically change the reach of the essence, but it will affect how quickly the essence permeates the space. If you need an immediate change in energy, add six to ten drops of an essence to your carrier. A gentler, slower effect can be reached with two to four drops.

Flower essences can also be added to essential oil diffusers to spread their energy into the atmosphere of a room. They can be used on their own or in tandem with essential oils if you would like to enjoy a scent or augment the power of the essences. Add new essences just as you would essential oils; different styles of oil diffusers will require different care. You can also try adding essences to fountains and other water features or adding a drop to the top of a candle before lighting it.

I learned an alternative method of diffusing essences from Deborah Craydon, coauthor of *Floral Acupuncture,* who has experimented extensively with the sacred pattern of interlocking circles known as the Flower of Life. She notes that when you place a stock bottle of a flower essence (or other vibrational remedy) in the center of the Flower of Life, the energy of the essence will be broadcast through your space.

Wearing Essences

A novel approach to working with flower essences is to wear them—that is, to wear a small vial or other container filled with water to which you have added a couple of drops of essence. Small glass vial pendants and perfume bottles can be found with some diligence, and craft stores often have supplies for making your own. It is even possible to simply carry a small dropper bottle in a pocket or purse. I was recently gifted a pendant carved from quartz crystal with a hollow center and a tight-fitting cap. Quartz vials like this are becoming increasingly available, and they make an excellent means of dispersing and magnifying the energy from an essence all day long. Some essence makers, including Australian Bush Flower Essences and Delta Gardens, offer ready-made pendants filled with single essences or essence blends aligned for specific goals.

Wearing a flower essence is a bit subtler than taking it orally, applying it topically, or some of the other methods of application. In a sense the effect is much more diffuse, although it stays with you all day, and it can help maintain and deepen the effects of the essence between the more conventional doses. This method is especially effective when the essences are worn over the heart, throat, or solar plexus chakras, as these points represent areas in your subtle anatomy where emotional energy is stored and processed.[10] Wearing an essence also helps you build a rapport with the plant spirit of the essence; it's as though you have a direct link to the consciousness of the plant with you everywhere you go.

We'll talk more about wearing essences for magickal purposes in chapter 8; see page 173.

Meditating with Essences

Essences are excellent partners for meditation. You can take a couple of drops under your tongue, place a drop or two on pulse points or chakras, diffuse them in your meditation space, or introduce them to your meditation via any of the other methods we've discussed. Additionally, you can meditate on the flowers or gaze upon a photo of the flowers in meditation, with or without the physical essence, to help you tap in to their energy. It is also possible to meditate while holding a bottle of flower essence, as this draws the plant spirit energy into your field. The dark-colored glass does dampen and filter the energy of the essence a bit (thus protecting it from outside energies that might interfere with the quality of the essence), but consciously asking to connect to the essence and/or the plant spirit while holding the bottle in meditation has profound results. Best of all, this technique doesn't require you to consume or expend any of the essence itself, making it the most economical choice for using an essence.

Other Uses

There are boundless possibilities for using flower essences in your everyday life and for the benefit of plants, animals, and the environment. You are limited only by your imagination.

In the garden, a few drops of flower essences can be added to your watering can, or you can spray plants with them. You can even use a dropper to offer a few drops of an essence to the soil at the base of the plant. Flower essences can help plants grow and thrive, offering a remedy to illness and injury just as they do for humans. Using flower essences in the garden also enhances your relationship to the spirits of the plants that you grow, and it may reduce shock from pruning or replanting, improve crop yield, boost the potency of herbs, and deter pests.

Animals are usually very willing to receive the healing of flower essences, and entire books are devoted to the subject. Many of the same methods for selecting and applying essences for human benefit can be adapted for your furry, feathered, and scaly friends. Always be mindful of the dosage for small animals, as the preservatives in the essences can be detrimental to their well-being. One of the safest ways to use the essences is to dilute them and apply them topically or spray them in the environment where your pets spend time. You can spray them on a bed or in a crate so the animal has the choice to soak up the essence energy whenever they like.

Using flower essences in your environment is a rewarding practice that can be accomplished via diffusing and spraying essences, or else by the magickal practices described in chapter 8. You can cleanse the energy in a room, alleviate sick building syndrome, and release earth-bound spirits or other energies from your space with flower essences. They also offer the opportunity to clear karmic patterns and other memories stored in buildings and other sites. As in the garden, working with flower essences in your environment affords you the chance to partner with the spirits of place more consciously and conscientiously. Essences can be given as offerings to help you establish a working relationship with the devas and spirits of place to support both personal and planetary well-being.

In the next chapter we'll look at more ways to use flower essences by exploring their applications in magick and ritual.

8

Flower Essences in Magick

Plants are at the heart of many traditional practices in witchcraft and magick, including the making of charms, talismans, and amulets. Initially I thought the magickal use of plants was merely the principle of correspondence in action, but over the course of my studies I learned that the plant spirits themselves play a role in these interactions, although not every magician may be aware of them.

Because flower essences are such intentional products of communing with plant spirits, they are potent materia magica that can be incorporated into magick and spellcraft in a variety of manners. They offer sustainable, safe, and effective means for working with plant spirits, and throughout this chapter you'll find inspiration for ways to incorporate them into your magickal practice.

MAKING FLOWER POTIONS

For many people the word *potion* conjures images of bubbling cauldrons and alchemical laboratories. The word is derived from the Latin *potio,* meaning "drink" or "poisonous draft," and nowadays refers to liquids of many types used in magick. From medicinal tinctures and teas to essential oils and flower essences, potions are composed of natural substances derived from plant, stone, and animal alike and often made to correspond to specific astrological timing. They can be made for internal or external use, and safety can vary contingent upon the ingredients.

Flower and vibrational essences are among the safest varieties of potions available, since they contain little, if any, botanical material and seldom have unpleasant effects.

The process of making flower essences is itself an act of potion making. Essences can also be incorporated into other potions for virtually any use, from teas and tinctures aimed toward healing to magickal baths and anointing potions. They offer profound effects and potent spiritual energy in just a few precious drops, which makes them an economical way to produce potions. Essences enliven magickal brews, since they contain the pure imprint of the consciousness or spirit of the plants from which they are made. They also blend easily with other essences as well as with other, more traditional potion-making ingredients.

Magickal Potions vs. Therapeutic Essences

While all flower essences constitute potions from a broad definition, I tend to differentiate flower essence potions—that is, essences of a more magickal nature—from therapeutic essences in my healing practice. For me, an essence combination is truly a potion when blended *and empowered* with magickal intent; in other words, flower essence potions, with or without other magickal ingredients, are those blends made in a ritual setting and magickally consecrated or charged with a purpose in mind. (See chapter 9 for instructions on charging essence potions.) Generally speaking, when consulting with a client and using traditional methods for essence selection, I use a more clinical approach. However, there is some overlap between the therapeutic and magickal fields; sometimes I'll blend a client's therapeutic dosage bottle in a magickal setting to create a highly potent and charged blend.

Note that while this distinction is the one I use for my own practice, I invite you to create your own definitions based on your own experience.

Essences offer alternatives to working with raw botanical ingredients. They can allow access to plants that are otherwise hard to get, and they offer a much safer route for working with the traditional baneful herbs of witchcraft. Further, using essences as potions and potion-making ingredients is economical in the long run, as very little essence is required. And they have a wide range of applications: Use them to anoint yourself and your tools, to sanctify your ritual space, to ward your home, and to dress candles, charm bags, and other magickal creations. We'll talk about some of these applications here. Consult chapters 9 and 10 for inspiration in creating your own flower essence potions and spagyrics.

DRESSING CANDLES WITH ESSENCES

Incorporating flower essences into candle magick is a simple way to forge a connection to the plant spirits who are best suited to assisting you in your work, and it is an effective way to augment your candle magick. I started by adding a couple drops of an essence to candles lit in my devotional spaces, like household shrines and altars to deities. In cases where I didn't have the appropriate herb in my magickal cabinet, I started to use the essences as a means of offering that plant's gifts to the beings enshrined: rose for Aphrodite, violet for Yemayá, and so forth. In time I noticed the essences not only were effective as offerings to gods and spirits but also infused the room with their energy. Soon I moved on to pairing essences with candle spells with good results.

There is an art to dressing candles (also called "fixing" candles), with many magickal traditions prescribing their own sets of rules and regulations. Typically, freestanding candles, like taper, chime, and pillar candles, are rubbed with oil and sometimes rolled in herbs as a means of ritually charging them with magickal intention. The direction in which the oil is applied is important. To imbue a candle with the goal of drawing something toward you, you would apply the oil from the top to the bottom or from the ends toward the middle, effectively mimicking the act of attraction. To remove or otherwise send away some influence, you would rub the oil from the bottom to the top or from the middle outward to each end. To use flower essences in candle dressings such as these, you might add a couple of drops of an essence (or a combination of essences) to the magickal oil.

I often use jar candles in my spiritual practice. I dress them with herbs and oils by simply sprinkling a small amount of the ingredients on top of the wax. Using flower essences in these candles is quite easy, too; you need only dispense a couple of drops onto the surface of the wax. Just be sure to avoid the wick, as it may not light if it is saturated with the essence. I usually let the candle sit for several minutes and visualize the energy of the essence expanding to fill the wax before I light it.

Candle dressing with essences is an alternative way to work with toxic plants and baneful herbs, as well as being a scent-free option for people with sensitive respiratory systems. It is also a discreet way to augment the power of any candle without attracting attention from others in your space, as the essence will not be visible, unlike herbs and oils. I find that although essences have a much subtler presence than herbs and essential oils, they produce wonderful results, often by working on your interior landscape and helping heal the underlying patterns of the psyche that might otherwise stand in the way of manifesting your goals. Additionally, using essences in your candle dressing helps forge a much stronger bond with your plant spirit allies or familiars.

CLEANSING ENERGY AND CREATING SACRED SPACE WITH ESSENCES

Many people use flower essences and other vibrational remedies for their space-clearing properties. Essences can be sprayed, infused, or even just dispense from the dropper to cleanse the energy and help create an appropriate atmosphere for healing, spellcraft, and ritual. Many essence producers offer ready-made energy-clearing blends in atomizer bottles, and you can easily mix your own to meet your personal needs.

Several hours before a ritual or spell, I sometimes will diffuse a cleansing essence in the ritual space using either the bowl of water or crystal cluster method (see pages 161–62). This is more effective in closed environments, as the energy of the essence permeates the room and leaves it fresh and clean in advance of the magickal working. You can also spray a room with an essence blend, or use essences with other cleansing methods, such as adding a couple of drops on your incense or herb bundle, candle, or holy water or to cleansing sprays made with essential oils. Some essences suited to general cleansing include crab apple, garlic, lemon, lemon balm, lilac, lotus, sage, and walnut. Diffusing essences in this manner also helps invoke the presence of the plant spirits, devas, and other spirit allies that can be helpful in your work.

However, beyond merely spraying and diffusing essences to purify the energy in your home or ritual space, essences can be used to otherwise elevate and coordinate the energies of your sacred space to support the specific intention of your magickal working. You can diffuse or spray flower essences that correspond to your work, such as rose or basil for love magick or dill or tomato essence for money drawing spells. Essences can also be used to delineate the boundary of your sacred space, such as applying them around the circle, especially at the four quarters (see "Casting a Circle" on the following page). In many magickal traditions the ritual act of calling the quarters takes place as a means to strengthen, stabilize, and protect the magickal or ceremonial space. Specific guardians or guides can be invoked at each of the four cardinal directions; they may range from animal, elemental, or plant spirits to specific deities of the tradition or framework you work within.

When using essences to augment this ritual act, you can use small vessels of water or quartz clusters to diffuse or project essences at these points; you may also add essences to candles or merely place essence bottles at the points of the four directions. I sometimes call on plant spirits aligned with the appropriate elements at the four quarters in my rituals. Placing the essence in the corresponding direction anchors the presence of the plant spirit as guardian and guide during the ritual. Although I recommend experimenting to find the plant spirits and essences that best fit the needs of your practice, here are some suggested correspondences:*

- ★ **North (earth):** oak, potato, tobacco, yew
- ★ **East (fire):** angelica, basil, blackthorn, poppy, St. John's wort
- ★ **South (air):** dill, foxglove, hazel, Queen Anne's lace, vervain
- ★ **West (water):** apple, blackberry, cannabis, water lily, willow
- ★ **Center (spirit):** belladonna, cacao, datura, lotus, rose

You can write your own quarter calls to summon the plant spirits that are most appropriate for your ritual. Consider partnering plant spirits of single type, such as only banes or balms or trees. You can set appropriate essences in place ahead of the ritual working as part of the setup, or you might dispense them during the quarter calls themselves.

☽ Casting a Circle ⋯★⋯⋯★⋯

The expression *casting a circle* is used by many magickal and spiritual traditions to describe the ritualized act of creating a sacred space for performing your spiritual work. This practice is usually followed by *calling the quarters,* wherein the archetypal forces of the cardinal directions and their associated elements or other attributes are invoked to protect and strengthen the circle.

To cast a circle, many traditions use a wand, staff, or ritual blade. While these tools are all part of my regular practice, I often will use the index and middle finger of my dominant hand to direct the energy. If you find a fallen branch or twig of the plant you're partnering with to make the essence, you can also use that to cast your circle.

---

*Different traditions associate the elements with different directions. Most commonly, you find earth in the north, air in the east, fire in the south, and water in the west. This is an elemental setup known as the middle world orientation. The orientation I use most often is the underworld orientation, as listed above, with fire and air having swapped places. This arrangement of the elements is more alchemical and dynamic in nature. Ultimately, as my teacher Christopher Penczak has emphasized on more than one occasion, the elements reside in a direction that can't be pointed to, which means you can experiment with different directional associations for the various elements. You might even dispense with elemental correspondences and choose to call plant spirits based on the qualities they bring to the circle.

To begin, hold your tool or extend your fingers while facing the northern quadrant of the space around the plant. If you don't know which way is north, you can merely designate a starting point. Trace a circular boundary with the point of your tool while walking clockwise around the space; visualize a brilliant light or flame flowing from your tool and creating a boundary. I prefer to trace this boundary three times, often while reciting a simple incantation. Here is a sample one that you can use:

> I conjure this circle as a vessel for my magick. May it be a safe haven, free of all harmful influence.
>
> I cast this circle to allow only the energies of Love, Will, and Wisdom, a sanctuary for the gods and for the spirit of this plant.
>
> May this circle be a doorway beyond time and space, a perfect temple for magick and transformation.
>
> As above, so below. This circle is sealed.

These words can be adapted to suit an array of circumstances according to your preference. Once the circle is erected, you can call the quarters by facing each cardinal direction, beginning in the north and moving clockwise, to invite the protection, guidance, and blessings of the element associated with that direction. A sample quarter call using flower essences and plant spirits can be found on page 172, but you can also make a simple petition to the direction, element, or other power to guard your circle. Following this, you may choose to invoke any deities with whom you have a working relationship. This effectively invites them into the sacred temple you've created, thus allowing them to impart their blessings to the essence-making process.

If at any point you choose to leave the circle, you can cut a doorway with the same tool you used to create the circle; imagine that you are cutting out a door-like shape, walk through, and then trace the line of the opening in reverse from the outside. This allows you to pass through the circle without diminishing its power. You can repeat this process when you return to the circle.

When you've finished making your essence, it will be time to devoke your deities, release the quarters, and release the circle. Politely thank the higher power(s) you've called upon for their blessings and guidance, and bid them farewell. Similarly, turn to each cardinal direction, beginning in the north and moving counterclockwise, and release the quarters by thanking each guardian for standing watch throughout your rite. Finally, take your ritual tool and trace the outline of the circle, starting north and moving counterclockwise, and say:

> I release this circle, sending its energy out into the world around me. The circle is open but never broken.

☽ Calling the Quarters with Plant Spirits ⋯⋆⋯⋆⋯

For this exercise, I've selected four trees as the plant spirits to represent the directions and elements. For each direction you call to, spend a moment attuning to the plant spirit, element, and direction embodied in the work. Then extend your nondominant hand with fingers splayed to represent the pentagram, ripe with all its elemental imagery, to receive the guardian spirit of that direction.

> I call to the tree spirit of the north, mighty Oak. O guardian of earth, may your steadfast strength support me throughout this rite. Hail and welcome!

> I call to the tree spirit of the east, mighty Blackthorn. O guardian of fire, may your brilliance and warmth lend inspiration throughout this rite. Hail and welcome!

> I call to the tree spirit of the south, mighty Hazel. O guardian of air, may your deft cunning bring the gift of clarity throughout this rite. Hail and welcome!

> I call to the tree spirit of the west, mighty Willow. O guardian of water, may your wisdom and compassion be overflowing throughout this rite. Hail and welcome!

To release or dismiss the quarters, raise your dominant hand with fingers spread to represent sending the guardians on their way as you recite the devocations. Begin in the north and move counterclockwise as you release the quarters.

> Mighty Oak, guardian of the north and the element of earth, thank you for standing watch throughout this rite. Hail and farewell.

Mighty Willow, guardian of the west and the element of water, thank you for standing watch throughout this rite. Hail and farewell.

Mighty Hazel, guardian of the south and the element of air, thank you for standing watch throughout this rite. Hail and farewell.

Mighty Blackthorn, guardian of the east and the element of fire, thank you for standing watch throughout this rite. Hail and farewell.

AMULETS, TALISMANS, AND CHARMS

Although the definitions of the terms *amulets, talismans,* and *charms* differ among magickal traditions, they generally refer to magickal objects that are carried or worn to obtain specific results. In my tradition we use *charm* as an umbrella term for all such tools. The word *talisman* most often refers to magickal objects that are worn or carried to draw or invite a specific goal, whereas *amulets* are said to banish or repel a particular influence. For many witches, plants are central to the creation of charms; botanical materials, such as bits of root, berry, and bark, are empowered so they may be worn or carried to ward off or draw specific intentions.

Wearing flower essences as amulets and talismans has become one of my favorite ways to experiment with new essences or blends. In its simplest form, you make an amulet or talisman from a small bottle (dram-sized works perfectly) containing a few drops of essence and then carry or wear the bottle as you go about your day to achieve a particular goal.* I like to use small perfume bottles made of quartz crystal, as it is a natural amplifier.

You can also use an essence to ritually charge an object that can be worn or carried as an amulet and talisman, such as stones, sigils, jewelry, spell pouches, and so on. (See the following exercise for instructions.)

The making and use of magickal objects, such as charms, talismans,

---

*Machaelle Small Wright, creator of Perelandra Essences, provides a similar tool called the Essence of Perelandra Infusion Pump, a small bottle of an essence blend that you carry close to your body to continuously infuse the energy of the essence into your entire system.

and amulets, is a complex art with much room for creativity. While a thorough discussion is outside the scope of this work, know that a properly cleansed and empowered object can be infused with the energy of a flower essence or similar vibrational elixir to produce powerful results. Perhaps the easiest medium to use for this is quartz crystal, which naturally coheres, amplifies, and transmits energies that are programmed into its crystal structure. Similar principles are at work when you fashion charms from other materials, too.

☽ Charging Crystals with Essences

Rocks, crystals, and gemstones have long been used as charms, and they can be ritually consecrated and impregnated with virtually any source of energy, from the magician's own intention to the energy of the stars and planets. The simplest way to create a flower essence charm is to charge one with the energy of an essence. Crystals, particularly quartz, are an excellent tool for this, as they amplify and transmit whatever energies or intentions they are imbued with. To create a crystal amulet or talisman charged with flower essence energy, you'll need a freshly cleansed crystal and the essence (or blend) that matches your intention or needs.

The simplest means of charging a crystal with a flower essence is merely to cleanse the stone and place one or more drops of the essence on its surface. Maintain a focused intention for the essence to program or charge the crystal with its energy. Gently rub the essence onto the surface to spread it around, then allow it to dry. Or, if you are using a stone that is sensitive to moisture, put the essence in an atomizer and spray it over crystal from a safe distance to avoid saturating the stone.

For a more magickal approach, you can cast a circle and call the quarters, or perform a full-length ritual wherein the primary magickal act is the charging of your stone (or other material) with the flower essence. If possible, you can time the ritual according to the phase of the moon, day of the week, or planetary hour that aligns with your intention.

Some magickal traditions suggest "feeding" magickal items to maintain their efficacy, such as offering iron filings to lodestones or periodically anointing charm bags or spell pouches with oils. In the same fashion, your crystal will benefit from receiving more of the flower essence to maintain the pattern within it. You may simply add a drop (or spray) of the essence before wearing or carrying it once or twice a week, or you might choose to reempower the charm in ritual once each lunar cycle.

When the crystal has fulfilled its function and you'd like to wipe it clean of any of the essence's vibrations, cleanse it thoroughly before charging it for another purpose. With a quartz crystal, I bury it in salt at least overnight or for up to a week, and then I gently rinse it in alternating warm and cool water. Other stones may be sensitive to salt or water; please refer to the cleansing instructions in my book *Crystal Basics* (pages 98–110) for more information on cleansing stones.

The basic procedure described above can be adapted for virtually any variety of talisman or amulet.

BURNING ESSENCES

Burning essences in a cauldron or thurible is a powerful, intense method for releasing their effects. This technique is often used for cleansing, countermagick, and healing. You add the essences to a base of alcohol in a fireproof container, and the resulting mixture will ignite and burn for a good amount of time. The base is usually a small amount of salt (sea salt or Epsom salts) lightly saturated with alcohol, such as rubbing alcohol, Florida water (an alcohol-based cologne or eau de toilette infused with essential oils and used in some magickal practices), or high-proof rum. Other botanical ingredients can be added, too. Be sure to use a sturdy vessel, such as a cast-iron pot or cauldron—small ones are safer, as they will contain smaller amounts of fuel and burn for shorter amounts of time. Ignite the vessel with an extra-long match or lighter, or with a taper candle, to avoid getting too close to the flames.

Fire can be somewhat contrary to the delicate, water nature of flower essences, so setting your intention and inviting the plant spirits to assist you in your magickal work is crucial here. I tend to use essences alone in a base of neutral alcohol, though I sometimes combine them with other ingredients, such as dried herbs or essential oils, if they are all aligned toward a single purpose. Once the flame is lit, the energy of the essences expands outward quite rapidly, which stands in stark contrast to the slow and gentle method of diffusing essences in water, and it tends to produce rapid but short-lived effects.

Two groupings of essences seem to take better to this method than others. The first is tree essences. Since these plants have long been felled and fed to flame, I think their spirits already have a kinship with the nature of fire. The second is essences made from flowers that correspond to the element of fire or the fiery planets (Mars and the sun) and signs (Leo, Aries, and Sagittarius). Examples include calendula, garlic, gorse, nettle, St. John's wort, and sunflower. One blend worth exploring as a sacred fire is based on the nine trees featured in the longer version of the Wiccan Rede: apple, birch, fir, hawthorn, hazel, oak, rowan, vine, and willow.* Essences for these plants are all readily available on the market, and you may be fortunate enough to be able to make some yourself. The combination of these nine essences can be used not only for cleansing or general healing but also as a sacred flame to celebrate holy days, such as the eight sabbats comprising the wheel of the year in many witchcraft traditions.

An alternative means of burning essences is to add them to incense, whether store-bought sticks and cones or homemade loose incense. Adding a couple of drops of essence can boost an incense's efficacy and yields excellent results in ritual and spellcraft. I sometimes add an essence that matches the incense I'm burning, such as adding rose essence to a rose incense, as well as using flower essence blends that match the intention of my ritual. Be sure to allow your incense several minutes to dry before lighting it. Adding a flower essence to incense

---

*The Wiccan Rede is an ethical guideline followed by many adherents of Wicca and related witchcraft traditions. In its simplest form, it reads something along the lines of, "An' it harm none, do what ye will." Longer versions can be found, usually written as poems that describe other elements of witchcraft philosophy and practice. While today many will assume that the vine described in the Rede is grape, it is likely that the real identity of vine in this poem is blackberry, as it was common throughout the British Isles before grapevine was introduced. In spite of the historic precedence, I have found that grapevine is a better energetic fit than blackberry, as it has a woodier stalk and often exhibits the vertical growth (when properly supported) that characterizes tree spirits.

with a synthetically derived scent (most inexpensive incense is made without the actual botanical ingredient it's meant to smell like) imparts the vibration of the plant itself.

PLANT SPIRIT BOTTLES

This particular magickal practice involves partnering with a plant spirit to create a vessel to house the plant's spirit or consciousness. The idea of the plant spirit bottle draws upon a diverse array of spiritual and esoteric traditions, including the archetypal djinn or genie from Middle Eastern lore, the traditions of indigenous healers and ayahuasqueros of South America, and the alchemical practice of crafting a homunculus (Latin for "little person").[1] In occult lore, this spirit is a sort of servitor, fetch, or familiar with a deep working relationship with the witch or magus. Though the technique does not traditionally employ flower essences, the use of essences magnifies the power of a plant spirit bottle greatly. Ideally, use this technique only when you've already established a relationship with a particular plant spirit, rather than as a first introduction to it.

The mechanics of making a plant spirit bottle are relatively simple: add plant material to a bottle, then fill the bottle with high-proof alcohol to preserve it and seal it. The idea is to add a representative of each part of the plant: root, stem, leaf, twig, bark, seed, flower, fruit, and so on. This means you'll have to craft the bottle slowly over time, as you probably won't find fruit and flower on the plant at the same time, so leave room in the bottle when you begin it. Each time you add a new ingredient, be sure to seal the bottle tightly.

Over time you'll notice that the plant spirit embodied in the bottle requests or requires special care, such as cleansing, feeding, or even a visit with its counterparts in nature. One of the simplest ways to feed the bottle is with flower essences.

Using the associated flower essence at the initial making of the bottle enables you to harness the holographically imprinted plant spirit consciousness within the essence to enliven or awaken the bottle itself. The essence functions as a sort of magickal or spiritual shortcut to establishing a deeper relationship with the plant spirit and for inviting the consciousness of that spirit to reside in your bottle. I like to use a variety of essences for making plant spirit bottles; if I have essences of the same flower made by different makers, I'll add a little of each to the bottle when I make it.

Christopher Penczak suggests making another form of plant spirit bottle that is an amalgam of all your plant spirit allies. I'd suggest working with your three primary ones—a single bane, balm, and tree—to get started. You can add more as time goes by and other plants come into season. Penczak writes that this version of a plant spirit bottle "eventually takes on a personality and presence that is more than any one plant, and becomes a tutor and interface for the entirety of the Green World."[2]

An alternative form of the plant spirit bottle can be made from flower essences alone. It becomes a sort of touchstone for the essences that form part of your personal journey. I have started one that is made from a few drops of the mother tincture of each of the flower essences I've made. I keep it in a special place and consult with the consciousness imprinted in it when I need inspiration or guidance. Making a composite mother tincture in this way results in a sort of collective consciousness of the plants with which you work, rather like a direct line to the oversoul of your own personal essences. I frequently commune with the oversoul of my own line of flower essences (after all, they have an architect, too), and this plant spirit bottle is a way for me to be in direct communion with the spiritual presence that oversees all my own essences.

It's not necessary to use only the mother tincture for making a plant spirit bottle for your flower essences. You can make one out of stock and dosage bottles, too. Just be sure to have some clarity about which ones you're adding and why; otherwise your additions can muddy the waters, so to speak.

If you work closely with a single line of essences, try adding two drops of each one to a plant spirit bottle to represent the collective consciousness of that entire line of essences. The resulting plant spirit bottle becomes a sort of guide or overseer for your work with that essence line. I've tried this successfully with the Bach flowers and the essences from Chalice Well. But note that for those versions made from an entire line of essences, taking the complete line at once is not usually very helpful therapeutically. The effect is rather like trying to listen to dozens of songs played at the same time. Instead, consider it a way to commune with the overarching spiritual presence of a collection of essences.

You can use the liquid from your plant spirit bottle in ritual and spellcraft, but it generally should not be taken internally unless made entirely from nontoxic plants. The liquid can cleanse, consecrate, or otherwise bless ritual tools, people, and places. You might also work with the plant spirit bottle to assist you in meditation and journey work for a variety of purposes. The spirit of the plant(s) embodied within the bottle can be called upon for healing, for protection, and as an aid to your spells and rituals. The deeper the bond you have with the plant spirit(s), the more effectively you'll be able to work together. You can place the bottle under or near the bed as you sleep for a powerful dreamtime experience, too.

FLOWER ESSENCES IN WITCHES' SACRAMENTS AND RITUALS

Flower essences can enhance our ritual and spiritual practice or sacraments to support and enhance our connection to the mysteries. Sacraments are sacred actions, oaths, or ritual dramas that enhance our experience of divine mystery. In witchcraft, one of the most widely practiced sacraments is the Great Rite, which we will discuss in a moment; however, a wide array of other sacraments, both greater and lesser, can be found among a variety of spiritual traditions.

Adding flower essences to your sacraments and rituals is a subtle, though powerful, way to lend more power to your magickal practice. They can be woven into your practice in passive ways, such as by adding a few drops to the contents of a chalice or cauldron, or they can be featured as tools for further focusing your intent and willpower for the sacraments themselves.

Four sacraments are common to many forms of witchcraft and other magickal traditions: anointing, the Great Rite, Cakes and Ale (and related practices), and offerings. Let's take a look at how you might use flower essences to enhance each of them.

Anointing

Anointing is usually performed as an act of blessing or consecration The act of anointing marks something as sacred, perhaps even as separate from the mundane. We anoint our tools as part of their ritualized cleansing and empowerment to confer sanctity and imbue them with our unique magick. Some magickal traditions anoint participants upon their entrance into a sacred space to helps shift their frame of mind into the magickal and spiritual. Flower essences can easily be incorporated into these sacred acts, as they are powerful tools for shifting consciousness and helping us commune with the spirit realm.

Many spiritual traditions make use of oils, infusions, or holy water for a variety of anointing rituals, such as rites to celebrate birth, death, initiation, and other mysteries, and flower essences can simply be added to them. Bear in mind that essences will not fully incorporate into oil, as they are prepared as aqueous solutions. Vigorous shaking or stirring will help, dispersing the essence into much smaller droplets. I generally prepare essence-infused oils in advance so they can marinate; the energy of the flower essence will more fully permeate the oil within a few hours or even overnight. Essences added to water- or alcohol-based mixtures will be ready to use more or less immediately. The essence-enhanced mixture can then be used as it normally would, whether it is sprinkled or dabbed/rubbed on the forehead and palms of participants. In some traditions, for example, rituals may include anointing participants by drawing a sacred symbol, such as an equal-armed cross or pentagram, on their forehead or palms with a sacred oil.

If you're going to anoint yourself, your tools, or participants in a ritual, select an essence or blend to fit the theme of the ritual. Perhaps you can choose flowers relevant to the tides of the season if you are celebrating one of the sabbats. You may also select essences with cleansing properties, such as crab apple or garlic, or those with sacralizing effects, such as cacao. You can also pick essences that match the theme or purpose of your magickal working; this will help attune everyone present to the ritual and help cohere and unify the consciousness of the group. Anointing with flower essences, or with a mixture containing flower essences, will draw in the virtues of the plant spirits contained within those essences to create a more harmonious and magickal environment for any celebration or working that ensues.

Great Rite

In the forms of witchcraft known as Wicca and its offshoots, there is a popular, albeit sometimes polarizing, ritual sacrament known as the Great Rite. At its heart, the Great Rite is the celebration of union. It is the poetic representation of complementary forces coming together to create something new. For many practitioners, these two forces traditionally have been interpreted as the God and the Goddess, the masculine and the feminine forces that course through the universe. However, the Great Rite is fundamentally symbolic of any two energies or entities that come together in the act of creation. It could be my fingers on the keyboard to create a manuscript or the blessings of the heavens (rain, air, and sunshine) and the earth (soil and nutrients) to help a seed germinate.

The Great Rite is usually enacted within the sacred space of the magick circle. The officiating witch will plunge the blade of a ritual knife, or athame, into a chalice, often while reciting a poetic script that describes the union of forces in nature. Some traditions use a wand in lieu of a knife. The modern ritual owes its symbolism to the esoteric writings and rituals of occultist Aleister Crowley, and it was popularized in British traditional witchcraft. The modern rite also draws inspiration from the ancient ceremony of *hieros gamos,* wherein a human (often a king or ruler) is symbolically wed to the divine; a human representative tends to stand in for the Great Mother herself. This ritual was meant to reinforce the sovereignty of the ruler and ensure the fertility and resiliency of the land. In modern ritual, the union of complementary forces can be used as a sort of magickal engine for powering spellwork or other ritual activity.

There has been a lot of pushback against the Great Rite as the witchcraft community grows and strives to be more inclusive. Since the blade-in-chalice imagery has long evoked male-female intercourse, alternative ritual scripts and actions have been developed to represent the Great Rite in token. It is important to remember that the cup and blade are just symbols; neither is inherently male or female. Although you can ascribe procreative interpretations to the Great Rite, its focus on fertility is not innately sexual. As a result, we can work with symbols and traditions that are more inclusive for all people. This has led to a rise in alternative gestures and tools to enact the Great Rite. Paul Beyerl, herbalist and Wiccan elder, suggests burning powdered alder and ash together on charcoal, for in Germanic lore the first woman and first man were created from the wood of these trees.[3] Gardnerian witch and author Jason Mankey developed a version of the Great Rite using three chalices, my own interpretation of which is described below.

The chalice is usually filled with water, wine, juice, or another liquid for the Great Rite. I know many witches and occultists who add flower essences, herbal tinctures, or other ingredients to their chalices to enhance the ritual. You can add a single essence or a blend of essences that represents the nature of your ritual. For seasonal celebrations, such as the eight sabbats of the wheel of the year, consider using essences made from flowers associated with the season or plants whose myth and lore underscore the themes of the celebration. For any rituals with strong astrological themes, like the equinoxes and solstices (wherein the sun enters a cardinal sign), you can choose essences with matching astrological correspondences. Similarly, opt for flowers whose astrological correspondences match the current lunar transits for rituals that celebrate the cycle of the moon. You can also choose flower essences that correspond with the magickal intention of any spellcraft that will take place in the circle.

A more advanced approach to using the flower essences in the Great Rite is to add one or more essences to the chalice and use another essence or blend to anoint the blade. Thus, you can energetically attune each tool to the forces they represent. Try partnering them based on their planetary and elemental correspondences, such as lunar flowers with solar ones, Venus with Mars, or watery and fiery flowers. Here are some possible pairings, with the chalice's essence listed first:

* ★ Alder and ash
* ★ Datura and sunflower
* ★ Rose and nettle
* ★ Holly and oak
* ★ Mugwort and oak
* ★ Lemon balm and St. John's wort
* ★ Night-blooming cereus and saguaro
* ★ Witch's Goddess and Witch's God blends (see page 210)

☽ Great Rite (Chalice and Blade Version)

In the more traditional versions of the Great Rite, especially as performed in group settings, a high priest will wield the knife, with a high priestess holding the cup aloft. Since each of us contains both masculine and feminine forces (as well as a wide array of other complementary powers) within us, I've written this ritual to be performed by a single person. Feel free to adapt it to your needs. The Great Rite is usually performed as part of a larger ritual and thus takes place within the bounds of the magick circle.

With your altar set up for ritual according to your traditions and preference, fill the chalice with a libation, such as water, juice, or wine. Add to it several drops of the flower essence(s) that you've selected for your ritual. When you reach the point in your ritual where it is appropriate to perform the Great Rite, hold the cup in one hand and the knife in the other, usually the nondominant and dominant hands, respectively. Raise the blade and recite the following:

As the blade is to the cup, the sky is to the land, and Truth is to Love. I draw together the Goddess and the God. May their union yield life and magick. So mote it be.

Plunge the knife into the chalice three times; some traditions will invite you to draw a pentagram within the chalice and/or tap the rim of the cup thrice before drinking from it or pouring a small amount of the libation out for the land, the spirits, and the gods. Return the chalice to the altar and proceed with your ritual.

☽ Great Rite (Three Chalices Version)

As a means of emphasizing that the Great Rite is neither explicitly sexual nor heteronormative, there has been recent exploration of other ways to enact the rite. I am indebted to Jason Mankey for providing a template for the Great Rite using three chalices in his book *Transformative Witchcraft*.[4] Two chalices are filled with beverages (Jason recommends two complementary drinks), while the third is left empty so it can be filled during the ritual. I find this version perfect for working with flower essences because a different essence can be added to each chalice and invoked by name, if you desire, during the ritual. As in the previous version, I've written this for a single person to perform, but you can adapt it to the needs of your magickal work. This version could easily be performed by three people, each holding a different chalice.

Prepare the altar for your ritual, including three chalices. Fill two with libations and flower essences, while leaving the third one empty. Hold one cup in each hand and say:

We now celebrate the original magick, the magick of joining, when two become one and worlds are born.

Pour the libations together into the empty vessel, taking care not to spill. Raise the newly filled cup aloft and say:

May the Goddess and the God bless this elixir of life that it may be a reminder of their power and grace. So mote it be.

Return the chalice to the altar and proceed with your ritual.

Cakes and Ale

The ritual act called Cakes and Ale, or Cakes and Wine, is often performed in tandem with or immediately following the Great Rite in many traditional forms of witchcraft. This ritual is called *houzel* by some branches of witchcraft, and it shares symbolism with the sacrament of communion in Christianity. Food and drink are consecrated as the body and blood, or form and essence, of the gods. For witches, eating and drinking the sacramental feast reminds us of the divinity already within us. The sharing of food and drink is usually performed toward the end of a ritual, as it is both celebratory of the magick enacted as well as grounding after the magickal work itself.

It is easy to add flower essences to the chalice used for the drink; in fact, in some covens the contents of the chalice from the Great Rite are shared among members in the rite of Cakes and Ale. The cakes—or bread, cookies, or crackers—that are shared, if homemade, could also include a few drops of flower essences. Both the cakes and the beverage should be blessed before being eaten, and it is traditional to first offer the food and drink to the land, the spirits, and the gods before any is shared among those gathered in the circle.

Offerings

I consider offerings made to gods, spirits, familiars, and ancestors to be a simple but important sacrament. Not every magickal tradition makes use of offerings, but for those that engage more directly with the spirit world, offerings are often of vital importance. Flower essences are powerful ways to supplement your offerings to spirits and to the land.

I usually add a couple of drops of a flower essence to most offerings that I make. In my household shrine, wherein I honor the genii locorum, or spirits of place, I feed beneficent spirits—whether they dwell in or near the home—with gifts of water, candlelight, and food. I tend to pick flower essences that appeal more generally to the spirit world, like many of the baneful plants, or essences that are attuned to the tides of the seasons. One of my standard essences for offerings to the spirit world is a flying blend (see page 204), though I also like to use mugwort, mandrake, lilac, and foxglove. Lilac and foxglove are also excellent choices for offerings to the spirits of the land and to the elementals, nature spirits, and devas.

You can add essences to your offerings to specific deities, angels, or spirits, too. Try to match the flower to the recipient of the offering; some examples include rose for Aphrodite, mugwort for Diana, cacao for Quetzalcoatl, and oak for the Horned God. Add a few drops to a clean glass or other vessel placed on a shrine or altar. Offerings to the spirits of nature can be poured onto the land or into a body of water, or they can be left in the garden or woods.

The benefits to using flower essences for offerings are twofold.

First, they energize and enliven the gifts you are giving. The best offerings are those that have thought and energy put into them. Whether you are giving clean water, freshly brewed coffee, or a fine wine to your spirit allies, essences add a new layer of intention and energy to those gifts to feed the spirits and strengthen your relationships with them. Second, adding a few drops of an essence to an offering acts as a means to diffuse the essence in your space. This helps sanctify and uplift the energy in your altar, shrine, or sacred space, and the effects spill over to help the humans and other residents in your space, too.

FLOWER ESSENCE SPELLS AND RITUALS

As illustrated throughout this chapter, flower essences can be incorporated into a magickal practice in a variety of ways. Ultimately, the manner in which you work with them will be shaped by your personal spiritual and magickal practices. Before closing this chapter, I'll offer you five sample spells and rituals featuring flower essences.

☽ Rose Bath for Drawing Love

Supplies: pink candle, rose flower essence, matches or a lighter, rose petals

Love has been one of the most popular themes in magick throughout the ages, and rose is perhaps the most universally praised ingredient in love spells. I've designed an easy love spell that uses rose petals and rose flower essence; use whichever rose essence you like, from the simple wild rose of the Bach line to a homemade rose flower essence from your backyard. To supercharge your love spell, try using a rose flower essence spagyric (see chapter 10). The universal themes shared by rose essences open the heart and flood the spirit with love. Bathing in rose flower essence will help you receive rose's virtues of love and beauty, thus drawing more of the same into your life. This spell can be guided to invite a new romantic partner or for learning to love yourself more; all you have to do is focus on the way you'd like to see love manifest in your life.

Begin to fill the bathtub with water, adjusting the temperature as you like it. Place your candle, flower essence, and rose petals in easy reach—and don't forget the matches or lighter. Spend a few moments calming your mind and focusing your will as the water rises; if you like, hold the candle between your hands and charge it with your intention to draw love into your life. When the tub is full, light the candle and state your intention aloud. Add at least eight drops of rose flower essence to the tub, then stir the water with your hand in a figure-eight pattern. Scatter a handful of rose petals on the surface of the water and allow them to steep for a few moments before climbing in.

As you soak in the water, ensure that every part of you gets wet, from the tips of your toes to the top of your head. Envision the energy of rose inundating every part of you with love, so much so that any unloving thoughts or feelings find their way out of you so rose can take their place. Stay focused on loving thoughts and images while you enjoy your rose bath, and when your mind wanders, bring it back to the purpose of your magick.

When you've finished your bath, let the water drain while you're still in the tub. Picture every unloving thought that you have released flowing down the drain. Feel yourself lighter, freer, and more loving. Dry off and treat yourself well, knowing that your call to love will be answered.

☽ Prosperity Candle Spell

Supplies: flower essences of calendula, dill, sassafras, sunflower, and tomato; container for blending the flower essences (dosage bottle or spray bottle), plus a carrier oil, if desired; green candle; two aventurine stones; two pyrite stones; matches or a lighter

This simple candle spell involves dressing a candle with flower essences and surrounding it with symbols of abundance (in this case, the gemstones aventurine and pyrite). The essences listed above all relate to prosperity and abundance in different ways. Calendula is a chalice-shaped blossom that helps us receive the abundance, confidence, and sovereignty of the sun. Dill reproduces prolifically, and it has long been touted as an herb of abundance; as an essence it helps us clarify and magnify our goals. Sassafras essence encourages us to find the sweetness in life; it helps us celebrate the rewards of our labor, including the financial ones. Sunflower is a symbol of solar sovereignty, and it is a popular ingredient in money magick. Tomato is sometimes used in rituals for abundance and prosperity, and as a flower essence it breaks down blockages to health, success, and wealth.

Ideally, perform this spell during the waxing moon on a Thursday, for its associations of expansion and wealth from Jupiter, or on a Sunday, for its solar vibes of success. Gather your supplies and prepare a blend of all the flower essences; you might make a dosage bottle with them or add a few drops of each essence to a carrier oil and mix it thoroughly. Sometimes I like to make a spray bottle of a candle dressing blend so I can spray the essences onto the outside of the candle before rubbing them in (and you can add essential oils and other ingredients when making sprays, too). You can prepare the blend ahead of time and charge it as a proper flower essence potion, if you like.

To begin your spell, gather and cleanse all the necessary supplies. Cast a circle and call the quarters as appropriate for your tradition. Hold the candle between your hands and charge it with the intention to draw prosperity and financial abundance; feel free to carve symbols of abundance in the candle wax. Next, coat the candle in your flower essence blend. Be sure not to saturate the wick or the top of the wax, as you don't want to prevent the candle from lighting. Set the candle on a surface and surround it with your stones. Hold your hands over the candle and crystals and fill the entire setup with your intention to draw prosperity and abundance. Light the candle and recite:

> With this candle burning bright,
> With these sacred essences five,
> May abundance come to light,
> More than enough for me to thrive.

Continue chanting the incantation while watching the candle flame. You will feel the energy rise within and around you, and eventually it will reach a natural stopping point. When you are ready to conclude your spell, offer gratitude to the plant spirits (and stone spirits) that have assisted in your working, release the quarters and circle, and allow the candle to finish burning. For ongoing support while the spell is unfolding, use the blend of essences daily.

☽ Protection Bottle with Tree Essences

Supplies: white candle; matches or a lighter; small glass bottle (preferably one that you can attach to a cord or chain to wear); salt; small bowl of water; small iron nail or piece of hematite; flower essences of oak, walnut, and yew; preservative, such as vinegar or brandy (optional)

This spell is inspired by the classic witch's bottle, a traditional apotropaic device made of glass or ceramic and filled with iron nails or needles, thorns or spines, protective and/or poisonous plants, and personal effects like hair, fingernail clippings, or urine, as well as a variety of other ingredients. The personal effects would act as a sort of magickal decoy to attract any harmful energy sent your way, which would subsequently be tangled up in the nails or thorns and neutralized by the other ingredients. I've modified this practice to make a simpler amulet to deflect harm and lend strength. The spell bottle relies on three protective flower essences and iron, in the form of a nail or hematite, an iron oxide mineral. Larger versions can be made with several nails or pins— nine or thirteen being a traditional number—and a preservative, such as brandy or vinegar, to top off the bottle. I prefer vinegar, as it is used for cleansing and protection in many traditions of folk magick.

Gather your supplies and prepare them for use on a Saturday in the waning moon. Cast a circle and call the quarters as appropriate for your tradition. Light your candle. Cleanse and consecrate the bottle with tokens of the four elements: sprinkle with salt and water and pass it through smoke and flame. Charge the piece of iron for protection, calling upon the defensive nature of this Martian metal to keep you safe, and place it into the bottle. Imbue a pinch of salt with the power to cleanse away evil and harm and add it to the bottle, too. Next, add your flower essences one at a time and request that the spirit of each tree protect you from harm. If you have a tiny bottle, you may be able to fill it with a dropperful of each essence, but if your bottle is large, add nine or thirteen drops of each essence and fill it the rest of the way with your choice of preservative.

Now that the bottle is full, close it tightly. If you are going to place the bottle somewhere in your home (like a bright windowsill) or bury it in the earth, seal the lid with wax from your white candle. If you are making it into an amulet to wear, you might consider adding glue or another sealant to ensure that it stays closed. When the bottle is sealed, recite this (or something similar):

> I, [name], ask in the name of [God/ Goddess/deity of your choosing]
> that this bottle completely neutralize and protect me from all harm, for
> the good of all and harming none. So mote it be.

Thank the plant spirits for their participation in making this protective charm, as well as any guardians, spirits, or deities that you evoked. Release the quarters and the circle, and use your protection bottle as you see fit. Eventually, you should dispose of the contents of the bottle someplace away from your home and then make a new bottle.

☽ Psychic Vision Spell with Mugwort Essence ⭐ ⭐

Supplies: mugwort flower essence, dried mugwort, purple pouch or cloth, moonstone, star anise pod

Mugwort essence is a helpful aid for developing psychic skills and honing your intuition. Both mugwort and moonstone have lunar qualities that assist in opening your inner vision and parting the veil to the spirit world, while star anise is strongly stimulating to the third-eye chakra. Perform this ritual at night as close to the full moon as possible, preferably under the moon's light.

Cleanse all the ingredients before performing this spell. To begin, lay out all of the ingredients under the light of the full moon and still your mind. Take a few drops of the mugwort flower essence, and use another drop to anoint your third-eye chakra. Take enough dried mugwort into your hands to fill the spell pouch, and silently invite the spirit of mugwort to open the doors to psychic vision. Place the dried herb into the pouch. Next, hold the moonstone in your hand and lift it toward the moon. Focus on the moonlight and see it filling the gemstone with its power. Bury the stone and the star anise amid the dried mugwort in the pouch and tie it tightly. Anoint the pouch with seven drops of mugwort flower essence (seven being a number attuned to lunar energies), and then, while holding the pouch up to the moon, recite the following incantation:

> By petal and stone, seed and moonlight,
> Sharpen my vision with psychic sight.
> Bring vision of spirit and form into view.
> Let my inner vision be clear and true.

Cup the pouch in both hands and hold it against your brow; allow the energy of the freshly charged spell pouch—and the mugwort flower essence—to gently stir your psychic senses.

Afterward, clear away your working area and keep your psychic vision spell pouch in a safe place away from direct sun. Consider keeping it on your altar or wherever you store your divination tools. You can meditate with the pouch to prepare for psychic readings or divination, or you can hold or carry the pouch while practicing psychic skills. Try placing it under your pillow for psychically inspired and prophetic dreams. Whenever you use the spell pouch, be sure to take a few drops of mugwort flower essence yourself for an added boost.

Feed the pouch at least once each month, when the moon is full, with seven drops of mugwort flower essence. You can also feed it on Mondays— the day of the moon—or when you are preparing to use the pouch for a psychic boost.

☽ Uncrossing Ritual ⋯★⋯⋯★⋯

Supplies: small cauldron or fireproof vessel; Epsom salts; rubbing alcohol; flower essences of cinquefoil, rue, and dill; and matches or torch lighter

When it seems as if everything is going wrong, or as though there are ill wishes or harmful magick sent your way, an uncrossing may be in order. Uncrossing work removes those crossed, stagnant, and harmful influences in our lives, and it often invites protection and healing. I've selected three essences to use in this uncrossing: cinquefoil, rue, and dill. Cinquefoil and rue are traditional ingredients in work for protection and uncrossing, and their essences are excellent for fortifying the aura. Dill factors into apotropaic magick and also in recovery from psychic attack; as an essence it is celebrated for reclaiming willpower and banishing the mentality of victimhood. Other essences like agrimony, blackthorn, yew, and many baneful plants may also be helpful in an uncrossing ritual. Ideally, perform your uncrossing ritual on a Saturday during the waning moon; if possible, do so in the hour of Saturn or Mars. If the situation is urgent, forgo ideal astrological timing and perform the ritual as soon as possible.

Fill your cauldron or vessel with a small amount of Epsom salts. Add a splash of rubbing alcohol and set up your working space with your flower essences close at hand. Many practitioners prefer to perform this kind of working in the confines of the magick circle, so cast a circle and call the quarters as you deem appropriate for your practice. You may call upon the gods and spirits of your tradition or simply connect to the power of the cosmos. When you are ready to enact the uncrossing, spend a few moments reflecting on your intention and focusing your will. Call upon the spirits of the essences you are using with the following incantation, and add a couple drops of each essence to the cauldron as you call upon its spirit:

I call to the spirits of cinquefoil, rue, and dill for protection, power, and healing.

May cinquefoil's virtues seal my aura against attack and clear away harm.

May rue offer me the support to bear the woes of life and avert harm from others.

May dill remind me to reclaim my power and help me heal and prosper. By the power of spirit and flame may evil be transmuted.

Use matches or a lighter to set the contents of the cauldron ablaze (with caution), and visualize the energy of the essences rapidly expanding from the cauldron. Allow the light, warmth, and energy conveyed by the flames to cleanse and clear your aura and the energy of your space as you picture the fire burning off and transmuting harmful, stagnant, or otherwise unhealthy energies. Meditate on your intention while holding the visualization of the fire cleansing and clearing yourself and your space until the flames die out.

Express gratitude to the plant spirits and any other guides and guardians you may have invoked. Release the circle and quarters, if you've called them, and dispose of the salt remaining in the cauldron.

9

Flower Essence Formulary

The art of blending flower essences yields formulas for every occasion. You can create essence blends to support your home life, the workplace, and emergency situations. You can tailor them for family, friends, clients, and pets. Many flower essence producers have ranges of combination essences made to treat specific circumstances or manifest certain results. There are blends for protection, abundance, peace, and communicating with angels. Each of these blends is, in one sense or another, a sort of potion that helps you tap in to the plants' virtues to create healing and boost your magickal or spiritual intentions.

It is worth noting that it was originally considered imprudent to create ready-made blends of flower essences, with the notable exception of Dr. Bach's Rescue Remedy. Apart from this blend, which is made to treat the effects of shock, trauma, and stress universally, traditional flower essence therapy based upon Bach's princeps and praxis aims to tailor the use of essences to the needs and psyche of the individual; after all, not everyone working toward the same outcome is faced with the same thoughts and feelings about it. However, advancements in flower essence therapy over the past forty years have resulted in a number of flower essence makers and practitioners creating their own blends that work in a more generalized manner. These ready-made formulas tend to address the most universal feelings connected to a particular goal or situation, and they are sometimes used for their spiritual qualities rather than merely for balancing certain negative psychological states.

Additionally, essences can be used outside of the therapeutic framework as materia magica. In these instances, blends are not necessarily created to address the current psychological state of a particular person. Instead, they are a form of plant spirit medicine aimed at producing a magickal or spiritual result. Flower essence blends are excellent for potion making because they are pharmakeia at its finest: medicine, magick, and more all in one.

FROM
MEDICINE TO MAGICK

While all flower essences and vibrational remedies are arguably potions of one sort or another, the key difference for me between a collection of ingredients and a potion is the intention behind it. Formulating therapeutic combinations of flower essences for friends and clients is a kind of potion making, but it differs in spirit from making a formula of essences designed for magickal or ritual use. One of the key differences is the act of charging or consecrating a potion.

As discussed in chapter 7, potions are charged with an intention in a ritualized manner. The term *charge* in this sense means not merely to fill with energy, as in charging a battery; rather, it means to instruct, command, or impose a task. While most practitioners, intentionally or not, will imbue a potion or other magickal device with their energy and the energy of whatever archetypal forces they are working with, charging comes from the idea of informing your potion—and the plant spirits working through it—about exactly what you'd like them to do.

Charging your potion can be as simple as closing your eyes, holding the bottle containing your blend between your hands, and visualizing the outcome or goal for which the potion is intended. Rituals for charging potions can be more elaborate, too. They might take place in your sacred space within a magick circle, wherein you'll bless or consecrate the potion with symbols of the elements or whatever other forces you might choose for the specific blend you've made. You can create your own rhyming incantations, or you might choose to simply speak straight from the heart. When you're done, affirm that the potion has been charged and that its purpose will be carried out.

☽ *Charging Potions* ⋯⋯★⋯⋯⋯⋯★⋯

When formulating flower essence blends as potions, it is helpful to select the best astrological timing available, usually by aligning your work with the appropriate planetary ruler for the day of the week and hour of the day (information about planetary days and hours is easily available online and in many books on magickal practice). Prepare your working space or altar by arranging your potion-making ingredients and cleansing the area.

For a simple potion-charging ritual, create sacred space by casting a circle and calling the quarters (see pages 170 and 172). You may also call upon divinity in some way, perhaps as the Great Mother and the Horned God of all things wild, or whatever deity or spirit feels best for your practice. Following that, state your intention for your work, such as "May this flower essence blend bring healing and transformation to _____," or "I stand within this circle to create a potion to grant prosperity and abundance." As you add each ingredient to your bottle or other vessel, stop to reflect upon its nature. Silently or aloud, speak to the conscious spirit embodied within that ingredient, whether it is an essence, tincture, dried herb, oil, or stone. Invite it to bring the specific quality you seek in your magickal elixir. When you have finished adding each ingredient, mix them all together—if I'm using a dropper bottle, I usually do this by succussion (hitting or tapping the base of the bottle against the palm of the hand resulting in a vigorous shaking).

Finally, it is time to empower the mixture as a whole, filling it with the energy of your overall intent. You might hold the potion between your hands or place your hands above it; alternatively, you might use a magickal tool such as a wand, athame, or crystal to focus and direct your magickal intention into the potion. Visualize your desired outcome or purpose for the potion; mentally and spiritually distill the energy behind this purpose and channel it through your hands or magickal implement, directing it into the bottle for a moment or two. When you are finished, you might draw a symbol such as an equal-armed cross, lemniscate, or pentagram over the bottle to seal in the energy.

Affirm that your essence potion is ready:

This potion is now charged with my intent and ready to bring magick and healing. So mote it be.

Say your farewells to any spirits, deities, or guides that you have called into your sacred space. Release the quarters and magick circle if you have made use of them. Your charging ritual is complete.

GENERAL FORMULAS

The blends in this section have univeral effects and are likely to be helpful for everyday situations, both magickal and mundane. Prepare bottles of these blends just as you would any other dosage bottle, following the instructions on page 101. You can keep these formulas on hand so that you are ready to face anything the world may offer you each day.

Witchy Rescue Remedy

Ingredients: foxglove, lemon balm, nettle, periwinkle, potato

The most famous of all flower essences blends is Dr. Bach's Rescue Remedy, a formula that consists of cherry plum, clematis, impatiens, rock rose, and star-of-Bethlehem. Each of these essences contributes to the blend in a way that makes it the ideal ally for times of emergency, acute trauma, and crisis. My own "witchy" version works similarly and can be used in a wide variety of situations to bring clarity, calm, and healing no matter what obstacles and upsets you might face.

Lemon balm flower essence calms a racing mind and releases tension and fear. Nettle bolsters your defenses and grants additional stamina during times of stress, and it is helpful when you feel "under attack" from your life's circumstances. Foxglove calms emotions when relationships are under strain; it also helps you stay clear and aligned with higher purpose during crisis. Energetically, it is very protective of the heart. Periwinkle is helpful for managing crisis; it alleviates feelings of overwhelm and dissociative states and allows you to think clearly. It also reminds you to make use of your magickal prowess to improve any situation. Finally, potato, one of my favorite nightshades, is called for whenever you feel spacey, ungrounded, or impractical; it helps when you are having trouble coping with reality.

Mix equal amounts (two to four drops) of each essence in a one-ounce dropper bottle filled with water and your favorite preservative.

Take the blend at the onset of crisis or emergency. It can be used for any setback great or small, from stubbing your toe to crashing your car, and it helps you stay levelheaded rather than falling into flights of panic, worry, or other kinds of distress.

Protection Potion

Ingredients: angelica, cinquefoil, rue, walnut, yarrow, yew

These six flower essences provide a powerful elixir of protection that serves a broad range of circumstances. Taken before you leave your home, it prevents outside forces from intruding upon your energy field. Taken at the end of the day, it helps remove any foreign energies you may have picked up along the way. Try spraying this blend in your aura, wearing a small vial of it, or charging a crystal with it for additional support.

Use five drops of each essence (as five is a protective number) in a one-ounce dropper bottle filled with water and your preservative of choice. Combine the ingredients on a Saturday in the waning moon for optimum astrological timing to boost the efficacy of your protection potion.

Purification Blend

Ingredients: crab apple, garlic, hyssop

Crab apple, garlic, and hyssop are my three favorite essences for all-purpose cleansing. Each of them helps clear away harmful, stagnant, and otherwise unpleasant energies. Crab apple addresses feelings of being unclean, while garlic and hyssop work more strongly on removing external energies.

Combine equal amounts (two or more drops each) of all three essences in a dropper bottle or spray bottle filled with water and your preservative of choice; add just a tiny amount of salt for additional cleansing power. Spray or diffuse this blend to clear energy from your environment, and take it at the first sign of illness or infection to clear away the emotional and spiritual components of the condition. I add a couple drops to my neti pot, too, whenever the need arises, and I've found it to reduce the symptoms of seasonal allergies and sinus infections significantly.

Meditation Blend

Ingredients: hellebore, lavender, lotus, monkshood, white chestnut

From time to time we all need a little assistance with our meditation practice. Each of these five essences offers help with staying focused and receptive. Hellebore supports us by cultivating stillness and breaking our addiction to validation from the outside world (read: screen addiction). Lavender invites a sense of calm focus and a gentle nudge that helps us listen to our inner voice during reflective moments. Lotus is perhaps the greatest of meditation enhancers, as it opens the crown chakra and enhances our awareness of our connection to divinity. Monkshood gives us a chance to retreat from the busyness of the world. White chestnut is perhaps the best essence to calm an overactive mind by gently easing idle mental chatter. (And I've included white chestnut in this blend, even though it's not listed in the directory of essences in chapter 11, because it is one of the Bach remedies and thus readily available.)

Mix your meditation blend in a one-ounce dropper bottle filled with water and the preservative of your choice. Use two to four drops each of hellebore, lavender, monkshood, and white chestnut, and use double that amount of lotus for added benefit. Take the blend at least fifteen minutes before you begin your meditation practice, perhaps while you prepare your space, and take it once more just as you start.

Sweet Dreams Elixir

Ingredients: chamomile, lavender, lemon balm, mugwort, passionflower, poppy, St. John's wort

For most of my life I've struggled to sleep soundly through the night. Even as a child, I would give up and grab a book to read for hours until my body and mind finally wearied themselves enough to drift off to sleep. This particular blend of essences is rather broad-spectrum, working to balance the mind, body, and spirit for a restful night filled with pleasant dreams. The essences in this elixir help calm an overactive mind, ward off nightmares, and ensure that you are less likely to wake during the night. While there is no single essence that is best suited to everyone's sleep cycle, this blend works well for me and my loved ones.

Combine two or three drops of each essence in a one-ounce dropper bottle filled with water and your favorite preservative. I recommend taking a few drops of the formula an hour or more before bedtime—perhaps in your favorite herbal tea—to start the process of readying the mind for bedtime. Take it again as you head to bed for a peaceful night of sleep.

Garden Blend

Ingredients: foxglove, garlic, lady's mantle, lilac, oak

My garden responds well to flower essences, and I've taken to using this blend regularly for all my plants. Foxglove and lilac both nourish the devas of the plants, and they encourage healthy growth. Oak is strengthening and protective to plants and encourages them to continue to grow healthily. The other two essences work more preventively. Lady's mantle helps plants succeed when all else fails, and it also boosts the effects of the other essences. Garlic flower essence helps control pests; if pests persist, try adding Bach's crab apple essence to the combination. Additionally, consider adding olive flower essence to the blend for germinating seeds, as this essence supplies a boost of energy to offset the expenditure of energy and effort on the part of the nascent plants.

To make your garden blend, add equal parts (two to four drops) of each of the essences to a one-ounce dropper bottle filled with water and a preservative of your choice. Add a dropperful or two of the blend to your watering can or a spray bottle and water your plants as appropriate. For pest control, spray the affected parts of the plant liberally. If your plants are undergoing any trauma, damage, or a change of scenery, offer them a couple drops of Rescue Remedy in addition to the garden blend.

City Witch Blend

Ingredients: echinacea, olive, rosemary, tobacco

Flower essences are sometimes described as "nature in a bottle," as they offer not only the vibrational effects of particular flowers but also a dose of balancing energy from Mother Nature herself. Nature is the living embodiment of the Great Mother, and it is said to be the source of inspiration, power, and the magick for many witches. But feeling "witchy" can be difficult when you are in an urban setting, and traveling into nature is not an option for everyone. This blend of four essences is exceptional for anyone who feels disconnected from nature or is otherwise unable to recharge in a natural setting.

Echinacea flower essence provides balance, support, and a connection to natural energies, and it also enhances your magickal prowess. Olive is sacred to Athena, who is a patron goddess of cities. Its essence is helpful for the symptoms of overwork and burnout that can result from not having adequate opportunity to recharge, with or without nature's assistance. Rosemary helps you remember who you are, what came before you, and the soul's innate link to magick and the natural world—even when you cannot see or sense that connection. Tobacco flower essence opens the heart and restores the soul's connection to the natural world. It also softens rigidity and the desire for power and control, thereby inviting you to work with the world around you instead of against it.

Mix two to four drops of each of these essences in a one-ounce dropper bottle filled with water and your favorite preservative. Take it orally to recharge whenever you need a dose of nature's nourishing energies, or diffuse or spray it in your space. Spraying it before meditation or ritual is a lovely way to connect to Mother Earth. This essence is also helpful for dealing with the effects of travel and jet lag, and it invites you to slow down and appreciate life whenever possible.

FLYING ESSENCE BLENDS

Flying ointments, or *unguenta sabbati,* are a staple of witchcraft lore. According to records from witch trials, these arcane and mysterious concoctions are said to have allowed witches to fly to the sabbat and consort with spirits and devils alike. They are, in fact, salves or unguents that, when applied to the skin, produce vivid hallucinations and the physical sensations of flying. Most recipes contain poisonous ingredients and baneful plants, like belladonna, henbane, and mandrake, and they are potentially quite toxic if misused.

Preparing and using flying ointments may be dangerous or even illegal, so many magickal practitioners turn to flower essences as alternatives to using deadly botanicals. Formulas of flower essences offer a vibrational substitute to psychoactive plants, and they work to subtly support and enhance spiritual practice. Flying essence formulas can be used to support meditation, lucid dreaming, psychic development, spirit communication, astral travel and shamanic journeying, and many other endeavors.

More than sixty extant recipes for historical flying ointments have been discovered so far, and practitioners continue to develop new formulas for modern use. Below you'll find a table of sample ingredients that can be used in flower essence formulas to enhance soul flight, astral projection, and shamanic travel. Among those plants listed you'll find many baneful herbs as well as some balms and trees. Even the plants that are nontoxic in nature may have some sinister lore associated with them, or they may offer a powerful magickal effect when combined with other plants. Consult the table to find some inspiration when crafting your own flying essence formulas. (Note that many of the essences listed below are not part of the directory of essences in chapter 11 but have been included here for reference.)

INGREDIENTS FOR FLYING ESSENCE FORMULAS

COMMON NAME	LATIN NAME
Agrimony	Agrimonia eupatoria
Angelica*	Angelica archangelica
Angel's trumpet*	Brugmansia spp.
Baneberry	Actaea spicata
Belladonna	Atropa belladonna
Bittersweet nightshade	Solanum dulcamara
Black nightshade	Solanum nigrum
Blue lotus*	Nymphaea caerulea
Cannabis	Cannabis spp.
Celery	Apium graveolens
Cinquefoil	Potentilla spp.
Clematis*	Clematis vitalba

*These plants are not traditionally used in the herbal salves of European witchcraft but show promise in flying essence formulas. Many have a rich tradition of use for shamanic journeys and soul flight among indigenous peoples, while others are psychically stimulating or otherwise appropriate for use in flying essences.

INGREDIENTS FOR FLYING ESSENCE FORMULAS (continued)

COMMON NAME	LATIN NAME
Coleus*	Plectranthus scutellarioides
Datura	Datura spp.
Elder*	Sambucus spp.
Enchanter's nightshade	Circaea lutetiana
False hellebore	Veratrum spp.
Fir*	Abies spp.
Fly agaric	Amanita muscaria
Foxglove*	Digitalis purpurea
Hellebore*	Helleborus spp.
Hemlock	Conium maculatum
Henbane	Hyoscyamus spp.
Hops*	Humulus lupulus
Lemon balm*	Melissa officinalis
Liberty cap mushroom*	Psilocybe spp.
Lily	Lilium spp.
Lotus*	Nelumbo nucifera
Mandrake	Mandragora spp.
Mayapple*	Podophyllum peltatum
Mistletoe	Viscum album
Monkshood	Aconitum napellus
Morning glory*	Ipomoea spp.
Mugwort	Artemisia vulgaris
Parsley	Petroselinum crispum
Periwinkle*	Vinca minor
Petunia*	Petunia violacea
Poplar	Populus spp.
Poppy	Papaver spp.
Purslane	Portulaca spp.
Queen Anne's lace*	Daucus carota
Syrian rue*	Peganum harmala
Tobacco	Nicotiana spp.

*These plants are not traditionally used in the herbal salves of European witchcraft but show promise in flying essence formulas. Many have a rich tradition of use for shamanic journeys and soul flight among indigenous peoples, while others are psychically stimulating or otherwise appropriate for use in flying essences.

INGREDIENTS FOR FLYING ESSENCE FORMULAS (continued)

COMMON NAME	LATIN NAME
Tomato*	*Solanum lycopersicum*
Vervain	*Verbena officinalis*
Vine (grape)*	*Vitis vinifera*
Water hemlock	*Cicuta maculata*
Water lily	*Nymphaea* spp.
Wormwood	*Artemisia absinthium*
Yew	*Taxus baccata*

*These plants are not traditionally used in the herbal salves of European witchcraft but show promise in flying essence formulas. Many have a rich tradition of use for shamanic journeys and soul flight among indigenous peoples, while others are psychically stimulating or otherwise appropriate for use in flying essences.

When making flying blends, I recommend getting to know each component individually. Take each essence internally or apply topically before meditation so you can acquaint yourself with its effects and the personality of the plant spirit. When you are ready to formulate your flying essence, the best effects come from doing so ritually. Call upon the plant spirits themselves to offer their wisdom and guidance as you prepare the blend.

To use a flying essence, simply take a few drops before you begin your meditation, trance, journey, or ritual. There is no universal dosage, especially since those blends made from predominantly baneful plants will be more intense than those made with a blend of banes and balms. You may also diffuse or spray the essence blend during your meditation or apply them to pulse points or the crown of your head. An alternative to taking flying essences internally is to mix them into a one-ounce jar of unscented lotion, using the same amounts that you would for a one-ounce dropper bottle, and apply them to your skin, like you would with a traditional flying ointment. It isn't necessary to coat the entire body—just rub some on your hands, chest, and forehead or anywhere else that you are guided to.

You can also use flying essences before bed to intensify the dream state. You may then experience vivid imagery, lucid dreams, and contact with spirits, guides, ancestors, and angels.

Therapeutically speaking, most flying essence formulas will address patterns of toxicity in your life. It's a case of fighting fire with fire, or in this case addressing toxic beliefs, behaviors, and influences with the wisdom of the baneful plant spirits. Flying essences can combat illusion, deception, and gaslighting, and they help you cut out toxic people and situations. Most of the blends that contain nightshades are adept for shadow work, and they'll help you heal emotional trauma at the deepest level.

On the following pages you'll find some sample recipes. Use these as a starting point for crafting your own flying essence formulas. You'll also find a couple of blends to take after your journey or meditation to help you become more grounded and fully embodied. These "return blends" enable you to restore your awareness of ordinary reality and recall and integrate the experiences you've had in other realms.

Flying Blend #1

Ingredients: black nightshade, cinquefoil, datura, lemon balm, yew

This is my favorite blend, as it contains a mixture of banes, balms, and a tree spirit. I find it balanced, protective, and deeply transformational. Cinquefoil and lemon balm offer protection and grace as you engage in spirit flight or other spiritual journeys, while the more baneful ingredients open the gateways into other realms. I use equal amounts of each essence, usually two or three drops for a one-ounce dropper bottle filled with water and a preservative.

Flying Blend #2

Ingredients: belladonna, datura, henbane, mandrake

This blend is inspired by the formula that Sarah Anne Lawless offers through her Bane Folk line of essences. She uses two different species of datura in her blend, though I've had success using only *Datura stramonium*. I mix two drops of each of the essences in a one-ounce dropper bottle filled with water and a preservative and shake it thoroughly. This is a simple but very effective recipe, and it is also useful as a therapeutic blend. Lawless recommends using it to overcome obstacles, heal from trauma and grief, and see through illusion and deception.

Flying Blend #3

Ingredients: datura, monkshood, yarrow

This simple and effective recipe comes from Christopher Penczak's *The Plant Spirit Familiar.*[1] Penczak's recipe calls for five drops of datura, three drops of monkshood, and four drops of yarrow mixed in a one-ounce dropper bottle filled with water and preservative. Take three to ten drops prior to meditation, ritual, or another visionary experience.

Flying Blend #4: Egyptian Wine

Ingredients: henbane, lotus or water lily, mandrake, vine (grape)

The ingredients for this flying essence are inspired by a ritual wine prepared by the ancient Egyptians.[2] In addition to supporting astral travel or spirit flight, this formula can also help you commune with the gods, particularly the Egyptian pantheon. Try adding it to offerings to the gods and spirits with whom you work to forge a deeper relationship and for enhancing visionary experiences with those beings. I usually use about four drops of henbane, lotus, and mandrake, and half as much of vine; mix these together in a one-ounce dropper bottle filled with water and preservative. Too much vine essence can make it hard to maintain a trance state, but a small amount is helpful, especially if you find yourself having difficulty letting go enough of control for a true visionary state to occur. If possible, use blue lotus (*Nymphaea caerulea*), as that is what the Egyptians would have used; otherwise substitute true lotus (*Nelumbo nucifera*).

Flying Blend #5: Balm Version

Ingredients: angelica, basil, cinquefoil, lavender, lemon balm, lotus, mugwort, vervain, yarrow

I formulated this combination of essences for those who are sensitive or have an aversion to working with baneful plants. Each of these essences works in a different way to support spirit flight and astral travel. Use seven drops of lotus, four drops each of mugwort and lemon balm, and two drops of each of the other essences and mix together in a one-ounce dropper bottle that contains water and your choice of preservative.

Return Formula #1

Ingredients: potato, rose, St. John's wort, star-of-Bethlehem

The first return essence I ever encountered was this recipe from *The Plant Spirit Familiar.* I worked with it as a follow-up for flying essences, and I also started to use it to ground after any intense ritual, magickal, or spiritual experience, whether or not essences were involved. The blend helps you be more incarnate and embodied afterward, while also integrating the magick of your experience. Add five drops each of St. John's wort and rose essences, two drops of star-of-Bethlehem (one of the Bach flower essences and easily obtainable), and a single drop of potato flower essence to a one-ounce dropper bottle filled with water and preservative.[3]

Return Formula #2

Ingredients: clematis, potato, rue

I use a very simple blend of equal parts of clematis, potato, and rue mixed in a one-ounce dropper bottle filled with water and preservative. Clematis is a Bach remedy that calls the consciousness back from dreamy, distant states, and potato similarly grounds the soul back into the body. Rue is an essential ally after journey work, as it grounds, cleanses, and protects the aura to remove any unwanted or foreign energies/entities that you may have picked up along the way.

RITUAL AND MAGICKAL FORMULAS

The essence blends in this section are inspired by magickal and ritual intentions, ranging from drawing love and money to connecting with the gods and ancestors of your craft. Some of the recipes are simple and straightforward, coming directly from the use of the same botanicals in herbal magick, while others are built upon other mythic or vibrational currents embodied within the component essences. Enjoy experimenting with these formulas, or use them as inspiration to make your own.

Money Magick

Ingredients: dill, oak, peppermint, sassafras

Each of the plants in this formula is traditionally used in folk magick to attract prosperity and abundance, and their essences can offer help in the same manner. This formula helps you make internal shifts so that you can accept the universal abundance that is your birthright, and it helps you creatively pursue sustainable means of manifesting that abundance in your life. Mix eight drops of each essence into a one-ounce bottle filled with water and a preservative on a Thursday during the waxing moon. Use it to anoint a green candle for a simple money spell. You can also take several drops of the formula before you start work as well as during meditations for inspiration about ways to increase your wealth and well-being.

Open Doors

Ingredients: blackberry, iris, mistletoe, tomato, vervain

This formula consists of five flower essences that help channel your creativity, enthusiasm, and power into achieving success. Tomato helps break down barriers to seeking rewarding experiences in life, while mistletoe was historically believed to magickally unlock any door. Vervain is the remedy against overenthusiasm, ensuring that you'll be able to put the right amount of effort and intensity into any project and avoid becoming burned out. Blackberry is one of the best aids for boosting manifestation among flower essences, and iris is a powerful tool for channeling creativity and inspiration.

Mix seven drops of each essence into a one-ounce dropper bottle containing water and a preservative on or shortly after the new moon. Use this essence anytime you need a gentle boost of inspiration and motivation or in rituals aimed at removing obstacles and opening the path. Take two to four drops under the tongue each morning upon rising for a full lunar cycle following an obstacle-removing ritual for added power and follow-through.

Love Potion

Ingredients: damiana, hibiscus, jasmine, red clover, rose, trillium, violet

This combination of seven essences offers a well-rounded and loving energy to support emotional balance and set the stage to attract or strengthen a romantic relationship. These essences are made from flowers with a long history of inspiring love, beauty, and pleasure, and they work together to offer a delightful love potion that helps you love yourself from within. Together, they ignite confidence and may make you more attractive to a potential mate. Combine the essences in equal parts in a one-ounce dropper bottle filled with water and your favorite preservative on a Friday (the day of Venus) during the waxing moon. Add a small amount of honey or glycerin to the bottle to sweeten the blend, as well as to sweeten your heart with the love that blossoms with every drop you taste.

Countermagick Formula

Ingredients: cinquefoil, dill, nettle, rue, thistle

The plants used in this formula have been used in magickal herbalism to break curses, avert the evil eye, and restore health and wellness after psychic attack. Working with their flower essences is a wonderful way to harness their curse-breaking qualities. This blend can be used for rituals of uncrossing, jinx breaking, and curse removal. It offers a reversal of fortune when you feel as though the world is out to get you. The action of the formula is twofold: it energetically clears and removes harmful energies while also changing the way you perceive the situation. As a result, you'll feel more empowered, as though life is under control again. The combination is fairly protective, too, and it can be used to prevent future sources of psychic and magickal harm from targeting you.

Combine several drops of each essence in equal measure in a one-ounce dropper bottle filled with water and a preservative; apple cider vinegar is an excellent choice for the preservative, as it is energetically cleansing and protective. Mix and consecrate your blend on a Saturday in the waning moon if possible, and take two to four drops by mouth several times a day when you feel you are the target of magickal or psychic attack. You can also spray it in your aura, add it to the bath, or dab it onto your wrists and behind your ears for maximum effect.

Elemental Balance

Balms: St. John's wort (fire), rose (water), peppermint (air), red clover (earth), lotus (spirit)

Banes: buttercup (fire), water hemlock (water), lily of the valley (air), potato (earth), mandrake (spirit)

Trees: oak (fire), willow (water), hazel (air), pine (earth), cacao (spirit)

Here I'm offering a different elemental balance formula for each class of plant spirits (balms, banes, trees). Each includes a representative of the four earthly elements plus spirit or quintessence. These correspondences come from my own practice, but you are welcome to make changes according to the essences you have on hand and the correspondences you prefer. Taking any of the elemental formulas helps restore harmony and balance in all areas of your life, as represented by the alchemical elements. Of the three formulas, the balms tend to work the most gently, and they address the personality and overt parts of the psyche. The banes work more on the shadow and hidden aspects of the psyche, often by dredging up hidden traumas to address long-standing imbalances. The tree formula is grounding and aligning, and it works on all areas of the self—body, mind and spirit—with equal measure.

Make your blend with four drops of each essence in a one-ounce dropper bottle that contains water and preservative, calling upon the plant spirits and the corresponding elemental forces as you mix and consecrate your blend. Take two drops in the morning and evening for general balance, as well as for boosting magickal proficiency.

The Mighty Dead

Ingredients: belladonna, dandelion, elder, poppy, wormwood

This blend of five essences assists in ancestral healing and communication. It is not limited to the ancestors of your bloodline; it can also help connect you to your spiritual lineage, as well as those on the other side who offer guidance, support, and inspiration whether or not you bear any direct relation to them. The Mighty Dead are akin to the saints of witchcraft; they are the ancestors who guide and guard the traditions of the craft, from the famous—or infamous—characters known to history to those forgotten in the sands of time.

Add this essence to offerings on an ancestor altar or shrine or to libations poured onto the land, or take it before meditation or journey work to commune with the spirits on the other side of the veil. This blend may also be useful for helping lost spirits cross over and for catalyzing ancestral healing.

To prepare it, add two to four drops of each essence to a one-ounce dropper bottle filled with water and a preservative. Ideally, mix and consecrate the essence on a Saturday to take advantage of its Saturnian connection to endings and death.

The Witch's Goddess

Ingredients: birch, black nightshade, elder, magnolia, mugwort, red clover, rose

These seven flowers are all sacred to the Goddess, and each one connects to different archetypal roles that she has played throughout history. This flower essence formula enables you to tap in to the Great Goddess as creatrix and destroyer, sovereign of the cosmos. Take a few drops before invoking her, or add the blend to the chalice used in the Great Rite or other sacraments. This flower essence formula can also be used to consecrate tools dedicated to the Great Mother or added to the bath for a rite of cleansing before rituals that honor her.

To prepare it, mix seven drops of each flower essence in a dropper bottle filled with water and a preservative. You can enhance this elixir by adding a few drops of a gem elixir or homeopathic remedy prepared from silver. If you are making it for use as a spray, add a few drops of rose essential oil or another floral scent to bring a new dimension to its work.

The Witch's God

Ingredients: basil, holly, mistletoe, oak, sunflower, yarrow

This blend has a powerful connection to the divine masculine and the Horned God of the witches. It combines his dual nature into one potion, making it perfect for any ritual that invokes or honors any of his aspects. Try placing a few drops of this formula on the athame or wand as part of the Great Rite, or use it to anoint and consecrate any tools dedicated to the god of the craft.

To prepare it, combine five drops of each essence in a one-ounce bottle filled with water and a preservative. You can enhance this recipe with a few drops of a gem elixir or homeopathic remedy prepared from gold. If you are preparing it as a spray, a couple drops of oak absolute and basil essential oil would be a powerful addition to the formula.

Light-Bringer

Ingredients: apple, cacao, elder, mullein, St. John's wort

A large part of my personal spiritual journey has been exploring the role of the light-bringer archetype from cultures around the world. The most widely known is Lucifer, fallen and rebellious angel of the morning star. Though he is nowadays conflated with adversarial figures, a Theosophical retelling of his myth illustrates his descent from the celestial sphere to the terrestrial one as a metaphor for bringing the light of spirit into matter, thereby preparing Earth for the incoming incarnation of humanity. Other light-bearing figures include Hekate as Hekate Phosphoros, the torch-bearer; Prometheus, who stole fire from heaven to offer it to humanity; and Quetzalcoatl, whose gift of cacao brought enlightenment to humankind. Luciferian figures in myths from across the globe symbolize shining light into the darkness and bearing a torch to lead others to enlightenment, often at the risk of personal sacrifice.

The five flowers I've chosen for this recipe all have connections to various light-bringers, and they help you hold your light in a world that occasionally feels quite dark. Apple cleanses feelings of impurity and represents the acquisition of wisdom; as a flower of Venus, it is doubly symbolic in this blend. Cacao is an essence also connected to Venus through the myth of Quetzalcoatl (see the profile of cacao on page 270 for a brief retelling of this myth). As an essence, it nourishes the light-body and helps us remember our innate divinity. Prometheus is said to have hidden the fire of Mount Olympus inside the hollow stem of elder.

The flower essence of this holy tree helps you share your light with the world. Mullein has taken on associations with Hekate, and the plant's inflorescence resembles candles or torches; it protects and illuminates while assuaging fear. Finally, St. John's wort is perhaps the flower most symbolic of light and illumination. This essence expands your ability to draw in and radiate light no matter the circumstances.

Add two to four drops of each essence to a one-ounce bottle containing water and a preservative. For additional potency, add a few drops of emerald gem elixir or a tiny chip of emerald to the bottle. Take a few drops or spray the light-bringer formulas in the aura whenever you need help shining. The blend is protective, nourishing, and enlightening. It offers hope, solace, and magick in times of despair. Use it for inspiration when you feel dull or languorous, as well as any time you are called to lead others to shine more light into the world.

SABBAT FORMULAS

The eight sabbats are the traditional holidays celebrated by many pagans, witches, and other magickal folk. The essences in these formulas have been chosen for their attunement to the particular holiday. Some, for example, come from flowers that bloom on or around the seasonal holiday, while others carry the symbolism of the festival. Ideally, acquire or make the individual essences ahead of time, and prepare the blends by mixing and consecrating them in sacred space on the holiday, drawing the tides of light and dark and life and death—unique to that very day—into your blend.* When making the sabbat formulas, mix equal parts of each essence (I suggest eight drops to represent the eight sabbats) in a one-ounce dropper bottle filled with water and preservative.

You can incorporate the sabbat blends into your seasonal celebrations

*If you'd like to use a commercial vibrational essence made with those natural tides of energy, two essence producers make excellent ones: the Wheel of Life collection made by Chalice Well Essences in Glastonbury, England, and the Sovereignty Essences produced by Green Man Essences in Wales. Refer to the appendix for more information about where to find these and other essences.

in a variety of ways. Add them to the sacrament within the chalice, spray or diffuse them in your ritual space, anoint yourself and other celebrants as they enter the circle, or take them internally to attune to the seasonal tides. You may add them to food and drink outside of ritual, too. The essences can also be taken at any time in the year whenever you find yourself in need of the magick and healing represented by that sabbat.

One final note: the dates provided for the sabbats in the descriptions below correspond to their celebrations in the Northern Hemisphere. Celebrants in the Southern Hemisphere will find the dates reversed. I recommend finding the flowers that best represent the natural tides of energy in your region when making these blends—or indeed, when making *any* essences.

Yule Essence

Ingredients: ash, gorse, holly, mistletoe, pine

Yule, also known as Midwinter, is the celebration of the winter solstice (approximately December 21) as the sun enters the sign of Capricorn. This essence blend hails the imminent return of the sun's light while inviting us to surrender to the stillness of winter with strength and ease. Ash, holly, mistletoe, and pine are all traditional plants connected to Yule, while gorse's yellow blooms signify the return of the sun. Take the essence whenever you have need of stillness, inspiration, and hope, as it helps conceive new ideas and energies.

Imbolc Essence

Ingredients: angelica, daffodil, rosemary, snowdrop, willow

Imbolc, also called Candlemas or Brigid's Day, is usually celebrated on February 1 or 2. It traditionally marks the end of winter as the first signs of leaf and bloom emerge from the snow. The flowers in this blend (daffodil, snowdrop) bloom around this time of year, while angelica and rosemary share the fiery symbolism of the goddess Brigid. Willow's flexible branches are connected to weaving, another symbol of the goddess. Use this blend to offer some seasonal support and instill the hope and renewal that Imbolc represents. It can also help you birth new ideas and projects.

Ostara Essence

Ingredients: chamomile, cherry blossom, iris, violet

Ostara is one of several names given to the vernal equinox, which takes place around March 21. It symbolizes the budding growth and flourishing of new life that springtime offers. All the flowers in this blend tend to bloom around this time of year—in fact, you can add or substitute any flowers native to your region that blossom during the equinox. Taking this essence adds a sense of movement, growth, and vitality to whatever you may be focusing on.

Beltane Essence

Ingredients: birch, hawthorn, lilac, lily of the valley, rowan

Beltane, or May Day, is usually celebrated on May 1 and is symbolic of the marriage between the Goddess and the God. Flowers, dancing, sex, and revelry are all associated with this holiday, and the flowers in this essence attune you to the tides of the season. Many other flowers are also in bloom at this time of year, and you can add any that feel appropriate to symbolize the height of spring in your region. The Beltane essence blend invites you to embody joy and pleasure, and it also encourages you to tap in to your natural creativity and fertility in whatever way you choose.

Midsummer Essence

Ingredients: heather, mugwort, oak, St. John's wort, vervain

Midsummer, also called Litha, takes place on the summer solstice, which represents the height of solar energy and the apex of the tides of light and life. The flowers in this blend are all connected to the sun and the solstice. Taking this essence helps you reach your highest potential in both a magickal and material sense, helping you pursue your sense of purpose with passion and zeal.

Lammas Essence

Ingredients: calendula, hazel, poppy, sunflower, yarrow

Lammas, or Lughnasagh, is the first of the three harvests, focusing on the harvest of grains. It is usually celebrated on August 1 or 2, and festivities are related to grain and baking. The flowers in this blend all bloom in late summer and early fall, making them well suited to celebrating this sabbat. For an extra boost, consider adding a flower essence made from maize or another grain. The Lammas blend helps you soak up the last of the warmth before autumn and winter set in, and it helps initiate the process of letting go. Take this essence to reap the rewards of your work without losing sight of the bigger goals on the horizon.

Mabon Essence

Ingredients: blackberry, enchanter's nightshade, passionflower, rue, sage, vine

Mabon is a modern name given to the celebration of the autumnal equinox, which takes place around September 21. The second of the harvest festivals, Mabon celebrates the reaping of the fruits of the season, and it is often considered a festival of thanksgiving. Blackberry and vine (i.e., grape) are traditionally related to this sabbat, while enchanter's nightshade, passionflower, rue, and sage each help us connect to the themes and tides of the season. Take the Mabon essence to instill gratitude deep within your heart as well as to help you find enjoyment in your work. Use it to bring things to fruition before letting them go.

Samhain Essence

Ingredients: apple, elder, juniper, pomegranate, wormwood, yew

For many witches, occultists, and other magickal practitioners, Samhain is the holiest of sabbats. It coincides with Halloween and is celebrated on October 31 or November 1, as it sits directly opposite Beltane on the wheel of the year. Samhain is the funeral feast of the dying god, as well as the final harvest: the culling of the flock before winter falls. The flower essences in this blend all relate to endings, death, and release. Many also carry a link to the underworld and the Mighty Dead. Take this essence to initiate cycles of release as well as for building a connection to helpers and guides on the other side of the veil.

10

Plant Spirit Alchemy

Flower essences are, in a sense, born from the same current as the ancient alchemical traditions. The alchemical work of Paracelsus, notably his famous doctrine of signatures, led to the formative principles of modern homeopathy. This, in turn, inspired Dr. Edward Bach to create his flower essences, which follow similar patterns of potentization-through-dilution as homeopathic remedies. The themes and rituals of alchemy and the Hermetic arts have also strongly influenced many modern witches, myself included, and it isn't hard to imagine that the cunning folk and magicians of bygone eras similarly drew inspiration from the alchemical symbolism of the grimoire traditions in their spiritual and therapeutic praxes.

Within the ontology of alchemy, we learn that there are five elements and three substances—or three primes—that constitute all things in the manifest world. The five elements are earth, air, fire, water, and quintessence (also known as spirit, ether, akasha, and many other names). As these five primal forces combine in various ways, they help create the many levels of reality all around and within us. The three primes, or *tria prima,* are sulfur, mercury, and salt—not the literal sulfur, mercury, and salt that we are accustomed to, but metaphorical ideas relating to the practice of alchemy itself. These three substances are separated and recombined in the Great Work of alchemy to create spagyrics and ultimately the *lapis philosophorum,* or philosopher's stone.

The tria prima each have their own range of meanings and symbolism. Sulfur represents the fire element and the spiritual nature of matter. It is the spirit of matter itself and a representation of the superego in Freudian psychology. Mercury is the volatile element of air; it is the mind or soul inherent in matter and represents the mental level of existence. When sulfur and mercury combine, we achieve salt. Salt offers solidity and symbolizes both elemental earth and water. While sulfur and mercury are the spirit and soul, salt is the body. It is a representation of the material plane, the physical manifestation of our spiritual and mental natures.

SPAGYRICS AND FLOWER ESSENCES

In the alchemical tradition, plant matter is broken down into the three constituent primes, which are then further refined and recombined. This process takes place in three stages, called separation, purification, and cohobation, and it yields a potent spiritual medicine: the spagyric. Paracelsus pioneered the work of producing spagyrics, whose name he derived from the Greek *spao,* meaning "to divide," and *ageiro,* "to combine," thus following the ancient alchemical methodology of *solve et coagula:* to dissolve and congeal.[1] Through the stages of separating, refining, and reuniting the three primes, the resulting elixir—the spagyric—is made more potent, and it can be used for healing or spiritual practice.

In a sense, the art of making flower essences is profoundly alchemical. We begin the process with pure water and raw plant matter. Through spiritual union with the plant spirit or deva, we extract the spiritual imprint of the plant into the water. Following this, we preserve and potentize (dilute) the essence for therapeutic use. This is akin to the stages of separation and refinement in the alchemical tradition. The end result is a concentrated dose of the plant's spirit—its alchemical sulfur—imprinted upon the water. Other processes of making botanical medicines, such deriving essential oils and tinctures, yield the mercury and the salt of the plant. When we recombine the sulfur, mercury, and salt, we achieve what I call a *flower essence spagyric*—a more potent elixir, medicinally and vibrationally. A flower essence spagyric contains both the vibration of the plant and its active phytochemicals, so it works to bring healing to the body, mind, and spirit simultaneously.

Let's take a deeper look at the tria prima as they relate to the alchemical art of flower essence spagyrics.

Salt: The Soma

The salt of the plant is its *soma,* or body. Metaphorically, it is the son—the divine child born of the union of mercury and sulfur. In traditional alchemical methods, the raw plant material is subjected to processes such as maceration, extraction, or circulation to separate the salt from the sulfur and mercury with some sort of solvent, such as alcohol or water. The resulting liquid contains both sulfur and mercury, while the salt must be further extracted from the leftover plant matter, usually via calcination (burning). Although this same process can be used for a flower essence spagyric, I tend to favor an infusion or tincture of the plant to represent its soma or salt.

In making flower essence spagyrics, any physical extraction or tincture of the plant can serve as its alchemical salt. You can make an infusion by steeping the plant in water or a decoction by heating or boiling the plant matter on the stove. Tinctures made in alcohol, vinegar, or glycerin can also represent the soma or salt of the plant in a flower essence spagyric. Hydrosols or hydrolates of the corresponding flower essence can also be used, as can juices, wines, and cordials. (If you use juice from fresh fruit, try to render the juice yourself, and be sure to add an adequate amount of preservative to your finished stock bottles of spagyric.)

Some plants are dangerous to use via normal extraction methods, including monkshood (aconite), belladonna, datura, hemlock, henbane, mandrake, wormwood, and yew. In these cases, homeopathic preparations can be used instead. Even with homeopathic preparations it may be possible to have reactions to some plants, so be sure to research appropriately and use scant amounts of potentially harmful plants at the correct dilution.

Making Tinctures

The simplest method of tincturing a plant requires a glass jar with a tight-fitting lid. Collect the useful parts of the plant; usually these are chosen for their medicinal potency, but be sure to harvest flowers, too, if they are available. Ensure that you collect from your plants with permission, making an offering if it feels appropriate. Wash the plant material thoroughly and discard any unwanted bits. Chop larger plant matter into smaller pieces and place the plant material in the jar. Fill the jar with your solvent of choice, such as vodka, brandy, or vinegar, aiming for a roughly equal ratio of plant to solvent. (If you are using dried herbs, use one-fourth the amount of plant matter to alcohol.) Seal the jar and leave it in a safe place to infuse for six to eight weeks; shake it intermittently to mix the components and encourage extraction of the herb's medicinal qualities. Finally, strain out the plant matter. Store the tincture in a sealed glass container in a cool, dark location.

Mercury: The Psyche

In the alchemical arts, mercury represents the psyche of a substance—that is, its mind or soul. The psyche symbolizes the personality and vital energy of the substance. It is volatile and ephemeral, unless it is bound to or supported by sulfur. In making flower essence spagyrics, the essential oil represents the psyche of the plant and thus is our mercurial component.

Essential oils are volatile, hydrophobic liquids that contain the concentrated scent and energy of the plant. Using them in flower essence spagyrics requires a certain amount of care and consideration. Most essential oils are unfit for internal use, although others may be safe if only a drop or two is used for a one-ounce dropper bottle of spagyric. Some oils that may be relatively safe to use in a spagyric that you intend to consume include angelica, basil, chamomile, elder, hyssop, jasmine, lavender, lemon and other citrus, lemon balm, peppermint, rose, rosemary, sage, and violet.*

When it comes to harnessing the mercury of baneful plants, essential oils are not always available, nor would they be safe if they were. Even with otherwise safe herbs, essential oils can pose toxicity threats if mishandled, so it is vital to exercise care when working with them. My first recommendation is to consider using such spagyrics for external use only, such as spraying them in your ritual space (be careful not to inhale them) or anointing your tools with them. In these cases, you could use a fragrance oil, rather than the essential oil, for baneful plants.

If you cannot find an essential oil for a particular plant, or if the essential oil would be dangerous to use in the manner you would like, there are some alternatives. You may be able to make a safe infusion of the plant in a food-grade carrier oil. This infused oil won't carry the same potency as an essential oil, either chemically or spiritually, but it can be magickally empowered to make up for this deficit (see the exercise on page 221). If possible, use fresh leaves, flowers, or roots for the infusion, and place the oil near the plant, out of direct light if possible. Infuse for several hours or even overnight for a low-potency infuscion and for several days or weeks for a medicinal-strength infusion if it is safe to do so. Strain the oil thoroughly before use.

Another method is to use a safe substitute, such as an essential oil from a nontoxic plant that is somehow related, either botanically or magickally. In the wise words of my friend Dan Lupacchino, some nonbaneful plants can actually help open us up to deeper spiritual connections with the banes themselves. Members of the nightshade family can be substituted by capsicum (hot pepper), which is also a nightshade. Rose otto, though expensive, can substitute for other members of the

---

*For a more extensive list of essential oils that are generally recognized as safe for consumption by the U.S. Food and Drug Administration (FDA), see section 182.20 of the Code of Federal Regulations (search online for the term *21CFR182.20*). Oils that appear on this list are not necessarily safe to consume in any large quantity but may be safe in highly dilute concentrations. If you have any doubts, dilute the essential oil in question in a food-grade carrier oil or alcohol, shake it well, and leave it to infuse for several hours or even days. Use only a couple drops of this diluted solution to make your spagyric.

rose family, such as rowan, while juniper berry essential oil might make a viable replacement for yew essential oil. Some plants, like parsley, are generally helpful in forging links to baneful plants, thus making it a good candidate if you need a substitution for a more toxic plant—especially a member of the carrot family to which parsley also belongs. You can always consult with the spirits of the plants themselves to see what they prefer.

You may also consider using a fragrance oil of a plant, or a related plant, if the essential oil is unavailable. Be sure not to consume any spagyrics made from fragrance oils or toxic essential oils.

Since it is not possible for most practitioners to distill or extract their own essential oils, consider purchasing the best-quality oils that you can reasonably afford. Many store-bought essential oils are not very active, vibrationally speaking, so it is best to ritually empower them before using them to craft your flower essence spagyric. See the box below for instructions.

☽ Ensouling an Essential Oil

All the components of a flower essence spagyric should be filled with vital energy. That is not always the case for commercial essential oils, but you can ensoul them—that is, consecrate and enliven them—through ritual. You may choose to empower the entire bottle of essential oil at your first opportunity or wait to consecrate it for each specific use. For the purpose of making a spagyric, I'd suggest doing it separately so you can spend time meditating with the essential oil, tincture, and flower essence individually to get to know the characters of the tria prima before uniting them. If you are using an infused oil or fragrance oil as a substitute for an essential oil, you can empower them through this same ensoulment ritual.

To begin, you will need a working altar or other surface, the glyph for mercury (☿) copied onto paper or wood, and any other ritual tools you might like. I like to burn incense for this ritual, as the mercury of the tria prima and the smoke of incense both correlate to the air element. You can add a drop or two of the essential oil to the incense to attune it to the plant spirit you will be evoking.

Place your bottle of essential oil atop the symbol for mercury and arrange the altar in a fashion that is meaningful to you. Light the incense (if you are using it) and then cast a circle, call the quarters, and evoke deity according to your preference. I prefer to use my athame to cast the circle and direct energy in this ritual, as it is often associated with the element of air.

Remove the cap from the bottle of oil and intone these words:

I call to the spirit of [name of plant]. Join me in this sacred space for the consecration and empowerment of this essential oil. I call to the archetype of mercury, the prime of air and the psyche of all matter, to help me ensoul this oil to carry the volatile nature of the mercury of [name of plant].

Trace the symbol for mercury over the bottle, either with your finger or with a ritual blade, and visualize the glyph hanging in the air over the bottle, blazing with etheric flame. Aim the point of your blade or the tip of your finger at the bottle. Breathe in deeply, imagining that you are filling your lungs not just with air but also with the mercurial essence of the air element. As you exhale, direct this energy down your extended arm, through your hand, and out the tip of your blade or finger into the bottle. Repeat twice more, for a total of three breaths.

Draw the mercury symbol over the bottle once more and say:

This oil is now empowered as the living mercury of [name of plant]. May it embody all the essential qualities of the mercury of [name of plant] and become the vessel for [name of plant]'s psyche.

Draw an equal-armed cross over the bottle of essential oil and say:

I fix this oil as the living mercury of [name of plant]. So mote it be.

Return the lid to the bottle. Deconstruct the sacred space according to your traditions. Keep the ensouled essential oil in a special place where it will not be contaminated by external energies, the same as you would store flower essences.

Sulfur: The Pneuma

For our purposes, the sulfur is the vibrational essence of the plant. In alchemy, sulfur is the *pneuma,* or spirit of the substance itself. It is associated with the transpersonal spiritual force breathed into existence by the Creator. If soma/salt gives form and psyche/mercury gives personality, then pneuma/sulfur provides the animating essence of life itself. This is the perfect depiction of the spiritual consciousness that imprints during essence making. The collective, rather than personal, level of consciousness interacts with the flowers and the water to produce a flower essence. Even the fiery nature of sulfur speaks to the light of the sun (or moon) used to transfer the spiritual energy of the plant to the water.

When making flower essence spagyrics, you can use homemade flower essences just as easily as those made by professionals. Homemade flower essences are in some ways preferable because you have your hands in the making of more of the spagyric components. Essences you've made yourself also allow you to use the mother essence directly in the bottling of your spagyric, yielding a true stock bottle potency.

While traditionally made flower essences contain the vibrational imprint of a single species of plant, spagyric-style essences are greatly enhanced when made from blends of closely related species. Blends of essences—especially those that are botanically related—can enhance the function of your spagyric. When I make spagyric flower essences, I like for the sulfur to be composed of several flower essences by different makers, which often means blending the essences of closely related plants. The first spagyric I made was that of rose, and I combined essences of the red roses from the garden at my new home with the Bach wild rose essence and an essence called Blend of Roses from Chalice Well Essences. The latter was, as you might imagine, made from a collection of different roses, and you can find similar varietal blends for other flowers, like sage and yarrow. Uniting the various incarnations of a plant species in your spagyric can be powerful, tapping in to the collective force of the pneuma of the plant itself.

Bringing together a mixture of essences as the pneuma of your spagyric creates an essence blend that anchors a wider range of frequencies embodied within one plant; it's a bit like an essence made from the oversoul of the plant group, rather than the individual soul of a single species or varietal. For some plants, such as rose and oak, this can be done without muddying the waters vibrationally. Others may not produce such clear results—experimentation and communing with the plant spirits themselves are the only ways to know for sure.

USING FLOWER ESSENCE SPAGYRICS

Traditionally made flower essences are profound tools of healing that perfectly embody the gifts of the plant spirits themselves. They do not require embellishment to do their job with ease and grace. However, we have nothing to lose by augmenting these remedies so they can work on several levels beyond the vibrational. Since flower essence spagyrics contain both the spiritual energy of the plant spirit and the phytochemicals from the plant, they work on psychological and physiological patterns at the same time. As a result, flower essence spagyrics are fast-acting tools for healing and magickal practice.

Being made from the whole plant (or at the very least from more than merely the flowers floating in water), flower essence spagyrics help us forge a stronger and deeper relationship with the plant spirits themselves. A well-made spagyric that is ritually mixed and consecrated confers the virtues of the plant spirit. The elixir becomes the living embodiment of the body, mind, and soul of the plant. Taking this sacred plant medicine similarly impacts all three areas of our own lives, too.

Comparing Essences and Spagyrics

Let's compare the actions of traditional flower essences and flower essence spagyrics before discussing their applications. Both the essence and the spagyric are made from water that has been imprinted with the energy of the plant spirit. Both forms are made with the same conscious reverence for the deva or consciousness of the plant, and both offer their benefits to our mind and soul. Both forms of essences are also subject to the process of potentiation-through-dilution as described in the law of infinitesimals. Stock bottles of both can be diluted into dosage bottles for personal and professional use. For the most part, flower essences and their alchemical counterparts can be applied in similar ways (so long as spagyrics are derived from non-toxic plants): they can be taken internally, applied topically, sprayed, added to the bath, added to food and drink, and used in magick and ritual.

Despite the commonalities between these two types of preparations, there are marked differences in their makeup and therapeutic effects. The first is the most obvious: spagyrics are chemically active, while essences are only vibrational in nature. This means that more care must be taken in their use. While ordinary flower essences offer no contraindications and do not interfere with other therapies or medications, flower essence spagyrics contain phytochemicals that may pose some concerns. For example, someone with a rose allergy would have no problem taking a flower essence, but the spagyric, which contains volatile oils and other compounds extracted from roses, could cause a severe reaction. Some plants are known to interact with one another and with prescription medication, so it is vital to research this aspect thoroughly if you intend to take spagyrics full-strength at the medicinal dosage. Some of these effects can be mitigated by taking them only after they have been further diluted into dosage bottles—two drops to a one-ounce dropper bottle, prepared as described in chapter 5.

Traditionally made flower essences work predominantly at the psychological level. They influence our emotional and mental patterns, and that effect trickles down to the material level to manifest changes in our pathology over time. Though some essences do have a clearer effect on our bodies, they are vibrational remedies, not chemical ones. Often, it can take weeks or even months for the spiritual qualities of an essence to work their way through the psyche and begin to make lasting change at the physical level. Flower essence spagyrics, on the other hand, influence the body, mind, and spirit simultaneously. Even when diluted, they still contain active chemical compounds that produce tangible effects beyond what vibrational essences offer. This means that the spagyrics work much more quickly than the essences.

Guidelines for Use

In light of the information above about how flower essence spagyrics work, here are some guidelines for using them safely:

★ Flower essence spagyrics have two dosages for internal use: medicinal and vibrational. The medicinal dosage for many plants is fifteen to thirty drops twice per day, though this varies from one plant to the next; you may need to consult with a medical herbalist to ensure safe dosage. The vibrational dosage is generally two drops up to four times per day.

★ Take the spagyric directly under the tongue or add it to a beverage, such as water or tea, and drink it.

★ Flower essence spagyrics can be diluted to produce stock bottles for safer consumption. The recommended dosage at this dilution is identical to that of traditional flower essences.

★ Combining spagyrics is not recommended unless you are familiar with their energy and physiological influences. Do your research to ensure the flower essence spagyrics that you mix are safe together. I usually limit the number of spagyrics in dosage bottles. In most cases a single spagyric can be combined with several traditional flower essences to produce good results.

★ Never prescribe or blend a spagyric for someone else if you are unsure about its safety for them. Never give one to someone else if you would not trust its safety for yourself.

★ Do not overuse flower essence spagyrics. Not only do they carry the possibility of chemical interactions, but they also have strong emotional and spiritual effects. Overstimulation from overuse can lead to spiritual burnout.

Magickal and Ritual Uses

Flower essence spagyrics offer more than enhanced therapeutic applications. They are a refined and magnified connection to the plant spirits themselves, lending themselves well to magick and shamanic journeys. When I first encountered flower essence preparations resembling the spagyrics described here, I was hesitant to use them. One of my dear friends, Elena, a fellow flower essence enthusiast herself, had pointed me to the Flower Essence Tinctures from Floracopeia, which combine tinctures and essential oils with blends of vibrational essences. I'm a bit of a purist about many things, and I often prefer to work with single essences, rather than complex blends when trying out products from a new essence maker. However, Elena's personal recommendation made me curious enough to try them out. I bought a couple and began to experiment. I noticed that they worked with immediacy. I also noticed how much more energetic they felt, as though they were somehow more directly tuned in to the frequency of the plants' consciousness.

Flower essence spagyrics have the same power. Using them in your spiritual practice affords a stronger connection to the plant spirits—especially when you invest the time and effort to make your own spagyric essences by creating a tincture, empowering the ingredients, and marrying the body, mind, and spirit of the plant together. The prime ritual use I've found for these enhanced essences is for direct communion with the plant spirits. You can use a couple of drops under the tongue or topically, such as on the wrists or brow, before meditation to support communication with the spirit of the plant from which the essence is made. You can add a couple of drops to a glass of water to use as an offering in shrines. Diffusing the essence through any of the methods described earlier in the book (see chapter 7) creates an atmosphere that the plant spirit will find most inviting, facilitating any sort of ritual work with that spirit.

Flower essence spagyrics can also be used like more traditional materia magica, as described in chapter 8. Use them to dress candles, consecrate ritual tools, empower spell pouches, or program (or charge) crystals. Add a small amount of the flower essence spagyric to your homemade incense, potions, or philters. Place a few drops on a scrying mirror or crystal ball to call the spirit of the plant to assist you in divination; this is particularly helpful if you are more visually inclined and are looking to implement another means of communication with the spirit of the plant. Let creativity and inspiration lead your practice with these sacred alchemical preparations, while remembering to do so safely.

MAKING FLOWER ESSENCE SPAGYRICS

Before making your flower essence spagyric, spend time getting to know each of the components that comprise it. Take the flower essence for several days, if not weeks, to see how its vibration affects your energy field. Inhale the scent of the essential oil in meditation. Diffuse it into the room or anoint candles with the oil; if it is safe, use it on your skin or in your bath—but only if it is properly diluted. Meditate with the tincture; take it in your morning beverage or place a couple drops under the tongue—so long as it is nontoxic. Once you have established a relationship with the individual aspects of the tria prima of your plant spirit ally, you can prepare for the ritual to make your flower essence spagyric.

Although an effective blend can be produced simply by marrying the tincture, essential oil, and flower essence, the real potency of a flower essence spagyric comes from uniting the separate components of salt, mercury, and sulfur together in sacred space. You can make the spagyric even more potent by performing the ritual blending under the most auspicious astrological timing. For example, the Saturnian qualities of an oak flower essence spagyric can be enhanced if it is made on Saturday in the hour of Saturn.* The spagyric of jasmine might best be made under the light of the full moon, while the fiery nature of St. John's wort would be at its height if made into a spagyric on the summer solstice when the sun reaches its zenith. You can consult the flower essence directory in chapter 11 for the appropriate elemental and astrological correspondences for each plant to help you plan when to make your spagyric.

The tools required for making a spagyric are not much different from those required to make an ordinary flower essence. You'll need a dropper bottle to make a stock bottle, or a glass jar or bottle if you plan to make a larger quantity of the elixir. You'll probably want a funnel for adding the tincture. Make sure that all your tools are sterile, as the spagyric contains botanical matter that can become contaminated

---

*The system of planetary hours can be found online, and many apps and websites will calculate the planetary hours for you.

if exposed to microorganisms. An easy way to sterilize your bottles and tools is to boil any glass or metal implements for five to ten minutes. I usually add the dropper caps with rubber bulbs for the last minute of boiling so as not to damage them. Carefully remove the implements from the water and allow them to cool and dry. You will also need tools for the ritual consecration of the spagyric, such as candles, incense, and sigils representing salt, mercury, and sulfur.

Measurements and Ratios

Making flower essence spagyrics is not an exact science. Because they are rooted in vibrational energy, they do not require as much finesse or precision as the conventional approach to making alchemical spagyric elixirs. This is not to say that you can throw caution to the wind; however, there is much more room for creativity. So, when you're considering how much of each of the tria prima to add to your spagyric essence, consider the following guidelines.

Salt

Salt is the base for the flower essence spagyric. Most tinctures are preserved in alcohol or vinegar, thus rendering them an effective stabilizer for the entire spagyric. By the same token, a liqueur or cordial made from the plant or flower also works to preserve the elixir. My friend Candice Covington produces the most amazing flower essence cordials in which she uses a liqueur infused with the same flower from which the essence is made.

If you are using an infusion, decoction, or fresh juice from the plant, plan on adding enough alcohol to preserve it safely. I aim for a one-to-one ratio to ensure that the final spagyric will be shelf-stable. If you are using a homeopathic remedy or diluting the salt because of toxicity, consider using only two to twelve drops of that liquid for a one-ounce dropper bottle filled with a preservative of your choice. When I am doing this, I fill the dropper with the homeopathic remedy or dilution ahead of the spagyric-making ritual so that I'm ready to dispense the drops when it's time.

Mercury

The mercury of the spagyric is easily the component that requires the most caution, as essential oils can be toxic even in minute doses. So long as the oil is relatively safe, you can use a couple of drops directly in your stock bottle of flower essence spagyric; two or three drops in a one-ounce dropper bottle is ample, and a single drop is often sufficient. If your oil is potentially hazardous even at that dosage, consider diluting it in a carrier oil or alcohol, using several drops of the essential oil per ounce of carrier oil or alcohol. Then you can use several drops of the diluted oil in your spagyric to serve as the mercury. Bear in mind that you can always use your spagyric exclusively for external applications if you are uncertain of the safety of the essential oil or any other component.

If your spagyric is stabilized with alcohol, the essential oil will readily incorporate. However, that is not true for other stabilizers, such as vinegar, in which case you should be sure to shake your bottle thoroughly before each use.

Sulfur

The flower essence in your spagyric is the component that requires the least amount of care when it comes to dosage. The measurements are typically the same as for when you are preparing conventional flower essences (refer to chapter 5 for more details). If you use the mother essence, you'll typically need only two to four drops in a one-ounce dropper bottle. If you use a stock bottle of the essence, you can be much more flexible in deciding how much to add. I don't usually plan how many drops of the flower essence I will add to my spagyrics. Instead, I ask the spirit of the plant to guide me in the moment, and I just let the drops flow without second-guessing how much comes out. Often I find a number that matches the number of petals on the flower itself.

Finishing and Storing the Spagyric

After blending and consecrating the elixir in ritual, you will have a fully realized flower essence spagyric. This alchemical elixir should be succussed (shaken) thoroughly to fully incorporate the essential oil. Label the bottle properly and record all the ingredients used, as well as any relevant astrological timing. Store it out of direct light, preferably in a place where it will be safe from accidents and unwanted energies. Your spagyrics are sacred potions that hold the body, mind, and spirit of the plant in each drop.

☽ Making a Flower Essence Spagyric ···✶········✶··

Gather together your tria prima: the flower essence (sulfur), essential oil (mercury), and tincture (salt), or whatever substitutes you may be using for them. Prepare for the ritual by cleansing the space ahead of time. You may want to add symbols of the four elements or other ritual tools according to your tradition or preference. You will need the glyphs for salt (⊖), mercury (☿), and sulfur (🜍) transcribed on paper or wood. I like to burn an incense that corresponds to the plant from which the spagyric is made and to light candles. If possible, I also like to place some fresh or dried flowers, leaves, or other parts of the plant on the altar for the ritual.

Set the altar with your ingredients, placing the sigils of the tria prima in a triangle in the center of the altar and arranging the incense, candles, and any other ritual tools as you deem appropriate. Cast a circle, call the quarters, and evoke deity according to your preference. Then call the plant spirit to join you in the sacred space. Silently or aloud state your intention to create a flower essence spagyric, with words such as:

> Within this hallowed temple and before the gods [or spirits or any other deity or ally you have evoked], I ask for the blessings and guidance of the spirit of [name of plant] to blend and consecrate this flower essence spagyric.

Place your dropper bottle filled with the salt (tincture) atop the glyph for salt. Recite the following:

> I call upon the alchemical salt of [name of plant]. I ask that this tincture be the perfect matrix to represent the soma of [name of plant]. May this salt be the living body of [name of plant].

Draw the sigil for salt over the bottle.

Move the consecrated bottle onto the sigil for mercury. Add the appropriate amount of essential oil to your dropper bottle and recite the following:

I call upon the power of the alchemical mercury of [name of plant].
May it enjoin with the salt within this bottle, adding the psyche of the
[name of plant] to this elixir.

Draw the sigil for mercury over the bottle.

Move the bottle containing the tincture and essential oil onto the sigil for sulfur. Connect to the consciousness of the plant, intending that it guide you in adding the correct amount of flower essence to the elixir. Recite the following:

I call upon the alchemical sulfur of [name of plant]. May this flower
essence carry the pneuma, the very spirit, of [name of plant], as it
combines with the salt and the mercury of this plant to produce a flower
essence spagyric.

Draw the sigil for sulfur over the bottle. Cap it tightly, and shake the bottle vigorously.

Move the bottle into the center of the triangle formed by the three sigils. Hold both hands over it and visualize it filled with the energy of the body, mind, and spirit of the plant. When the spagyric has been thoroughly energized, say:

I fix this elixir with the consecrated energies of the sulfur, mercury, and
salt of [name of plant]. May this spagyric unite the body, mind, and
spirit of this plant to create a healing elixir. So mote it be.

Draw an equal-armed cross over the bottle to seal the consecration.

Once you are done, thank the plant spirit for its participation and guidance. Devoke the deities, release the quarters and the circle, and return to ordinary consciousness. You may want to keep your spagyric on the altar for some time or move it to another safe space between uses.

SAMPLE SPAGYRIC RECIPES

Here are three flower essence spagyrics that you can make at home, with a basic walk-through of how to make each one. Use this information as a guide; listen to the spirit of each plant to adapt the directions to suit your needs and the materials you have available. The following recipes yield a one-ounce dropper bottle. With each one, you'll find some suggestions for practical uses, both mundane and magickal; these suggestions work in addition to the information provided in the directory of flower essences found in chapter 11.

Elderflower

Ingredients: elder tincture (flower, berry, or both), elderflower essential oil, elderflower essence

I've chosen elder as an example because of its magickal and medicinal potency. All of the ingredients are readily available if you are not able to make them at home. Tinctures made from the dried or fresh flowers will produce a spagyric that is more uplifting and spiritually oriented, while those made with the berries will have a more body-centered effect. Elderflower liqueur can be used as the preservative for your flower essence spagyric for an extra level of elder-infused energy; elderflower syrups can be added instead for a nonalcoholic alternative.

Making the flower essence spagyric is relatively straightforward. Follow the instructions on page 231. I might suggest adorning the altar with leafy sprigs, blooms, and clusters of berries freshly harvested from elder—but only if the plant spirit gives you permission first. Use a single drop of the essential oil in the bottle. The most auspicious days to make the spagyric are Beltane (May 1) or the summer solstice (around June 21); otherwise, try making the spagyric on a Tuesday or in the hour of Mars.

Elder as a flower essence spagyric is excellent for promoting recovery from illness. The spirit of elder nourishes us profoundly on each level, physical, psychological, and spiritual, and she helps us tap in to our inherent magick and power. This spagyric is also a powerful offering for spirits. Use a drop or two in a glass of water as an offering to the elder plant whenever you request to harvest from it. The spagyric can similarly be added to offerings of water made at household shrines, at ancestral altars, or during ritual. Added to ritual incense, this elixir may also improve the visual manifestation of spirits being conjured.

Lavender

Ingredients: lavender tincture or infusion, lavender essential oil, lavender flower essence

Lavender flower essence spagyric is likely to be the easiest to make at home, as the components are readily available and affordable. Nevertheless, it might be worth growing some lavender at home so you can cultivate a relationship with it before making an essence from the flowers on your own. For the spagyric's salt, use either a simple infusion or a tincture made from the dried flowers. The essential oil is safe to use neat (undiluted), so several drops can be added to your spagyric to represent the mercury of the plant.

Lavender is traditionally ruled by the planet Mercury, but it has such loving energy (and is often associated with love and romance) that I like to combine the planetary influences of Mercury and Venus; this also underscores the spagyric's use in psychological well-being and nerve support. I recommend performing your spagyric-making ritual in the hour of Venus on Mercury's day (Wednesday) or in the hour of Mercury on Venus's day (Friday).

A flower essence spagyric made from lavender is soothing to body, mind, and soul. It is a tonic for the physical and etheric nervous system. Use it when you feel anxious or tense; taken before bed, it can improve sleep. As a spiritual tonic, lavender flower essence spagyric promotes an unparalleled level of clarity and focus. It can help you maintain an unwavering awareness of your spiritual self and inner wisdom in spite of the chaos of the world around you. Added to the bath, it is cleansing and rejuvenating, and it can be added to a mister to clear the energy of your home or office. Sprayed on the face, it is an instant stress buster. Indeed, lavender flower essence spagyric is a versatile elixir that you can work into many areas of your life.

Oak

Ingredients: oak leaf and flower infusion or tincture, oakwood absolute, oak flower essence

There are many oak species and oak essences available, most famously the English oak (*Quercus robur*) from the Bach line of essences. I have several oak flower essences in my toolbox, including some I've made from local trees, and I recommend making this spagyric from a blend of oak flower essences so you can tap in to the spiritual archetype of all oak trees. Oakwood absolute can be found without too much difficulty, but it should be used in highly dilute form—you can add a single drop to your spagyric, or dilute a couple drops in oil or alcohol and add just a drop or two of that dilution to your spagyric.

After some experimentation I've found that the best tincture for this spagyric is made from a combination of young, fresh leaves and flowers. Accordingly, you will need to make this tincture yourself—you'll need to plan ahead so you can gather the flowers and leaves from your local oak trees. Before harvesting, connect to the spirit of oak and ask permission to take from its body. Leave an offering before you commence. Gather enough flowers and some leaves to fill a small jar, and cover with alcohol to extract the tincture. My preference is to use brandy, as it is usually aged in barrels made of oakwood. If you prefer to make a simple infusion rather than a tincture, make a strong tea from the fresh leaves and flowers by steeping them in hot water for fifteen minutes and then straining the liquid.

To make your flower essence spagyric, follow the instructions on page 231. Oak is typically allied with the archetypes of the god of the forest, the Horned God and the Green Man, so consider evoking an aspect of the divine masculine to oversee this working. Oak is associated with the planets Mars, Jupiter, and Saturn, so Wednesday, Thursday, and Saturday may be auspicious days for making the spagyric. Oak energy is most active in the warmer half of the year, from the vernal equinox to the autumnal equinox; this gives you a wide window for the ritual.

Once it is compounded and consecrated, use your oak flower essence spagyric any time you need strength and support. Not only is it a naturally protective plant spirit, but oak is also attuned to many gods and spirits. Using the flower essence spagyric can help you petition the divine to assist you in any magickal working. It is a wonderful addition to offerings, sacraments, and spells associated with the archetype of the Horned God in his many guises. Medicinally, oak is often used for rebuilding and strengthening tissues in the body, with the tannins supporting the body's natural boundaries, the skin and mucous membranes.[2] The flower essence spagyric strengthens our natural defenses against outside energies, so it can be taken when we feel depleted or we are targeted by unwanted attention and malefic forces. Sprayed, sprinkled, or diffused around the home, the spagyric will maintain an energetic barrier to protect everyone within. Oak is a warrior essence that gives us the strength and resilience to keep moving forward.

11

Directory of One Hundred Flower Essences

Mother Nature tends her balms, banes, and trees in wild spaces and cultivated gardens around the world. Each plant has healing potential, and every plant spirit offers its own mystery and magick. As flower essence therapy grows in popularity, more and more essences make their way to the marketplace. Accordingly, I've selected one hundred plants (and fungi) whose essences are fairly easy to obtain to discuss in detail in this chapter. Each entry includes a mix of information about flower essence therapy and magickal herbalism. You'll find the plant's common and Latin names, plant spirit classification (i.e., balm, bane, or tree), astrological and elemental signatures, associated chakras, and therapeutic indications, as well as a summary of magickal uses. Elemental, planetary, and zodiacal signatures are listed in the order in which they appear in chapter 6. My hope is that the essences listed in this chapter will provide a strong starting point for your practice and inspire you to collaborate with Mother Nature and the spirits of the land to weave profound magick and healing into your life.

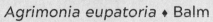

Agrimony

Agrimonia eupatoria ♦ Balm

Elemental signatures: water, fire

Planetary signature: Jupiter

Zodiacal signatures: Cancer, Sagittarius, Pisces

Chakras: root, solar plexus

Magickal uses: healing, protection, reversal, hex breaking, good fortune, changing your luck

Therapeutic indications: avoidance, escapism, hiding behind a cheerful face, perfectionism, uptightness, emotional dishonesty, addiction, anxiety, restlessness, insomnia

AGRIMONY, A MEMBER OF THE ROSE FAMILY, is a deciduous perennial herb. It has dark green leaves with toothed margins, and the entire plant is covered in soft hairs. The flowers are borne on tall spikes; they are five-petaled and yellow and produce burr-like seeds that stick to clothing and fur. Agrimony is common throughout Europe, Asia, and parts of northern Africa. Closely related species are also found in North America and other parts of the world. This plant has been employed in medicine and magick for millennia, and it was one of Dr. Bach's original twelve healers.

As one of Dr. Bach's earliest flower essences, agrimony is indicated when anxiety, fear, and pain are hidden beneath a cheerful appearance. It helps you become more honest about your emotions and encourages you to lean into the discomfort of everyday life and embrace the full range of human emotion. This essence is helpful for releasing perfectionism and enforcing healthy emotional boundaries. Because it offers a sense of emotional honesty and transparency, agrimony essence is useful when you endeavor to release familiar or societal conditioning about what is polite or appropriate, as these patterns from childhood can teach you to repress your true feelings. It invokes a sense of optimism, good cheer, and joy, and it is often the perfect essence for anyone in the role of diplomat or peacemaker.

In folk magick, agrimony is considered the herb par excellence for undoing harmful magick directed toward you. In many European magickal traditions, the herb can be burned to turn away hexes, curses, and the evil eye. It is both protective and cleansing, and it will return harmful spells to their senders, acting as a sort of karmic catalyst. Agrimony is also burned or hung in the home to banish unwelcome spirits; it may also be used to exorcise entities attached to the aura. As an essence, it can be sprayed or diffused to cleanse and protect the home, and a few drops applied to the palms can be swept through the aura to dislodge stagnant energies and foreign entities. Try combining the essences of agrimony and rue for an especially potent remedy for the evil eye; not only do they deflect the baleful energy, but they also help you heal and return to balance.

Agrimony flower essence is indicated for people faced with addiction, especially when that addiction serves as a means of avoiding or anesthetizing emotions. Many occultists and healers recognize that addiction has a palpable presence, a veritable spirit in its own right. In the same way that agrimony was used in magickal herbalism to banish and exorcise spirits, the essence is helpful in tackling the spirit of addiction. It helps treat the root cause of the behavior and addresses the consciousness or spiritual energy of the addiction itself.

In addition to protection, agrimony is also thought to confer the strength and courage you need to face what is dangerous or unknown. The essence leads you toward this same sense of courage, providing the optimism and courage you need to plumb the depths of the pain that you feel unable to share with others. Many people who resonate with agrimony flower essence prefer to hide their pain and avoid conflict of all sorts. The expansive, jovial nature of this plant spirit offers the requisite strength for being more transparent and learning to better communicate your needs and desires. Agrimony flower essence can bolster your sense of resolve and help you go after what you really desire.

The hooked seeds of the agrimony plant yield a signature sometimes used in money magick for drawing business and "hooking" customers; in a similar vein, the flower essence can help boost your charisma and help you make a more authentic connection in a sales environment. Add it to blends alongside other essences traditionally associated with abundance to spray or diffuse in your business or office to increase traffic and boost sales.

Agrimony is known for changing the environment around you.[1] When things look dire or grim, this plant leads to a reversal of fortune; magickally speaking, it can open doors that were once closed to you.

Therapeutically, agrimony essence is helpful when the prognosis is daunting or confusing. Flower essence therapist Pablo Noriega writes that taking agrimony "in processes in which the root of the complaint is unclear—processes that present contradictory symptoms that are difficult to bring together into a coherent story—allows us to dismiss appearances and define their origin."[2] The action of delving deep below the surface of the situation is agrimony's real magick; this plant spirit can help you resolve the pain you feel within, thereby transforming your outer world, too.

Alder
Alnus glutinosa ♦ Tree

Elemental signatures: water, fire

Planetary signature: Venus

Zodiacal signatures: Aries, Pisces

Chakras: sacral, solar plexus, heart

Magickal uses: protection, courage, neutralizing psychic attack, communication with fairies and other spirits, binding, breaking love spells

Therapeutic indications: anxiety and tension, lack of clarity, strong emotions that disturb focus, difficulty seeing below the surface of a situation, inability to find meaning in life events, leaks or tears in the aura

ALDER IS A DECIDUOUS TREE belonging to the birch family, Betulaceae. Its leaves are simple and alternate with serrated margins, and its flowers are separate male and female catkins that bloom on the same tree. Alder is typically found throughout the Northern

Hemisphere in wet and desolate places. It prefers to grow in and near swamps, creeks, ravines, and riverbanks—virtually anywhere it can get its roots into water. This water-loving tree colonizes remote places and is a hardy member of many forests.

Alder is steeped in mystery and lore. It is simultaneously a tree of blessings and of misfortune. In part, this owes to the liminal spaces it inhabits; alder is a mysterious tree that is connected to fairy lore and to the dead. When cut, its wood oxidizes to a deep red or orange color, almost as if the tree bleeds when harmed. This has led to the idea that it is unlucky to fell an alder tree. Alder is also used in defensive magick, especially in preventing psychic or magickal attack, even if it is sent unconsciously. It is also used in binding magick, particularly to prevent harm or poison from spreading, and some folk magick involves breaking alder sticks to symbolically break ties with a home (when moving out) or family (presumably because they have wronged you in some way).

Alder flower essence overlaps with some of these magickal themes. Like many tree essences, it is protective and confers strength to help you meet life's challenges. It is also associated with mental and emotional clarity. It tends to focus its effects on the sacral, solar plexus, and heart chakras, as it draws its energy to the abdominal region as a whole.[3] Alder essence promotes relaxation, even to the extent that it may release physical tension as a result of the release at the mental and emotional level. It offers a reprieve from nervousness and anxiety of unknown origins, such as those arising from external sources of psychic harm. Alder is also tied to themes of survival and self identity; taking the essence promotes happiness and joy and increasing overall well-being, making alder essence perfect for recovery from psychic attack or any other source of stress.[4]

Alderwood provides clues to its action as an essence. First, the tree's affinity for water is a clear signature for the essence's work on the emotional level. The wood is prized for its ability to maintain its strength in water and therefore is used for the foundations of bridges and in other situations where wood will be exposed to water. Alder flower essence enables you to reach deep into your psyche to stay rooted when exploring unknown emotions. Even when emotional currents feel as though they might sweep you away, alder essence helps you maintain your strength and clarity. It offers clear perception, even when you otherwise feel too limited by circumstances or past experience to navigate clearly. It leads you to find meaning in life's lessons, often by plunging deep below the surface of a scenario to see the spiritual underpinnings of life's events.

The second important signature in alder's wood lies in its oxidation to shades of red. The words *alder* and *alnus* are taken from a Germanic root meaning "rust" or "red," referring to the reddening of the wood when cut. Alder flower essence helps stanch the flow of overactive, out-of-control, or unwelcome energies and emotions. Psychically, this can be seen as a leaking or bleeding in the human energy field, and it is often a symptom of trauma or psychic attack. This makes alder flower essence helpful in emergency situations when thoughts and feelings arise rather uncontrollably, often clouding judgment. Alder steers you back toward clarity and confidence.

Alder is often connected to the energies of the divine feminine in magick and ritual. Germanic lore records that the first woman was made of alder, and the first man from ash. Alderwood's oxidation may evoke imagery of menstruation, thereby linking the tree to the womb among ancient people. It is also linked to the planet Venus, another signature for the Goddess. Taking alder essence can help you attune to the energies of the Great Goddess, and it is a welcome addition to the chalice for this reason. In spite of its Venusian associations, alder is an ingredient in breaking love spells, and its flower essence can be used in similar fashion.

Alder flower essence's protective qualities extend beyond the human realm. This tree spirit is a pioneer in the landscape, and it favors nutrient-poor soils that other trees cannot tolerate. Thanks to the nitrogen-fixing bacteria in its roots, alder makes the earth more fertile and paves the way for other plants to flourish. Use alder flower essence to protect, uplift, and nourish the elementals and spirits of the landscape. It is particularly effective as an offering to the spirits of lakes, streams, marshes, and any other watery areas. It can help energetically heal and balance land that has been disturbed by human activity or natural disaster.

Angelica

Angelica archangelica ♦ Balm

Elemental signature: fire

Planetary signature: sun

Zodiacal signature: Leo

Chakras: solar plexus, crown

Magickal uses: protection, uncrossing, exorcism, healing, recovery from psychic attack, psychic development, astral travel

Therapeutic indications: feeling unsafe, sense of being cut off, lack of guidance, abandonment, isolation, disorientation, low self-confidence

ANGELICA IS A MEMBER OF THE CARROT FAMILY, Apiaceae, that likely originated in Syria and has subsequently spread through many parts of the world. It is a biennial, though cultivated specimens often live longer. It has the characteristic hollow stems and umbelliferous inflorescence of Apiaceae, and all parts of the plant exude a pleasing, pungent scent. Its flowers are small and white, clustered in globe-like umbels that bloom in the plant's second year. Angelica is used around the world for medicinal, culinary, and magickal uses.

I learned from my friend and mentor Christopher Penczak that angelica is one of the premier essences for protection. It helps you feel safe, healthy, and protected while also encouraging you to radiate your best self outward. Angelica flower essence defends against outside influences and keeps them from taking root in your energy field as well as in your mind and body. The solar nature of this flower essence helps you get in touch with your inner nature, your divine light, and it brings this light out in all circumstances. Thus, angelica flower essence doesn't merely seal your energy field against harmful external forces; it encourages your sense of sovereignty to blossom so your own light can shine no matter the circumstances you face.

Angelica is named after St. Michael the Archangel, who is a divine protector and sometimes considered to be a divine healer and physician, especially as he presides over springs, rivers, and pools that he has imbued with healing properties. Taking the essence invokes angelic protection and guidance; the plant's umbel-shaped blooms highlight the innate connection between the ordinary self and the network of spiritual guides and guardians that will support you. This essence works on the level of spiritual connection to counteract feelings of isolation, abandonment, and insecurity. By inspiring authentic relationships with the spirit world, angelica flower essence helps you overcome the sense of separation that you experience by incarnating in the material world. Angelica helps invoke the higher self, sometimes called the Holy Guardian Angel or the watcher self (evoking the term *watcher angel* of biblical lore). When you learn to operate with a deeper connection to the higher self, your intuition and psychic faculties are greatly magnified. Angelica therefore helps raise psychic awareness.

The hollow stem and deep taproot of angelica signify its ability to help you move into higher realms while simultaneously staying grounded. Herbalist Pam Montgomery writes, "For those people who always have their head in the clouds, Angelica can help them move into their body and vice versa; Angelica can help those who are stuck to the Earth access loftier realms."[5] She also notes that it helped her color-blind friend see the color purple; perhaps it helps us see what we couldn't see before—the true colors of someone or something.

I find angelica very helpful for astral travel and shamanic journeying. Taking a few drops of the essence beforehand both facilitates the journey itself and offers protection while you're outside your body. The bright, beneficent nature of this essence makes it a helpful adjunct when you are working with baneful flower essences, as it offers balance to the dark and shadowy witching herbs. The hollow stems are a portal through which you can journey, and the essence can thus be helpful in making the journey to the witches' sabbat via spirit flight. In some parts of Germany, the stems are collected in a rite that may be connected to the old sabbat celebration on Walpurgisnacht; I've had the experience of riding a giant stalk of angelica like a broomstick after taking the essence for journey work.

Angelica's connection to the angelic realm can awaken the memory of the watcher angels who taught the arts of magick and witchcraft to humankind and gave rise to the race of witches. Angelica flower essence seems to evoke the primal memory of this rebellious act among the watcher angels, and it awakens the witch blood within. Angelica flower essence helps you reclaim your sovereign power through your magick, and it facilitates contact with the spirit world, especially angels and plant spirits. This essence is a loving, protective, and powerful ally on the witch's path.

Angel's Trumpet
Brugmansia spp. ♦ Bane

Elemental signature: spirit

Planetary signature: Pluto

Zodiacal signature: Scorpio

Chakra: crown

Magickal uses: spirit communication (especially ancestors and angels), rituals related to death and dying, transformation, divination, channeling, astral travel

Therapeutic indications: materialism, fear of letting go, fear of change, fear of death, fear of the supernatural or spiritual or paranormal, denial of the spiritual world, ignoring the spiritual impetus for change, excessive responsibility, sacrifice of self-care, reluctance to delegate, resentfulness, bitterness

MEMBERS OF THE GENUS *Brugmansia* are often called angel's trumpet, a moniker that describes their large, trumpet-shaped flowers. These plants have woody stems and can grow ten to thirty-five feet tall. The flowers are large and pendulous; their five-pointed corolla hangs downward toward the ground. The plants are strongly poisonous and have been used as entheogens for millennia. All extant species of angel's trumpet show evidence of being cultigens, meaning they all show signs of having been altered by humankind for cultivation. No truly wild, undomesticated species exists today, which indicates that angel's trumpet has been used for spiritual purposes far into prehistory.

Angel's trumpet has a long history of magickal and ritual use in its native South America. Although it is toxic, indigenous people have employed it for its entheogenic properties. Taking the plant ritually induces a violent fit and visions, often of the deceased. Traditional uses include ancestral communication, communing with the gods and spirits, and shamanic rites for acquiring an external soul (which resembles the fetch or familiar spirit of European witchcraft in form and function). Among the Jívaro people, angel's trumpet was administered to young boys so they could be reprimanded by the ancestors.[6] The plant was also used to stupefy servants before burying them alive with their deceased masters, and the spirit of the plant was believed to reveal treasures that had been preserved in graves.[7]

In flower essence therapy, angel's trumpet is connected to death and dying. This essence is often reserved for end-of-life care, as it addresses fears and attachments that prevent you from experiencing a peaceful death. An essence of surrender, angel's trumpet releases the hold of materialism, dissolves resistance, and assuages the fear of death itself. Patrica Kaminski and Richard Katz write that angel's trumpet "is used especially for the soul's capacity to experience death, or any profound transformation, in a way which is conscious and free."[8] Paralleling its traditional use for preparing people to face the grave without fear or resistance, the essence of angel's trumpet assists you in facing endings great and small.

Because of its ability to help with transition, angel's trumpet essence is an ideal support for people who have undergone trauma of all varieties. Working with this essence can help survivors of natural disasters, such as floods, hurricanes, and earthquakes; it also supports survivors of abuse. For anyone who is experiencing life differently from how they once knew it, including those who have gone through a divorce, loss of job, or move across the country, angel's trumpet helps you look at the bigger picture from the perspective of the higher self. This can offer a healthy sense of detachment and objectivity from the source of trauma or transition, thereby enabling you to better surrender to the process of transformation. It helps you open your heart and find meaning amid pain and stress.

On a more mundane level, angel's trumpet flower essence helps you let loose and let go when faced with responsibility or when you fear trusting others to get the job done. This essence may be the best remedy for anyone who sacrifices their well-being and freedom for their career; it invites you to be more flexible and patient with others instead of shouldering all the responsibility yourself. In particular, this essence is indicated for people who worry about disappointing others or fear that things will not be done well if they do not do it themselves. This mind-set can yield a state of bitterness, resentment, and impatience, which angel's trumpet counteracts by softening the heart and inviting vulnerability; the essence reminds you when to ask for help and when to practice self-care.[9] This essence also helps you exercise discernment and learn to prioritize your actions for the true needs of the situation, rather than what your ego projects the needs to be.

Like the daturas, its botanical relative, angel's trumpet assists in spirit flight and astral travel. As signified by its five-petaled flowers, it opens doorways to other realms. Although most often used for exiting the material plane, the essence also helps you transcend the physical so you can communicate with other realms more effectively. It also helps release worldly attachments to make for easier and more accurate spirit communication; it helps eliminate the projection from the ego so your psychic perception shines through. *Brugmansia* species are traditionally grown in high altitudes, indicating their proximity to the heavens, the abode of the gods and spirits. The essence helps you commune with spirit guides, angels, devas, ascended masters, gods, ancestors, and extraterrestrial intelligences. Flower essence healer Diane Stein recommends angel's trumpet essence for receiving wisdom from the stars as well as for promoting psychic communication of all types, including mediumship, telepathy, and channeling.[10]

This flower essence is helpful for anyone who has an ingrained fear of the spiritual or supernatural. Whether arising from religious programming or negative experiences, a fear of the occult or paranormal can prevent a practitioner from truly growing. This essence helps you face those fears and remember that not every spiritual experience is warm and fuzzy. Angel's trumpet is sometimes a volatile plant spirit, and the indigenous people of South America often described the plant's indwelling essence as an evil and violent spirit. Although most commercially available essences made from showy hybrids produce gentler effects, some of the cultivars, particularly *Brugmansia sanguinea,* have a more rugged energy in their essences. This plant reminds you that it is not always easy to communicate with the gods, and it serves to help you through challenging periods of change and transition. This flower essence is a potent ally for shamanic rituals for rebirth, initiation, and communion with the spirit world.

Apple
Malus spp. ♦ Tree

Elemental signature: water

Planetary signature: Venus

Zodiacal signature: Libra

Chakra: heart

Magickal uses: healing, love, protection, immortality, wisdom, increasing magickal power

Therapeutic indications: feeling unclean or impure, obsession with appearance or with cleaning, temptation to stray from moral or spiritual principles, spiritual or psychic toxicity, crudeness or lack of refinement, inability to acknowledge growth or change in oneself, trouble maintaining focus or motivation, being spread too thin or overworked, fear, feeling vulnerable

THE APPLE IS A MEMBER OF THE ROSE FAMILY, Rosaceae, and has been an important food source for thousands of years of human history. There are roughly thirty-five species of apples and several thousand varieties cultivated and found wild around the world. The five-petaled flowers are usually pale pink with yellow anthers; they have the classic appearance of a member of the rose family. Apple trees sport a proliferation of flowers in the spring that gradually mature into fruits ready to harvest in the fall.

Apple trees are steeped in legend and lore. Apples have featured in a variety of myths, from the forbidden fruit of biblical lore to the golden apples of the Hesperides, which Gaea gifted to Hera and Zeus at their wedding. The Romans held apples in such high esteem that the goddess Pomona was named in their honor. Apples are sacred to many deities, particularly those associated with fertility, abundance, and the harvest. They are sacred to goddesses of love and romance, too.

Dr. Bach prepared one of his remedies from the crab apple (*Malus sylvestris*), and he considered it to be the remedy for cleansing, recommending it for times when you feel unclean, impure, or otherwise contaminated. Crab apple is also indicated when you are fixated on your wellness or appearance or with rituals of cleansing. The essences derived from other species of apple tend to overlap with this description, and it appears that apple essence overall is both cleansing and nourishing.

Taking apple flower essence results in increased motivation and a clearer sense of purpose. It helps clear away temptation and distraction, both internal and external. It centers you in your heart so that mental distractions will not keep you from being spread too thinly to properly enact your willpower and find motivation to follow through on your ventures.

Apple is a nourishing, detoxifying essence that is a valuable support for overall physical, psychological, and spiritual health. The branches, flowers, and fruit of the apple tree have been used in magick for healing for millennia, and apple flower essence is a valuable ally in any sort of healing magick or wellness routine. It inspires a sense of peaceful clarity that fuels health on every level, in part by encouraging the mind-set that health and healing are attainable. Apple flower essence is particularly adept at clearing away "the fear that magnetizes fear."[11] In other words, it targets the kinds of fears that we tend to experience as self-fulfilling prophecies, like when we fear that a problem or illness will recur, and the stress and anxiety we feal about that possibility leads to its recurrence. Apple flower essence can also be helpful in cases of hypochondria or just in treating fears related to health more generally.

I find apple flower essence to be deeply linked to themes of wisdom, inspiration, temptation, and liberation. If we look at the mythological record, apple is intimately tied to Luciferian images across cultures. The apple is said to be the fruit that the serpent tempted Eve to eat. Golden apples are also found in the sacred garden of the Hesperides, the nymphs of the evening star—another name for the planet Venus, which is the ruling planet of this sacred tree. Lucifer is both morning star and evening star, the embodiment of the planet Venus. Apple flower essence helps you synthesize these Luciferian images by feeding your soul and encouraging inner wisdom to blossom. This quest for wisdom is often born out of experience, both good and bad, including giving in to temptation. Apple represents the dichotomy of the base or crude contrasted with the most sacred and refined. Taking the essence is said to distill qualities of fineness out of your cruder aspects, bringing them out for you to see and admire.[12] Apple flower essence ultimately frees you of feelings of being impure, unloved, unworthy, or unrefined by helping your inner light shine.

Magickally, apple flower essence is excellent for clearing space, cleansing yourself and your tools, and offering clarity before ritual begins. Add it to potions or spells for healing and love. Apple traditionally represents immortality, longevity, and youth, and by preserving your health, the flower essence touches upon similar themes. In love magick, apples help inspire and deepen love in every way. Apple flower essence, in turn, opens your heart and clears away toxic beliefs or behaviors related to love, romance, and sex. It helps you find peace and beauty in the body by clearing away feelings of being contaminated or otherwise impure. Apple flower essence is an excellent addition to offerings to the dead and to deities associated with abundance, fertility, and love. Use it in the chalice to celebrate Samhain/Halloween, which is sometimes referred to as the Feast of Apples.

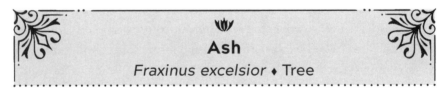

Ash
Fraxinus excelsior ♦ Tree

Elemental signatures: fire, water

Planetary signatures: sun, Mercury, Uranus, Neptune

Zodiacal signature: Pisces

Chakras: root, heart

Magickal uses: protection, curse breaking, fertility, healing, prosperity, love, luck, baby blessings, animal healing

Therapeutic indications: weakness, inability to stand up for yourself, difficulty saying no, being overcritical, feeling out of place or out of touch with your environment, practicality that supersedes spirituality

THE ASH, ALSO CALLED THE COMMON ASH or the European ash, is a flowering tree in the olive family. Its native range stretches throughout mainland Europe and the British Isles. Ash grows to be incredibly tall, upward of 130 feet, and it has strong, durable wood. The tree bears leaves in groups of nine and thirteen and drops them early in the fall.

Sacred to cultures throughout Europe, ash is considered one of the most beneficent and protective of trees and features in many myths. Alongside oak and hawthorn, it was part of the Celtic Druids' sacred trinity of trees; ash is also the World Tree, or Yggdrasil, for the Germanic peoples. It has been variously used to confer protection, prosperity, healing, love, and blessings of all sorts. Several traditions use ash for blessing babies, either by placing the sap on the infant's tongue or by bathing the child in water heated over an ash-wood fire. The flower essence is a suitable substitute for this practice, as it can be dropped in the mouth, sprayed, or added to bathwater for blessings.

Ash has an abundance of uses in healing magick, from being made into wands that draw out illness to being used in spellcraft to transfer sickness to another target. One folk remedy recommends placing ash leaves in a bowl of water and leaving this in your room overnight; it is thought that the ash will avert illness and maintain health. Ash flower essence can be diffused in the room of the sick to help them convalesce, and it may be taken internally to maintain good health. Taking ash essence before healing sessions of any modality encourages you to be a more sensitive, conscientious, and compassionate healer.

Ash is strongly energizing to both the heart and root chakras, thereby endowing you with a stronger sense of what is happening around you and renewing your ability to cope with the world.[13] Ash essence also increases the love within your heart and helps you express your feelings compassionately. This flower essence helps you feel more at home in your body and in tune with the world around you. It encourages greater flexibility and adaptability, and it helps you cultivate greater consideration for those around you. Naturally, ash was once a popular ingredient in love magick, and the flower essence can be used to foster more loving thoughts starting from the inside out.

Ash wood is incredibly strong and durable. The tree's name is derived from the root word *aesc,* meaning "spear" in Old English, for it was preferred for making weapons on account of its hardiness. In turn, ash flower essence promotes inner strength and stability. It helps you cultivate the strength to stand up for yourself and exercise boundaries with tact and compassion. The ash tree, in spite of its great height, doesn't prevent lower plants from receiving sunlight; in a similar fashion, ash flower essence helps you find a way to be in tune with your surroundings even when you are exercising strength and power. During my flower essence training with Sue Lilly, I used ash flower essence to help me enforce boundaries at work in a manner that didn't upset the balance of power. Ash is apotropaic in nature, and it is a fine ingredient in protection potions. It was once believed that eating the buds of the ash tree made you invulnerable to witchcraft,[14] and taking the flower essence stabilizes the energy field as a whole and makes you less sensitive to people and events in your environment.

Ash has long been a protective amulet for travelers; carrying the leaves would ensure a safe return after a long journey. Since it is also connected to the planet Mercury—the planet of travel—and to the World Tree, ash essence facilitates movement between the three worlds via shamanic journey. Ash is also linked to yuletide celebrations. It was burned as the Yule log in some regions, and wassailing cups were occasionally carved from its wood. Today, you can use the flower essence to attune to the winter solstice and celebrate the changing of the seasons and the rebirth of the light.

Basil
Ocimum basilicum ♦ Balm

Elemental signature: fire
Planetary signatures: Mars, Jupiter
Zodiacal signature: Scorpio

Chakras: root, sacral, solar plexus

Magickal uses: love and romance, sex magick, consecration, renewal, protection, courage, exorcism, wealth, astral travel, truth

Therapeutic indications: issues with authority, lack of enthusiasm, aggression, difficulty processing or understanding emotions, compartmentalization of sexuality, disparity between sex and spirituality, shame or guilt related to sexuality, objectification, clandestine behavior, sex addiction

BASIL IS A MEMBER OF THE MINT FAMILY, beloved for its flavor and aroma. An annual or tender perennial, it is cultivated for culinary and medicinal uses, and it is often grown in gardens to attract pollinators. Sweet basil, also known as Genovese basil or great basil, has a sweet flavor and an aroma akin to that of anise. Basil is now grown in many cultivars around the world with a wide range of scents and tastes. Its name is derived from the Latin *basilius,* as well as the earlier Greek *basilikón phutón,* meaning "royal plant" or "kingly plant." Its etymological origins have been conflated with *basilisk,* as the herb was once thought to be an antidote to the venom of this mythical deadly serpent. Magickally, basil has a wide range of uses, from love and sex magick to bestowing blessings, protection, and wealth.

Some of the most common uses for basil in magick include spells and divinations related to romance and sex. The leaves were burned as a means of divining the fidelity of one's mate, and the herb was also used to attract love and ensure fidelity. The scent of basil is said to inspire sympathy between two people and is used as a remedy for lovers' quarrels. Basil's flower essence can also soothe disputes between partners. It is typically used to integrate sexuality with spirituality; it helps when you tend to view these integral parts of the self as opposing forces. It also addresses infidelity, objectification, degradation, abuse, or otherwise destructive sexual behaviors. It works to undo the damage of compartmentalizing sexuality, thereby ameliorating shame, guilt, and feeling unclean as a result of desire and sexuality. Basil essence underscores the holiness of the body and the sacredness of sex. It helps you understand that sexuality of all expressions among consenting adults is sacred, good, and undeserving of judgment. Basil essence thus deepens expressions of love, sex, and intimacy between parters, and it helps sex become a sacred, pleasurable, and joyous act.

Another traditional use for basil in magick is for blessing and protecting the home and family. Sprigs of basil are used to sprinkle holy water in acts of blessings and benedictions. Sprinkling or spraying the flower essence of basil can offer a similar effect. In American folk magick, an infusion made from basil leaves is sprinkled on the doorstep to draw money, success, and luck to the home, while simultaneously driving out evil and protecting the entire family.[15] Add a few drops of basil flower essence and pink salt to a vessel of water to make a magickal floor wash that yields similar results. Basil essence is invigorating and rejuvenating, and it inspires renewal from the soul level outward; try adding a few drops of the essence to the chalice on Candlemas to tap in to the current of springtide energy that is beginning to rise.

Many of basil's properties are ultimately built upon its role as an herb of sovereignty. The plant wears a tall crown of flowers that rise heavenward. The fiery signature of the plant connotes raw power—the power to rule oneself and others. This is not to say that basil flower essence has a dictatorial effect; instead, it crowns you with your own inner authority born from the union of the currents of light and dark, yin and yang, life and death, that dwell within. Basil reminds you that you are love incarnate, and love is the divine law that regulates the cosmos. Basil flower essence invites you to turn inward to find guidance, thus breaking the cycle of seeking approval and direction from an outside source. The regal nature of this flower essence counteracts tendencies toward cruelty, inhumanity, aggression, and violence. Instead, basil flower essence instills patterns of compassionate leadership, mercy, and courage, and it helps you to be assertive when the need arises.

Basil flower essence represents the sacred marriage, or *hieros gamos*. It marries together the polarities that dwell within by honoring both light and dark, life and death, in balanced union. Symbolically, it represents the union between the sacred king, the embodiment of the divine masculine in his archetype as the ruler, and the Goddess as Sovereignty, she who grants the power to rule. The king draws his power from the embodiment of the land, the Great Goddess, and likewise, basil helps you marry the territory of your life. Basil flower essence also helps enthusiasm flourish, and it invites you to channel that energy into helpful and creative outlets. The word *enthusiasm* means "to be filled with the presence of a god" or, less literally, "divinely inspired." This divine inspiration is the direct result of harmonizing the opposing forces that dwell within the psyche; only when you are sovereign over all aspects of yourself can you truly fulfill your mission on Earth and draw forth your innate divinity.

Use basil flower essence in rituals to draw upon the power of the fire element or to call upon fire elementals such as salamanders and dragons. Because of its associations with the sacred marriage, it is also an excellent addition to the chalice for the Great Rite, which symbolizes the union between the God and the Goddess. It helps you move forward when you feel stuck, so try adding it to road-opener spells and potions. Bathing with the flower essence is extremely purifying and protective, and it is a wonderful way to prepare for ritual. Similarly, you can diffuse or spray the essence in your ritual space to create an atmosphere ready for magick. The essence also improves discernment, and it can be used in spells for truth and justice. Witches were said to have drunk the juice of basil before embarking upon their flights to the sabbat, and taking a drop or two of basil flower essence several minutes prior to taking a flying essence blend (see chapter 9 for a discussion of flying essences) can improve your experience and protect you on your astral journey.

Belladonna
Atropa belladonna ♦ Bane

Elemental signature: spirit

Planetary signatures: Mars, Saturn

Zodiacal signature: Scorpio

Chakras: heart, third eye, crown

Magickal uses: protection, cord cutting, shamanic journey, increasing psychic power, victory, love, seduction

Therapeutic indications: poor self-image, feeling unworthy of love and
beauty, repeating karma, self-fulfilling prophecies, emotional pain,
depression

BELLADONNA IS THE MOST FAMOUS of nightshades. Also known
as deadly nightshade, it is a perennial herb native to Europe, northern Africa, and some parts of Asia; nowadays it is also found in the
wild in the United States and India, where it has escaped cultivation.
Related species may be found in many parts of the world. The flowers
are purple-tinged brown with five petals; they are bell-shaped and hang
as solitary blossoms. The berries are an enticing, shiny black, resembling
polished spheres of obsidian. All parts of this plant are poisonous.

The name *belladonna* means "beautiful woman" in Italian, a reference to an old and dangerous beauty custom of applying the juice of the
berries to the eyes to dilate the pupils. The herb has a long-standing connection to love and lust, and many magickal herbalists experience the
spirit of this plant as a beautiful woman. Its energy is often described as
seductive, lustful, and sexual. Belladonna as a flower essence can be used
in magick for love and beauty. It helps conquer negative body image and
feelings of unworthiness caused by past trauma, as it supports you in
plumbing the depths of pain and shadow to find what makes you beautiful. Belladonna flower essence can also be used in spells to promote
honesty and boost attraction in relationships.

Belladonna flower essence opens the gates between worlds. The
genus *Atropa* and its poisonous alkaloid atropine are both named for
the Greek goddess Atropos; she is one of the three Fates, or Moirai.
Atropos cuts the thread of life with her shears, thus making her
responsible for the end of our time on Earth and the beginning of our
journey into the afterlife. Accordingly, belladonna's five-petaled flowers represent the doorway between the living and dead, which makes
it a powerful flower essence for working with the Mighty Dead, the
ancestors of the craft. It also helps with any sort of journey work, such
as astral travel or shamanic journeying, as belladonna was one of the
traditional ingredients in the flying ointments used by witches. It was
used in some cultures to assist in shape-shifting, and it can help you

achieve altered states of consciousness for meditation, healing, and lucid dreaming.

The toxicity of this plant makes it helpful for combating toxic energies and situations in your life—a case of fighting fire with fire, not unlike the homeopathic law of similars. The image of the Fate who cuts the thread of life can be transformed into one of cutting the cords that tie you to harmful people, places, and memories. Belladonna plants cleanse the environment by eliminating toxins in water, and the essence works in the same way to draw out mental, emotional, and spiritual toxins from the human energy field. Belladonna can also help you enforce boundaries, and it is a useful ingredient in banishing spells. Energetically, the essence also clears out trapped karmic energies from the spine and chakra column, thereby helping you become free of the karmic patterns stemming from a toxic past that continue to play out in your life.

Belladonna may be one of the most powerful protective essences. The black berries borne by this plant have long been carried or used in potions to deflect harm. Infusions of deadly nightshade were used by the priests of Bellona, the Roman goddess of war, after whom the plant might be named. Roman warriors also used belladonna to increase their courage and work them into a frenzy as they went into battle, helping ensure their victory. Because of this, the plant has adopted the astrological correspondence of Mars, and the flower essence can be used for courage, bravery, and victory when you are faced with danger. In Germany, belladonna was once known as *walkenbaum,* a name derived from that of the Walküre, or Valkyrie, the female warrior spirits who claim the souls of the deceased.[16]

Therapeutically, belladonna essence represents emotional breakthrough. By removing the illusory appeal that harmful, unhealthy, and unfulfilling people, careers, places, and habits have, it allows you to release them and make space for the next chapter of your life. Belladonna provides insight and understanding into family dynamics and history so you can heal childhood trauma and break generational curses. It was once used medicinally as a narcotic for pain, and magickally it was used to chase away demons, a metaphor for depression, psychosis, and spiritual disease.[17] This flower essence works to give you the strength and inner honesty to lean into the discomfort required to heal the deepest of emotional traumas and dig through the psyche to find the root causes of your pain.

Birch
Betula spp. ◆ Tree

Elemental signature: water

Planetary signatures: sun, moon, Venus

Zodiacal signatures: Leo, Capricorn

Chakra: heart

Magickal uses: love, beauty, fertility, new beginnings, purification, protection, birth, renewal

Therapeutic indications: fear of rejection, feeling disconnected, focus on imperfection, perceiving the self or others as ugly, difficulty seeing beauty in the world, intolerance, lack of empathy, indecisiveness, lack of determination

BIRCHES ARE GENERALLY SMALL-TO-MEDIUM-SIZE, deciduous trees praised for their fine wood. Many species are easily identified by their bark, which is usually marked with horizontal patterns and is quite papery. Birches are relatively short-lived, for trees, but they are valuable pioneer species and are often host to mushrooms. Several birches are found as flower essences, including the silver birch (*B. pendula*) and paper birch (*B. papyrifera*).

Birch is almost universally associated with the Goddess and all manner of feminine energies and traits in folklore and magick. This has earned the tree the nickname of "Lady of the Woods." Birch cradles were once popular to protect newborn children with the tree's maternal energy. Lore tells us that damaging a birch tree might invite the wrath of the Goddess herself. In spite of this warning, birch is a very loving tree, and its wood, bark, and leaves are often used in magick related to beauty and romance. Birch is also employed in rituals for fertility and new beginnings, as well as for protection and purification.

As a flower essence, birch is intimately tied to themes of beauty and relationship. The birch family as a whole invites better understanding and healing in relationships.[18] Birches of all types tend to foster trust, tolerance, empathy, and reconciliation. Use birch flower essence to take ownership of issues in your relationships; the essence can also make you more aware of when it is time to move on from a relationship that no longer serves you.

Silver birch in particular is useful for cultivating the awareness and appreciation of beauty. My teachers Sue and Simon Lilly expand upon this theme in describing birch as follows:

> The spirit of birch brings the ability to experience beauty and calmness. . . . The experience of beauty is more than a simple appreciation of form: it is an acknowledgment and realisation that everything that is rejoices in its own nature, its own life—that simply being is sufficient to create endless joy within oneself. Beauty is the acknowledgement of this simple goodness of being, both in oneself and in others. Without the Awareness of Beauty there can be only separation and division.[19]

Thus, birch flower essence can mitigate judgment of oneself and others and clear away a sense of separation and fear of rejection. By revealing the innate beauty in yourself and the world around you, birch flower essence brings a feeling of deep and abiding peace no matter what is happening around you. Birch invites better communication by allowing you to feel comfortable enough to share your most authentic self, and it helps you communicate with greater tact and empathy. This flower essence helps you find common ground to support reconciliation and improve relationships all around.

Birch is a helpful ally for finding direction and motivation, too. Taking birch essence improves your sense of determination and heightens your awareness of your purpose.[20] It is useful when you stand at a crossroads in life, as it combats the feeling of aimlessness by revealing the path of purpose to you. Birch enables you to see the way to creating more beauty and love in your life, and in the world at large. Birch is calming, clarifying, and relaxing in a way that helps you get in touch with your true self, that part of you that is intimately connected to the bigger picture and radiates light and beauty.

Use birch flower essence in rituals designed to connect to the divine feminine in her myriad forms. It is an appropriate essence for blessing women in all stages of life, as well as for helping men and male-identified people connect with their inner spark of the divine feminine. Birch flower essence is excellent in the bath for rituals that inspire love and beauty, and it is a perfect essence for consecrating the chalice and broomstick or besom. Use birch flower essence in potions or with candle rituals aimed at creativity, inspiration, and new beginnings.

Bittersweet Nightshade
Solanum dulcamara ♦ Bane

Elemental signature: water

Planetary signatures: Mercury, Saturn, Uranus

Zodiacal signature: Aquarius

Chakra: solar plexus

Magickal uses: protection, binding, destruction, spirit communication, psychic development, ancestor magick, shamanic journey, luck and gambling

Therapeutic indications: shyness, feeling trapped, longing for change but difficulty leaving one's comfort zone, impulsiveness, difficulty addressing the shadow self

BITTERSWEET NIGHTSHADE IS A PERENNIAL VINE with a woody stem and arrow-shaped leaves. The flowers are five-petaled, as is the case for many nightshades, with purple petals and bright yellow stamens. It is native to parts of Africa, Asia, and Europe, but this tenacious plant has spread worldwide. It is considered an invasive weed in many countries.

Bittersweet nightshade has long been associated with magick and witchcraft, and its most widespread use is against maleficia and the evil eye. The woody stems were gathered in bundles or fashioned into wreaths to be hung to protect the home. Small pieces of the vine were woven into collars to protect livestock from harmful magick and from otherworldly creatures. The flower essence can similarly help prevent psychic attack and thwart baneful magick.

With its vining growth, bittersweet nightshade lends itself well to magick aimed to bind and detain those who would harm us. Spraying the essence in your space creates a sort of psychic trap, wherein negative entities, thoughtforms, and intentions get tangled in its energy. In Sweden, this plant is traditionally used for harmful and destructive magick,[21] and its essence can be used to target your harmful beliefs and thoughts in a similar fashion, as it will completely envelop them over time, as though the beliefs are slowly choked away by the vines of this nightshade.

As a flower essence, bittersweet nightshade is helpful for people who feel stuck in their everyday lives. It helps those who are shy or trapped by routine stretch beyond their comfort zone, encouraging an adventurous spirit. The essence also helps those who are too adventurous and impulsive, teaching moderation and imparting a reasonable amount of caution and discernment. This flower essence helps you find your way out of struggle, danger, and fear. Its ability to offer boldness and help you assess risk also makes it helpful for conjuring luck, especially when gambling. Try anointing a piece of aventurine with the essence and carry it with you when playing games of chance.

The climbing habit of the plant represents the ability to climb out of the depths of despair. This essence helps you face your shadow self with honesty and a willingness to heal. It helps you see the unseen; like the tendrils that reach out, it helps you feel your way through the darkness of the unconscious mind. It is also helpful for shamanic journeying and astral travel. The signature of this vine is one of climbing to other planes of consciousness, like climbing down to the underworld or climbing into the light of spiritual awareness.

The purple flowers of bittersweet nightshade indicate a psychic connection. Folkloric herbalist Corinne Boyer suggests using the flower essence to induce prophetic dreams; for best results, she recommends making the essence at night, just before the new moon.[22] Bittersweet nightshade essence can also promote spirit communication and may help you forge a stronger connection to your ancestors.

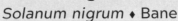

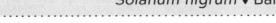

Black Nightshade
Solanum nigrum ♦ Bane

Elemental signatures: earth, spirit

Planetary signature: Saturn

Zodiacal signature: Scorpio

Chakra: third eye

Magickal uses: protection, lunar magick, cord cutting, past-life and generational healing, honoring the dead, connecting to the Dark Goddess

Therapeutic indications: low self-worth, distorted view of body, challenging mother-child relationships, prolonged tiredness, feeling overwhelmed, inability to nurture, fear, aversion to or misunderstanding of femininity

BLACK NIGHTSHADE IS A small-to-medium-size, short-lived perennial plant with an herbaceous stem (though older specimens may have a woody stem), and it has the characteristic five-petaled flowers of the nightshade family. Its blooms are crowned by prominent yellow anthers, and the petals themselves curve backward and are occasionally tinged green. The berries of black nightshade start green and ripen to a satiny black. Some populations of this plant have berries that are edible when ripe, but the alkaloid contents vary from one plant to the next.* While it is much less toxic than deadly nightshade (*Atropa belladonna*), you should not ingest any part of black nightshade without adequate research.

European black nightshade is associated with magick related to protection, death, and the moon. It has been associated with the darker, fiercer aspects of the divine feminine, and the flower essence is use-

---

*The plant described here belongs to a group of related species and subspecies referred to as *Solanum nigrum* complex; the type species (*S. nigrum*) is sometimes called European black nightshade to differentiate it from other members of this complex. The members of this group are visually similar and hybridize easily. Many black nightshades have served as sources of traditional food and medicine in parts of Africa and Asia.

ful for attuning to goddesses aligned with the archetypes of the Dark Goddess. Black nightshade is a powerful ally for attuning to themes associated with motherhood, and its essence helps you examine and transform mother-child relationships. This flower essence is helpful for birthing and nurturing in all areas of life—not just in a procreative sense. Work with this flower essence to increase your feelings of self-worth and confidence so you can better conceive of new ideas and carry your projects to fruition.

Black nightshade flower essence is often used to promote a healthier body image. It tackles ingrained beliefs about your value being tied to your body's ability and beauty. Black nightshade enables you to see the beauty and joy in your body, and it helps you engage with your body intentionally, compassionately, and sensually. The essence may be helpful for alleviating sexual trauma and shame by helping you claim your power and sexuality. It is also deeply tied to issues of subjugation and oppression of all things feminine; it slowly dissolves patterns of ingrained misogyny and allows people of any gender to be in touch with their inner feminin-ity and claim their connection to the Divine Mother.

Black nightshade often grows in desolate, liminal spaces, like aban-doned lots, deserted fields, and roadsides. It is frequently found as a garden weed, and its persistence speaks to some of its use as a flower essence. Black nightshade flower essence is helpful when you feel tired, overwhelmed, or fearful; it teaches persistence, courage, and compas-sion. It is also useful for releasing issues stemming from past lives and unresolved karma. It is adept at countermagick and recovery from malefic witchcraft, whether occurring in this life or previous ones. It may also help you release fears related to spirituality and the occult.

Black nightshade flower essence can be used in meditations, ritu-als, or journeys to assist you in communicating with the ancestors and the Mighty Dead. This makes it appropriate for use in celebrating Samhain or Halloween. The essence can also be sprayed through the aura to dislodge harmful energies resulting from others' magick as well as for releasing your own fears related to magick. It can promote vivid dreams—often lucid ones—and is a gentle guide and protective ally for exploring the underworld.

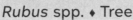

Blackberry

Rubus spp. ♦ Tree

Elemental signature: water

Planetary signature: Venus

Zodiacal signatures: Aries, Virgo

Chakra: heart

Magickal uses: protection, preventing psychic attack, love, healing, increasing magickal power, aligning with your true will, purifying the mind, justice, past-life recall

Therapeutic indications: lack of motivation, procrastination, indecisiveness, frustration, lethargy, feeling unworthy due to lack of productivity, fear of death and dying, infertility

BLACKBERRY, A MEMBER OF the rose family, grows thorny canes that form dense patches of bramble and briar. It bears white (sometimes tinged pink), five-petaled flowers that transform into dark berries. Blackberry has a long history with humankind as food, medicine, and a magickal ingredient. A lot of lore surrounds this plant, linking it to figures such as the fairy folk and the devil. Tunnels and arches of blackberry canes were thought to remove sickness, though they could sometimes provide passage to the land of the fairy folk. Stories also tell of the devil's disdain for this plant, for he landed in a patch of blackberry brambles when he fell from heaven.

Blackberry flower essence can offer protection and healing to the witch who partners with it. The thorny brambles of this plant signify its ability to ward off baneful magick and avert harm. It does this in part by purifying the mind and granting freedom from judgment and bias; this permits you to see things more clearly as they are and take the necessary steps to maintain your health, safety, and success.

Much of the lore around the flowers of the blackberry relate to matters of the heart. Folk herbalist Corinne Boyer recommends using the flowers in love magick "where one is desiring to draw love to oneself, but is in need of protection as well, possibly from a past tragedy."[23] An essence made under the light of the full moon will feel especially maternal and loving, making it a soothing balm for heartache and grief. The flowers are sometimes employed in healing magick to help those who have lost children, and the flower essence can be helpful to someone who has endured miscarriage, abortion, or hysterectomy.[24]

As a flower essence, blackberry is typically associated with finding a lasting connection with one's true will. It is often prescribed for people who have dreams of grandeur but are unable to carry them out to fruition. Often, these people lack motivation, or they use such schemes as a form of escapism. Blackberry invites a sense of resolve that counteracts indecision, lethargy, and procrastination so you can manifest your heart's desire. It is an excellent remedy for the witch or magician whose magick fizzles out because they fail to follow up in the mundane world. Blackberry flower essence grounds your light and your magick from the mental and spiritual planes into the world of form, thereby enhancing any form of spell or ritual.

This essence boosts confidence and self-worth by reminding you that you are capable of manifesting the world you wish to see. It helps you triumph over enemies and obstacles (and it can be a helpful remedy if you are experiencing psychic attack). Work with blackberry essence to explore past lives, forge a deeper relationship with the divine feminine, and initiate contact with the fairies and spirits of the land.

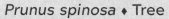

Blackthorn
Prunus spinosa ♦ Tree

Elemental signature: fire

Planetary signatures: Mars, Saturn

Zodiacal signature: Aries

Chakras: root, heart

Magickal uses: protection, curse breaking, connecting to the Dark Goddess

Therapeutic indications: low energy, unstable emotional body, pessimism, stagnation, weakness, despair

BLACKTHORN BELONGS TO THE PLUM GENUS within the rose family (Rosaceae). It has shiny, dark-colored bark; prominent spines; and dense masses of white, five-petaled flowers. The blooms transform into dark purple-black or blue-black fruits called sloes. Blackthorn is common in the English countryside, and it was traditionally grown in hedges to form a boundary between one's property and the outside world, which signals the apotropaic uses of blackthorn in both magickal herbalism and flower essence therapy.

Blackthorn is traditionally used to ward off evil, to break curses, and in all manner of offensive and defensive magick. Branches of blackthorn were commonly made into "blasting rods," or wands used to focus the magician's will to cause or avert harm. The spines have also been used in myriad ways to promote protection, such as warding the home against malefic magick and evil spirits. The essence is similarly protective, and it balances power and strength with a willingness to be vulnerable. As a member of the rose family, blackthorn exerts an influence on the heart center, helping it feel safe even when under attack from the emotions or expectations of other people. This essence synthesizes strength and beauty, making it easier for you to let your guard down to reveal your inner beauty and forge authentic connections with others.

The dense wood of the blackthorn tree has been prized for making clubs and tools, and it resonates with themes of strength and power. Therefore, the essence of blackthorn is strongly empowering, and it enables you to gather your strength and resources to push through challenging circumstances. Taking the essence is energizing and revitalizing, and it helps improve circulation of the blood and oxygenation of the cells.[25] It has a stabilizing effect on the emotions, which can in turn invite a sense of balance and feelings of joy and optimism. According to Sue and Simon Lilly, the spirit of this plant "epitomizes the delicacy and strength of the force of life," and blackthorn's strong spines emphasize the essence's ability to root spirit into matter.[26]

Use blackthorn essence when you are faced with the "dark night of the soul" or any scenario that elicits despair and hopelessness. It brings a grounded strength and heart-centered light to allow you to face your shadow self and combat your most deeply held fears. It is also helpful in addressing self-destructive behaviors and serves to break down illusions grasped by the ego.

Blackthorn is sometimes allied with the fairy folk and with the darker, more feral aspects of the Goddess. The bitterness of its autumnal fruit and dark, shiny wood connote a sense of the dark and wild Goddess, the fierce and devouring Crone. Blackthorn flower essence can be used to attune to cycles associated with this aspect of the divine feminine, such as the waning or dark moon and Samhain or Halloween. Use the essence as an offering to the Crone for assistance with magick for healing and harming alike.

Borage
Borago officinalis ♦ Balm

Elemental signatures: air, fire

Planetary signature: Jupiter

Zodiacal signature: Leo

Chakra: heart

Magickal uses: courage, strength, hope, peaceful home, conflict resolution

Therapeutic indications: shyness, reticence, being withdrawn or antisocial, melancholy, dread, depression, fear of failure, fear of conflict or confrontation, lack of meaning in life, grief, discouragement, low confidence

BORAGE IS A POPULAR MEDICINAL HERB and garden flower that hails from the Mediterranean and is now grown in many parts of the world. It has fuzzy leaves and stems with star-shaped flowers in a brilliant shade of blue. While it is praised for its medicinal qualities, its stems and leaves contain small amounts of toxic alkaloids that are hazardous if consumed in large quantities.

Borage is the quintessential flower of courage. To ensure bravery and banish fear, ancient Roman soldiers ate the plant before battle, and medieval knights brandished scabbards with borage flowers embroidered on them.[27] Most of the magickal and medicinal folklore of this balm relates to lifting the spirits, improving mood, and dispelling melancholy. As a flower essence, borage is adept at helping you achieve lighthearted joy and tenacity. It offers a renewed outlook on life and strength of character that comes from being boldly openhearted.

Borage flower essence sweeps away feelings of melancholy, dread, and depression, and it is ideal for anyone who feels shy, reticent, or withdrawn. Flower essence maker and practitioner David Dalton writes that this essence "excels when one feels burdened by the recurring daily events of life that tax the soul" and that it is helpful for anyone who is overworked, feeling trapped, or facing failure, repetition, and frustration.[28] Borage eases feelings of emotional heaviness, grief, and despair, making it a popular essence for treating a wide range of emotional states. When you feel lethargic, depressed, or just generally glum, borage offers buoyancy to the heart, mind, and soul to help you rise above discouraging situations.

Borage is sometimes used in folk magick for creating a peaceful home, and the essence can be added to floor washes or used for dressing spell pouches, talismans, or candles for the same purpose. It fosters a state of being openhearted, joyful, and filled with peace. Borage flower essence is sometimes indicated for cases of conflict and confrontation, and it can be used in spells aimed at resolving conflict, and perhaps even for court cases to ensure that all parties find peaceful resolutions.

Buttercup
Ranunculus acris ♦ Bane

Elemental signature: fire

Planetary signatures: sun, Mercury, Jupiter

Zodiacal signatures: Leo, Sagittarius

Chakra: solar plexus

Magickal uses: happiness, prosperity, love, pleasure

Therapeutic indications: low self-esteem, self-deprecation, cynicism, impatience, bitterness, patterns of lack or shortage, feeling slighted,

ungratefulness, difficulty accepting help, disconnection from the
inner child, inability to see and share your inner radiance

BUTTERCUP IS A PERENNIAL HERB with bright yellow flowers that
is common in fields and meadows around the world; it was originally
native to Europe and Asia but has been naturalized in many other
regions. The flowers have five petals and five sepals, the latter starting
green and maturing to yellow. Buttercup blossoms are strongly reflective, a characteristic owed to their unique petals. All species of buttercup are toxic; they are strong irritants that may affect both livestock
and humans.

The unusually reflective flowers of buttercup have commanded the
attention of countless children through the ages. A common game is to
hold a buttercup below the chin, and if the chin reflects the flower's yellow hue, one is said to have a fondness for butter. Buttercups represent
richness, indulgence, and abundance. The flowers are used in magick
for cultivating happiness, pleasure, love, and prosperity. As a flower
essence, buttercup also relates to your ability to experience and enjoy
the richness that life has to offer. Buttercup invites you to experience
good cheer, joy, and the sweetness of life. It helps you recognize and
appreciate the resources that dwell within and around you at all times.

Buttercup flower essence is chiefly used for cases of low self-esteem
or lack of appreciation. It clears away self-doubt and helps you find happiness amid the small, everyday moments of life. It invites you to see
your inner light and radiance and recognize the gifts you have to share
with the world. In doing so, it teaches you to celebrate your value, skills,
and unique gifts. Buttercup essence raises self-esteem and ends cycles of
self-deprecation and ingratitude. It helps you maintain a sense of abundance and prosperity, and it can help you find innovative and joyful
ways to succeed in life.

Buttercup flower essence also leads you to a balance between shyness and confidence. If you are overconfident—or overindulgent in
life—buttercup leads you to be more present in the small things, teaching you to revel in the little indulgences and stop trying to project an
image of success on those around you. If you are shy or lack confidence,

buttercup essence helps you feel worthy of success and gently nudges you to step in to your power. It is helpful when you are confronted with high expectations from authority figures, and it helps you exercise boundaries and learn to say no when appropriate.[29]

The bright, solar nature of buttercup flower essence helps you discover hidden talents, express joy, and nurture the light of the soul. The essence assists in the assimilation of all things: food and nutrients, new ideas, and spiritual energies. For this reason, it helps you feed each part of your being, and it is particularly nourishing to the inner child. The essence promotes a sense of childlike wonder and playfulness that brings exquisite joy and light into the world.

Use the essence in rituals and spells for joy and abundance. You can couple it with other ingredients that attract money and opportunity for a more holistic approach to prosperity and abundance. Buttercup flower essence is also useful in fairy magick and bringing light and hope to troubling circumstances. Among the baneful plants, buttercup is unique in its brilliance and lightheartedness.

Cacao
Theobroma cacao ♦ Tree

Elemental signature: all

Planetary signatures: Venus, Uranus

Zodiacal signatures: Taurus, Libra

Chakra: heart

Magickal uses: psychic development, lucid dreaming, sex magick, communion with gods, restoring balance with nature

Therapeutic indications: oversensitivity, numbness, self-sacrifice, self-neglect, feeling selfish for taking care of yourself, poor body image, denial of pleasure, low sex drive, low creativity, lack of inspiration, unhealthy cravings

THE CACAO TREE, source of our beloved chocolate, grows in a natural range from Mexico into the Amazon Basin in South America. This tropical evergreen bears five-petaled flowers that are white with a pinkish calyx. Mature trees may produce upward of six thousand flowers each year, but only approximately twenty of those blooms may yield fruit. The flowers are unusual, for they grow directly out of the trunk and older branches of the tree. Although cacao is properly categorized as a tree, its spirit shares many traits with the entheogenic banes, as it can affect the consciousness when used ceremonially.

The mythic origins of the cacao tree point toward Luciferian gnosis. The god Quetzalcoatl, the personification of light, justice, and the morning star, who is often depicted as a plumed serpent, figures prominently in the mythology of cacao. He is said to have gifted the cacao tree to humanity after stealing it from his twin brother, Xolotl, god of death, darkness, and the evening star. His transgression is akin to that of the Titan Prometheus, who stole fire from heaven and gave it to humanity. Cacao is considered a sacred gift, one that brings enlightenment, healing, and riches to humankind, not unlike the virtues offered by Luciferian figures throughout the world.

Cacao is the essence of communion. The flowers' unusual manner of growth—directly out of the woody bark of the trunk and largest branches on the tree—gestures toward the theme of direct communion with divinity. Taking this essence allows you to have your own personal experience of the gods and spirits. Myths from Central America tell that cacao will rise from the forest when humanity has lost its connection to nature, and the medicine of the plant will restore that relationship. Cacao flower clears the way for you to live in harmony with spiritual truth and the natural order of the cosmos.

The flowers are not borne on intermediary branches, which signifies their ability to break down the religious programming that many of us have, wherein we hand the power to communicate with the gods to intermediaries such as priests. Cacao initiates us into the mystery of priesthood by allowing us to hear the voices of the gods, but only after revealing to us our own innate divinity. The genus name of cacao, *Theobroma,* means "food of the gods" in Greek, and this flower essence nourishes and strengthens the god-self (or higher self, upper soul, and so on) within each of us.

Cacao water was once used in baptisms, though the specifics of this ritual are not well preserved today. Cacao flower essence makes an excellent substitute, and a few drops can be added to pure, consecrated water as a baptismal sacrament to bless and empower anyone undergoing periods of rebirth and transformation.

Therapeutically, cacao essence is indicated when you have lost touch with your true nature. It reminds you that the body is no less important or divine than the spirit. For those who engage in self-sacrifice or self-neglect of any sort, cacao is the perfect remedy. If you ignore your needs or feel selfish practicing self-care, cacao helps you see the body as holy, good, and beautiful. Cacao can help workaholics slow their pace, learn to take naps, and listen to the needs of their physical vessel.

Cacao is great for curbing unhealthy cravings, as it helps you learn to nourish your body in a healthy and holistic manner. Many times cravings for sweets arise from a lack of sweetness in life. Cacao flower essence reveals the sweetness hidden within the heart and sweeps away the obstacles that prevent spiritual growth and flourishing health. It is helpful in cases of low self-esteem, negative body image, or other unhealthy attitudes about the body and sense of self-identity.

Cacao flower essence helps moderate between extremes of sensitivity and numbness. It can help soften conditions characterized by pain and oversensitivity; for this reason, cacao can be used for seasonal allergies and other environmental sensitivities. When you experience emotional numbness and self-denial, cacao flower essence opens the path to restoring sensitivity and worthiness. Cacao is helpful for people in roles like that of counselor and therapist, as it promotes sensitive attunement not only to the needs of the self but to others' needs, too.

Themes of sense and pleasure fall under the domain of Venus, and cacao is inclined toward all manners of Venusian traits. The essence teaches you to indulge your senses and seek beauty, as these are valid methods for honoring your inner divinity. Cacao flower essence transforms sensitivity and numbness into the state of sensuality. Because it also addresses issues related to body image, this essence opens the door to seeing your innate beauty and worth and encourages you to express love through your physical form. It promotes union with the divine within, as well as union with others; it can be used to heighten pleasure and elevate sex and eroticism into spiritual acts. Because it attunes you to the needs of others, cacao flower essence is a wonderful companion for physical intimacy and for sex magick. It can be added to the chalice for the symbolic Great Rite or used by partners engaged in more literal acts of the Great Rite.

This flower essence feeds the light body and nourishes your most holy and divine nature. Because of this, it sharpens your psychic senses and makes dreams more vivid and easier to recall. Taken before bed, cacao flower essence can also promote lucid dreaming and other forms of dreamtime journeys. It can also be balancing to the metabolism and is sometimes recommended for people experiencing any sort of hormonal change, such as puberty, menopause, and menstrual cycles.[30] Cacao makes an utterly exquisite and transcendent essence that brings you closer to bliss and wholeness on all levels.

Calendula
Calendula officinalis ♦ Balm

Elemental signature: fire

Planetary signature: sun

Zodiacal signature: Leo

Chakra: solar plexus

Magickal uses: success, wealth, popularity, attraction, healing

Therapeutic indications: blunt or argumentative communication, unwillingness to listen, harsh or abusive choice of words, frequent misunderstandings, coldness or lack of emotional warmth, sense of isolation, lack of imagination

CALENDULA, ALSO CALLED MARIGOLD and pot marigold, is a member of the aster family (Asteraceae or Compositae). It is an annual plant with brilliant orange flowers whose petals are arranged in a chalice-like shape. The plant is relatively short-lived, and its flowers do not last as long as sunflowers. However, it blooms for much of its life cycle, producing many flowers in a short amount of time. Because it has been cultivated so widely and for so long, it is hard to determine the native range of calendula, though it is likely to have been somewhere in southern Europe.

Calendula is a solar herb that is used in magick mainly for healing, success, and wealth. The round, golden flowers resemble coins when dried, and they are an excellent addition to rituals for prosperity and wealth. With their chalice shape, the flowers are inherently receptive, and the essence makes you more receptive to the blessings of the universe. These cheerful blooms invite peace, joy, and success; the flower essence can counteract grief and help you draw in more solar energy to augment your life force for healing magick or to adapt to the change of the seasons.

Therapeutically speaking, calendula flower essence is largely used to invite you to be more receptive and compassionate in your communication. It is indicated for people who are too blunt, argumentative, or unwilling to listen to what others have to say. Use this essence in times of conflict, impatience, and misunderstanding, and it will foster tolerance, compassion, warmth, and intimacy. The essence enables you to balance speaking and listening and improves personal relationships in all areas.

The therapeutic uses of calendula flower essence align with the traditional magickal uses, which include working with it to make yourself more popular and desirable, as well as to stop gossip. Albertus Magnus, a thirteenth-century Dominican friar and philosopher, described a talisman made from calendula petals and several other ingredients that, when carried, renders no one "able to have a word to speak against the bearer thereof, but words of peace."[31] A German spell uses the root of calendula to make a person more desirable, popular, and attractive to potential mates.[32] If taking the flower essence improves your communication by enhancing your receptivity, compassion, and warmth, then it is a natural progression for it to make you a more attractive mate by allowing you to become more magnetic and radiant and inspiring social success, prosperity, and love. While taking the essence over time will naturally manifest these results, calendula flower essence can also be added to spells and rituals aimed at popularity, success, love, faithfulness, stopping gossip, and conquering challenging circumstances.

Though solar herbs tend to be masculine, calendula's form points to a more feminine signature, and it offers a softening in your speech. Flower essence pioneer Patricia Kaminski writes that calendula "is a notable member of the daisy family because it does not have the radial, star-like blossoms that last a long while, but instead forms soft, curving golden chalices with exceptional life force and repeated blooming. While most plants in the daisy family . . . have more masculine, solar qualities, this extraordinary flower is appropriately called Mary's Gold because it embraces the sun in a feminine manner. Calendula flower essence creates a nurturing, listening and holding place for the 'sun force' of another's individuality."[33] This flower essence can help you better embody the principles of the divine feminine and hold this current of energy throughout your everyday life; it helps you hold your ground through sensitivity, compassion, and radiance so as to combat the hard, cold, and imbalanced masculine energy of the world at large.

Calendula flower essence is deeply tied to the powers of inspiration and creation. It reminds you of the sacred, creative power of your words. The essence also activates your visual and imaginative skills; calendula once held a reputation for being able to heal conditions of the eyes and head and to cleanse your energy if you merely gazed upon the fresh flowers. This visual connection helps you see and process from more than just your intellect. Calendula flower essence links the heart and mind and brings you in touch with your inner truth. It also opens and relaxes the heart-mind and helps you better express your truth. It is a valuable ally for anyone who uses their words or spends time in a creative field, including writers, public speakers, performers, teachers, and artists. The chalice-shaped flowers symbolize the essence's action of making you more receptive to inspiration and the creative potential within you.

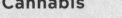

Cannabis
Cannabis indica, C. sativa ♦ Bane

Elemental signature: water

Planetary signatures: sun, moon, Saturn, Neptune

Zodiacal signature: Pisces

Chakras: heart, crown

Magickal uses: peace, happiness, healing, friendship, love, community, psychic development, inspiration, creativity, shamanic journey, spirit communication

Therapeutic indications: attachment, desire, gluttony, wasting of resources, selfishness, seriousness, fear of authority figures, lack of focus, narrow-mindedness, anxiety, depression, dissociation, exhaustion, jet lag, vertigo, ascension symptoms

CANNABIS, THE PLANT WITH A THOUSAND EPITHETS, is a flowering annual herb native to central or southeast Asia. It is grown worldwide today, and it has been cultivated as fiber, food, and medicine for thousands of years, making it one of the oldest plants to form an agricultural relationship with humankind. Many legends the world over attesting to the sanctity of cannabis survive to the present day, and it has been held sacred to numerous gods from disparate cultures, especially Shiva, Parvati, Kali Ma, Freya, Ashera, Ba'al, Amaterasu, and Jah.[34] This unique scenario of a holy plant with such a long history of co-creating with humanity has allowed cannabis to come forward as a plant spirit especially invested in the health and harmony of humankind as a whole.

As a medicinal plant, cannabis has been used to relieve pain, treat anxiety, reduce nausea in chemotherapy patients, increase appetite, reduce muscle spasms, combat depression, and alleviate post-traumatic stress disorder, among many other applications. Spiritually, cannabis expands the consciousness and induces euphoria; people around the globe have harnessed the psychoactive qualities of cannabis to improve their psychic perception, commune with the spirit world, and elevate their consciousness to be closer to that of the gods.

An Indian myth tells us that cannabis sprouted when droplets of amrita, the sacred and magickal nectar that fed the gods, fell from the heavens. Another tale tells of Vishnu churning an ocean to obtain amrita and bring back the lost goddess Lakshmi; the event did return the goddess, as well as giving birth to fourteen precious substances, including the first cannabis plant. Amrita and cannabis were both associated with pleasure, delight, and spiritual awakening. Cannabis was even believed to bestow supernatural powers on those who use it.[35] Perhaps the coveted amrita was the first cannabis flower essence.

Magickally speaking, cannabis is associated with spiritual power, psychic development, and shamanic journeys. Cannabis seed, also known as hemp seed, was until recently used in divinatory practices in Europe, and the smoke of cannabis fueled many an oracle through the ages. The flower essence also supports psychic perception, as it expands the consciousness and widens the perception of the user. It enhances meditation and brings visions of the future, especially when used to anoint the brow or empower a scrying mirror or crystal ball. Try combining it with mugwort flower essence for clearer psychic visions and successful scrying sessions.

The psychoactive qualities of cannabis often promote warm, fuzzy feelings of friendship, love, and community. Occultist and writer Melanie Marquis writes that the "cannabis plant embodies a spirit of kindness and compassion, understanding and unity. It is very much a helper plant for humankind, providing us not only with a sustainable source of food, fiber, fuel, and medicine, but also offering us a reason to get together in the shared comfort of a joyful experience, promoting peace, friendship, and community."[36] As an essence, cannabis imparts this same sense of unity, friendship, and compassion. It is a loving plant spirit that helps combat seriousness by inviting you to lighten up and open your heart to the shared human experience. It can be used in magick for friendship, love of both romantic and platonic natures, and healing communities. It brings people closer together, and it may even act as an aphrodisiac.

Cannabis flower essence is a shamanic tool par excellence. Some ancient shamanic practices employed cannabis as a power plant, while literature from ancient China describes cannabis as making the body light, thus enabling humankind to converse with ghosts and discarnate spirits. In *Witchcraft Medicine,* ethnobotanist Wolf-Dieter Storl discusses the connection between plants and various customs regarding death and dying. Storl explains that burial customs of western Asia once featured cannabis smoke, as the smoke "relaxes the soul enough from the physical construct of the body, making it possible to accompany the deceased part of the way into the regions beyond."[37] Similarly, in India the cannabis plant is sacred to the god Harshana (or Harṣaṇa), who oversees funeral rites. It was used at funerals to permit mourners to witness Shiva claim the souls of the dead and then to dance ecstatically with the god and his retinue of demons and devas.[38] In medieval Europe, cannabis was added to medicinal poplar salves and flying ointments, both of which likely produced both analgesic and psychoactive effects. Cannabis as a flower essence also encourages soul flight and shamanic journeys. Consider adding it to a flying blend (see chapter 9), alongside plants such as datura and tobacco—both historically mixed with cannabis and smoked by the holy men of some sects in India.

A story handed down in some sects of Mahayana Buddhism tells of the Buddha living off a single hemp seed per day; scholars also theorize that the sacred soma plant depicted with the Buddha may actually be cannabis.[39] In the same way that the seeds of cannabis fed the Buddha, the flower essence nourishes you on the soul level so you can have the strength and endurance needed to pursue self-realization. I have personally reaped these benefits of cannabis flower essence. My friend, the late Jamie Lynn Thomas, introduced me to cannabis flower essences at a trade show in 2017. It was my first large public appearance, and I was more than a little travel weary. She offered me a few samples of her essences and directed me to place a few drops of one made from a strain called "Shark's Breath" in a glass of water and to dab that water on the soles of my feet. After I got back to my hotel room, I did just that—and I felt more refreshed than I would have if I'd taken a long nap.

Therapeutically, cannabis flower essence eases tension, anxiety, insomnia, depression, and a slew of other conditions. It helps you get back in touch with your body and the present moment. Smoking cannabis can distort your perception of time, but the essence helps you release an unhealthy attachment to linear time. Cannabis flower essence is evolutionary; it has assisted humankind adapt and innovate for millennia, and it will continue to do so into the future. For this reason, its flower essence alleviates ascension symptoms that result from the onslaught of new energies reaching Earth and human consciousness today.

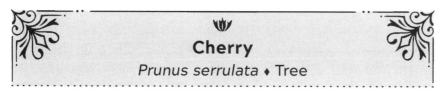

Cherry
Prunus serrulata ◆ Tree

Elemental signatures: air, water, spirit

Planetary signature: Venus

Zodiacal signature: Taurus

Chakras: heart, crown

Magickal uses: love, beauty, innocence, compassion, cleansing

Therapeutic indications: tension or resentment from social pressures, conformity, unwillingness to relax, rebelliousness, attachment, fear of aging and death, difficulty coming to terms with impermanence, grief, lack of empathy, bitterness, inability to forgive, lack of innocence, feeling unclean or impure, being stuck in the past

THE BLOSSOM OF THE JAPANESE FLOWERING CHERRY, known as sakura, is celebrated as a national symbol in the Land of the Rising Sun. More than two hundred varieties are cultivated in Japan, and many are appreciated in other countries around the world as well. Also called the hill cherry and East Asian cherry, this member of the rose family is a small, deciduous tree with densely packed branches rising from a single trunk. Wild cultivars have the five-petaled flowers that are typical of the Rosaceae, often ranging from white to pink, while domestic cultivars may have more sensational blooms. The flowers are short-lived, often lasting about a week, and they appear and fall before the trees' leaves open each spring.

Cherry blossoms symbolize transience and the ephemeral beauty of the world. As a result, they have also taken on the cultural associations of compassion, empathy, and being able to embody both appreciation and sadness when contemplating impermanence. The flower essence of cherry blossom perfectly synthesizes these qualities and helps you cultivate greater empathy, acceptance, and clarity.

Cherry blossom flower essence can help you release fears related to impermanence and death. The trees themselves lose all their leaves and appear as lifeless, branching forms during the winter. As springtime approaches, they explode into a cloud of petals that will soon fall. Cherry blossoms almost command you to be more present in the here-and-now and appreciate that all things come and go in their own time. The essence derived from these delicate flowers plants a seed of trust that there is existence beyond the material, and it can be helpful for addressing fear of death and healing grief. Cherry blossom flower essence also offers profound healing for anger, bitterness, or any other attachment to the past. It inspires you to be more compassionate with yourself and others, especially by recognizing that everyone is affected by loss and impermanence.

When you accept that all things are impermanent in one way or another, a profound sense of clarity and relaxation can take hold, making cherry blossom flower essence helpful for handling stress and tension, too. This essence is particularly well suited to dealing with stresses and social pressures that come from the expectation to conform. It balances the desire to rebel with the need for conformity by helping you remain true to your individuality amid the backdrop of community.[40] Cherry blossom essence can also help you free yourself from unhealthy social obligations and maintain appropriate energy connections and boundaries. This essence invites you release resentment that results from social pressures, and it can mitigate the fatigue and loss of motivation that occur when you consistently resort to conformity. It stimulates a creativity and desire to contribute to the welfare of your community, or perhaps the world at large, by using your unique skills and talents. It helps you remain true to yourself in a changing world, imparting balance and harmony and helping you overcome an attachment to a dualistic worldview.

Cherry blossoms may be used in magick related to love, beauty, forgiveness, and innocence. Author and magickal expert Tess Whitehurst writes that since these flowers "emanate the energy of divine love in an uncommonly pure and potent way, they can be magickally employed to remind us of this love. This lifts our spirits and establishes the energetic atmosphere that will bring greater harmony and blessings into every area of our lives."[41] Like all members of the rose family, sakura are excellent for inspiring love and romance, as well as for attaining inner and outer beauty. Their essence is gently cleansing; it bathes you in a radiant light that helps you release anything that doesn't serve you. As a result, your inner purity, innocence, and beauty shine forth.

Use this essence for springtime celebrations; it is a perfect accompaniment to rituals for Ostara (vernal equinox) as well as in spells for love. Diffuse cherry blossom flower essence in your home for greater peace and to help you detach from the noise of the world and unwind after a day of work.

Cinquefoil
Potentilla reptans, Potentilla spp. ♦ Balm

Elemental signature: fire

Planetary signatures: sun, Mercury, Jupiter

Zodiacal signature: Virgo

Chakras: solar plexus, throat, third eye

Magickal uses: protection, luck, psychic development, love, money, power, wisdom, cleansing, curse breaking

Therapeutic indications: feeling unlucky or stuck, sluggishness or unclear communication, feeling vulnerable to strong or ill-intentioned people, motivation arising from fear, lack of fulfillment in daily tasks, overattachment to material objects, difficulty manifesting your desires

THE NAME *CINQUEFOIL,* MEANING "five leaf," refers to a genus of plants in the rose family. They're known by many other names as well, including tormentil, potentilla, silverweed, barren strawberry, and, especially among practitioners of hoodoo, conjure, and American folk magick, five-finger grass. The classic cinquefoil

(*Potentilla reptans*) has pinnate leaves with serrated margins, usually arranged in groups of five that are vaguely reminiscent of the shape of the hand with the fingers splayed. Yellow, five-petaled flowers resemble the archetypal form of the wild rose. It is found in cooler regions around the world.

Cinquefoil has many magickal attributions, some dating to the medieval period. Herbalist and witch Paul Beyerl asserts that it was connected to medieval witches and their acts of maleficia.[42] English lore holds that wearing a crown of cinquefoil permits one to see fairies.[43] In hoodoo and conjure, this herb has a wide array of magickal proficiencies, including obtaining love, luck, money, power, and wisdom. It is also used in magickal cleansings and the breaking of curses and jinxes.

The essence of this plant is helpful when you need a dose of Mercurial luck and a boost to your communication skills. The dried herb is traditionally carried to bring eloquence, especially when you are asking favors of others. For this reason it is often used in magick related to court cases. I find that taking the essence helps me find the best words for any given situation. Steve Johnson, founder of Alaskan Essences, describes a close relative of cinquefoil as "an important essence for those who have chosen a path of service and healing through communication," saying that it helps "words become living expressions of higher knowledge and spiritual truth."*[44]

Cinquefoil is considered a powerful herb of protection and cleansing, and I find the essence equally as effective. The five-part leaf resembles a hand held up, as if to signal "stop," which likely signifies its protective qualities. The essence is used to clear your energy field from dense, stagnant, and unhealthy energy. These vulnerable spots in the aura can serve as anchor points for other unhealthy energies—and entities—to attach themselves. Cinquefoil essence helps you release the

---

*The plant Johnson was describing is tundra rose or shrubby cinquefoil (*Dasiphora fruticosa*). At the time that Johnson's book was published, tundra rose was classified as *Potentilla fruticosa*. Energetically, I find a fair amount of similarity between essences made from tundra rose and the traditional cinquefoil.

inner causes of these patterns, thereby making you less attractive and vulnerable to people and spirits that might siphon off your health, happiness, and power. Some varieties of cinquefoil flower essence are indicated when a person is motivated by fear, especially the fear of death and dying, as well as when daily life is uninspired, joyless, and unpleasant. These can typically be symptoms of "crossed conditions," a term in hoodoo that signifies having your health, love, success, luck, or power impacted by malicious magick or intent.

Traditional uncrossing remedies often incorporate cinquefoil; as signified by its bright yellow flowers, this essence can restore hope and align you with the healing power of love. It shines a light on your fears and clears the stagnant energies in the aura caused by prolonged fear and misfortune. Take the essence orally, add it to your bath, or spray it liberally in the aura as part of an uncrossing ritual or for general protection and cleansing. Cinquefoil essence can remove attached entities and thoughtforms, too.

Cinquefoil flower essence is helpful for protection during magickal and spiritual pursuits, such as astral travel, shamanic journeying, and spirit flight. The juice of the plant was once used in spells to aid in spirit flight, and the dried leaves have long been considered talismans to protect travelers in the material sense. The flower essence helps prevent interaction with harmful spirits during your more vulnerable out-of-body travels. The essence also enhances other psychic endeavors by stimulating the third-eye chakra; it may help you more clearly see auras and experience clairvoyant visions.[45]

Cinquefoil flower essence is a powerful aid to manifestation and magick of all sorts. I learned early on in my magickal studies that the dried herb can be added to virtually any spell to boost its effects. The hand-shaped leaves lend a sense of agency and power in your magick; the essence helps you manipulate (from the Latin *manus,* meaning "hand") energy and intention to create your desired outcome. However, overconcern with material gain and power are also indications for taking this flower essence. It can rein in out-of-control impulses and desires and clear away attachments to material objects.

✿
Clematis
Clematis vitalba ♦ Bane

Elemental signature: water

Planetary signatures: moon, Mercury, Saturn

Zodiacal signature: Cancer

Chakra: throat

Magickal uses: ecstatic meditation, astral travel, protection for travelers, mental powers, dreaming, cleansing the aura and chakras

Therapeutic indications: daydreaming, dwelling in the future, being distant, drowsiness, absentmindedness, boredom, tendency toward fantasy

CLEMATIS, A MEMBER OF THE BUTTERCUP FAMILY, is a perennial climber native to England and other parts of western Europe. It is sometimes also known as traveler's joy, old man's beard, or beggar's grass. It grows slowly but will gradually engulf trees and other plants, especially along roadside hedges. It was traditionally used for basketmaking and as the raw material for making rope. Though poisonous, the dried stems can be smoked and the young shoots occasionally eaten if prepared properly. There are some instances of clematis being used in traditional medicine, too. Contact with the plant causes blisters to appear on the skin, and even the scent can cause the eyes and nose to water profusely. Ingestion is not generally fatal, but it is unpleasant.

Clematis was one of the first remedies prepared by Dr. Bach, and it was one of only two essences made from plants that are outright poisonous or baneful, the other being star-of-Bethlehem. Bach found clematis to be the appropriate essence for those who were daydreamy, distant, ungrounded, or otherwise not fully present. He described the sort of person who required clematis thus: "Those who are dreamy, drowsy, not fully awake, no great interest in life. Quiet people, not really happy in their present circumstances, living more in the future than the present; living in hopes of happier times, when their ideals may come true."[46]

It is a component of Rescue Remedy, helping people overcome faint and faraway feelings and bringing them back to fuller awareness. Bach went so far as to recommend moistening the lips of the unconscious with clematis flower essence, having had success doing so with his own patients.[47]

Precious little magickal lore is attributed to clematis, though there are some uses that display connections with Bach's use of the essence. Clematis was once used to revive people rendered unconscious by close contact with ghosts.[48] Perhaps the unpleasant effects of the plant could physically revive someone, though the toxicity and ability to grow into a dense hedge might have served as a metaphysical deterrent against invading spirits. It is often said that clematis does the devil's work by invading other plants and choking the life from them. The manner in which clematis crowds out other plants is reminiscent of the way fantasies can overtake more productive thoughts and actions, and hence Bach's indications for its essence.

The astrological associations of the plant point toward its magickal uses. In Bach flower therapy, the essence is often equated with the sign of Cancer and the moon. Author and flower essence practitioner Gaye Mack suggests that the indifference of the clematis type, characterized by being ungrounded and dreamy, illustrates a lunar connection through its connection to night and dreams themselves.[49] Bach also described this essence as the remedy for "the ecstatic," describing the rapture and otherworldly perspective of the clematis person. Though the essence is meant to ground you into everyday life, taking it consciously before bed may facilitate ecstatic and prophetic dreams. Likewise, the essence may be used both to facilitate astral travel and shamanic journeys and to draw the consciousness back to the body afterward. Because of its practical nature, clematis urges you to act on the information or images received in meditation or dreams in order to help create the life you want, rather than simply imagining it.

The liminal nature of clematis, as well as its toxicity, leads to associations with Saturn. It creates a dense border as a hedgerow plant, suggesting that this plant spirit confers protection from harm. Its prolific blooms along the roadside are the impetus for the nickname "traveler's joy," and it is a helpful plant ally for offering protection along the journeys we take in life.

In the Victorian language of flowers, clematis symbolizes cleverness, ingenuity, and trickery—all very Mercurial traits. Taking the essence does in fact boost mental alertness if you are prone to being absentminded.

Finally, clematis flower essence is cleansing to the human energy field. Essences made from several clematis species all support strong cleansing, especially of the central channel along which life force and kundalini flow.[50] Essences made from several varieties of clematis also support karmic healing and help you transform and release the pain of trauma and abuse; these events may be what precipitates a propensity to become an escapist or daydreamer.

❦ Daffodil

Narcissus spp. ♦ Bane

Elemental signature: water

Planetary signatures: sun, Mercury, Venus, Mars, Saturn

Zodiacal signature: Aries

Chakras: solar plexus, throat, crown

Magickal uses: communication, love, fertility, luck, inspiration, clairaudience

Therapeutic indications: dishonesty, inability to hear the truth, egotism

WITH THEIR CHARMING BLOOMS and long green leaves that emerge from buried bulbs, daffodils are emblematic of springtime. Their flowers are six-petaled and usually yellow, with a conspicuous trumpet-shaped corona emerging from the center. All members of the genus *Narcissus* contain toxic alkaloids such as lycorine; the poisonous compounds are most concentrated in the bulbs, and lesser quantities are found in the leaves. Accordingly, the cheerful-looking daffodil is considered a baneful herb. There is much debate over the origin of the genus name *Narcissus*. Many modern sources attribute it to the Greek myth of Narcissus, the beautiful youth who fell in love with his own reflection. Other sources claim that the name of the plant is derived from the Greek word *narkao,* meaning "to numb" (as in *narcotic*).[51]

Daffodils are sometimes employed in magick as a means of attracting love and luck, as well as for increasing fertility. Medieval writings attribute apotropaic powers to the daffodil; it was believed to prevent evil from entering the home and to guard against melancholy. Despite its bright, cheerful color, the flower became associated with Saturn, the underworld, and the deceased. In his 1890 book *The Golden Bough,* anthropologist James George Frazer called the daffodil the "Chaplet of Infernal Gods."[52] The ancient Greeks considered the flower to be a portent of death, and even today it is often planted as a memorial to deceased loved ones. The flower essence can offer much-needed levity when working with underworld deities, while still facilitating communication with them.

The flower essence of daffodil deals primarily with communication. It is among the best flowers to use when you feel too shy or lack the confidence to speak honestly. It's a great help when used before presentations or any sort of public speaking. The essence promotes concise and clear communication through any medium—written, spoken, or otherwise. Daffodil essence also grants you better perspective, so you can see where you fit into the bigger picture; in turn, you can more clearly understand your needs and communicate them to those around you. It is a wonderful essence for speaking and hearing the truth. On the one hand, it enables you to be conscious of your own baggage and find healing by sharing your story with others. On the other hand, it invites you to listen more closely to what others are—and *aren't*—saying. It helps you really listen to the truth behind the words being shared with you. The essence is great for therapists and healers of all kinds, as it enables you to hold space compassionately for others.

On a more subtle level, this essence helps align the subtle bodies with the higher self, thereby clearing the way for you to hear your inner guidance. It strengthens the conical flow of energy from the higher planes into the crown chakra.[53] It promotes greater connection and sensitivity to the voice of divinity—both within and without.

Taking the essence before meditation can facilitate your practice and enhance your ability to hear the still, small voice of the god-self within. It promotes clairaudient faculties, and it is a helpful essence to take before psychic endeavors, such as dowsing and other forms of divination. Some people find that daffodil essence promotes animal communication, too.

Daffodil flower essence is a wonderful balm for relationship troubles, as it helps you listen to your partner(s) with an open heart and mind. It can give you the courage to speak up about issues that need to be dealt with in order for your relationship to grow and flourish. The plant is considered an anaphrodisiac, as it lessens the libido, and the flower essence is indicated for those who rely on physical intimacy and sex as a means of avoiding communication to resolve conflict.

Taking daffodil essence boosts confidence, creativity, and inspiration. Try working with daffodil essence when you have low self-esteem or when you are struggling to overcome egotism. It helps you find your place in the world with equal parts of confidence and humility. The essence is excellent for anyone struggling to communicate their identity or their story, such as coming out of the closet or disclosing other personal details that you fear may alienate others or incite judgment from those around you. Daffodil invites you to be open and honest, but not without a filter; it helps you share as much as is appropriate in any given circumstance. This flower essence also helps you establish a healthy self-image and exercise healthy boundaries.

Work with daffodil essence to help resolve patterns of indecision, financial hardship, and periods of melancholy. Daffodil encourages hope, joy, and optimism grow in any circumstance by feeding your self-worth. By showing you that you are deserving of joy and happiness, daffodil essence allows you to manifest greater abundance, opportunity, and success in your everyday life. Over time, it can help you find your spiritual practice in your everyday life. It helps you make magick out of the mundane by drawing out your inner spark of divinity in each moment.

Damiana

Turnera aphrodisiaca, T. diffusa ♦ Balm

Elemental signature: fire

Planetary signature: Pluto

Zodiacal signature: Scorpio

Chakra: sacral

Magickal uses: love, lust, sex magick, Great Rite, clairvoyance, psychic development

Therapeutic indications: neediness, feelings of inadequacy, imbalanced sex drive, lack or deprivation of sensuality, detachment

DAMIANA IS A FLOWERING EVERGREEN SHRUB that belongs to the passionflower family. It sports bright yellow, five-petaled flowers and is native to Central and South America as well as the southwestern United States and the Caribbean. Most of its magickal lore is associated with love and lust, and the plant has been used in medical herbalism as an aphrodisiac. In American folk magick systems such as conjure and hoodoo, damiana is a prime ingredient for spells for attracting love, improving your sex life, and bringing back a lover who is drifting away.[54] It is also a traditional herbal remedy for treating scorpion stings, and I find that this use underscores the astrological associations of this plant, as it is an herb of Scorpio.

As a flower essence, damiana is focused on love, sex, and sensuality. For those of us with unhealthy attitudes about sex or those who crave touch and sensual fulfillment, damiana flower essence comes to the rescue. Cynthia Athina Kemp Scherer, founder of Desert Alchemy, describes damiana as "an aid for the soul that cries out for physical touch, sex, or sensuality."[55] The essence is recommended for anyone who denies these needs or is otherwise out of touch with their sensuality. Damiana reminds you that sensual touch is not necessarily sexual, and it can help retrain and reprogram your expectations about touch; this makes damiana flower essence useful for people with a history of sex abuse.

Damiana flower essence can help you feel more comfortable in your body, too. Taking this essence can help people who deny physical gratification in favor of mental pursuits; on the flip side, it is equally effective for people who are oversexed. Damiana can help you find sexual equilibrium. It is a grounding essence that also helps you resolve feelings of shame about sex and helps you learn to cultivate pleasure from the five senses.

Magickally speaking, damiana flower essence has its best applications in workings related to love, romance, and sexuality. It can be added to the chalice during the symbolic enactment of the Great Rite and used by participants in sex magick. Damiana fosters authentic connection during these intimate moments. The flower essence also opens the chakras and can induce visions or sharpen other psychic senses; try diffusing damiana with other appropriate essences when you are seeking to practice shamanic journeying or psychic readings. It can be helpful to take alongside flying essence blends (see chapter 9) to ground your experience into your body, especially as you make your return to ordinary consciousness.

Dandelion
Taraxacum officinale ◆ Balm

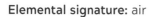

Elemental signature: air

Planetary signatures: Mercury, Jupiter

Zodiacal signatures: Sagittarius, Aquarius

Chakras: sacral, solar plexus

Magickal uses: healing, luck, wishes, summoning spirits, happiness, success, money

Therapeutic indications: tension, rigidity, perfectionism, fear of surrendering control, unrealistic expectations, stubbornness, difficulty listening to and honoring the body's needs

DANDELION IS A TENACIOUS PERENNIAL belonging to the aster family (Asteraceae or Compositae). Its name comes from French *dent de lion,* meaning "lion's tooth"—an allusion to the serrated margins of its leaves. Dandelion has a deep taproot and yellow composite flowers held aloft by tall stalks; the blooms give way to the fuzzy seed heads beloved by those who seek to have their wishes granted. This plant is now widespread around the world, and it has been used as both food and medicine for millennia.

Magickal lore about dandelion often connects it to healing, wish granting, luck, and happiness. The whimsical, jovial nature of the plant has inspired countless children to pluck the seed heads and blow their wishes, alongside dandelion seeds, out into the world. Modern magickal practitioners use dandelion for a wide range of purposes, from success, victory, communication, and clarity to healing and protecting animal companions. Because the plant is ruled by Jupiter, it is also used in spells for success and money.

Dandelions have tough, deep-reaching taproots that are celebrated by herbalists for their medicinal qualities and cursed by gardeners trying to eradicate these plants from their lawns. The roots of dandelions point to the plant spirit's relationship to the underworld and the deep unconscious. The flower essence helps you release lower, unhealthy energies by examining the source of these emotions, allowing you to gain a better understanding of where jealousy, bitterness, anger, and resentment come from. The root is also a signature for karmic and generational healing, as dandelion flower essence helps you resolve old emotions carried from past lives and invites you to move beyond past traumas that you carry with you. This flower essence also brings light to the depths of the soul in order to release fears of inadequacy.

Therapeutically, dandelion is one of the best essences for addressing patterns of tension, rigidity, and stubbornness. It releases tension in the mind and body alike by addressing the root cause of stiffness and transmuting this rigidity into flexibility and adaptability, thereby offering greater strength and endurance. Dandelion flower essence dissolves stiffness that stems from unrealistic expectations. It helps overplanners, perfectionists, and obsessive do-ers learn to listen to the needs of their body and get in touch with their emotions. This flower essence transmutes unrealistic expectations into realistic ones by helping you envision your life holistically, preparing for the flaws that are inevitable. Dandelion essence is vital for relaxation, especially in today's world, where picture-perfect social media posts fuel our desire to keep planning and doing.

Witch and plant spirit expert Cyndi Brannen writes that the "persistence of dandelion to grow anywhere and its refusal to yield to attempts to destroy it are a mighty lesson in living our truth. . . . Dandelion reminds us that conformity is quite boring and requires way too much effort. Thus, the message of dandelion is just to be you—from your emotional roots to your intellectual curiosities."[56] Dandelion flower essence helps you channel a natural intensity and love for life into surrendering into the moment; doing so is a great way to reclaim your power and your identity. Dandelion essence also helps you stand in your truth as a means of addressing the fear of losing control. Taking the essence over time teaches you to accept imperfection as a natural and healthy part of life.

Dandelions are traditionally used as offerings to Hekate, and they are sometimes used in magick to summon spirits. A few drops of the essence potentizes offerings to Hekate, and it can also be used on ancestral shrines or altars to feed the spirits of the dead. Dandelion flower essence can be sprayed or diffused to prepare for ritual, as it keeps you grounded and helps you be more fully present, despite any accidents or imperfections in the ritual itself; simultaneously, dandelion essence cleanses the ritual space and helps participants establish rapport with the spirit world. Dandelion essence is a valuable ally for attuning to the elementals of air (often referred to as sylphs), and it reminds you to use each breath intentionally, thereby nourishing body, mind, and spirit.

Datura
Datura spp. ♦ Bane

Elemental signature: spirit
Planetary signatures: moon, Venus, Saturn, Neptune, Pluto
Zodiacal signatures: Scorpio, Pisces
Chakras: third eye, crown
Magickal uses: death and rebirth, past-life recall, psychic development,

spirit communication, shamanic journey, soul retrieval, attunement to
nature, love, lust, protection

Therapeutic indications: uncertainty, lack of faith, sense of obligation
that supercedes fulfilling personal wants and needs, lack of
imagination, despair, burnout, repetitive karmic cycles, loss of
memory, persistent painful memories, trauma, obsessive thinking,
self-destructive behavior, nightmares

DATURA IS A GENUS OF PLANTS in the nightshade family; their
common name is the same as their genus name, but they're often also
called jimsonweed or thorn apple. Most daturas are night-blooming
perennials with fragrant, trumpet-shaped, white flowers that bloom
after sunset and wither when touched by dawn's light. The flowers
exhibit fivefold symmetry, and some varieties may be purple, yellow,
or bicolored. The common name thorn apple dervies from the spiny,
walnut-size seedpod.

The nature of datura flower essence is expansive, visionary, and
initiatory. When ingested, datura causes intense euphoria and hallucinations, though the experience is often unpleasant and cannot be
remembered. The essence is similarly expansive, invoking a Neptunian
nature that Cynthia Athina Kemp Scherer, founder of Desert Alchemy,
says can help us "go beyond our perspective of a situation, or even perception of ourselves, to be able to find limitless possibilities that exist
beyond that perception."[57]

Datura can be fatal even in small doses, making the flower essence
the safest method for working with this baneful plant. Its association
with death and destruction gestures toward its use in communing with
the spirits of the dead. Datura essence also helps us let go of deceased
loved ones, allowing us to move through the grieving process and find
healing. Taking the essence over time provides understanding of the
cycle of birth, death, and rebirth and facilitates past-life recall.[58] The
trumpetlike flowers facilitate communication with other forms of consciousness, from ancestral spirits to the indwelling consciousness of
plants, stones, and the land. This essence also promotes psychic development, as it stimulates clairvoyance and clairaudience. It promotes

vivid dreams, but it can be used to prevent nightmares and address the fear of the dark.

The flower essence of datura is among the best for facilitating shamanic journeys and astral travel. It opens the gates to the upper and lower worlds, but it can be a challenging plant spirit to work with if you are untrained in the art of spirit flight.[59] I like to use it in blends inspired by the witch's flying ointments alongside essences made from other familiar witching herbs. In shamanic journeys, I find that datura essence also assists with soul retrieval, or the art of finding and reintegrating soul fragments lost during trauma. The sweetness of this flower draws the lost parts of the self back together.

Datura is used by some indigenous people to induce ritual intoxication for rites of passage. One of its hallmark effects is loss of memory, and it was once administered medicinally to women undergoing labor to initiate "twilight sleep," wherein they were completely divorced from the experience of labor and retained no memory of the pain.[60] Accordingly, as a flower essence, this plant spirit offers solace in times when your memory and perception fail you. It can be used to help you forget and release trauma and awareness of old wounds just as easily as it helps you remember that your true nature is not defined by your traumas or your stories.

Datura is one of the best flower essences to turn to when you are faced with the need to release something familiar; it helps you learn to redefine yourself beyond roles such as father, manager, daughter, executive, server, and so on. Not unlike its close cousin, angel's trumpet (which was once categorized in the genus *Datura*), this flower offers a lesson in surrender. Working with datura enables you to embrace uncertainty and the realm of possibility that exists within not knowing.[61] This flower essence invites you to ask yourself what you want to do and who you want to be when you are no longer bound and defined by the way things were. Datura lights the path through the dark to help you find your purpose beyond the limitations of trauma and loss.

Magicians, mystics, and shamans have used datura for both creative and destructive endeavors throughout history. It is often associated with the Hindu god Shiva and the goddess Kali, who are both described in similar terms as creators and destroyers. Datura is said to have sprouted from Shiva's chest, and his devotees make offerings of its flowers and seedpods. Datura essence can help create a sense of new identity, and it can also break down destructive influences in your life, including your own self-destructive habits and beliefs. The essence also promotes connection to the archetype of the Dark Goddess in her many guises, such as Hekate and Ereshkigal.

Datura is often used magickally in workings for love. Its seductive scent indicates a Venusian element in its energy, and many people describe the spirit of datura to be a powerful maiden capable of inducing love and lust. In Mexico, datura flowers are used in love potions, and the flower essence can be used to this end as well. When taken with focused intent, datura flower essence teaches you to release resistance to love and attachment to an idealized, imaginary partner. Try combining this essence with essences of rose and tobacco for a powerful love-drawing elixir.

Dill
Anethum graveolens ♦ Balm

Elemental signatures: air, fire

Planetary signature: Mercury

Zodiacal signature: Gemini

Chakras: solar plexus, throat

Magickal uses: abundance, money, luck, love, mental powers, psychic development, protection, jinx breaking, uncrossing, recovery from psychic attack

Therapeutic indications: overwhelm, overstimulation, hypersensitivity, insomnia, congestion, restlessness, fascination with death, victim mentality, not having or doing enough

DILL IS AN ANNUAL HERB that belongs to the carrot family, alongside Queen Anne's lace and angelica. It is widely cultivated for its culinary, medicinal, and magickal properties. As a magickal herb, dill is chiefly associated with abundance and prosperity, which is owed to its prolific seed production. Dill as an essence also helps magnify and multiply energies, and it is helpful in clarifying and refining the mind and will, thus leading to more competent magickal skills. Work with dill flower essence for magickal intentions such as money, luck, love, and protection to multiply those influences in your life.

Dill is said to bring clarity of thought and is a helpful herbal ally for those pursuing magickal knowledge.[62] This plant unites the mind and the will, which is emphasized in its dual elemental signatures of air and fire. As a flower essence, dill is known to promote discernment. It helps the mind discriminate amid a cacophony of sensory input. This essence sharpens and refines your perception and mental processes, resulting in a deftness akin to that of the athame or ritual knife—the tool associated with the air element. Dill lifts and expands the consciousness, helping to elevate it from the primitive, reptilian parts of the brain. This evolutionary, expansive quality is illustrated by the way the flowers expand out from a common point, creating delightful umbels of tiny flowers.

Dill flower essence can help you process psychic information more clearly. It helps harmonize your psychic nature with the modern world, allowing you to deepen clairvoyant and clairsentient skills and apply them to your everyday life. Truly an evolutionary flower essence, dill can also help you maintain clarity in fast-paced, ever-changing environments. This flower essence is particularly indicated for anyone feeling overwhelmed, overstimulated, or restless. Its Mercurial nature helps you keep calm and clear in demanding situations. It is helpful for people who are weighed down by life, especially those suffering from depression or obsessed with death, or anyone who has a fear of alienation or abandonment. Dill essence brings light to the psyche and helps you integrate information, energy, and spiritual messages without needing to go into seclusion.

Dill essence is an excellent ally when you are targeted by harmful magick, psychic attack, or crossed conditions. In folk magick, dill leaves are used to break jinxes and remove crossed conditions that affect romance.[63] There is also some lore that tells us that dill "robs witches of their will," thereby averting malefic magick. Although this belief is rooted in dill's use in treating colic medicinally, it comes from a time when colic was thought to be caused by malefic magick.[64] Dill's abundant seed production seems like the perfect signature for boosting the potency of magick in recovery from psychic attack and baleful magick; it magnifies the restorative power of your magick and helps the good things in your life multiply.

As a flower essence, dill is recommended for people who have given up their personal power and live as victims.[65] It helps you reclaim your power, in turn bringing shifts in your relationships, both platonic and romantic. Psychic attack is another means by which you lose your power, and dill flower essence can help you recover from such experiences with grace and ease. Part of this is owed to dill's abundant seed production, as described above, which highlights how this plant magnifies positive influences while mitigating harmful ones.

Dill is often used in love magick; an infusion of the seeds can be added to the bath to make a person irresistible. I believe that as a flower essence, dill also makes us more attractive, because it helps us become more confident and composed as it helps us claim our power and exercise healthy communication in relationships. Try combining dill flower essence with other love-drawing plants to manifest a healthy, happy relationship.

Echinacea
Echinacea purpurea ♦ Balm

Elemental signatures: earth, air
Planetary signatures: Jupiter, Pluto
Zodiacal signature: Sagittarius
Chakras: third eye, crown
Magickal uses: healing, protection, strengthening
Therapeutic indications: trauma, abuse, attack, loss of dignity, fractured sense of self

ECHINACEA, ALSO CALLED CONEFLOWER, is native to North America. It is a member of the aster family, Asteraceae or Compositae, and is a popular remedy in folk herbalism. Echinacea bears magenta-pink flowers with orange centers. The disk flowers each carry a long, spiny-looking palea, which gives reason for the genus name *Echinacea,* derived from the Greek *ekhinos,* meaning "spiny" or "hedgehog."

Because it is native to North America, there is precious little magickal lore surrounding echinacea. Author and witch Scott Cunningham reports that echinacea was used by Native Americans as an offering to the spirits to strengthen their rituals and ensure the outcome.[66] Modern practitioners often use the herb for healing and protection magick. The former is owed to its medicinal properties as an immune booster, and the latter likely owes to its strong and tenacious stems and spiny inflorescence. Much in the way that the plant is believed to strengthen the immune system, it strengthens our magickal prowess. Take the flower essence before casting a spell or performing a ritual to enhance your magickal proficiency. Adding the essence to potions, oils, mojo bags, and candle dressings can augment the efficacy of the other ingredients, too.

Echinacea's primary use as a flower essence relates to self-identity. It redefines your relationship to the soul and the higher self and stimulates awareness of the true self, providing context for self-identity beyond what the ego defines. The essence of echinacea provides a sense of balance, support, and connection, especially when you feel cut off from nature, community, and family.[67] For this reason, it is an excellent ally for witches and magicians practicing in urban areas who feel disconnected from the natural world.

Echinacea flower essence provides support to the spiritual immune system in the same manner that the herb works on physical well-being. The immune system copes with changes by monitoring and defending the body from unhealthy change, and a healthy immune system can adapt to changing external environments with ease. On a subtle level, echinacea flower essence helps you accept change without losing self-awareness or suffering a loss of identity. As a flower essence, it facilitates acceptance of new changes, new abilities, and new ways of seeing things; ultimately this helps you develop more effective psychic senses.

Echinacea flower essence stimulates and strengthens the etheric body, sweeping away old and disharmonious energies stored there. The etheric body often contains echoes of old traumas and deeply held wounds; echinacea frees you from these old, stale energies to restore a sense of self and purpose no longer burdened by the weight of the past. This makes echinacea one of the best essences for use when you are faced with trauma. It is the remedy for any sort of violence or assault to your sense of self, whether that comes from physical abuse, injury, illness, or any other painful experience. When these events take place, you may suffer from a loss of dignity and close down your connection to the higher realms. Echinacea offers emotional support and protection while you are in a weakened or vulnerable state; simultaneously, this essence gives you the hope and resiliency to rebuild your spiritual and emotional foundations.

Echinacea works swiftly, and it is helpful in emergency situations. Ultimately, this flower essence works to build a healthy sense of identity rooted in inner peace and spiritual connection. Its effect can be described as "picking up the pieces of identity and putting them back together,"[68] suggesting that this essence can be used for soul retrieval and integrating suppressed or hidden parts of the psyche. It clears away fear, such as the fear of trauma or abuse happening again. It confers the strength you need to heal from trauma and abuse, as well as the strength and perspicacity required for authentic spiritual growth and psychic development. This flower essence works to gently open the upper chakras, especially the crown and third eye, and it can be used to boost clairvoyance. It also addresses fears that arise from psychic development, including the fear that you will gain frightening or harmful information through clairvoyance.

Elder
Sambucus nigra, S. canadensis ♦ Tree

Elemental signatures: fire, air
Planetary signatures: Mars, Venus
Zodiacal signature: Libra
Chakra: third eye

Magickal uses: healing, protection, house blessing, spirit communication and conjuration, clairvoyance, beauty, past-life recall, ancestral healing, boosting magickal power, shamanic journey

Therapeutic indications: intolerance, low self-esteem, negative self-image, lack of vitality, not feeling comfortable in your own skin, aggression, anxiety, sorrow, feeling disconnected from family or ancestral line

ELDER GROWS AS A SHRUB or tree. It has hollow stems and a proliferation of small white flowers arranged in umbels. The flowers yield dark blue-black berries that are famed for their immune-boosting properties. Elder abounds throughout central Florida, where I live, and it has become a trusted ally in my practice with plant spirit medicine.

In folklore, elder is considered sacred to the Goddess, especially in her aspect as the Dark Mother and the Crone. Elder essence can help you forge a deep connection to the Goddess and to the Earth, attuning you to the tides of life and death that ebb and flow with the changing of the seasons. Elder is also associated with the fairy folk and the devil. Elder has a dual nature; once a sacred plant, it was later demonized with the spread of Christianity. These dual forces are embodied in the essence, which helps you explore the dark and unsettling shadow self while teaching you to hold the light of the divine within.

As a magickal herb, elder is traditionally employed in protection and healing magick. It exorcises illness and drives away all manner of evil, including baneful magick and harmful spirits. Elder tree is thought to be the residence of a variety of spirits, and taking elderflower essence can open the channels of communication with the spirit world. Be sure to ask permission before harvesting any part of this plant, even the flowers for essence making, as it is said that the spirits who reside in elder trees may punish unwary humans who harvest without permission. Elder essence also confers second sight; it clears blockages from the third-eye chakra and boosts psychic perception. In addition to clairvoyance and spirit communication, essence of elder helps you understand and interpret dreams with greater fluency.

Elder is closely associated with death and dying in many traditions. Carole Guyett, author of *Sacred Plant Initiations,* notes that elder offers ancestral healing and assists the dead in crossing over.[69] It can facilitate a smoother transition for people who are close to death, and it can ease the grief and fear that their loved ones experience. Try making an offering of a few drops of elderflower essence in your libation of choice when you are preparing to help release earthbound spirits. Anyone who works with the dead and dying or with ghosts can benefit from the spiritual protection and psychic boost that elder essence provides.

As a flower essence, elder is often associated with self-image and self-worth. It shifts negative perceptions of the self (especially when they are related to appearance) and gives you permission to be comfortable in your own skin. It promotes a sense of youthful vitality and assists in recuperation. This flower essence is both calming and stabilizing, and is can be helpful in cases of aggression, anxiety, and intolerance. It catalyzes forgiveness and promotes modesty and humility. The value you find within then radiates outward, dissolving judgment and instilling respect, consideration, and appreciation for those around you.

Elder may be shrouded in dark and devilish folklore, but it is a flower essence of extraordinary light. In many regions, elderflowers bloom around the time of the summer solstice, thus connoting the light and warmth carried within. It is an essence of death and rebirth, and it enables you to hold the light for others. Molly Sheehan, founder of Green Hope Farm Flower Essences, describes this essence as an immense and ancient chalice of light that defies the dark.[70] When Prometheus stole fire from the gods, he is said to have hidden it within the hollow stem of the elder. Similarly, taking this essence reminds you of the hidden light within, so that you can carry light into the shadows. Like the fire-stealing Titan Prometheus or the fallen angel Lucifer, this essence helps you share your light. When you feel misunderstood or targeted for the work that you do, elder essence offers comfort and support. Thus, elderflower essence boosts your magickal potency, increasing the energy that can flow through you as you empty yourself of thoughts of inadequacy.

Add elderflower essence to potions of protection and healing, or use it in any magickal work to boost its power. A few drops of elder can enhance offerings to ancestors, spirits, guardians, gods, or other spiritual allies. Apply some of the essence to your brow to open your psychic vision. Take it internally or spray it around your space for assistance in shamanic journeys, past-life regressions, and attuning to the spirits of the land.

᭦
Enchanter's Nightshade
Circaea lutetiana ♦ Bane

Elemental signatures: earth, water

Astrological signatures: Saturn, Capricorn, Aquarius

Chakra: third eye

Magickal uses: balance, revealing secrets, binding, hexing, transformation, love, manifestation, boosting magickal power

Therapeutic indications: fear of shadows or light, fixation on light and positivity, toxic positivity, spiritual bypassing, avoidance of deep recesses of the mind, addiction or attachment to expansion, spiritual burnout

ENCHANTER'S NIGHTSHADE IS NOT a true nightshade, instead belonging to the willow herb or evening primrose family (Onagraceae). It grows in shady places with only dappled light; it favors a balance of sunlight and shadow to thrive. Enchanter's nightshade is a small, sprawling herb with tiny two-petaled flowers, each one notched or split nearly in two. The Latin name for this plant derives from that of the Greek sorceress Circe, and it is known by a number of folk names, such as witch's grass, Paris nightshade, sorcerer of Paris, great witch herb, and magic wood herb; the name *Paris,* here, refers to the legendary prince of Troy, who started the Trojan War by kidnapping Helen. While it is not toxic, it does contain a high amount of astringent tannins.

Enchanter's nightshade is a curious plant that seems underappreciated today. It's propensity for shadow and inedibility on account of its tannins make it a baneful herb, albeit a rather tame one. Historically, enchanter's nightshade has been used in magick for love and attraction, as its seeds form burrs that cling to clothing and fur, as well as for binding and hexing. It is sometimes used as a substitute for true nightshades, especially when a nontoxic option is needed or preferred. This plant is used today as a general boost to magick and manifestation, owing to its connection to the mythical enchantress Circe. Taking the flower essence helps you cultivate greater magickal power by unifying opposing forces within you and initiating a state of self-mastery. Add it to any spell for a gentle boost, and take it to develop confidence in your magickal and spiritual abilities.

Enchanter's nightshade is rumored to have been one of the ingredients in Circe's potion that transformed Odysseus's men into pigs. As a flower essence, it is strongly associated with inner transformation. This plant spirit helps you manifest the person you wish to be by cultivating greater balance and granting you the self-love and courage you need to be your true self.[71] It is said to release the magick of your true potential and to help you experience connection and communion with all life. By better connecting you to the natural world, enchanter's nightshade essence can promote better communication with plant and animal spirit allies, and it may be used in meditation, trance, and journey to catalyze shape-shifting. I find that it promotes a rich and vivid dreamtime landscape when taken before bed.

The real magick of enchanter's nightshade flower essence comes from its balancing properties; it invites a state of dynamic equilibrium between the polarities of light and darkness. This essence heals imbalances that result from too much exposure to or fixation on the light, and as a result it enables you to find peace, protection, and security in the shadow by releasing fear.[72] It is a great essence for combating patterns of toxic positivity and spiritual bypassing, as it offers grounding via the shadow and a genuine experience of balance. The two-petaled flowers have a strong signature for uniting polar and dualistic forces; the essence reminds you that neither side of the spectrum is more powerful or important than the other, and that the union of opposites creates something greater than the sum of its parts. Take enchanter's nightshade essence to release stale trauma, as well as to overcome feelings of both isolation and being too exposed.

The dualistic and balancing nature of enchanter's nightshade makes it an apt addition to floral potions for the equinoxes, and I find it better attuned to the autumnal equinox. It could be used to mitigate the harm of others' actions, both from its Saturnian (and therefore karmic) influence and because it helps mediate between light and dark, yin and yang, action and inaction. Take the essence before spellcraft or ritual to perform your magick with greater confidence and therefore to improve your magickal results. You can also use the essence to reveal secrets or discover the unknown.

Fir
Abies alba, Abies spp. ♦ Tree

Elemental signatures: earth, water

Planetary signature: Pluto

Zodiacal signature: Capricorn

Chakra: crown

Magickal uses: protection, strength, rebirth, healing, shamanic journey

Therapeutic indications: disconnection from your skills or abilities, pessimism, feeling unsure of the best course of action, indifference, stunted creativity, rationalizing or ignoring feelings

FIRS ARE A GENUS OF TREES in the pine family characterized by short, flattened needles; an erect habit; and cones that stand upright on their branches. They are widespread around the world, and they are beloved for their aromatic foliage—so much so that many species are used as Christmas trees. Fir is rarely used as medicine, and some species can be toxic if mishandled.

Fir is used in magick mostly for protection, healing, and purification. It is connected to the World Tree in some myths and has been praised for its connections to the divine. Fir is sacred to the Keresan people (one of the Pueblo communities) of the American Southwest; in the Keresan mythos, the fir tree was created by the Maize Mother, the principle goddess, and ascending the tree allowed humankind to rise from the lower world.[73] This tale points to fir essence's ability to assist in shamanic journeying and astral travel, especially if you seek to reach the upper world or soar among the stars. Appropriately, the genus name, *Abies,* is taken from a Latin expression meaning "to rise" or "rising one," referring to the great height of the tree.

Fir flower essence is simultaneously grounding and uplifting. It opens the crown chakra and ignites a flow of energy between the root and crown chakras that cleanses and clears the entire energy field. The essence is energizing, providing the drive and empowerment necessary to manifest your desires with your innate wisdom and skills. The tree is traditionally used in protection magick, and the flower essence is similarly protective. Fir essence is protective inasmuch that it brings you into harmony with your inherent skills, thereby ensuring safety and success in all that you do.[74] This flower essence inspires optimism and positive action, granting not only the aspiration for happiness, but the follow-through for achieving it.

Fir also invites practicality, curiosity, and creativity. It brings subconscious beliefs into conscious awareness, and it is helpful to take when you feel disconnected from your passion, purpose, or feelings. Fir essence offers objective insight when you are over-rationalizing or outright ignoring your emotions and their causes. It is gently cleansing, and it can illuminate the path to fulfillment through self-exploration and self-realization.

Fly Agaric

Amanita muscaria ◆ Bane

Elemental signature: air

Planetary signatures: Mercury, Jupiter, Saturn

Zodiacal signature: Gemini

Chakras: root, third eye, crown

Magickal uses: shamanic journey, spirit flight, sovereignty, power, psychic development, purification

Therapeutic indications: narrow-mindedness, rejection, insecurity, fear of criticism, difficulty with expression and communication, old religious programming

ALTHOUGH NOT PROPERLY A FLOWER—nor even a plant—the fly agaric is a powerful witching "herb." Fly agaric is the fruiting body of *Amanita muscaria,* the quintessential mushroom with a wide red cap adorned with white warts. Fly agaric is easily the most widely depicted of fungi, and it is considered humankind's oldest entheogen. Like all mushroom essences, it should be made as a lunar or nocturnal infusion; under the full moon is ideal.

Fly agaric features heavily in the hymns of the Rig Veda, where it is equated with soma, the elixir of the gods. Soma and fly agaric also feature in the cult of Indra, the Hindu god of the skies, storms, and thunder. Shamanic cultures around the world have employed this mushroom as an entheogen, taking advantage of its psychoactive properties. Interestingly, the Maya called the mushroom by names that translate as "lightning mushroom" and "lord of lightning," a parallel shared with its association with Indra in Vedic literature. This connection is underscored by its astrological correspondence of Jupiter, the Roman god of thunder.

Magickal uses for fly agaric are mostly limited to its entheogenic aspects, though it is also employed for psychic development and magick related to sovereignty and power. It is among the ingredients used in the traditional flying ointments of European witchcraft and may have featured into the rituals of early Gardnerian Wicca and in the traditional witchcraft of the British Isles.[75] As a flower essence, fly agaric has a powerful ability to open the third eye that enhances psychic development and psychic travel, such as spirit flight or shamanic journeying. It also purifies the body and mind and clears stale patterns from the energy field.

The essence is used in healing for issues related to expansion and contraction.[76] It helps you open up when you feel constricted or contracted, such as after childhood trauma centered around authority figures (parents, teachers, priests, and so on). It is also sometimes recommended for cases of sex abuse. The essence can be used to treat the pain of rejection and the resulting insecurity, fear of criticism, and difficulty with self-expression. It also can be used to overturn religious programming from childhood.[77] With its expansive nature, it helps with rigid thinking and rigidity in the body.

Fly agaric essence can combat excessive openness by resetting the natural cycles of expansion and contraction. When you are too flighty or imaginative, fly agaric essence can initiate concrete action based upon the information you receive from intuitive and imaginative states. It is a great essence for writers and other creators, as it helps you narrow the focus to achieve tangible results with your craft. The contractive nature is perfect for editing, too, helping you pare down the writing to the essential words.

Fly agaric essence alleviates the intensity of painful emotions by purifying the emotional body; it is most effective when these painful emotional experiences stem from reliving past trauma. It also floods the physical and subtle bodies with light to facilitate astral travel. Work with fly agaric in flying essences to assist in spirit flight. You can also meditate with the essence to connect to the archetypes of the thunder gods, as it helps open your consciousness so you can receive the expanse of the sky itself.

Foxglove
Digitalis purpurea ♦ Bane

Elemental signature: air

Planetary signatures: Venus, Pluto,

Zodiacal signature: Taurus

Chakra: heart

Magickal uses: protection, healing the heart, communication with nature spirits, fairy magick

Therapeutic indications: feeling disconnected, mental fog, confusion, narrow-mindedness, feeling heartbroken, shame, strained relationships, emotional crisis, strong fear (especially fear of change and the unknown), loss of perspective, anxiety about material well-being

FOXGLOVE IS A BIENNIAL PLANT that bears tall spikes of purple-to-pink, bell-shaped flowers in its second year. This plant has enchanted humankind for centuries, and folk etymologies connect foxglove to the stealth of foxes, as well as to the fairy realm ("folk's gloves").

Magickally, foxglove is largely used for connecting and communicating with the fairy folk and with nature spirits. Grown in the garden, it is regarded as inviting to the fair folk and the spirits of the land. Adding the flower essence to your watering can will improve the health of your garden by nurturing the spirits of the plants. Adding a few drops to the ritual cup or chalice makes for a powerful sacrament that connects you to the realm of the green spirits; Christopher Penczak describes a ritual in which the cup-shaped flowers of foxglove are used as a sort of chalice to enhance communication with plant spirits. He describes it as "the holy grail of the green" and states that foxglove "attunes the heart spiritually to the green heart of the land."[78]

In Wales, it was once common practice to protect the home by using dye made from foxglove to paint a cross pattern on stone floors; this was thought to prevent evil from entering the home.[79] A nontoxic alternative is to add several drops of foxglove flower essence to water and use it to mop the floor. You could also add some of the essence to water to diffuse in the home, pour some at the thresholds, or spray it in the air to offer protection.

One of the principal effects of foxglove essence is greater alignment of mind, body, and spirit. It works predominantly on the mental levels, lifting your perspective to that of the higher self, which results in new ideas and offers a visionary new manner of seeing the world. This essence resolves mental rigidity by releasing attachment to the way things have been and offering insight into the best ways to mediate conflict and move forward. Energetically, foxglove flower essence aligns the flow of energy in the body and aura; it draws this energy downward from the crown chakra to the ground. This alignment with the spiritual and mental planes offers clarity and harmony, and it affords better communication in the material and immaterial planes. It also helps build a bridge between the human kingdom and the realm of the nature spirits. Foxglove acts as a translator and mediator between worlds, thereby facilitating communication with plant spirits and other spiritual beings.

Foxglove has been used medicinally for heart conditions since the nineteenth century. As an essence, it is particularly suited to the health of the heart chakra and emotional body. This essence helps nourish you back to wholeness when you feel brokenhearted or emotionally drained. Medicinally, digitalis protects against heart attack; vibrationally, the essence protects the heart against emotional crisis. Foxglove strengthens the heart and prevents it from closing down. It is one of the best remedies to work with when you are experiencing relationship turmoil or strong emotions like grief, anger, confusion, denial, anxiety, and shame. It helps you learn to stand up for yourself while also exercising compassion and sensitivity. Foxglove may be one of the best essences for conflict resolution and compromise, as it promotes sincerity, compassion, and sensitivity for all parties.

In homeopathy, foxglove is used to treat fears related to moving and death. The flower essence is similarly indicated for fear, especially fear of the unknown. Since it opens the heart and helps you align with spirit, a side effect of the essence is greater trust and surrender. This, in turn, helps alleviate fears related to your material well-being. The essence helps promote peace, fulfilling relationships, and pride in the self.

Gardenia
Gardenia jasminoides, Gardenia spp. ♦ Tree

Elemental signature: water

Planetary signatures: moon, Venus

Zodiacal signature: Cancer

Chakras: heart, throat

Magickal uses: healing, love, peace, spirit contact, manifestation, money, divination

Therapeutic indications: indifference, selfishness, unrest, discomfort with or tendency to avoid silence and stillness, blocked or troubled communication, sense of failure, fear of financial hardship, difficulty bringing plans to fruition

THE CLASSIC GARDENIA, *Gardenia jasminoides,* is an evergreen shrub or small tree with dark green, glossy, waxy leaves and fragrant white blooms. It is a member of the coffee family, with a native range throughout many parts of Asia. Wild gardenias usually have six-petaled blooms, though cultivated varieties often display double that number. Other members of the genus *Gardenia* are distributed through tropical and subtropical regions of Africa, Asia, and the Pacific Islands.

Gardenias entered the Western materia magica only through colonialism, which brought the plant into the Western world in the mid-eighteenth century. The seductive fragrance of the flowers allies them with Venus, while their immaculate white color represents lunar energies. Gardenia blossoms are often used magickally for healing, peace, love, and manifestation. The essence can be sprayed or diffused in spaces dedicated to healing and recovery to assist those recuperating from illness and injury by inducing a sense of abiding peace.

Some modern-day practitioners use gardenia flowers in love spells and for attracting new friends. The essence inspires peace, compassion, and loving-kindness, which opens the heart to give and receive love of the highest order, thus helping attract people who are similarly compassionate and caring into your life. As an essence this flower also renews passion for and interest in your partner(s), and it can help you work past romantic plateaus. Gardenia inspires the throat chakra to convey messages of compassion, thus enhancing communication between friends, family, and romantic partners. Bathing with the essence is a wonderful way to invite more love into your life.

Gardenia is sometimes used in money magick and for manifestation. Keeping the dried petals in a purse or wallet is believed to assuage the fear of running out of money. The flower essence also works to ameliorate financial worries; it is an essence of inspiration and creativity that supports your ability to plan for the future. Gardenia essence helps you integrate your personal life with your long-range plans, and it encompasses personal and family-oriented goals with professional ones to ensure balance in all aspects of life. This essence can help you translate ideals and desires into concrete, achievable plans. It is especially useful for teachers, writers, and public speakers; it awakens talents for engaging with language and communication and helps you hone your craft. Gardenia also fosters healthy and effective student-teacher relationships that are rooted in compassion and a desire to help one another learn and grow.

Gardenia flower has among the highest vibrations among the green world, alongside flowers such as rose, lotus, and lemon balm. As an essence, it supports communion with the higher realms and facilitates divination, especially by scrying or spirit communication. Adding gardenia essence to the bath can support you in opening and attuning your mind and spirit to spiritual matters. Gardenia's glossy leaves are a signature for self-reflection, and this essence helps you take inventory of your spiritual progress, as well as your progress in mundane matters. Taking the essence after intense spiritual experiences, changes in consciousness, or after any sort of vibrational or magickal healing session helps you integrate and anchor positive changes while offering you insight so that you can adjust your course for continued growth and healing.

Garlic
Allium sativum ◆ Balm

Elemental signature: fire

Planetary signature: Mars

Zodiacal signature: Aries

Chakra: sacral

Magickal uses: cleansing, protection, courage, curse breaking, exorcism, cursing, underworld magick, lust

Therapeutic indications: fear, paranoia, weakness, parasitic conditions such as spirit attachment or possession, contamination, low energy, overactive or oversensitive psychic abilities, low immune response

GARLIC IS THE TYPE SPECIES of the genus *Allium*, to which onions, leeks, and scallions also belong. It is a fragrant perennial herb that grows from a bulb, and it has been prized for its magickal, medicinal, and culinary uses for millennia. Garlic flowers appear on tall, erect spikes in rounded clusters of white, pink, purple, or bluish starlike blossoms. The mythic origin of garlic is preserved in Islamic lore, which states that it sprouted from the footprint of the devil when he was cast out of heaven.

Garlic's most famous magickal uses are apotropaic. The strong smell, owing to its sulfur content, lends itself to the ability to drive away unwanted influences. Garlic has been used to ward off unwanted visitors of all varieties, from unwelcome houseguests to thieves, malefic witches, poisoners, spirits, and the devil himself. The herb is used to avert the evil eye and evict spirits. Soldiers once carried it into battle to prevent fatal blows from their enemies, an act that highlights the herb's Martian influence.

As a flower essence, garlic is perhaps one of the strongest for combating fear, weakness, and low vitality. It is indicated for parasitic conditions, such as poor psychic defenses resulting in psychic attack or attached entities. When used as a spray, it renders the aura antagonistic to invading influences, thereby preventing psychic attack.[80] Try diffusing or spraying the essence to rid a home or building of unwanted spirits; it can be useful when combined with rituals of exorcism and purification. Some practitioners also use garlic flower essence in cases of low immune response, especially when a client is faced with infection.[81] It may also be used in the garden to remove unwanted pests.

Working with garlic essence promotes vitality and focus. It increases overall health and well-being by first removing harmful energies and entities and then invigorating the body, mind, and spirit so that you make a full recovery. The essence works wonders for clients who are scattered or too psychically open and for those who have experienced rapid spiritual growth without sufficient time to integrate and heal.

The sulfur borne by garlic points to its connections with the liminal goddess Hekate. Offerings of garlic were traditionally left at crossroads as a means of honoring her, and even today, many witches and occultists associate sulfur with Hekate and the underworld, and some use garlic to clear the way to travel into Hekate's realm. This pungent herb is said to grow in her garden, and its essence can be combined with that of other baneful plants under her influence to make a potent magickal blend that can mitigate challenging or unpleasant effects; it cleanses and strengthens the energy field as the baneful plants bring toxic patterns to the surface. Combining several drops each of garlic and potato essences can yield a useful tonic to counteract strong reactions to other essences or any intense spiritual experience.

Garlic flower essence is extremely cleansing and purifying. On a psychological level, it helps you release the unhelpful thoughts you perpetuate, especially with regard to fear, nervousness, insecurity, and anger. The essence draws out positive thoughts to balance and displace the negative patterns, and it reminds you to dream big and imagine positive outcomes. Over time, garlic can help you support the manifestation process and increase the efficacy of your spellwork because it reduces the inner doubts and fears that can derail success.

Gorse
Ulex europaeus ♦ Tree

Elemental signatures: fire, earth

Planetary signatures: sun, Mars, Jupiter

Zodiacal signatures: Aries, Sagittarius

Chakra: solar plexus

Magickal uses: protection, love

Therapeutic indications: hopelessness, resignation, pessimism, joylessness, lack of passion and/or motivation, feeling disheartened, depleted energy, low willpower, withholding or feeling withdrawn from life

GORSE IS A THORNY EVERGREEN member of the pea family. Its leaves form specialized spines that protect and support the plant as it grows. Gorse sports brilliant yellow flowers, scented like coconut, that bloom year-round. The young shoots are used as fodder for livestock, and the plants are sometimes burned as fuel. Gorse, also known as furze, is native to most of western Europe. Though it usually has a shrubby habit, some gorse specimens grow tall enough and with enough verticality to resemble trees.

Gorse is one of the four helpers (and later seven helpers) that Dr. Bach added as complements to his original twelve healing remedies. He prescribed gorse in cases of extreme hopelessness and resignation, noting that it was helpful for people who experienced chronic illness and believed there was no hope of relief.[82] For those who have tried everything to get better to no avail, gorse offers motivation and hope so that they can make an effort to be well again.

Gorse thrives in extreme conditions and desolate places; its brilliant blooms bring hope and sunshine to the wasteland, itself a signature for the action of this flower essence. Julian Barnard, an expert in Bach's remedies, describes the nature of gorse essence in his book *Bach Flower Remedies: Form & Function:* "To raise the energy of the Gorse state, to prick the person back to life, a powerful plant is needed, with a ferocious will to live; something brilliant, resilient, touch and tenacious, a flower that is sensitive and delicate yet strong and ablaze with light."[83] Gorse flower grants hope and imparts conviction and willpower to anyone dispossessed of these qualities.

Gorse is traditionally associated with protection and love in herbal lore. An old saying goes, "When gorse is out of flower, kissing's out of fashion." Since it produces flowers virtually all year long, it is thought to bring joy, passion, and romance into relationships. Gorse flowers are often added to bridal bouquets to ensure a romantic union, and the flower essence can restore faith after lost love. It may be that gorse holds space for hidden places in otherwise desolate spaces where illicit trysts may unfold, pointing toward an interesting link between the desolation and hopelessness of the gorse state and the life-affirming act of making love.[84]

As an apotropaic plant, gorse can be grown in hedges to create a nearly impermeable boundary. It grows so densely, it's said, that even fairies and harmful spirits cannot cross a hedge of gorse. The spines of the plant serve an additional purpose; they interlock in such a way that each branch and each plant supports another. They form a network of support that ensures the safety of the plants, much in the same way that people who benefit from the flower essence of gorse must be supported by those around them.[85] Magickally speaking, the flower essence can be used to conjure spiritual support while instilling hope. It is helpful when you need protection against dire or bleak situations. Simultaneously, gorse strengthens resolve, brings light to the mind, uplifts the heart, and activates enthusiasm and dynamism.[86]

There is a curious bit of lore regarding gorse and attracting money.

Pliny the Elder recorded a method for extracting gold dust from water using gorse, and the golden-yellow blooms have been long connected to sunshine and success. As a result, some magicians use gorse flowers in money magick. Gorse flower essence is best added to money spells when you have dire and urgent need for financial gain; it will boost your resolve to hustle for a payout while maintaining hope that a positive result is possible.

Gorse is a flower of renewal and regeneration. It is known to bloom through the winter, presaging the return of the sun's light after the winter solstice. The essence is excellent for attuning to and celebrating the rebirth of the sun at the Midwinter (approximately December 21) and Imbolc (February 2) sabbats. The height of its bloom is usually later in the spring, but the sheer vibrancy of the flowers makes it a wonderful addition to the chalice during celebrations of the vernal equinox (Ostara) and Beltane (May Day).

Hawthorn
Crataegus monogyna ◆ Tree

Elemental signature: fire

Planetary signatures: Venus, Mars

Zodiacal signature: Taurus

Chakra: heart

Magickal uses: protection, healing, love, divination, fairy magick, exorcism, cursing, curse breaking, communion with the Goddess, communication with the dead

Therapeutic indications: yearning, unrequited love, heartbreak, closed heart, inability to express love and affection, lack of appreciation, ungratefulness, feeling as though life is a struggle, materialism, inability to forgive

THE GENUS *CRATAEGUS* COMPRISES roughly two hundred species of small trees, including the species *C. monogyna,* know as common hawthorn. The name *hawthorn* comes from *haw* or *haga,* meaning "hedge" in Old English, though the tree is also known as whitethorn,

May thorn, quick thorn, May tree, and occasionally thorn apple (not to be confused with datura, which is also called thorn apple). Like its relatives in the rose family, hawthorn has five-petaled flowers, famed for their unusual and somewhat unpleasant odor; they bloom in May in many temperate regions.

Hawthorn lore teeters between light and dark. The more pleasant tales of hawthorn depict it as a tree of healing, love, and connection to other worlds. Hawthorn fruit and flowers were sometimes used in divination, especially to dream of your future love, while their thorns have been used to defend against malice and harm, to break curses, and to cast out spirits and other malevolent beings. On the other hand, hawthorn is clearly connected to death, misfortune, and darkness. The flowers' scent is somewhat like that of decay, and the tree has been sacred to the darker aspects of the Goddess. A popular superstition holds that misfortune and death are sure to follow a flowering hawthorn branch brought indoors in the spring.

As a flower essence, hawthorn is mostly related to matters of the heart. It is among the most important remedies for bringing the heart chakra into perfect balance. It heals a broken heart and opens one that is closed to love. Hawthorn flower essence calms, protects, and cleanses the heart chakra and emotional body. It dissolves barriers to expressing love and affection, and it allows you to be more receptive to the love and beauty all around you. It also promotes trust and forgiveness, and it alleviates stress of all varieties. When your heart is full of yearning, hawthorn brings it into the present moment. This flower essence enables you to cultivate appreciation for the resources already at your disposal and thus combats materialistic impulses.

Magickally speaking, hawthorn essence can be added to spells for protection, love, beauty, and healing. Dew collected from the blossoms on the morning of May 1 was once used as a facewash to ensure a clear complexion and draw love; in a similar fashion, you can add a few drops of the flower essence to a bowl of water and bless it to grant yourself beauty, charm, and love. As noted, thorns from this tree have been used for protection and for driving out spirits for centuries; you can use the flower essence alongside other cleansing and protective essences to encourage unwanted presences to leave your home or land. Hawthorn flower essence can be added to offerings for the fairy folk and spirits of the land, too.

Hazel
Corylus avellana ♦ Tree

Elemental signature: air

Planetary signatures: sun, Mercury

Zodiacal signature: Virgo

Chakra: throat

Magickal uses: inspiration, wisdom, divination, protection, good fortune

Therapeutic indications: sluggish mind, poor memory, stunted communication, poor focus, writer's block, feeling uncertain or directionless, egotism, controlling behavior or desire to be controlled, repressed emotions, overattachment to ideas and expectations

THE HAZEL TREE IS PRIZED for its beloved nuts, a source of nutrition and spiritual sustenance. Native to the cooler climates of the Northern Hemisphere, it bears separate male and female flowers on the same branch. Male blossoms are greenish-yellow catkins overflowing with golden pollen; each catkin consists of more than two hundred individual flowers. Female flowers are solitary and resemble a green bud with scarlet styles protruding like a starburst. Hazel blooms much earlier than its neighboring trees, with the male catkins appearing as early as January or February, giving the flower essence a connection to Candlemas.

The lithe and twisted hazel has a long-standing connection to magick and medicine. The most well-known myth involving hazel is the Celtic story of the Salmon of Wisdom. The salmon lived in a sacred well surrounded by hazel trees. After feasting on nine hazelnuts that fell into the water, the salmon gained all the wisdom of the world, and to feast on that salmon would grant you all the knowledge contained therein. Accordingly, hazel has been a symbol of wisdom, inspiration, and learning. It grants the bardic gift of poetry and eloquence and was thought to magickally confer the ability to understand the language of all things. Use it to heal imbalances of the throat chakra and to support communication on every level. Hazel essence opens the doors to communicating with spirits and devas, too, as it helps you understand all languages, even the language of energy and symbol used by many nonhuman entities.

Hazel flower essence is related to the realm of the mind and wisdom, and taking it offers inspiration and boosts mental faculties. Sue and Simon Lilly write that hazel "brings the flowering of skills. It gives the ability to receive and communicate wisdom and so is excellent for both student and teacher."[87] It helps expand the mind and assists you in integrating new knowledge and skills as you learn them, thereby enhancing memory and recall.

The first time I met the spirit of the hazel tree in meditation, I was shown the scene from the myth of Fionn MacCumhaill in which the hero Fionn gains the wisdom of the hazel tree by ingesting a single drop of fat from the salmon that ate the hazelnuts. The story speaks to the lessons of hazel essence regarding mental clarity and focus in your communication. When your message is clear and concise, the integrity of that message can be translated from one medium to the next with no loss of meaning. Taking hazel essence helps you refine your ability to compose and communicate your thoughts in this way. Try taking inspiration from the myth by adding nine drops of the essence to a glass of water or cup of tea—one drop for each hazelnut eaten by the Salmon of Wisdom—and then drinking it to receive the blessing of hazel.

Hazel flower essence is associated with freedom from attachment, control, and expectation. It instills a sense of wonder and joy that makes every day an exploration, thereby opening the door to releasing egotism and subsequently dissolving patterns of uncertainty, directionlessness, and restlessness. This essence helps you to be truly present in each moment so you can receive the inspiration of everything around you. In this way, hazel is an essence of creativity, helping to break through writer's block and boost creativity and productivity on all levels.

As a magickal tool, hazel branches and twigs were attributed a wide range of uses and abilities. A forked, *Y*-shaped branch of hazel is the preferred divining rod of water witches and dowsers seeking underground wells and buried treasure. The essence can be used to bless tools for dowsing and divination, such as pendulums, dowsing rods, scrying mirrors, and runes. Taking the essence can enhance divination by allowing you to detach from expectation and come with a sense of impartiality and openness to whatever message may arise. Hazel is considered the best material for a magician's wand, and it will greatly focus and amplify the energy of whoever wields it. Try blessing your own wand with holy water to which you have added nine drops of hazel essence.

Much folklore regarding the protective nature of hazel persists into the present day. In particular, hazel twigs and wood were believed to prevent attack from serpents and to ward against thunderstorms. The tree is considered sacred to thunder and storm gods, such as Thor, and it is often used in weather magick. The essence may not prevent lightning from striking or snakes from biting, but it may be useful in recovering from feeling as though your ego was attacked or stung by sharp words or unexpected criticism. The tree is often referred to as "Lady Hazel" and is sacred to the Great Mother and to the fairy folk. Use the essence as an offering to build relationships with the fairy folk (and other spirits of the land) and to learn the mysteries of the Great Mother.

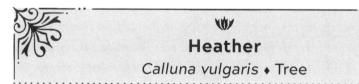

Heather
Calluna vulgaris ♦ Tree

Elemental signature: water

Planetary signature: Venus

Zodiacal signature: Taurus

Chakra: crown

Magickal uses: protection, purification, luck, weather magick, summoning ghosts, ancestral magick

Therapeutic indications: self-absorption, talkativeness, craving for attention, unconscious draining of others' energy

COMMON HEATHER, also called ling, is a low evergreen shrub with tiny magenta flowers clustered together densely in the late summer and fall. Though it grows across much of northern Eurasia and has naturalized in parts of North America, heather is regarded as emblematic of the Scottish countryside, and it has been an important botanical among the people of the British Isles, where it is used in thatched roofs, brooms, and rope as well as for bedding and fuel.

Like gorse (see page 313), heather is one of the four helpers (and later seven helpers) that Dr. Bach designated as complements to his original twelve remedies. Bach recommended heather for people whose self-centeredness drives others away. People in the heather state are lonely, and so they latch on to whoever will listen to them talk about their own life—and particularly their problems—until the listening party grows tired of it and leaves. Thus, heather types are lonely people who create a self-fulfilling prophecy: their overcompensation creates further loneliness.

People who unconsciously drain the psychic energy of others also benefit from heather. These psychic vampires are so hungry for recognition that they make up for it by siphoning more than just attention, and they can leave you feeling utterly drained. We see this in the signature of the plant, as described by author and essence-maker Julian Barnard: "[Heather's] flowers cluster on stalks crowding so densely that the impression is of a massed colour rather than individual plants. Heather forms a specialized habitat, where each plant shelters its neighbour, so there is a closeness there. It builds into a miniature forest, excluding other species. This indicates the tendency of Heather people to sap the vitality of others, with their need for closeness and constant chatter."[88] In extreme examples, a person in such a state may learn to manipulate psychic energy in order to manipulate others, compelling them to listen to their problems.[89] Heather flower essence nourishes the feeling of emptiness that drives these behaviors and cultivates compassion and self-sufficiency.

Magickally speaking, heather is used mostly in spells aimed at protection and luck. Dried heather, when carried, is said to prevent violent crime and keep intruders out. This appears to be an inversion of the indications for the flower essence, which can be taken when you intrude upon the energy of others. Try diffusing or wearing the essence if you will be around people who have a tendency to drain your energy, and it may help you be mindful of your own boundaries.* Perhaps it will even inspire them to be more mindful of their tendency to drain the energy of their audience.

Heather has a curious connection to the dead. Scott Cunningham notes that it is used to conjure ghosts,[90] while Tess Whitehurst suggests that it may be used for connecting with your ancestors and for attaining ancestral wisdom[91] One legend tells us that the color of the flowers is derived from blood spilled in battle, and thus the flower continues to mourn those precious lives lost. You might consider adding the essence to ancestral offerings as a means of honoring your loved ones on the other side. The flower essence works very strongly on bringing consciousness into the present moment and releasing pent-up feelings of loneliness and emptiness; many times these cycles of self-centeredness and loneliness are sparked by trauma, such as abuse. Heather reminds you of the power you carry and the ancestral line that brought it—and you—into being. The essence can even be used to transmute violent, angry vibrations into soft, nurturing ones.[92] It can transmute the pain of the past into wisdom for the present and future, thereby helping you break the cycle begotten by trauma.

Heather's long connection to luck is one of my favorite aspects to explore for co-creating with the plant spirit. In magick, I've always found dried heather to be the herb of right timing, which is essentially what luck is. You can call upon the plant spirit through the flower essence for attracting luck and manifest the perfect timing for your desired results. Because it flowers in late summer and autumn, heather flower essence can also be used in rituals for Lammas (August 1), while the fiery color is used by some to symbolize the summer solstice. Scottish lore says that witches would fly over fields of heather on Samhain, and that the plant was attributed to the Cailleach, a dark goddess of the wintertide. With this in mind, heather flower essence may offer comfort and warmth during the dark half of the year.

---

*Note that taking heather flower essence yourself will not stop others from draining your energy; it is not protective outright.

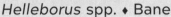

❀
Hellebore
Helleborus spp. ♦ Bane

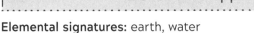

Elemental signatures: earth, water

Planetary signature: Saturn

Zodiacal signature: Capricorn

Chakras: solar plexus, heart

Magickal uses: protection, invisibility, glamoury, banishing, exorcism, mental powers, shamanic journey

Therapeutic indications: feeling invisible, unappreciated, or unloved; feeling uncomfortable with silence; avoiding being alone; shyness; inability to define goals; excitability; grief; screen addiction

HELLEBORES ARE A GENUS of evergreen members of the buttercup family (Ranunculaceae) that are native to Europe and Asia. They are characterized by leathery, palmate leaves with serrated margins and flowers that rise above the foliage; the blooms may last for many months. Most species belonging to the genus *Helleborus* are poisonous, as attested to by the Greek roots of the word, which comes from *heleīn,* meaning "to injure," and *borá,* meaning "food." Flower essences are often made from three species: *H. orientalis* (also called Lenten rose), *H. niger* (Christmas rose or black hellebore), and *H. viridis* (green hellebore).

Hellebore has been used in magick since antiquity, often in association with protection against harm, both magickal and mundane, and with exorcising malefic entities. One of its curious applications was in healing animals that had been poisoned,[93] a use probably based on the same principle at play in homeopathy—like fighting fire with fire. The essence is indeed protective, as are many baneful plants, and it can be used to fight against toxic patterns in the psyche as well as combat harmful energies and entities in your environs. It can also be added to spells and rituals designed to bless and offer healing to animals.

Hellebore was a magickal ingredient in spells and charms aimed at rendering the caster invisible. The signature for invisibility may be derived from green hellebore, whose flowers are hard to see in a field of green (alternatively, *H. niger* produces white flowers, often while there is still snow on the ground, and is thus equally hard to see). As a therapeutic ally, hellebore is used to address situations in which you feel invisible, unloved, unappreciated, or even misunderstood. Hellebore flower essence starts by turning your attention inward, inviting you to discover why you feel unseen or unappreciated. Such patterns often stem from not understanding the signals of appreciation that others give you or from being unable or unwilling to request help or affirmation. In both cases, the culprit is typically low self-worth in disguise. Hellebore reduces the shyness and unworthiness that prevents you from speaking up or being seen. It increases self-assurance by inviting greater self-awareness, poise, and clarity.[94]

I learned from my teacher and mentor Christopher Penczak that hellebore essence reveals the mystical power of silence. For anyone who resists stillness and silence, perhaps through the increasingly common scenario of screen addiction, hellebore gently leads you to find solace and peace. It is the essence of the solitary mystic; it shows you that, rather than climbing to a mountaintop, you can find that holy silence right where you are. Through silent reflection, hellebore guides you through self-discovery. It can help you discover goals and themes that give you a sense of direction and purpose.

Hellebore flower essence also assists astral projection and journey work. It is especially helpful in cutting out mental chatter, for an unquiet mind is a major obstacle in any form of psychic or spiritual endeavor. This stillness offers a doorway to your own personal eureka moments. In reducing tension and overexcitability, hellebore essence provides clear thinking and inspiration. In addition to working on the mind, it affects the chakra system as a whole, flooding your entire energy field with healing energy and expelling harmful or stagnant patterns that are inhibiting health and magickal prowess. Hellebore, especially the green variety, is well suited to combating harmful magick and the effects of the evil eye.[95]

Hemlock

Conium maculatum ◆ Bane

Elemental signature: water

Planetary signature: Saturn

Zodiacal signature: Aquarius

Chakras: sacral, crown

Magickal uses: astral travel, consecration, stalling or slowing a situation, quenching desires, hexing

Therapeutic indications: holding on to the past, difficulty releasing stubborn beliefs, feeling that life is moving too quickly, racing or dizzying thoughts, faithlessness

HEMLOCK, OFTEN KNOWN AS POISON HEMLOCK, is one of the most poisonous plants on Earth. A hardy biennial, it has the characteristic hollow stems and white umbels of members of the carrot family, Apiaceae. Its stalks are marked by purplish splotches that make it easy to recognize when compared to safer members of the carrot family, like Queen Anne's lace and angelica. Hemlock is widely naturalized outside its native range, and it should be approached with extreme caution. **Do not make an essence from this plant without taking extreme caution.***

There is very little lore about poison hemlock available today, probably owing to its extreme toxicity. Historically, hemlock was used as a poison, most famously the one administered to Socrates. The plant is sacred to Hekate, and it appears among the ingredients of several flying ointments. Some witches and magicians use the plant to ritually consecrate magickal knives and swords; the flower essence is a much safer alternative for this purpose.

---

*I do not recommend making this flower essence by a direct method at all; use one of the indirect methods described in chapter 5, and consider using an extra stage of dilution if the plant makes contact with the water. You can find a safe, commercially made poison hemlock essence from Pacific Essences, a producer based on Vancouver Island; its products are distributed internationally and can also be found online.

Magickally, hemlock is sometimes used to ritually paralyze a situation.[96] Paralysis is one of the symptoms of ingesting hemlock, and vibrationally it works on patterns of paralysis, rigidity, and being stuck. Taking the flower essence dissolves patterns of emotional, mental, and social paralysis, particularly when the feeling of being stuck or paralyzed arises during periods of intense change. It is especially effective when you believe that the change arises from forces outside your control.[97] Hemlock flower essence helps you confront the experience of freezing up, as this is usually a mechanism of denying or escaping the present moment. As a result, hemlock can release feelings of disempowerment or being swept away by situations that are beyond your control. Instead, hemlock essence helps cultivate an inner stillness that affords you space to claim your power in any situation, even when events cannot be changed or stopped.

Hemlock's genus name, *Conium,* derives from a Greek word meaning "whirling," referring to the dizziness associated with hemlock poisoning. These sensations account for its use in flying ointments; naturally, as a flower essence it is a much safer alternative for assisting astral travel and spirit flight. Hemlock flower essence also treats another sort of dizziness—the kind resulting from racing, uncontrolled thoughts. It prevents you from freezing up when you are faced with life's twists and turns by keeping you present in the moment and helping you expand your perspective beyond the limitations of the ego. Use this flower essence if you feel as though you can't keep up with the pace of life. Hemlock helps you cross the abyss of the subconscious mind to find clarity, stillness, and the perspicacity to keep moving forward.

❧ Henbane

Hyoscyamus niger ♦ Bane

Elemental signatures: water, fire

Planetary signature: Saturn

Zodiacal signatures: Capricorn, Aquarius

Chakra: third eye

Magickal uses: inspiration, weather magick, ancestral communication, astral projection, protection, banishing, rainmaking, inspiration

Therapeutic indications: persistent karmic and ancestral cycles, difficulty letting go, persistent chaos in your life, reliving trauma, fear of the unknown, difficulty making decisions, fear of relapse

HENBANE, A MEMBER OF THE nightshade family, has striking five-petaled flowers; they're yellowish but criss-crossed by a network of purplish-black veins leading to a darker center. The plant originated somewhere in Eurasia but is now widespread. All parts of the plant contain toxic tropanes, and it is also psychedelic in nature. In spite of its toxicity, henbane has featured in traditional medicine around the world.

One of the classic witching herbs, henbane is a traditional ingredient in flying ointments and other potions. It has medicinal and magickal uses that stretch back to ancient Egypt and Sumeria. The Greeks considered it sacred to the sun god Apollo, which earned it the name *Apollinaris*.[98] The closely related white henbane (*Hyoscyamus albus*) featured in the sacred incense burned to inspire the oracular powers of the priestess of Delphi, a temple dedicated to Apollo.

Henbane flower essence inspires oracular visions in meditation and dreams, and it facilitates contact with spirits, especially ancestral ones. The Saturnian nature of the flower aims toward karmic healing; taking the essence helps release the burdens of generational karma and inherited trauma. It also breaks generational curses and helps you learn the lessons taught to your ancestors, such that you no longer need to repeat their mistakes.

The flowers of henbane symbolize release and letting go, and similarly, the essence can help you release deeply held ideas, beliefs, and emotions. Henbane is effective whether these ideas or patterns have accumulated over lifetimes or are the result of experiences in this life. On a smaller scale, henbane flower essence grants you the resolve to walk away from toxic people and situations, such as leaving an unhealthy relationship or a detrimental work environment. I find that it can also provide deep healing to relationships with your family, particularly your parents.

Part of henbane's gift of letting go comes from its relationship to memory and identity. Greek myths describe crowns of henbane worn by the shades of the dead as they wandered the underworld. Describing the role of henbane, witch and herbalist Harold Roth writes, "The function of their crowns was to cause them to forget their lives—perhaps so that they would not try to return and haunt or attack the living. Those who remained behind in the world of the living also decorated the tombs of the dead with henbane. This may have been partly as a protective measure—the dead cannot return if they cannot remember who they were—but it may also have served symbolically as a help for the living to forget their loss."[99] More recently, the hyoscyamine obtained from henbane was used much like datura (see page 292) to induce twilight sleep in laboring women to ease and help them forget the pain of childbirth.

As a flower essence, henbane helps treat a variety of scenarios related to memory. It eases the throes of grief by alleviating painful memories and breaks through patterns of reliving difficult or distressing memories, making it useful in treating people who have undergone trauma of all sorts. It can also treat memory loss, helping you recall and reclaim a better perspective of the past.

Henbane essence helps you navigate through the unknown. This baneful plant has long been sanctified in the name of Hekate, the light-bearing goddess who stands at the crossroads. The veins in the flowers almost resemble a map, and the essence helps you assess where you are in relation to the bigger picture. Like Hekate's torches, this essence brings light to the unknown. It helps you surrender and find peace and faith in the midst of chaos and transition. Whenever you are faced with decisions—when you stand at the proverbial crossroads—henbane flower essence helps you attune to what you know and sense to be true before deciding on the ultimate path to take. This essence can help you weigh the options without experiencing choice paralysis. Henbane is also helpful for people who fear repeating past mistakes or relapsing into old behaviors.

Henbane, associated with both fire and water, is an odd mix of opposing images in magick and lore. On the one hand, henbane prefers dry soils and has a drying influence on physical tissues. On the other, its leaves are covered in hairs that trap moisture, and its pods resemble cauldrons (which could hold water). It is connected to gods of day (Apollo) and night (Hekate). It was once used to summon storms, another indication of its connections to water. Perhaps this relationship to storms contributes to the essence's predisposition for finding calm in turbulent situations; it helps you seek the eye of the storm and remain calm under pressure.

Magickally, henbane flower essence is useful for protection, ancestral communication, astral travel, and divination. It offers inspiration and is an excellent ally for poets. It can also be used in spells or rituals for finding courage, particularly for making important decisions in life.

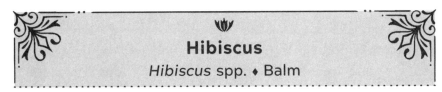

Hibiscus
Hibiscus spp. ♦ Balm

Elemental signatures: water, fire

Planetary signatures: Venus, Mars

Zodiacal signatures: Aries, Taurus, Libra

Chakras: root, sacral, heart

Magickal uses: love, passion, harmony

Therapeutic indications: loneliness, self-pity, doubt, stress, exhaustion, hopelessness, overwhelm, sexual dysfunction, puritanical attitudes about sex, low vitality

HIBISCUS BELONGS TO THE mallow family, and there are more than two hundred different species in the genus. The flowers are five-petaled, trumpet-shaped, and brightly colored. They have a prominent pistil rising from the center, around which the stamen emerges. While it is native to tropical and subtropical climates, many different forms of hibiscus are cultivated around the world. Flower essences are often made from the red-flowered *Hibiscus rosa-sinensis* and *Hibiscus syriacus*.

Hibiscus is absent from western European herbal lore, as it is native to more tropical climates. The flower is a symbol of the fierce goddess Kali in India, and it is used as an offering to both Kali and Ganesha.

Hibiscus often symbolizes love, desire, passion, and vitality. Modern-day witches often use the dried blossoms in magick for love, lust, and passion. The energy of the plant is very liberating, and it helps you break free from self-imposed restraints and restraining projections from your family, belief system, or culture.

Hibiscus flower essence is often used for healing from sexual trauma, especially among women. It can help alleviate psychological wounds caused by society's exploitation and commercialization of feminine sexuality.[100] Although the flower has a reputation of magickally inciting lust, the essence is much gentler, bringing warmth and caring to expressions of sensuality and sexuality. Hibiscus essence is helpful for overcoming feelings of betrayal, loss of innocence, and loss of faith, especially as a result of sexual or romantic experiences. Hibiscus flower essence kindles the flame of passion and a lust for life; it helps you fall in love with your time on Earth in every way.

The essence also offers a fresh perspective when life is stale, repetitive, or overwhelming. It balances the entire chakra system, providing a boost of energy when you need it and relaxing you when you feel over-stimulated and stressed out. The essence is like a light at the end of the tunnel, and it helps you adopt the mind-set of starting anew when undergoing life-changing events.[101] The flower symbolizes synthesis and togetherness, as depicted in the prominent pistil that carries the stamen on it; this union of the male and female organs of the flower rises upward, as if to point toward common roots and a common goal that each of us shares.

Use hibiscus flower essence whenever you feel as though your flower essence blends or your magickal practice need a boost in potency. It expedites the effects of other magickal ingredients, helping to catalyze change. This flower's elemental and planetary correspondences represent a union of opposites: fire and water, Venus and Mars. This alchemical union provides the raw fuel needed to energize your healing, magick, and spiritual practice. Take the essence if you feel too burned out to effectively perform magick as well as when you feel like you'd benefit from a little extra push toward your goals. Hibiscus may also be helpful in magick related to stalled legal matters.[102]

Holly

Ilex aquifolium, Ilex spp. ♦ Tree

Elemental signature: fire

Planetary signatures: Mars, Saturn

Zodiacal signature: Capricorn

Chakra: heart

Magickal uses: protection, luck, dream magick, love, connecting to the divine masculine

Therapeutic indications: jealousy, envy, thirst for revenge, isolation, suspicion, anger, resentment, hard-heartedness, frustration without knowing why, aggression, violence, longing for love

HOLLY IS AN EVERGREEN TREE or shrub well known for its sharp, prickly, glossy leaves and bright red berries. Its genus, *Ilex,* contains nearly five hundred species, each one an evergreen with glossy leaves. The flowers are small, waxy, and greenish white; they have four petals. This tree is a beloved holiday decoration that once was featured at the Roman festival of Saturnalia, a predecessor to the modern celebration of Christmas.

Holly is one of the thirty-eight essences prepared by Dr. Bach. It is predominantly used to open the heart to the experience of love. Bach considered it to be the remedy for those plagued by thoughts of jealousy, envy, suspicion, revenge, and all forms of frustration. He noted that it was particularly helpful when the cause for frustration was not readily apparent.[103] Holly flower essence is a supremely nurturing and loving remedy; it floods the heart with love, and the overflow of love moves through the body, mind, and spirit. This love is the divine, transcendent love that holds the universe together; it is the very substance of Source.

Among its magickal properties, holly is best known for its apotropaic effects. It has been used to ward off negative magick, repel storms and lightning, and neutralize poisons. It was used to pacify wild animals and prevent harm from malicious spirits, too. The protective signatures of the plant are quite obvious: the spiny leaves are defensive and the toxic red berries a warning.

As an essence, holly's protective influence is more refined. As Dr. Bach said, "Holly protects us from everything that is not universal love. Holly opens the heart and unites us with divine love."[104] This sentiment echoes a teaching I learned in Reiki: the best protection is an open heart. If you allow yourself to be completely and utterly united with the divine in a current of unconditional love, no harm can truly come to you, metaphysically speaking. Holly does indeed ward off negative energies, but it does so by displacing unloving, fearful, or violent energies with compassionate, loving energies instead.

Holly flower essence brings balance and clarity to the mind. It acts as a spiritual guide and clears away spiritual disturbances from the past, ultimately offering greater clarity, discernment, and justice.[105] This essence is also helpful in treating panic, fear, and anxiety that stem from a place of insecurity or a loss of control. Ultimately, the nurturing, protective nature of holly helps you overcome loneliness, fear, unhappiness, and other emotions by surrendering to love. Holly brings you to a sense of gratitude for all that you have and all that is yet to come.

Because of the seasonal associations with holly berries and leaves, the essence can be added to blends for yuletide celebrations to honor tides of cheer and goodwill and the rebirth of the sun at the solstice. Holly trees flourish in the low light of the underbrush, otherwise shadowed by taller trees, and yet they remain steadfast and evergreen; holly essence is thus well suited to winter celebrations. Add a few drops to the chalice as a sacramental elixir, or combine it with other wintertide flowers to attune to the season. Spray holly essence in your home and garden for protection and to refine the energy. Combine it with mistletoe and oak for a profound connection to the god of witchcraft, and use this blend to attune to the seasonal shifts throughout the year.

❀ Hyssop
Hyssopus officinalis ◆ Balm

Elemental signature: water

Planetary signatures: moon, Jupiter

Zodiacal signatures: Cancer, Sagittarius, Aquarius

Chakras: root, sacral, solar plexus

Magickal uses: cleansing, purification, protection, love

Therapeutic indications: shame, guilt, low self-esteem, self-blame, difficulty enjoying life, denial of pleasure, fear of success, perfectionism, sense of foreboding, self-sabotage

HYSSOP IS A MEMBER of the mint family and prized for its medicinal qualities. It generally grows as a small shrub with bright green, lanceolate leaves. The stem tends to be woody at the base, and the flowers are bright blue, often tinged with shades of pink or purple. Both the flowers and leaves are highly fragrant.

Hyssop has been celebrated since antiquity for its powers to cleanse and protect. The herb is traditionally used for rites of cleansing, like asperges, where it is gathered into bundles and used to sprinkle blessed water around a person, object, or place. Dried hyssop is also hung in windows or around the home to confer protection and ensure that the environment stays free from harmful influences. As a flower essence, hyssop is also cleansing. It helps clear the aura and chakras of lower emotions, and it can be sprayed or diffused around the home to sweep away stale, stagnant, or harmful energy. Hyssop flower essence is also helpful for anyone in the healing arts, as it prevents you from taking on the energy that you help others release and transform.

The flower essence of hyssop is specifically focused on feelings of guilt, blame, and shame. Rather than suppressing these feelings, it encourages a state of emotional honesty wherein guilt is acknowledged and released. Releasing guilt makes space for more constructive feelings and behaviors. Taking the essence over time can even improve relationships of all kinds, as it cultivates a deeper sense of connection to others.

Hyssop flower essence offers a greater sense of harmony and oneness, even stretching to remove collective guilt, fear, and other emotions carried within groups.

Hyssop essence ultimately alleviates deeply held tension that results from feeling unworthy or undeserving of happiness. It addresses tendencies toward perfectionism, especially those that stem from being inwardly fearful of being judged.[106] The essence enables you to let your guard down once you have faced internalized feelings of guilt. It encourages you to accept the love, forgiveness, and nurturing from both internal and external sources—all of which helps you overcome feelings of guilt, shame, and unworthiness. Hyssop flower essence invites you to forgive yourself for past errors and harmful actions; it asks you to reframe these mistakes as lessons and opportunities to learn. It breaks cycles of self-sabotage that are consciously or unconsciously perpetuated as a form of punishment for past mistakes. Through this action, hyssop helps connect you to the best parts of yourself, allows you to cultivate feelings of self-worth, and builds your self-esteem.

Hyssop was a traditional ingredient in medieval spells for purification and binding, particularly binding someone to love. The outcome was usually an all-or-nothing scenario; either the object of love was won or the spellcaster's loving feelings would be purged and purified.[107] In flower essence therapy, hyssop can be used to treat a similar all-or-nothing mentality related to love and sex. I've found it especially effective for targeting shame or guilt caused by carnal thoughts and deeds. Taking the essence helps you break through that shame and find pleasure, or it can release the desire that caused the shame in the first place.

In your magickal practice, consider using hyssop flower essence to cleanse your sacred space and to consecrate ritual tools. Added to a bath, it brings cleansing and renewal. Though it is not an outright Venusian herb, hyssop flower essence can be helpful in love magick because it brings a sense of deserving love, pleasure, and success. It wards against harm, especially the harm you project to yourself, and it is invaluable for establishing confidence and harmony when working in groups.

Iris

Iris spp. ✦ Balm

Elemental signature: water

Planetary signatures: moon, Mercury

Zodiacal signature: Leo

Chakras: solar plexus, throat, crown

Magickal uses: love, luck, money, inspiration, beauty, power, peace

Therapeutic indications: creative block, feeling lackluster or uninspired, repressed emotions, impaired expression, inability to speak up, resentment

IRISES, COMPRISING THE GENUS of the same name, account for nearly three hundred species of flowering plants in a wide array of colors. Many irises are blue-to-violet, often with tinges of yellow and gold in the center. The flowers usually have six petals, and they exhibit three large sepals that are retroflexed (i.e., they hang downward). Irises grow in a wide range, mostly in the Northern Hemisphere, and they remain popular garden plants today.

Iris flowers take their name from the Greek goddess of the rainbow, the sky, and the sea. Iris is a messenger goddess, often appearing winged; she bridges the human world with that of the Olympian gods to deliver messages. Iris flower essence shares qualities with this ancient goddess, for it inspires you to use your voice and share your message. The essence can help you speak up when you feel small, insignificant, or weak. It is an essence of empowerment.

Most flower essence authors and makers highlight the ways in which iris essence boosts creativity and expression by clearing away inner blockages. Iris essence helps you develop an awareness of the unbridled and infinite creative potential within, and it helps you cultivate a greater appreciation for yourself and your talents and abilities—even those that might still be latent. When you become frustrated with a creative block of any kind, iris flower essence eases the feelings of anger, despair, frustration, and tension that are directed inward, thereby alleviating additional self-created obstacles to enable creativity and inspiration to flow without effort. Flower essence experts Patricia Kaminski and Richard Katz state that iris flower essence "impels the soul to create and cultivate beauty, within itself and within the world."[108]

Work with iris flower essence for creative activities of all varieties—writing, painting, drawing, making music, acting, sculpting, and virtually any other artistic endeavor. I find it helpful for resolving writer's block, and I sometimes combine it with hazel and blackberry flower essences for that purpose. Iris's creativity is not limited to the arts, however. This flower essence also helps you break free from overanalytical, logical reasoning that might otherwise impede creative thinking. This essence is ideal for anyone who must have a rational explanation for everything, as it teaches you how to surrender to mystery and the splendor of life itself. Use it to help you solve any problem from a more creative perspective.

The iris draws from the symbolism of the rainbow, after which it is named, conferring hope. The flower is said to have three virtues, represented by its threefold symmetry: faith, wisdom, and valor.[109] Like the rainbow that unites heaven and earth, iris flower essence bridges spirit and matter, bringing illumination and protection to the body and soul of anyone who takes it. For this reason, it is a wonderful essence to use for blessing or christening babies and young children; the promise of spring borne by the iris flower confers grace and protection to all forms of new life and burgeoning growth. The springtide current within this essence makes it perfect for attuning to and celebrating Ostara, the vernal equinox.

In magick, many species of iris are used for love and romance. The roots of some species, known as orris root, Queen Elizabeth root, or Jezebel root, are used in hoodoo and other forms of folk magick to attract male lovers, as well as to bring luck in all matters of the heart. Adding orris root to the bath was thought to entice a partner to extend a marriage proposal. Iris flower essence is an excellent ally in love magick because it inspires appreciation of beauty, both within and without. When you truly see your own inner and outer beauty, you learn to exude greater confidence, which makes you more attractive to potential romantic partners. Iris is sometimes used in prosperity magick, too; as a flower essence, it can help you find creative solutions to financial woes while offering hope and faith that the universe will provide for you.

Essences made from a variety of irises tend to be cleansing and detoxifying. Iris is sometimes used medicinally as a strong emetic, and vibrationally speaking, the flower essence can also purge unwanted or unhealthy energies from the aura. Blue iris (*Iris versicolor*) offers emotional cleansing, often by bringing repressed and forgotten emotions to the surface to be purified through expression. Purple iris (*Iris germanica*) is adept at resolving feelings of resentment. One of the irises native to Florida (*Iris hexagona*) has proved itself to be a valuable ally in writing and creating, clearing away feelings of being unworthy or uninspired.

The ancient Romans used iris to consecrate sacred spaces, altars, and ritual tools. Modern-day magicians occasionally use iris oil to cleanse and consecrate wands, and iris flower essence is equally adept at this task. Orris root is sometimes used as a pendulum, and I find that iris flower essence is excellent for cleansing a pendulum and enabling it to bridge heaven and earth to better communicate truth in any scenario.

Iris essence enables you to take back your inner authority and live to your highest potential; work with it to reclaim your power. It is an essence of sovereignty, and the shape of the flowers may have inspired the fleur-de-lis and the scepter, both symbols of royalty and power. By connecting you to both heaven and earth, iris flower essence helps you speak your truth and create a life of beauty. It is noted for being universally applicable because it initiates and sustains development with flower essence therapy as a whole.[110]

Jasmine
Jasminum officinale ♦ Balm

Elemental signature: water
Planetary signatures: moon, Venus
Zodiacal signature: Cancer
Chakras: heart, crown

Magickal uses: love, creativity, joy, abundance, beauty, prophetic dreams

Therapeutic indications: low self-esteem, feeling unlovable, inability to see your own beauty, insecurity, inability to recognize the divine within yourself and others, judging yourself, having a mind-set that is too cerebral or too grounded to put spirituality into practice

JASMINE IS A HEAVENLY SCENTED, white-flowered member of the olive family. There are more than two hundred varieties, most of which are native to warmer regions in Eurasia and Oceania. Jasmine has been cultivated widely since antiquity, and its exact origin is unknown. Common jasmine has a climbing, twining habit, and it is a vigorous grower. Its flowers are five-petaled, appear in summer, and release their divine fragrance in the evening.

Like many white, night-blooming flowers, jasmine is considered sacred to the Goddess and is associated with the moon. Thanks to its five petals and heady fragrance, jasmine is also associated with the planet Venus. These days you'll find jasmine used to honor a diverse array of manifestations of the divine feminine, including Diana, Mary, and Kuan Yin. Accordingly, this flower is best used for rituals related to love, romance, beauty, and connecting to the divine feminine. The flower is said to attract a more spiritual love, rather than merely a physical one.[111] Jasmine is occasionally used in rites for abundance and joy, too; the flower essence can be added to an infusion of the flowers or a glass of champagne to make a quick and easy potion for manifesting joy.[112]

As a flower essence, jasmine is most closely indicated in cases of low self-esteem, poor body image, feeling unwanted or unloved, self-hatred, loneliness, and jealousy. It is effective when shyness, stemming from lack of confidence or poor self-image, keeps you from engaging with the world around you. It enables you to see and appreciate your own unique beauty, thereby boosting confidence and helping you express yourself. Take jasmine flower essence when you are hard on yourself, critical of your physical features, or fearful and judgmental of your inner darkness and trauma. It is also helpful in cases of emotional wounds resulting from sexual trauma. It can clear repressed sexual instincts and allow you to find healthy ways to express them.

Jasmine helps you focus on your innate spark of divinity, even leading you to see it in others, too. This leads to deeper connection, particularly when you are taking the essence as part of regular self-care rituals or for spells and ceremonies aimed at attracting or deepening romantic relationships. Jasmine flower essence can be added to the bath to boost self-esteem and help your inner goddess truly shine. By connecting you to your inner divinity, it can allow you to overcome a state of being too cerebral or too practical for engaging with your spiritual practice effectively. I think it makes an excellent remedy against "armchair occultism," as it helps you develop a personal, intimate relationship with the divine within and without.

Jasmine flower essence sparks creativity, mental clarity, and practicality. Diffuse it in your space when you are creating anything at all—a painting, poem, manuscript, or four-course meal—to help you stay centered in love and joy while expressing yourself through your creative process. You can also add it to the chalice or diffuse it during rituals to honor the moon or the Goddess in her myriad forms. Taking a few drops before bed may invite vivid, prophetic dreams, although be warned: some people (including me) find it too stimulating and may not be able to sleep well. Jasmine flower essence can be used in all rituals for love and beauty, as well as to attract friendship. Diffuse it or dress a candle with it in your space for a gentle dose of psychic protection and to heal the aura.

Juniper
Juniperus spp. ♦ Tree

Elemental signature: fire

Planetary signatures: sun, Mars, Saturn

Zodiacal signature: Leo

Chakras: root, sacral, heart, throat

Magickal uses: protection, exorcism, healing

Therapeutic indications: low self-esteem, fear of criticism, procrastination, resentment, remorse, jealousy, lack of confidence

JUNIPER IS A POPULAR EVERGREEN best known for its aromatic berries, which are used to flavor gin. Juniper trees vary in form, sometimes resembling a small shrub and other times a pyramidal tree. They live to be centuries old and thrive in soils where other plants fail.

Juniper has a long history of both culinary and magickal uses. The wood, resin, and berries are generally burned for protection, exorcism, and healing. The smoke, which is thought to banish darkness and simultaneously attract beneficent, healing energy, is excellent for cleansing sacred space before ritual, and it is especially attuned to preparing the space before the great sabbats of Samhain and Beltane.

As an essence, juniper is similarly cleansing and protective. Spray or diffuse it before a ritual to create a sacred atmosphere. It is also strengthening, thereby making you more resilient against outside influences. I've found the essence helpful for insecurity, fear, and low self-esteem. It nurtures your sense of self and the creative spark within while thwarting the feeling of not being good enough. It helps clarify your intentions and follow-through on your goals. As a result, it is an excellent remedy for procrastination. The essence helps you observe why cycles of procrastination have begun (which for me is usually some sort of insecurity), and it opens your heart to new sources of inspiration.

Juniper is an essential tree for repopulating wastelands and regenerating damaged or depleted landscapes. It was an early colonizer of the British Isles and is often employed when replanting after mining and industrial activity in the United States. Juniper thrives in places where other plants do not, and it also prevents erosion while dropping leaf litter that gradually improves soil quality. We can see these same processes echoed in the uses of juniper as an essence. When the sense of self is depleted or exhausted, often from long periods of effort or trauma from the distant past, juniper offers a road to renewal. It begins by helping you feel more rooted and capable. It reveals how the distant past has shaped the present; when you have felt powerless, this awareness fosters the sensitivity and innovation you need to move forward. The essence empowers you to achieve your goals and grants you a sense of purpose.

Juniper's connection to the past makes it a powerful tool for resolving feelings of guilt, shame, remorse, resentment, and jealousy. It can help initiate forgiveness through a better understanding of how and why the present circumstances arose. Juniper essence helps you accept and forgive your mistakes, as well as the mistakes of others.[113] I find juniper most helpful for self-forgiveness; with that gift, it can help you feel more confident in your abilities and take pride in your achievements. Just as the juniper tree helps restore barren land, the essence helps restore your faith in yourself and your ability to turn your life around.

In American folk magick practices, such as hoodoo and conjure, juniper is used predominantly for matters of love and sex. The berries are thought to bring luck and increase attraction in your affairs, as well as boosting male potency. In a similar vein, juniper flower essence releases the stress accumulated at the sacral chakra.[114] The essence also promotes a state of love and grace between lovers, elevating pleasure in a way that affirms and delights both partners.[115] Juniper essence also alleviates obsession with body image, objectification (especially of feminine traits), and issues of self-worth related to body image.[116] Over time, this essence brings confidence in yourself and invites you to be playful and loving in the bedroom and beyond.

Juniper is a powerful hex breaker in magickal herbalism. It is said that Mary and Joseph sought shelter under a juniper tree as they fled to Egypt; the tree blessed them with its power to chase away evil and counteract baneful magick. The flower essence of juniper helps you reclaim your power and cleanse both self and space, thereby rendering harmful magick powerless. It also elevates your consciousness, helping you rise above the baleful influences of harmful magick or hateful thoughts directed toward you. Ultimately, the gift of juniper is a more luminous inner state of being that calls you to rise in grace.[117]

❀ Lady's Mantle
Alchemilla vulgaris ♦ Balm

Elemental signatures: water, earth

Planetary signatures: Venus, Mars

Zodiacal signature: Cancer

Chakras: sacral, solar plexus, heart, third eye

Magickal uses: love, alchemy, connecting to plant spirits, boosting herbal magick

Therapeutic indications: being overly technical, feeling disconnected from Mother Earth, lack of respones to flower essence treatments, lack of focus, disconnection between mind and body, disconnection between reason and intuition, sexual trauma or reproductive illness, imbalance of masculine and feminine energy

LADY'S MANTLE, A MEMBER OF the rose family, is most widely recognized for its unusual leaves, which are palmate and corrugated; these leaves attract and hold dew in shining, gemlike droplets each morning. The plant has a spreading habit, unlike the verticality of most other members of Rosaceae, and its flowers are a bright yellowy green. They lack true petals and resemble tiny eight-rayed stars. It is native to temperate areas of Europe and Asia, with relatives being widespread in this region and beyond.

Traditionally, the plant is said to boost the efficacy of all magick. The dried leaf and dew collected from the leaves are used in spells for love, and the dew is also used to impart beauty and healing.

Lady's mantle is the patron of the alchemical arts—hence the genus name, *Alchemilla*. As noted, the plant collects drops of dew in its chalice-like leaves; this signature of collecting dew is reminiscent of Dr. Bach's earliest attempts to gather dew for making his second generation of essences. As an essence, lady's mantle enables you to better attune to flower essence use as a whole, as it represents the alchemical process of making essences themselves.

The green flowers, spreading habit, and dew-bearing leaves of the plant all suggest that it is deeply connected to the power of the Earth. It is said to align the human heart with the heart of Earth, allowing you to recognize that Earth is a living being. The essence is also used to enhance your connection to the divine feminine, particularly as represented by the archetype of Mother Earth, and it is sometimes recommended as an ally for anyone seeking protection from the Great Goddess. Christopher Penczak describes this plant spirit as a wise teacher who helps unlock the secret nature of herbs.[118] Patricia Kaminski says that lady's mantle allows the chalice of your heart to emanate the soul qualities of nature.[119] Indeed, lady's mantle may be the master essence for attuning to the power of the green world. Taking it before seeing clients or engaging in any sort of herbal magick or healing better attunes you to the plant kingdom and inspires you to work intuitively, rather than just relying on technical know-how.

The flower essence made from lady's mantle also balances feminine and masculine forces within the body, mind, and spirit. This plant's dual correspondences of Venus and Mars symbolize the synthesis of masculine and feminine principles within you. It may soften an aggressive personality or strengthen a softer one.[120]

The essence also strengthens the body-mind connection and marries together the rational and intuitive elements of the psyche.[121] Take it to mitigate the mental effects of stress and trauma as well as for inviting greater awareness and mindfulness. This essence is sometimes used in cases of reproductive illness or sexual trauma, particularly among women.[122] It also supports you in accessing information from the subconscious mind, improves focus and concentration, and helps you respond mindfully, rather than thoughtlessly, in any situation.

Use lady's mantle in flower essence blends when it seems that effects are slow or not forthcoming—assuming, of course, that the blend is the right match for the condition you're trying to affect. The essence is also wonderful for rituals honoring the Earth Mother and other manifestations of the Great Goddess. For beauty and grace, spray it on your face or add it to water and use it to rinse your skin. Try offering the essence to your garden if your plants won't thrive even though you're following all the rules and guidelines for growing them.

Lavender
Lavandula angustifolia ♦ Balm

Elemental signature: air

Planetary signature: Mercury

Zodiacal signatures: Virgo, Aquarius

Chakras: third eye, crown

Magickal uses: peace, love, purification, protection, psychic development

Therapeutic indications: stress, anxiety, nervous tension, poor boundaries, lack of mental clarity, confusion

LAVENDER IS AN EVER-POPULAR member of the mint family. It is native to the Mediterranean region and widely cultivated as an ornamental and culinary herb as well as for herbal medicine and the production of essential oils. The plant exhibits long, narrow leaves, and its flowers are appropriately lavender-colored and borne on tall, leafless spikes. Most varieties are low-growing, evergreen, relatively short-lived herbaceous perennials. The entire plant is highly aromatic.

Lavender is used in magick related to love, peace, protection, and purification. Its name is taken from the Latin *lavare,* meaning "to wash," implying its connection to cleanliness. It is a calming and stabilizing herb that helps clear the mind and spirit alike. At varying points in history, lavender has been used to both excite and temper passions, and it has taken on associations with marriage, fertility, and luck in love. It is probable that Hekate's priestesses knew and used the herb, and it continues to be popular in magick today.[123]

As a flower essence, lavender is best used to cleanse and clear the mind and energy field. It is helpful for oversensitive people, especially those who are drawn to spiritual pursuits but are unable to effectively acclimate to or process the energies involved in spiritual practice. Whenever you feel too sensitive or open, lavender flower essence helps you listen to the wisdom of your body and learn to regulate your own mental and spiritual energies so you don't feel overwhelmed. Dried lavender is often used in cleansing rituals and spells, and the flower essence can be diffused or sprayed in your home for spiritual purification. For people who take on too much energy or too much responsibility, lavender offers a sense of freedom and levity. Add it to the bath when you feel as though you've accumulated too much energy that doesn't belong to you. It is gently protective, and it envelops the aura in a gentle layer of defense against outside simulti and harmful energies.

Lavender flower essence is also a wonderful remedy against insomnia, as it slows repetitive thoughts and eases mental and physical tension alike.

Lavender flower essence concentrates its spiritual effects on the crown and third-eye chakras. It invites clarity at the psychic and spiritual levels, thereby facilitating psychic development and meditation. It boosts intuition, enhances communication with the higher self, and helps you become better aligned with divinity. The vertical nature of the flower spikes highlights the essence's connection to higher realms. This plant spirit offers a calm clarity that enables you to better contact and journey to the spirit realm; try it in flower essence blends for astral travel and spirit communication.

Folk tradition records this flower's use in love magick. It can draw a new romance, improve your odds of finding a mate, and promote peace and intimacy in existing relationships, too. The flower essence is said to remove old karmic patterns between two people, thereby allowing them to resolve conflict easily and quickly.[124] It is easy to see the correlation between the magickal properties of the herb and the therapeutic applications of the flower essence; both improve relationships and invite harmony, peace, and love.

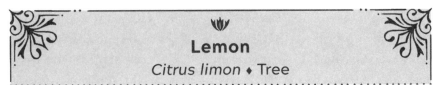

Lemon
Citrus limon ♦ Tree

Elemental signature: water
Planetary signatures: moon, Venus, Neptune
Zodiacal signatures: Cancer, Leo

Chakras: sacral, throat

Magickal uses: cleansing, harmony, friendship, protection, love

Therapeutic indications: mental fatigue, sluggish mind, lack of focus, dreaminess, indecisiveness, lack of humor, confusing or muddy emotions, shame or guilt related to pleasure

LEMON IS A CITRUS FRUIT that has been cultivated for nearly two thousand years. It originated as a hybrid between the bitter orange and citron, likely in India, China, or Myanmar. Like all citrus, it has whitish, waxy, five-petaled flowers with a heavenly aroma. The lemon tree's leaves are reddish when young and mature to a shiny green; its branches sport protective thorns.

Lemon's most widely recognized magickal properties are cleansing and apotropaic. The sharp, fresh scent has inspired countless magickal practitioners the world over to employ lemon juice, rind, flowers, and essential oil to cleanse and clear unwanted energies. Lemon flower essence is equally cleansing, and it purifes on all levels (it is sometimes even described as an aggressive cleanser).[125] Use it to purify your environment, ritual objects, personal energy field, and mind and to scrub away stress, tension, confusion, and shame. The ellipsoid shape and succulent nature of the fruit suggest that it can be employed as a prophylactic against the evil eye,[126] and the flower essence can be used both to turn back the effects of another's harmful intentions and to cleanse and heal after being targeted by psychic attack.

Lemon flower essence focuses its therapeutic effects on the mind. It clears mental fog, breaks through intellectual blocks, and offers clarity and focus. It stimulates and lightens the intellect by gently pushing aside emotional interference and helping to coordinate your thoughts.[127] In addition to boosting your capacity for logic, reasoning, and analysis, lemon flower essence also links the intellect with the imaginative and intuitive side of the mind to help you achieve breakthroughs and find artistic inspiration. It sharpens the wit and stimulates the throat chakra, thereby helping you speak with eloquence and grace. It also steers you toward decisive action and combats mental fatigue. Take it when studying or before an exam to boost your performance.

The whitish, five-petaled flowers of the lemon tree make it a text-book herb of Venus, and it has traditionally featured in magick for love, beauty, and friendship—all Venusian virtues. The fruit and flowers have been used to attract love and friendship, maintain fidelity, and increase attraction between partners. The flower essence is used by some practitioners in the bath for developing self-love and expressing inner beauty.[128] Lemon flower essence also has a reputation for releasing trauma related to sex and romance, and it helps release shame and guilt.[129] It balances yin and yang and masculine and feminine energy, which helps ensure harmony and balance in romantic and sexual relationships.

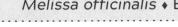

Lemon Balm
Melissa officinalis ♦ Balm

Elemental signature: spirit

Planetary signatures: moon, Venus, Jupiter

Zodiacal signatre: Cancer

Chakras: all, but especially root, sacral, solar plexus, and heart

Magickal uses: purification, love and beauty, prophecy, healing, good fortune, success, boosting magickal power

Therapeutic indications: stress, anxiety, restless thoughts, fear of resting, performance anxiety, insomnia, writer's block, melancholy, jet lag

LEMON BALM, ALSO CALLED MELISSA, is a perennial herb and a member of the mint family. It is native to southern Europe and throughout the Mediterannean, especially in mountainous regions, and has become naturalized in parts of Europe and North America. Lemon balm has wrinkly, heart-shaped leaves with serrated leaves and small yellow flowers that fade to pale lilac or white as they mature. It has a long history as a medicinal herb, having been used for everything from stress and insomnia to stomach complaints and menstrual problems.

The generic name *melissa* is derived from Greek and means "honeybee." Melissa was also the name of one of the nymphs who is said to have sheltered and nurtured the child Zeus; she discovered and taught the benefits of honey, giving her name to the bees themselves. Lemon balm's flowers are a favorite of bees, and the essence bears a deep affinity for the symbolism of the bee. Bees were once a widespread symbol of the Great Goddess, worshipped as Diana, Artemis, Cybele, and others. Priestesses and oracles once used the herb to help them receive prophetic messages from the Goddess, and today, lemon balm flower essence offers a deep link to the healing and mystery of the Great Mother. This flower also bears a lunar correspondence, and its essence is best suited to workings related to moon goddesses and the lunar cycle. Add a few drops to the chalice during full moon rituals, or use them to anoint the brow prior to drawing down the moon.

Lemon balm is associated with magick for love and beauty, success, healing, cleansing, and mental prowess. Use a few drops of the flower essence in a facewash to promote inner beauty and help attract an ideal partner. As a cleansing essence, it is powerful and gentle all at once. It can be used to enhance the effect of any magick, for it has a helpful and generous nature that supports all magickal endeavors. Christopher Penczak describes the spirit of lemon balm "like an attendant priestess, willing to aid and help us in whatever ways are necessary."[130] Alchemists once regarded it as the most potent of healing herbs, as it was said to store more life force than any other.[131] Paracelsus considered it the elixir of life, and it was said to restore vitality and grant immortality. As an essence, it helps you when you feel critically depleted, nourishing you to health, just as Melissa nurtured Zeus.

Therapeutically, lemon balm flower essence is an essential remedy against tension, anxiety, and stress. It is excellent for people who are high-strung and unable to relax. The essence helps reset and restore the ideal rhythm of activity and rest, slowing the mind and unwinding tension.[132] It calms the spirit and untangles the fears woven into the subconscious mind. Over time, this essence helps tease those fears to the surface, where they can be processed in dreams. Through this action, the essence can eliminate chronic anxiety, overactive mind, and ceaseless worry. Ultimately, it can grant peaceful sleep and allow you to release your resistance to the healing process.

Lemon balm is sometimes used in magick related to success, business, and creativity. As an essence, it addresses underlying worries and fears related to productivity. It helps you recognize that your worth is not contingent on what you can produce, thereby allowing you to be guilt-free when we rest. Lemon balm also addresses performance anxiety, making it a helpful ally for singers, actors, public speakers, and anyone else in the public eye. It helps you find a natural balance between work and rest, granting you the motivation and drive to rival that of the most industrious of bees, while still taking time to recharge and renew yourself. It is also helpful for those who travel, as it counteracts jet lag and keeps spirits high when you are engaging with new people.

Among flower essences, lemon balm may be the best suited to supporting our collective growth and evolution. The essence can reconcile your past with your present, as it helps you remember past-life experiences and understand the karmic underpinnings of situations in the present life. The essence aligns you with your soul's purpose, and it also aligns your desires with passion for truth.[133] By helping you to release fear and align with your soul's true purpose, lemon balm also promotes creativity and inspiration, making it my favorite remedy for writer's block. It reduces the ego's hold on the conscious mind and catalyzes spiritual growth. An aid to meditation, lemon balm also offers attunement to subtle energies. It awakens psychic abilities, promotes group unity, and is deeply nourishing on all levels.

Work with lemon balm flower essence to enhance and support the action of other essences. It lightens any situation, providing humor and good cheer. Consider adding the essence to flower essence blends that are challenging or intense in order to maintain humor, appreciation, and perspective along with the healing process.[134] It is an optimistic essence that brings countless gifts.

☙ Lilac

Syringa vulgaris ◆ Tree

Elemental signature: water

Planetary signatures: moon, Venus

Zodiacal signatures: Taurus, Leo

Chakra: all, but especially root and crown

Magickal uses: exorcism, protection, Earth healing, letting go, change, kundalini activation

Therapeutic indications: rigidity, nostalgia, clinging to the past, inability to move on, shouldering too much responsibility, soul amnesia, sadness, sense of burden, abandonment, isolation, holding grudges

LILACS ARE SMALL TREES in the olive family that sport spring blooms in shades of lilac, purple, and pink, among other colors. The common lilac, *Syringa vulgaris,* is native to the Balkan Peninsula, but it has naturalized in parts of Europe and North America. The flowers are usually four-petaled and grow in erect spikes. Lilac leaves are heart-shaped, attesting to gentle, loving energy exuded by these plants.

Lilac flower essence nourishes nature spirits and promotes attunement to the natural world. It invites you to recognize your place in the world, reminding you that you are one with all of creation. The essence can be added to a watering can to promote the health of your garden, as it supports not only the flora and fauna but the spiritual ecology that resides there, too.

Lilac is often associated with protection and exorcism.[135] As a spray, the flower essence guards your home and reinforces the work of other protective essences or spells. A simple exorcism spell for a haunted house once used fresh lilac blossoms; you can accomplish something similar by filling a bowl with fresh water, consecrating it, and adding several drops of lilac flower essence. As the bowl of water radiates the energy of the essence into the space, it dispels old energies and helps spirits move on. Lilac essence is also adept at reinforcing the aura and cleansing the energy field to neutralize the effects of old trauma stuck in the subtle bodies; this makes it an excellent remedy for oversensitivity, psychic attack, and negative thought patterns.[136]

In much the same way that it helps earthbound spirits move on from their past, lilac flower essence can be helpful for those who feel overly nostalgic, as though they are stuck in the past. Lilac helps those who seek distraction via old memories to be more present and to lovingly release old modes of perception.[137] This essence is especially helpful for freeing you from outdated expectations in relationships—expectations of both yourself and others. We all grow and change, and lilac essence permits us to see ourselves and others as we are now, not defined only by past behaviors. Lilac can be paired with blackberry in love magick to help you release past trauma, stay grounded in the present, and feel comfortable enough to be vulnerable for authentic connection.

Lilac's tall inflorescence suggests that the flower essence is intimately connected to the health and alignment of the spinal column. The essence promotes good posture and flexibility, and it extends this sense of alignment and flexibility to other areas of your well-being, too. It helps you become more flexible in the face of change and teaches you to let go of your need for control. Lilac is a pillar of strength that ushers you into alignment with the divine. It helps maintain a connection to the divine blueprint for any projects you engage with, thereby supporting you in learning to surrender control and rigidity. When you feel overworked or burdened with responsibility, lilac can help you learn to let go and to bend without breaking.

On an energetic level, lilac flower essence is similarly associated with alignment and movement. It aligns the subtle bodies of the aura, particularly the etheric, mental, and spiritual bodies. It also aligns and strengthens all the chakras, and it is especially nourishing to the root and crown. Lilac essence can initiate the flow of kundalini and raise the overall frequency of your energy fields. It invites you to integrate every part of your physical and spiritual anatomy into a unified and harmonious field of light, thus propelling you forward along the spiritual path.

Lilac flower essence helps you become more flexible and aligned by releasing unnecessary attachment to the past. It can help you overcome negative beliefs and a sense of powerlessness stemming from childhood.

Taking this essence can heal patterns of sadness, isolationism, abandonment, and depression. It is adept at helping you forgive and release grudges.

Lily of the Valley
Convallaria majalis ♦ Bane

Elemental signature: air

Planetary signature: Mercury

Zodiacal signature: Gemini

Chakras: heart, crown

Magickal uses: fairy magick, divination, happiness, justice, love, compassion

Therapeutic indications: feeling lost, sense of yearning, unrequited love, loss of trust, childhood trauma, bitterness and resentfulness, feelings of betrayal and despair, nightmares (especially in children), attraction to trouble, melancholy, feeling unwanted, rigidity, controlling behavior

LILY OF THE VALLEY IS A MEMBER of the asparagus family and a not-too-distant relative of Solomon's seal. It prefers shady woodlands, where its white and sweetly scented blossoms appear each spring. The flowers themselves are borne on stalks and hang like bells. They have six petals, which are fused together. Lily of the valley is native to temperate regions in the Northern Hemisphere and widely grown as an ornamental. It is toxic, as it contains cardiac glycosides and saponins, and thus care should be taken when using it as an essence.

Fairy bells, a common folk name for lily of the valley points the way to understanding the magickal and therapeutic nature of this plant. Lily of the valley is steeped in lore about the Good Folk. Fairies are said to play among stands of the plant and to use the rhythmically arranged stalks of flowers as ladders to reach the reeds they weave into cradles. There is a capricious, playful nature inherent in the plant and its essence, making it a wonderful ally for bringing peace and healing to the inner child. The essence offers protection for infants, children, teens, and pets, as it is associated with preserving the innocence of all those new to this world.[138] It allows them to feel safe, loved, and wanted.

A dear friend and fellow member of the Temple of Witchcraft, Lori, shared her love of this plant with me. She told me that the flower essence is a potent ally for transforming childhood trauma, as it focuses on returning to happiness and envisioning a better world. It helps you "see through the eyes of a child" and connects you with the inner radiance and vitality of the heart.[139] I've found that lily of the valley helps you regain a sense of wonder and awe; it is excellent for adults who have become so hardened that they are no longer able to perceive the wonder all around them. It brings you back to a state of innocence and wisdom, thereby releasing complicated notions of duty and control. A life without wonder is a life devoid of spirit, and lily of the valley flower essence helps you perceive that mystical quality all around you.

Traditional witch and poisonous plant expert Sarah Anne Lawless recently shared her findings from making a flower essence from this plant, writing that lily of the valley's medicine "can potentially help overcome the feelings of betrayal and despair over the lies of society that conceal hatred, racism, xenophobia, and inequality" and that it helps you "see the good in people and the good things people are doing to help each other right now."[140] Folklore tells us that this plant grows on the graves of people executed for crimes they did not commit; perhaps the essence can help us overcome injustice of all kinds by helping us cultivate innocence, within and without, and use that purity of heart to build a better world.

I work with lily of the valley when I need to be able to look for the good in others. While I don't find that this essence conceals the negative effects of people's actions, it does remind you that the human condition as a whole—our shared human experience—is not bereft of goodness. The fused petals imply a sense of unity, and lily of the valley flower essence helps you see that before we are anything else, we are all first and foremost humans. It also invites you to recognize that, generally speaking, most people are doing the best they can with the tools they have. It inspires you to want to lift up others and rise together in the face of adversity. Lily of the valley flower essence also has potential for helping you release the judgments you direct toward yourself; it helps free you from convention and the desire to seek social approval, instead directing you to live more authentically from your heart.

Try working with lily of the valley flower essence if you have difficulty saying no to those you love. Although this essence has a powerful heart-opening effect, it also imparts loving boundaries. The essence tempers love, compassion, and generosity with a gentle reminder that you are human, too, and that you must show yourself the same love and compassion you endeavor to give to others.

Lily of the valley is also used in divination. Taking the essence opens both the heart and crown chakras, stimulating the ability to tune in to the messages from spirit. The essence can also be used in offerings to fairy folk, nature spirits, and the souls of deceased children to honor their innate innocence and bring a sense of comfort to them from beyond the grave.

Lotus
Nelumbo nucifera ♦ Balm

Elemental signatures: water, spirit

Planetary signature: Neptune

Zodiacal signature: Pisces

Chakras: all, especially the crown

Magickal uses: purification, consecration, meditation, protection, astral travel, past-life recall, sovereignty, enlightenment

Therapeutic indications: disconnectedness, indecisiveness, lack of focus, muddy or unclear thinking, daydreaming, pride, egotism, being out of touch with reality, impatience (especially regarding spiritual development)

LOTUSES ARE ANCIENT FLOWERS once widespread throughout the world. Today only two species are extant, *Nelumbo nucifera* and *N. lutea*. The lotus grows in muddy water with leaves and flowers that stand above the water itself. It is the most venerated flower in human history, having been sacred to many cultures. The Egyptians depicted the lotus (actually the distantly related *Nymphaea lotus*) in their art,

354 ★ Directory of One Hundred Flower Essences

and it featured into Egyptian religion and myth. Isis was depicted in the lotus bud that rises above the waters, while her son Horus was shown cradled in a lotus leaf. The four sons of Horus are frequently depicted upon a white lotus blossom. In the Far East, the lotus is the seat of Brahma, Lakshmi, Buddha, and Kuan Yin.

There is precious little magickal lore about the lotus, as it was not widely available to occultists of the West until relatively recently. It is associated with purification, protection, and the enhancement of all spiritual endeavors, from meditation to past-life recall. Lotus essential oil is sometimes used to dress candles for protection and consecration. The flower essence can be used to the same end; as the candle burns, it will carry the spiritual light and energy of the lotus flower outward with the light and warmth of the flame. Such essence-infused candles can assist you in connecting to higher beings, such as your guides, spirits, and deities.

Lotus is one of the most universally supportive flower essences available. This potent remedy promotes openheartedness and helps you release judgment, stress, and egotism. It is one of the best for the health of the chakra system. The chakras are themselves sometimes visualized as lotuses; the Sanskrit name for the crown chakra, *sahasrara*, means "thousand-petaled lotus."* Appropriately, lotus flower essence opens the crown chakra and aligns all the centers of the subtle anatomy with the crown. It removes blockages in the chakras and restores healthy movement to these energy centers. It also aligns and coheres all other parts of the subtle anatomy, including the subtle bodies, meridians, and nadis.

Therapeutically, lotus flower essence is typically indicated for people who are ungrounded, unfocused, indecisive, and absentminded; it offers a gentle invitation to be grounded and practice mindfulness. The essence promotes focus and relaxation.

Sometimes likened to the philosopher's stone, lotus flower essence transmutes human consciousness.[141] It is considered among the most

---

*Curiously, the ancient Egyptian numeral representing the number one thousand was depicted as a water lily or lotus; the similarity to the thousand-petaled lotus of the Vedic chakra system is a beautiful synchronicity.

important flower essences available because it has such profound effects. It treats the entire person: body, mind, and spirit. It also boosts the efficacy of other essences, an effect owed in part to the manner in which it purifies and aligns all parts of the subtle anatomy, allowing you to integrate any healing modality with greater ease. Take it frequently to promote a general cleansing of body, mind, and spirit.

Lotus flower essence promotes spiritual pursuits and advances the higher functions of the psyche. It enhances meditation, assists psychic development, and steers the soul along its evolutionary path. Just as the lotus blossom rises out above the muddy water to bloom, so, too, does our inner divinity rise with it. It is a symbol of enlightenment, the attainment of Buddha-nature or Christ consciousness. Lotus's iridescent leaves repel water, allowing the plant to breathe, and reinforcing the signature of its transcendent nature.[142] Lotus essence helps you transcend your personal suffering by rising above it, and it reminds you that pain, attachment, and negativity can only affect you when you allow them to do so. Lotus remind you that the luminous nature of the soul is impervious to harmful vibrations.

Lotus also promotes psychic insight and spirit flight. The essence has been noted for its mind-altering, consciousness-expanding effects. Anointing the brow with the essence makes meditations more vivid and helps make psychic readings more accurate and informative. Lotus flower essence will assist all forms of out-of-body journeys, such as astral travel and dreamtime journeys. Try adding it to a flying blend alongside essences made from more traditional ingredients, such as mandrake, datura, and belladonna.

As you grow spiritually and magickally, lotus can help you avoid the pitfalls associated with the spiritual path. The essence promotes humility, thereby healing any tendency toward egotism, spiritual pride, and a sense of superiority.[143] It promotes sovereignty, helping you marry your will, love, and wisdom together so that you can accept responsibility as the architect of your own destiny. Lotus flower essence promotes objectivity and imparts wisdom, and it puts you in direct communion with your own inner divinity.

Magnolia
Magnolia grandiflora, Magnolia spp. ♦ Tree

Elemental signature: water

Planetary signature: moon

Zodiacal signature: Cancer

Chakras: root, crown

Magickal uses: love, lust, purification, connecting to the Great Goddess

Therapeutic indications: difficulty adapting, clinging to old habits or beliefs, feeling overwhelmed by circumstance, disconnection from your heritage, lack of positive female influence, feeling unimportant or undignified or undeserving

MAGNOLIAS ARE A FAMILY of more than two hundred flowering trees that have existed for millions of years. These plants adapted to reproduction by pollination before bees even existed; they evolved leathery petals that could withstand the attentions of bigger insects, such as beetles, rather than the more delicate pollinators we expect today. The southern magnolia (*M. grandiflora*), in particular, exhibits large white flowers with six to twelve petals, usually arranged in rows of four, with a whorl-shaped receptacle in the center that contains the reproductive parts of the flower. Magnolias typically have strong, sweet aromas and are used in magick, medicine, and spiritual practices around the world. Many magnolia flower essences are available today, with the greatest variety available from Flora of Asia. Although we'll focus on southern magnolia here, many of the general attributes apply to other varieties of magnolia.

With its oversized white blossoms and sweet, citronella aroma, southern magnolia is my favorite flower. Consequently, it is also one of my favorite flower essences and is easily the one that I, my students, and my clients use most often. Thanks to their primeval heritage—they are among the most ancient of flower trees—magnolia blossoms create an essence that awakens a memory of our primal nature and connection to the planet. Overall, the magnolia flower essence is grounding and stabilizing, and it exerts a protective influence, just as its tough leaves and leathery petals have protected the plant for aeons, and their overall heaviness lends an earthy quality to this essence.

Magnolia is sometimes used in love and lust magick. Its heady aroma attracts insects, but the flowers do not offer nectar as a reward. Instead, insects come and go on scent alone. As materia magica, magnolia is used to induce the thrill of the chase and is helpful for boosting confidence. The essence can help you come out of your shell and feel more attractive and deserving of love, as well as helping you enjoy the acts of flirting and courtship without feeling pressured for more. In American folk magick, the petals and leaves are employed to ensure a partner's fidelity. The essence can be taken to help you examine whether you've built a solid and loving foundation with your partner; thus, it can help you curtail feelings of insecurity in your relationships and ease worries or fears about a partner's faithfulness.

Magnolia flower essence offers a powerful remedy for anxiety, stress, and worry. It helps you tap in to the spiritual support that is everywhere within and around you. It is well suited for periods of change and transformation, as it keeps you rooted in the foundation you've built while supporting you in reaching upward toward the heavens as you grow. This flower essence teaches you the value of acceptance, thereby allowing you to release fear, worry, and resistance. It helps you seek meaning beyond the superficial appearance of any scenario by recognizing the divine origins of the soul.

Members of the magnolia family are all connected to the energy of the divine feminine, but this is especially the case for the southern magnolia. Its giant, white, bowl-like flowers are giant chalices, symbolizing the receptive, yin forces of the Goddess. Its essence catalyzes spiritual connection to the Great Goddess and helps you call upon her for claiming your own power, whether you identify as a woman, man, or otherwise. As a result, the essence also cultivates a sense of personal power, and it balances your ability to be independent with a recognition of the interdependence of all life. The sheer power of this flower to connect you to the divine allows you to transcend the obstacles on your spiritual path through surrender, dedication, and some added support from the Great Mother.

✿ Mandrake
Mandragora officinarum ✦ Bane

Elemental signatures: all, predominantly earth and spirit

Planetary signatures: Mercury, Venus, Saturn

Zodiacal signature: Scorpio

Chakras: sacral, crown

Magickal uses: protection, love, desire, fertility, success, healing, cursing

Therapeutic indications: dogmatism, contrarian attitude, empty spiritual practice, inability to commune with spiritual forces and beings, issues relating to power and sexuality

MANDRAKE IS THE WORLD'S most famous baneful plant, easily recognized by its large, forked taproot that occasionally resembles a humanoid shape. It is diminutive in nature, with wrinkly, deeply veined, oblong leaves that grow in a basal rosette emerging directly from the taproot. Two primary varieties exist: the black or autumn mandrake and the white or spring mandrake. The former has purple flowers that emerge in the fall, while the other has greenish-white or pale blue flowers appearing in the spring. The plant's native range is distributed throughout the eastern Mediterranean and the Middle East.

Of all magickal plants, mandrake has accrued one of the largest bodies of lore, which is populated by colorful and sinister stories. It has both malevolent and benevolent applications, being at once an important medicine and source of love and blessings and a home for malefic spirits and devils, too. Myths about the danger of mandrake have resulted in stories of it glowing in the night and emitting deadly shrieks when dug up. It is associated with Venusian goddesses, like Aphrodite and Hathor, and with patrons of witchcraft, including Hekate, Circe, Medea, Diana, and Mercury. Its root is employed in magick for love, lust, fertility, healing, protection, money, and success.

Mandrake is deeply connected to the spirit realms. It is a frequent ingredient in witch's salves and flying ointments, which were used to induce visionary experiences of flying to the witches' sabbat and communing with spirits. One of my first experiences with the flower essence resulted in exceptionally vivid dreams, which happened to be centered on flowers. I've found this essence to be a powerful aid for lucid dreaming, astral travel, and all manner of shamanic journeys. Because of the plant's large (and rather infamous) root, mandrake is attuned to chthonic energies and holds the keys to the underworld. Taking the essence before meditation, dreamwork, or journeying helps open the doors to the underworld for contact with ancestors, guides, and spirits that reside there.

Mandrake is a sort of emissary of the plant kingdom, a go-between for the worlds of human and plant. I've heard it called the "king of poisons," and it can be an intercessor when meeting other baneful plant spirits. Accordingly, it offers insight and assistance when you are working with plant spirits, especially those of other baneful plants. I sometimes turn to mandrake flower essence when I'm having trouble having or remembering meaningful experiences with plant spirits and other spirit allies; it also helps integrate the energy of other flower essences. In my own practice, taking mandrake essence introduced me to the spirit of datura—a plant I had longed to work with more deeply but had struggled to connect with. Adding mandrake essence to blends containing other baneful essences can help you integrate and process their wisdom and healing more effectively. The essence also opens your innate clairaudient skills, thereby facilitating communication with your spirit guides, ancestors, and other nonphysical entities. It is intimately linked to the underworld and to the Dark Goddess; use it to initiate a process of rebirth via shadow work, especially with the help of the Dark Goddess.

Mandrake flower essence confronts ingrained beliefs and challenges adherence to dogma. In this way, it helps you discover a more authentic experience of spirituality.[144] It can be helpful for people who assume a contrarian stance no matter the situation, even if they are not personally invested in either side of an argument; the essence works to reduce adversarial personality traits, replacing them with a sense of curiosity and mutual respect. It also helps you explore the nature of issues surrounding sex and power. Mandrake flower essence builds confidence by allowing you to see through the illusion of powerlessness.[145] It is helpful when your practice might be viewed as transgressive against mainstream institutions and culture; work with mandrake to release the fear and discomfort that arises from going against the grain. Mandrake flower essence also sheds light on the reasons behind emotional outbursts, while increasing your energy, creativity, and visionary skills.[146]

Mandrake essence is a magickal catalyst that can help you better connect to the spirit world for virtually any variety of magick. It connects you to the archetypes of the witch and attunes you to the very nature of magick itself. The roots were once soaked in water and the water then sprinkled on anything that needed help flourishing;[147] a few drops of the flower essence may be diluted in water to the same end. The essence catalyzes the effects of other flower essences—particularly the baneful ones—and it should be used with care, as sensitive people may find it intense. Try placing one or two drops on the crown chakra to best experience the visionary and consciousness-shifting benefits.

Mayapple (American Mandrake)
Podophyllum peltatum ◆ Bane

Elemental signature: fire

Plantary signatures: Venus, Saturn, Pluto

Zodiacal signature: Scorpio

Chakras: root, sacral

Magickal uses: protection, invisibility, keeping secrets, love, prosperity, shamanic journey

Therapeutic indications: need for shadow work, shame, depression, frustration, stubbornness, obsessive-compulsive disorder (OCD), impatience, transition, or lack of direction

MAYAPPLE, THOUGH SOMETIMES known as American mandrake, is not a true mandrake but a member of the barberry family. It is found in North American deciduous forests with plenty of shade and grows a large umbrella-like leaf on a single stalk. The flower, and eventually the fruit, can be found hidden beneath the large leaf. The flowers are waxy and white (occasionally with a rosy tint), and they have six to nine petals. Indigenous people used mayapple medicinally to treat parasites, as a purgative, and as an abortifacient. All parts of the plant except the ripe fruit are poisonous.

Little indigenous lore about the magickal or religious uses of mayapple has survived, but it is a common ingredient in hoodoo, conjure, and other forms of American folk magick. When European colonists came to North America, they found enough similarity between the uses and the environment in which mayapple grows to project some of the lore of traditional mandrake onto the mayapple. The roots are much thinner than those of the true mandrake and do not truly resemble the humanoid figure. They are sometimes bound together to make poppets for use in love magick, and a single, sticklike root is wrapped in a banknote and carried to draw money.

Dried mayapple fruit and roots may be used in magick related to secrets and invisibility. As a flower essence, mayapple deals with the hidden aspects of the psyche. The flowers are hidden beneath large leaves, the plant thrives in shadowy forests, and it dies back each year to be reborn in the spring. In the same way, the essence helps you withdraw into yourself to discover parts of the self you have forgotten or repressed. It takes persistence to find the flowers hidden beneath the large leaves, and mayapple flower essence endows you with the same persistence and tenacity to sort through the shadow self for deep healing. The essence connects you to the underworld and to the planet Pluto to help you dive deep into the recesses of the soul.

Mayapple flower essence is excellent for discovering the unexplored or repressed aspects of your identity, particularly those related to sexuality and gender identity. It cuts through the shame, guilt, and fear you might have around these issues and gives you permission to explore the nature of your desires. It helps you explore the nature of pleasure and protects you from the internalized phobias and judgments that come from society at large. Mayapple can be a valuable ally for members of the LGBTQ+ community in coming to terms with their identity and developing pride where shame once flourished.

Mayapple is strongly protective, as connoted by both its toxic nature and the shield-like leaves from which it derives its Latin species name, *peltatum*. Use the essence when you are feeling vulnerable, and it will simultaneously help you understand where the feelings of vulnerability arise from as well as protect you against outside energies. It can thus be used to treat patterns of depression, frustration, OCD, impatience, and stubbornness. Mayapple teaches the value of patience and divine timing; it helps you surrender to the unfolding of life events and offers deep insight when you feel you need additional clarity and support. This flower essence is a powerful ally for times of change and transition, as well as for overcoming the feeling of being lost or aimless; take the essence before meditation to meet the spirit of this kind and helpful plant for assistance in discovering your life's purpose.

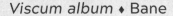

ꙮ
Mistletoe
Viscum album ◆ Bane

Elemental signature: air

Planetary signatures: sun, Jupiter

Zodiacal signatures: Capricorn, Aquarius

Chakras: solar plexus, heart

Magickal uses: protection, healing, love, fertility, removing obstacles

Therapeutic indications: loneliness, fear, insecurity, depression, low will to live, stunted creativity, repressed memories, spaciness, ungroundedness, inability to relate to others

MISTLETOE IS AN EVERGREEN, parasitic plant that attaches itself to trees, drawing water and nutrients from its host. It has smooth, oval-shaped leaves that grow in pairs along the stem, and its golden, honey-colored flowers attract pollinators when it blooms in late winter. White berries eventually replace the flowers, and they are clustered in small groups of two to six fruits. Mistletoe has been regarded as sacred and magickal for millennia, and it makes a powerful flower essence. Its host tree will influence the effects of the essence; mistletoe collected from oak will act differently than that which grows on apple or juniper. Nowadays it is possible to find entire collections of mistletoe essences made by producers across the globe.

This evergreen was among the most sacred of plants for the ancient Druids. Mistletoe growing on a sacred oak was regarded as a sign that the gods were present, and the Druids used mistletoe to create sacred drinks that could confer strength and courage, heal illness, counteract poisons, and make people and animals fertile.[148] The plant continues to feature in seasonal customs and folk magick in many parts of Europe. It is hung to ward off harm and illness and to attract love and boost fertility.

Mistletoe essence serves to link heaven and earth. It has no proper roots of its own; instead, it depends on the tree to which it is attached to provide nutrients and water. Its essence enables people predisposed to being spacy and ungrounded, people described as having their heads in the clouds, find viable methods for grounding. Mistletoe is also helpful for feelings of loneliness and insecurity. The flower essence helps connect you to the whole, often through an intermediary, such as a spiritual ally or a loved one, who can help open doors to connecting with others. The essence combats fear, depression, and feelings of weakness. It offers protection and nourishment from the heavens when you are tasked with challenging periods of growth and personal transformation. It also opens the door to higher consciousness; you can best use it for this by spraying it in the aura, meditating with a bottle held over your crown, or applying one or two drops of the essence to the crown chakra itself.

Mistletoe flower essence helps you develop creative solutions to challenging situations. It severs the hold that fear has over you, teaching the value of surrender and trust.

The white berries, which are often borne in pairs, are sometimes likened to testicles, thereby resulting in the herb's associations with fertility and sex. A North American relative of European mistletoe is held sacred to Erzulie, a Vodou *loa* (spirit or goddess) of love and pleasure.[149] The essence also has connections to these themes, for it helps balance sexuality with romance. Mistletoe essence increases your potency in all that you do, making you feel bold enough to pursue love and pleasure.

It also helps you maintain your individual identity among groups and relationships; this allows you to have a healthy and balanced dynamic within all your romantic and platonic relationships. The plant is often used in spells for fertility and in the Great Rite. When carried, it was believed to assist conception and pregnancy; as an essence, mistletoe helps you conceive of new ideas and boosts your magickal potency.

I find that mistletoe essence can be enhanced when partnered with a tree essence, especially oak. The two are powerfully synergistic and connect to the archetypes of the divine masculine, particularly the Horned God and Green Man. Add a drop or two of one or both essences to the athame or knife before plunging it into the chalice during the Great Rite to draw in the power of the god of the witches. Mistletoe is famously said to have opened locked doors, and the essence is one of opportunity, helping to overcome obstacles and open new doors on the path to spiritual growth.

Monkshood
Aconitum napellus ♦ Bane

Elemental signature: water

Planetary signatures: moon, Saturn, Neptune

Zodiacal signature: Capricorn

Chakras: heart, third eye, crown

Magickal uses: protection, glamoury, consecration, psychic development, leadership, wisdom, shamanic journey (especially to different times)

Therapeutic indications: dark night of the soul, irrational fear and phobias, fear of power and the abuse of power, dread about the future, anxiety, questioning the past

MONKSHOOD, ALSO CALLED aconite and wolfsbane, is a member of the buttercup family, Ranunculaceae. The plant has five-lobed leaves with serrated margins; its roots are thick and tuberous. The common name monkshood references the shape of the flowers, which resemble monks' hoods. Most monkshood has blue to purple flowers, though some cultivars have white blooms. All parts of the plant are extremely poisonous, and it must be handled with care.

Monkshood is a classic witching herb, annd much myth and magickal lore surround it. It is said to have sprung forth from the spittle of Cerberus, the three-headed dog who guards the gates of the underworld in Greek mythology. The plant was featured in the myths of Circe and Medea, and it has long been considered a powerful ally of witches and enchanters. Monkshood is one of the herbs in Hekate's garden, and it was held in high esteem by her priestesses. It is also linked to several other representations of the divine feminine. In Austria and France, for example, monkshood was called "chariot of Venus," a clear reference to the Great Mother and queen of the witches' sabbat. That name perhaps derives from the use of monkshood in witches' flying ointments, which allowed witches to fly to Mount Venus, the mythical location of the sabbat. Thus, witches once rode the "chariot of Venus" to journey to the sabbat. Another surviving Austrian folk name for monkshood translates as "heavenly mother's slipper," a nod to Mary, mother of Christ.[150]

Monkshood flower essence promotes communion with the divine. It can help you withdraw from the bustle and busyness of everyday life so you can better hear the whispers of spirit and the songs and stories of the ancient gods. The essence invokes a profound stillness, so much so that it enables psychic ability to flourish. The plant has an ancient association with shape-shifting and lycanthropy; it was believed to ward off werewolves or even cure the lycanthropic condition—hence the name wolfsbane. I find the essence helpful for shape-shifting during meditation or shamanic journeys, and it can boost your ability to cast a glamour.

One of monkshood's gifts is to release fears tied to the past and the future. It breaks through patterns of false prognostication—horrible visions of what may be caused by irrational fears and anxiety—to make you a clearer channel for the voice of the gods. The essence can invite you to experience time in a nonlinear fashion, especially during dreams. It helps you release deep karmic ties that have kept you from reaching your highest spiritual potential and may bring your karmic debts up to date.

On one hand, monkshood teaches acceptance, and on the other, it reminds you of the magick within you that can change the course of your destiny. It helps you use the power available to you responsibly. It is helpful for learning to maintain your own boundaries and to respect the boundaries of others. This makes monkshood essence invaluable for recovering from trauma, wherein your boundaries may be not only disrespected but violated outright. The essence sparks spiritual awakening as a means of transcending and healing trauma, but it does not result in spiritual bypassing. In fact, I find this essence capable of helping clients identify and break the patterns of bypassing.

Monkshood flower essence invites you to turn inward and find the depth of spiritual life therein. Like the hood or helmet that it resembles, this flower protects during spiritual endeavors, allowing the crown and third-eye chakras to open wide without worry of interference. As a result, it promotes psychic experiences, astral travel, and other spiritual phenomena. Out of this stillness and direct communion with the spiritual realms, monkshood empowers you to accept the role of spiritual teacher and leader. The essence promotes good judgment and helps you maintain integrity in all that you do. However, it also contends with fears of misusing power. It helps you keep your ego in check so that you can use spiritual, clerical, and social power—particularly of a sexual or magickal nature—ethically and responsibly. Taking the essence can also help you recover from having been abused or manipulated by someone in such a position of power; it may be particularly helpful for those recovering from experiences with cults and religious orders.

Monkshood essence combats materialism; it could be called the essence of the renunciate. It is helpful when you want to get away from everyday life, but rather than allowing you to become an escapist, the essence helps you channel that desire into productive and authentic spiritual development. As noted, monkshood is one of the classic ingredients in flying potions, and its flower essence similarly helps with spiritual travel and spirit flight. It especially seems to direct the attention inward, to the rich psychological landscape within. The plant has a number of funereal uses, including being offered to or planted in honor of the dead; taking the essence can help you commune with the deceased or visit the ancestral abode in the underworld. Monkshood also invokes the Mighty Dead, spiritual ancestors and the blessed deceased, to watch over your magick at the circle's edge. Try adding a few drops of the essence to offerings of water on ancestral altars, or take a few drops of the essence before invoking their presence in your rites.

Monkshood is sometimes used in the consecration of magickal tools, such as the athame and cauldron, and for this purpose, the flower essence is the safest preparation. Add a few drops to a container of holy water or a consecration oil to bless, protect, and empower your magickal tools. The essence will banish evil and harmful energies and infuse the tools with protective influences.

Morning Glory
Ipomoea purpurea, Ipomoea spp. ♦ Bane

Elemental signature: water

Planetary signatures: sun, Neptune

Zodiacal signature: Leo

Chakras: throat, third eye

Magickal uses: divination, inspiration, healing, success

Therapeutic indications: bad habits or addiction, inconsistency, shyness, difficulty communicating, irregular or erratic schedules that drain life force

MORNING GLORIES ARE A LARGE GROUP of flowers belonging to the Convolvulus family. They are vines with trumpet-shaped flowers, most recognizably in shades of blue and violet. The flowers open at dawn and have a fivefold symmetry in their flared corollas. They often attract moths and butterflies as pollinators. While the common morning glory (*Ipomoea purpurea*) is native to Mexico, hundreds of species and countless cultivars are grown in warm regions around the globe. Some species are considered noxious weeds in regions where they have naturalized.

The seeds of many species of morning glory contain psychedelic compounds, and they have been used as sacred medicine for contacting the spirit world in Central and South America for centuries. Ingesting the seeds is said to allow you to commune with the gods and receive messages from spirits for healing and prophecy. Art from the region often depicts members of this botanical family alongside gods and spirits, and the morning glory is associated with a mother goddess figure in some parts of Mexico. The plant is ruled by Neptune, the planet of the mystic, although the matutinal nature of the blooms also allows for a link to the sun.

The trumpet-shaped flowers are a signature for communication. Indigenous people in Central America use the medicine of this plant spirit to commune with their gods, and morning glory flower essence similarly provides contact with nonphysical beings, such as spirits, gods, and other beings of light. Flower essence healer Diane Stein suggests that this essence is helpful for connecting with the devas and spirits of nature as well as extraterrestrials.[151] The essence connects you to the very planet itself, allowing you to speak to the heart of Mother Earth to receive her wisdom and guidance in your everyday life. Morning glory permits you to learn the stories of every kingdom of earth: animal, vegetable, mineral, and beyond. It also is helpful for boosting memory and focus for more conventional studies, too.

Morning glory flower essence is helpful for people who have trouble getting up in the morning. It does more than merely shake off the inertia of sleep—it balances the nocturnal nature of the astral body with the diurnal forces of the etheric body.[152] An imbalance in this arena often manifests as erratic sleeping and eating habits as well as a tendency to stay up too late. Such inconsistencies in your schedule sap your life force and lead to burnout; they may also cause cravings for stimulants like caffeine. This flower's fivefold symmetry acts as a gateway to becoming more consciously incarnate and embodied. Morning glory flower essence helps reset the inner spiritual rhythms that influence your cycles of rest and activity and help you experience a natural energy boost in the morning. Try taking the essence as soon as you awake for complete renewal. Over time, the essence helps you form new and consistent habits and supports radiant health.

Morning glory flower essence may also treat bad habits, cravings, and addiction. A number of flower essence practitioners have found several species of morning glory to help conquer addiction to nicotine, caffeine, and other stimulants. The effect of the flower essence also invites clarity and simplicity by inviting you to separate needs from wants; it teaches you to focus on what really matters in each day and curtails cravings for empty stimuli and short-term gratification.

I've made several essences from various morning glories that grow wild in Florida, and each of them has a quality of exuberance. I've found that morning glories of all sorts are great for coming out of your shell. They inspire a sense of vitality and help you fall in love with life. Magickally, one type of morning glory is widely celebrated for its ability to improve life all around: *Ipomoea jalapa,* popularly called High John the Conqueror. It is used in hoodoo, conjure, and rootwork to gain personal mastery and to command your power for success and sovereignty. Morning glory flower essence similarly promotes a state of mastery by inviting you to step in to your body *and* your power; it encourages you to use your voice to create change, too.

Morning glory can be used in magick to promote communication and success. The vine overcomes obstacles and inertia by growing over them; in fact, it will form a dense blanket of cover that completely conceals obstacles it once faced. The essence helps you claim success in a similar way: by helping you find innovative ways to circumvent and transcend limitations. The essence is also useful for divination and psychic development; add thirteen drops to a bowl of water to use for scrying or anoint a crystal ball or scrying mirror with the essence.

Mugwort
Artemisia vulgaris ◆ Balm

Elemental signatures: fire, water
Planetary signatures: moon, Venus, Neptune
Zodiacal signatures: Cancer, Libra, Pisces
Chakra: third eye
Magickal uses: cleansing, protection, love, preventing weariness,

psychic development, clairvoyance, lucid dreaming, protection,
lunar magick

Therapeutic indications: tendency toward fantasy or hysteria, inability
to discern genuine psychic experience from projection, no psychic
filter, nightmares, blocked energy in the spine or aura or chakras,
misalignment of the spine

MUGWORT IS IN THE ASTER FAMILY, Asteraceae or Compositae. Mugwort plants tend toward tall and erect habits, with densely packed foliage. The leaves are feathery or forked, with a silvery dusting of hairs on the underside, and the flowers are clustered together in racemes or spikes. Individual florets are unassuming; each one is populated by small yellow or reddish petals. Species of mugwort are found in many parts of the world, and it is commonly found in liminal spaces, waste areas, and similar places alongside other witching herbs.

Mugwort has long been used for magick, medicine, and food. Its scent is pungent and fiery, and it often blooms around the time of the summer solstice and midsummer sabbat. For this reason, it is sometimes associated with the sun. The genus, *Artemisia,* is named after the goddess of the moon and hunt, Artemis, and its lunar associations are evidenced by the silvery leaves and connection to the subconscious. Occult herbalist Harold Roth says that mugwort "is like the sun shining in the dreamworld," and he highlights the way the correspondences are a union of opposites: fire and water, sun and moon, yin and yang, masculine and feminine.[153] Traditional magickal uses for mugwort relate largely to cleansing, protection, psychic development, and conjuring spirits. Among Germanic peoples, the plant was said to be the first and oldest of herbs and was sometimes called "mother of all herbs."

Mugwort has garnered the reputation for being among the best plant allies for psychic development. Practitioners drink the tea to open the third eye and place a bit of the herb under the pillows to heighten the dream state. Burned as an incense, it induces clairvoyance and facilitates communication with beneficent spirits. The flower essence works similarly to make the mind more receptive and aware of psychic information. Taken before bed, it makes dreams clearer and more vivid so you can use them to gain insight about everyday life. Taken regularly, the essence develops your psychic skills so you can access spiritual guidance more readily.

Mugwort flower essence is also indicated when you are unable to separate genuine psychic perception from projections—impressions or messages that you *want* to be true. It helps you practice discernment and acts as a sort of psychic filter. This makes it an excellent ally for sensitive people, empaths, and anyone with overactive or uncontrolled psychic senses. The essence also allows you to distinguish between physical, mundane experiences and nonphysical or psychic experiences. Take it to reduce the occurrence of nightmares and night terrors.

Mugwort is deeply cleansing, and it is used for purification in many cultures around the world. This herb is said to drive away all manners of evil, from demons and spirits to the harmful thoughts of other people. The flower essence can be sprayed or diffused as a substitute to burning the dried herb. Its energy smooths and evens out the energy of the auric field. The spirit of mugwort helps remove energy blockages, move energy from one place to the next, clear stuck and stagnant energy, and remove intrusive or foreign energies from your aura or your home.[154] A simple technique for making use of mugwort's propensity for cleansing the energy field is inspired by one taught by Pam Montgomery (itself based on herbalist Eliot Cowan's "Hole in One" method): try placing a drop of mugwort flower essence, or spraying a bit of it, at the spot where the skull and spine meet (called the foramen magnum); invite the spirit of the plant and the energy of the essence to flow down the spine, unwinding tension and releasing stuck energies to offer realignment of the spinal column and a renewal of the flow of life force within it.[155]

Mugwort flower essence is an excellent aid to divinatory work of all sorts. Scrying tools, like crystal balls, obsidian mirrors, or vessels of water, can be anointed with the essence and placed under the light of the full moon to consecrate and dedicate them to the art of clear seeing. The essence is also an appropriate one to use in celebrating

Midsummer; it can be added to the chalice alongside vervain to represent the height of solar magick and the impending return of the dark half of the year. You can take the essence to attune to the tides of the moon, and it is helpful to take it before drawing down the moon so you can better receive the power and magick of the Great Goddess.

Mullein
Verbascum thapsus ◆ Balm

Elemental signature: fire

Planetary signatures: sun, Saturn

Zodiacal signatures: Leo, Scorpio

Chakra: solar plexus

Magickal uses: protection, courage, love

Therapeutic indications: self-deception, fear of the truth, fear of vulnerability, looking for support in the wrong places, indecisiveness, moral weakness, deceiving others

MULLEIN IS A BIENNIAL PLANT in the figwort family native to Europe, Asia, and northern Africa; it has been naturalized in Australia and North America. It is hailed for its large, fuzzy leaves, which grow in a basal rosette. The yellow, five-petaled flowers are borne on a tall spike resembling a candle in the second year.

I fell in love with mullein the moment I met it. Those wide, fuzzy leaves are like a downy blanket, and the brilliant flowers stand like a fiery beacon. The leaves and inflorescence have been used as wicks and torches, further connecting the plant to the fire element and to light. Magickally, mullein is considered protective, healing, and illuminating. Folk magick traditions in America employ the herb for protection and control, as well as for divination and spirit conjuring, and in rare cases for jinxing or cursing. Odysseus is said to have used mullein to protect himself from Circe's magick, and lamps made with mullein wicks are thought to keep away all manners of evil spirits.

The flower essence has a protective and illuminating quality to it, too. Largely, the essence wards against self-deception and fear. It is especially effective when you are faced with a fear of being vulnerable. This flower essence offers a quiet strength and courage to help you face your fears. It provides a sense of self-reliance and reassurance that helps counteract the tendency to seek support from outside yourself, especially if you are prone to falling in with people who do not have your best interests at heart. Ultimately, mullein flower essence helps you step in to your truth and follow your sense of purpose unwaveringly. It teaches that real strength and protection come from authentic vulnerability.[156]

In herbal medicine, mullein is often used to treat the ears. As a flower essence, it addresses your inability to hear your inner voice. Mullein is helpful for people who have an underdeveloped sense of morality or a weakness of character. Use it when you are wrestling with your conscience, especially if you feel as though you may resort to dishonesty or deceit.[157] Mullein essence lights the path and encourages you to stand tall in your truth; it is an essence of authenticity, moral fortitude, and truth. You might consider using mullein in rituals aimed for these same principles, especially when it is combined with flowers connected to justice, success, and sovereignty.

Mullein flower essence is purifying to the aura and chakra system, especially with regard to the solar plexus. Applying it to the aura clears away dark, dense, and unhealthy energies to make space for increased light. The flower essence is evolutionary in that it prepares the physical and subtle bodies to receive more light. Consequently, the essence also expands the consciousness so that it is more receptive to psychic information, and it promotes clear thinking, better concentration, and innovative ideas.[158]

Dispense drops of mullein essence around your sacred space to maintain an atmosphere of integrity, power, and light in your magickal workings. Diffuse it or give it as an offering when conjuring spirits or other beings to keep away malefic forces and ensure honest communication from the spirit world. You might use the flower essence at Samhain or Halloween to represent the light and hope of the soul amid the dark half of the year; it symbolizes the magick of the witch that penetrates the depth of mystery.

Nettle

Urtica dioica ◆ Balm

Elemental signature: fire

Planetary signature: Mars

Zodiacal signatures: Scorpio, Aries

Chakras: root, sacral, solar plexus

Magickal uses: protection, banishing, binding, exorcism, luck, healing, cursing and countercursing

Therapeutic indications: anger, rage, spite, impatience, strong emotional pain (especially from a broken home life), irrational fear when life is going well, patterns of toxic relationships, feeling under attack, being highly sensitive or easily overwhelmed, tendency to push loved ones away, lashing out when feeling vulnerable

THE STINGING NETTLE is native to Europe, North America, and parts of Asia. Its leaves are dark green and soft with serrated margins; they are covered in silica-rich hairs that deliver a painful dose of formic acid. Nettles are dioecious, meaning they bear male and female flowers on separate plants. Most male plants have yellow (or sometimes purplish) flowers with four petal-like structures called tepals, while female flowers are grayish or whitish green, also with four tepals. In spite of their sting, nettles are classified as a balm, and they have a long history of use as food and medicine as well as for making textiles.

The magickal lore of this plant is largely inspired by its sting. Tradition holds that nettle is an ideal ally for work related to protection, banishing, and exorcism. Because of its connection to spinning and weaving, nettle is also an excellent plant spirit to turn to when you need to bind harm. The plant is very nutritious and is medicinally used to cleanse the body; magickally, it is adept at cleansing and purification, too.

Some of the lore surrounding nettle is linked to the fall of Lucifer and the serpent in Eden, which justifies the use of this plant for baneful magick. Some accounts assert that nettles sprouted where fallen angels landed on Earth. Nettle is also said to grow as a result of the devil's influence, favoring places where bodies lie buried or blood has been spilled. The devil himself reportedly gathered nettles on May Day, or Beltane, and after that day it was not wise to eat them; this story very likely comes from the need to harvest the greens before the plant flowers, because after flowering they become bitter. Irish lore tells that the serpent that tempted Eve to eat the forbidden fruit hid under nettles in Eden.

This serpentine connection is also present among the Iroquois people of North America, further highlighting the Luciferian energy of nettle. The Iroquois mixed nettles with snake's blood for "witching medicine," presumably to cause harm.[159] The pain inflicted by nettle's sting is reminscent of the serpent's strike, and both nettles and snakes have been used for harmful magick through the ages. Although this application for nettle foregrounds a more malefic side to the plant, this generous herb is even more helpful at undoing harmful magick and initiating the healing process thereafter, whether used in traditional herbal magick or taken as a flower essence.

Stinging nettle's flower essence is generally indicated for fiery and stinging emotions, like spite, rage, anger, impatience, and irritation. Nettle's downward-pointing flowers and sting are also indications of its ability to reach deep into repressed aspects of the psyche, especially by stimulating the lower three chakras.[160]

The fiery nature of this flower essence is also helpful for warming up cold, brooding, and distant temperaments. Nettle flower essence is at its best when used to facilitate recovery from painful events, toxic relationships, and old traumas rooted in the past. It is said to help you let go of harmful people and things that you insist on clinging to, often to the point of delaying or averting joy and peace in the present. This plant's connection to cursing may point to its ability to heal deep wounds arising from a broken home life, childhood trauma, and abuse. People affected by scenarios like these often feel cursed to repeat the same patterns later in life, and they may end up creating a self-fulfilling prophecy by pushing away their loved ones. Nettle essence helps those who feel stung by life learn to relax into patience and vulnerability. Over time, this flower essence eases the fear triggered by past experiences that they may feel when things are going well.

Another area in which nettle excels is helping sensitive people stay grounded and remain in touch with the world around them. Nettle flower essence helps those who are easily overwhelmed by too much sensory input learn to absorb, process, and integrate energy and information from their environment in healthy ways.[161] Empaths, highly sensitive people, and those who experience unbidden psychic information will all benefit from this flower essence.

Use nettle to defend your space and your personal energy field. As a flower essence, it is helpful in magick for protection and healing. Add it to witch's bottles or amulets designed to avert harmful influences, or use it to dress candles to recover from psychic attack. You can even use it on poppets for healing or for binding and neutralizing harm caused by the target of your spell.

Oak
Quercus spp. ♦ Tree

Elemental signatures: fire, earth

Planetary signature: Saturn

Zodiacal signature: Capricorn

Chakras: root, heart

Magickal uses: protection, strength, wisdom, healing, luck, prosperity and abundance, connecting to the land, fertility, justice

Therapeutic indications: overwork (while hiding signs of tiredness), struggling onward despite despondency, fighting adversity, pushing beyond your limits

OAK TREES ARE AMONG the most widely known of all trees in the landscape. Oaks comprise the genus *Quercus* in the beech family, Fagaceae, and there are hundreds of different species distributed around the world. The leaves of the trees are arranged spirally, and in most species the leaves are lobed. When oaks reach maturity (often at ten to twelve years of age) they begin to flower each spring. Oaks have separate male and female inflorescence on the same trees; the male flowers are long catkins, and the female flowers are inconspicuous and lack petals. They are pollinated by wind, and the seeds are borne in nuts called acorns, which reach maturity in six to eighteen months, depending on the species.

There is no dearth of lore regarding this holiest of trees. Sacred to practically all peoples who knew it, the oak has a long list of spiritual and magickal correspondences. Oak was regarded as the tree of thunder gods, like Zeus, Jupiter, Thor, and Perkunas, and that lore is preserved in the superstition that oak trees attract lightning. The tree is usually ascribed to Jupiter, but sometimes also to Saturn, Mars, and the sun. Oak is earthy, yet its connection to lighting and invigorating magick connect it to fire.

The English oak (*Quercus robur*) was one of Dr. Bach's remedies. Bach wrote that oak is indicated for "those who are struggling and fighting strongly to get well, or in connection with the affairs of their daily life. They will go on trying one thing after another, though their case may seem hopeless. . . . They are brave people, fighting against great difficulties, without loss of hope or effort."[162] The oak state is one of despondency and despair, yet the spirit is not broken. While these are generally positive qualities, oak remedy is needed when someone faced with just such a situation ignores their needs and begins to suffer burnout or breakdown.

Oak has long symbolized strength, and Bach's oak essence helps those people who seem to have an abundance of strength. However, the gift of the remedy isn't extra vigor or grit—it's perspective. Julian Barnard puts it best: "Those who take the remedy do not gain in strength and determination. They gain in understanding, and that allows them to look afresh at the chronic life difficulty they face. They begin to see a new way to grow."[163] Thus, oak flower essence offers balanced strength, tempering it with acceptance of your limits. It reminds you that it is okay to surrender and rest.

Oaks are often seen as stewards of the land. Ancient oak trees act as the wisdomkeepers and spiritual anchors of the landscape, and taking oak flower essence draws you into a state of communion with the spirits of the land. Oak trees are often home to a huge range of organisms, including birds, insects, moss and lichens, and countless others. A single large oak tree may be the home to scores of other living things, making it a sort of microcosm of the ecosystem in which it dwells. Taking oak flower essence helps you understand your place in your environment; it balances the ego self with the needs of the community. I think this also accounts for why oak teaches us to rest from time to time, because we are not alone in any of the work that we do. Accordingly, oak is used in magick for connecting to the spirits of the land, tree spirits, other nature spirits, and the fairy folk; oak essence can help attune you to these magickal beings, especially if it's an essence you've made locally.

Oak spirit is an excellent portal to the upper and lower worlds, for the tree's vast network of roots below the ground spreads like a second tree, inverted into the chthonic realm just as the branches touch the ouranic. Taking oak flower essence of any variety has a balancing effect that mirrors the tree's growth in the landscape. It starts by focusing its effects on the heart chakra and heart meridian, where it has a noted calming effect.[164] At the same time, oak essence reaches into the uppermost and lowermost chakras, those that lie in the aura outside the body itself. These centers represent your most rarefied consciousness and your connection to the Earth beneath us. Tree essence experts Sue and Simon Lilly describe this mechanism in oak, asserting that "oak helps with the absorption and integration of very profound, hidden energy levels that exist at the primal sources of being. Linking to the supraphysical levels of existence at either extreme of the individual auric field, oak funnels energy into the desire for growth in solid reality and the delight of expressing this in as many ways as possible."[165]

As a magickal ingredient, oak is usually used in spells and charms for protection, healing, strength, and fertility. Oak flower essence can be added to witch's bottles or used to anoint amulets meant to ward off harm. The regal and imposing stature of oak trees has led to bits of oak being used in magick for leadership; try taking oak essence when you need a boost in leadership skills or use it in magick aimed at leadership (like the leaders of your government, for example), as it will lend solidarity and resolve. Oak is also used in magick for money and abundance. Tess Whitehurst suggests that oak essence can be used to create shifts in your energy and consciousness that are necessary for earning and receiving money in a sustainable and fulfilling way.[166] Oak also features in spells for luck, courage, blessings, and wisdom—the essence is a wonderful way to bring it into your work.

Finally, oak essence is attuned to the positive attributes of the divine masculine. Astrologically, it is linked to Jupiter, Mars, and the sun, and it cultivates the positive qualities of each of them. Acorns have adorned priapic wands and are symbols of virility, masculinity, and power. Oak essence connects to the Horned God and the Green Man archetypes of the witch's god, and it symbolizes the height of life and power that peaks at the summer solstice. Oak may also be used to celebrate Lammas, or Lughnasagh (August 1), as oak trees in the British Isles are noted for their "Lammas growth"—a second round of new shoots that appears in late summer. Oak balances the masculine forces within you to cultivate restraint, wisdom, and endurance.

Olive
Olea europaea ♦ Tree

Elemental signature: fire
Planetary signatures: sun, Jupiter
Zodiacal signature: Leo
Chakras: root, solar plexus, throat
Magickal uses: protection, purification, healing, consecration, abundance, wealth, balance, success, peace and reconciliation, rebirth
Therapeutic indications: exhaustion, mental weariness, experiencing little or no relaxation or enjoyment, loss of enjoyment of work, resistance to rest, burnout

THE OLIVE TREE IS A CULTURALLY, economically, and spiritually important crop cultivated for its fruits, which are eaten and pressed to make olive oil. Olives are evergreen shrubs, growing short and squat unless cultivated into a habit that offers easier access to the fruit. The flowers themselves are small, white, and borne in dense clusters on the previous year's growth. They usually show fourfold symmetry, and the flowers may be perfect (with male and female reproductive organs) or staminate (with only the male stamen). Once pollinated, the perfect flowers develop into fruits, which may be harvested unripe (green) or ripe (black).

The cultivation of olive trees began roughly seven thousand years ago in the Mediterranean region. Over the course of time, these plants and the products thereof have accrued numerous holy and magickal associations. Olive oil has fueled lamps in countless temples throughout the ancient world, offering their light and warmth to gods and spirits of many traditions. The oil has been used in rituals of consecration, protection, and healing, and both fruit and oil have come to symbolize health, success, wealth, and abundance. An olive branch is now universally regarded as a token of peace, and the wood from the tree has long been used to make wands. The Greek sorceress Medea used a wand of olive wood to stir her potion of rebirth.[167]

Dr. Bach's original olive flower mother tincture was prepared by a colleague in Italy at Bach's behest and with Bach's instructions. Bach recommended olive essence for people who have suffered much, carrying on to the point of exhaustion such that daily life no longer offers them any pleasure.[168] Nora Weeks, his biographer and close friend and student, notes, "Bach proved that the flower of the Olive tree contained the life, warmth, and strength necessary to re-energise such people and give them back their health."[169]

Olive has been an important ally for me, as it is chief among essences used for treating exhaustion, burnout, and fatigue. My schedule is virtually always full, especially when I travel to teach and promote my works. When I start to feel a bit run-down, olive flower essence helps me bounce back. It is refreshing, invigorating, and bolstering, and it helps me move forward with my busy and fulfilling schedule. My friend and teacher Sue Lilly writes that olive essence benefits those with strong desires and great passions, and she suggests that it helps you learn to discover and apply these motivating forces in a creative and life-enhancing way. She also suggests that taking the essence helps balance your needs with the needs of others, while simultaneously mediating damaging or self-centered behavior with wisdom and empathy.[170]

Magickally speaking, the solar nature of olive makes it a wonderful essence for rituals of success, courage, and motivation, as well as for navigating conflict and finding peace and harmony. Some practitioners use olive essence to help clients get through crises and conflicts, such as divorce, while others suggest that olive essence offers valor, warmth, and radiance.[171] Diffuse it in the home when the environment feels heavy, low in energy, or dull; in addition to lifting the vibes in your home, olive flower essence confers a gentle blessing of protection, abundance, and healing to all who enter.

 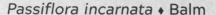

Passionflower

Passiflora incarnata ♦ Balm

Elemental signatures: water, spirit
Planetary signatures: Uranus, Neptune
Zodiacal signatures: Aquarius, Pisces
Chakras: third eye, crown
Magickal uses: sleep, healing, peace, friendship, love
Therapeutic indications: stress, physical and mental tension, anxiety, restlessness, mental chatter, slave to the clock, codependency, clingyness, religious zeal or fanaticism

PASSIONFLOWER IS A VINE that has three- or occasionally five-lobed leaves, gripping tendrils, and spectacular flowers. The stems have a square cross section, and the flowers are mostly purple, with white, blue, or even yellow components in some populations. The stunning blooms consist of prominent stamens, a frilly corona, five petals, and five sepals. The plant was named for the Passion of Christ, as early Spanish explorers in the New World superimposed Christian symbolism on the flower's anatomy.

In magick, passionflower is most often used for matters relating to peace, sleep, and love. Although its name might suggest that it incites passion, the plant does just the opposite: medicinally, magickally, and as a flower essence, it is deeply calming. The herb itself is used to calm troubles, cultivate peace, and invite new friendships. When burned as an incense before a gathering, passionflower predisposes groups toward peace. It is sometimes added to floor washes to reduce the potential for disagreements, too. The essence can similarly be sprayed or diffused to break up or prevent disharmony, and a few drops of the essence are perfect for use as a wash on the floors or furniture for a peaceful home or event.

In hoodoo and conjure, passionflower is said to symbolize a clinging love.[172] It is often added to spells to encourage affection and bring luck in love. As an essence, it treats the root of clinginess. The handlike lobes of its leaves and gripping tendrils act as vibrational signatures for being able to take control of your own life. Thus, the essence of passionflower breaks cycles of codependency. When you feel entangled in the drama of others, or if you continuously draw other people into drama of your making, passionflower essence teaches you to stand on your own. Rather than encourage isolationism, the essence encourages you to live in the moment without attachment to the past or worry for the future. In time, you'll find greater peace and confidence.

Passionflower has a reputation for aiding sleep. Taken as a tea or tincture, it dissolves tension and helps you sleep more soundly. Magickally, the plant can be placed in a sachet under the pillow for more restful sleep. The essence helps you let go of the events of the day, bringing peace to the mind and helping you fall asleep more easily.[173] It also reduces the frequency and severity of nightmares and promotes sweet dreams instead.

The essence stimulates the third eye and crown chakras, resulting in visionary states, both waking and dreaming. Passionflower may invite prophetic dreams rich with symbolism, while also promoting psychic development overall. It is helpful to take after psychic readings or other intuitive work, as it is subtly grounding and helps you integrate the information that you've received. Try taking it with potato or clematis essence if you require stronger grounding. The expansive effect that passionflower has on the mind and spirit leads you to greater compassion, equanimity, and charisma. The essence helps you have deeper and more authentic spiritual experiences overall.

However, it is also indicated for fanaticism and overzealous tendencies.

Taking passionflower essence yields acceptance and surrender. Many flowers subscribe to strict schedules, such as blooming at dawn and closing as the sun sets; passionflower blooms open sporadically, each one at its own pace. Similarly, people taking this essence will relax into the moment rather than worrying about when things will happen. In Hebrew, Greek, and Japanese, names for this plant translate to "clock flower" or "clock plant," for the flower's resemblance to the face of a clock. The flower essence helps you release stress related to timing and schedules, teaching you to be more present in the now. The flower has also been compared to the wheel of fortune; appropriately, the essence provides greater acceptance for those fateful events that you are unable to change.

Passionflower essence makes you a better magician by promoting empowerment and helping you be more present in your work. The essence fills the heart with divine love and leads you closer to embodying your true will. It helps make everyday life an act of magick and encourages you to fulfill your life's purpose. When life gets fast-paced and you feel as though you have no time for meditation, magick, ritual, or other spiritual endeavors, passionflower essence helps you find a way to slow down and make space for your practice. It is said to help you cultivate Christ or Buddha consciousness, as it opens the door to experiencing enlightenment. Ultimately, passionflower essence helps you embody your magick in all that you do, and to use your magick for creating a better life and a better world.

❁ Peppermint
Mentha piperita ◆ Balm

Elemental signature: air
Planetary signatures: Mercury, Venus, Jupiter
Zodiacal signatures: Taurus, Virgo
Chakra: solar plexus
Magickal uses: healing, protection, purification, money, success, peace and reconciliation

Therapeutic indications: sluggish mind, dull spirit, lethargy, slow
metabolism, poor memory, difficulty digesting and assimilating
new ideas

PEPPERMINT IS EASILY the best-known member of the mint family.
It has the square stem, opposite leaves, and quick-spreading rhizomes
that are characteristics of this family of plants. Its leaves are deeply
veined, somewhat wrinkly, and fuzzy, with serrated margins. The
flowers are four-lobed, pale lavender, and arranged in compact whorls
on short spikes. This species is the result of natural hybridization, and
the flowers are therefore sterile; the plant is able to reproduce only
clonally, by new runners and rhizomes.

Mints are generally used in magick related to healing, cleansing,
protection, and money. Peppermint is associated with the mind and
memory and has been used to boost mental performance since at least
the Roman era. Its fresh, clean scent contributes to its use in rituals
for cleansing, exorcism, and purification. The brilliant green leaves and
sharp scent also lend to its use in money magick, while its association
with Jupiter enables peppermint to be used for success. As a flower
essence, it offers clarity and may be added to blends for cleansing, especially at the mental level. The essence clears and cleanses the entire
energy field and brings fresh ideas that inspire success.

Medicinally, mints are often employed for their effects on the digestive system. Peppermint flower essence also improves digestion, metaphorically speaking, as it can help the mind digest and assimilate new
ideas. It overcomes patterns of mental lethargy and dullness that result
from being unable or unwilling to process information, beliefs, and
mental energies. Peppermint essence is refreshing and strongly stimulating to the mind; it ignites the higher nature of the mind for more lively,
vital, and penetrating thoughts.[174] The way peppermint's rhizomes creep
through the earth points to the essence's ability to navigate your innermost, hidden thoughts so you can break them down and assimilate or
eliminate them.

Peppermint flower essence balances your energy and may improve
metabolism. It helps mediate conflict between the instinctual level (the

gut) and the intellectual level (the brain). It can also help heal your relationship with food, particularly cravings for sweet things or the desire to eat for sheer stimulation when bored. The essence is also useful during the period of Mercury retrograde, and it alleviates many of the emotional and mental symptoms experienced by those who are sensitive to retrogrades.[175] Mint's Mercurial nature makes it a wonderful essence to take when traveling so you can better process and integrate the new experiences along your journey, a use that parallels the herb's traditional application in magick for safe travel.

❦ Periwinkle
Vinca minor ♦ Bane

Elemental signature: water

Planetary signatures: Venus, Saturn

Zodiacal signature: Aquarius

Chakras: sacral, crown

Magickal uses: protection, peace, love, healing, cleansing, magickal power

Therapeutic indications: gloom, despair, depression, confusion, feeling stagnant, stuck in the past, inability to learn from mistakes, grief, faulty memory, feeling smothered by outside forces or unpleasant memories

PERIWINKLE IS A LOW SHRUB with a woody stem, a vine-like habit, and evergreen leaves. It is native to Europe and Turkey, though it is widely naturalized around the world today. The plant sports pinwheel-shaped, five-petaled blooms of the characteristic shade of blue-lavender known as "periwinkle blue."

Periwinkle is traditionally used for remembrance, protection, blessings, and love magick, as well as for boosting magickal power. Much of the older lore is dedicated to periwinkle's ability to neutralize harmful magick and ill-wishing. Hung in the home or carried around the neck, this herb was said to exorcise evil spirits and avert the evil eye.

As a flower essence, periwinkle is gently protective and cleansing.

386 ★ Directory of One Hundred Flower Essences

Christopher Penczak recommends using periwinkle essence when practicing your psychic skills and giving readings. It offers psychic protection and helps you separate those energies that belong to you from those that you're merely tapping in to psychically. I find it helpful for healers for similar reasons; it allows you to be a more sensitive and psychically aware without taking on any of the energies or patterns you're helping your client release. Periwinkle seals the aura against leaks, and it helps you recenter after astral travel.[176] The essence is invaluable for recovering from psychic attack; its energy floods the aura with healing virtues to clear away psychic debris, much like the shrub's creeping habit chokes out the growth of other plants.

Periwinkle has folkloric connections to death, immortality, remembrance, and grief. Wreaths of periwinkle were placed on the heads of the deceased, particularly children. In the Victorian language of flowers, periwinkle is said to symbolize fond memories and friendship. As an essence, it can help you remember the good without being overly attached to the past. It is a powerful essence for transforming grief and loss, as it gives the gifts of perspective and healing. It is valuable for parents grieving loss or separation from children, as it keeps the memory of your loved ones alive without unhealthy attachments.

Periwinkle has a rich tradition of use in love spells. In hoodoo and related forms of folk magick, it is used to promote marital harmony and domestic bliss. The plant's Venusian qualities allow it to open the doors to love, romance, and pleasure. Its vining habit is sometimes described as clinging to walls in a loving and tender manner, thereby conferring the same qualities to the plant spirit.[177] The herb is traditionally sewn into the mattress or hidden beneath the bed to invite romance and passion, and the flower essence may be sprayed on the mattress and around the bedroom for similar purposes. Sprayed throughout the home, periwinkle essence also instills peace and happiness.

Periwinkle flower essence has an affinity with the mind, memory, and nervous system. One flower essence maker describes it as offering "nerves of steel" during periods of crisis, stress, and trauma,[178] while another writes that it can be used for experiences of emptiness, like dissociative states.[179] The essence helps you remember who you really are, and it elevates your consciousness, lifting it from the mire of confusion, depression, and despair. It is helpful when you feel as though circumstances are smothering you and making it hard to think clearly.

Periwinkle is also important for transmuting cycles that repeat. It can help you find the gift or lesson inherent in a situation (if such a lesson should exist, that is). It also helps you harvest wisdom from your experiences. Cynthia Athina Kemp Scherer, founder of Desert Alchemy, writes that periwinkle "supports us in extracting as much as we can from our experiences so they enrich us with a foundation upon which we can build something new."[180] This, in turn, prevents you from repeating the same mistakes and rushing into new things too quickly.

Periwinkle has long been used by cunning folk, witches, and magicians for healing and for boosting magickal power. Taking the essence regularly can help you learn to moderate your own energies better, as well as offer you better insight into directing the energies of the natural world for healing and magick. To boost magickal efficacy, try placing periwinkle essence on your palms before performing spellwork or rituals, or diffuse it in your ritual space.

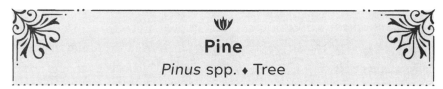

Pine
Pinus spp. ♦ Tree

Elemental signature: earth
Planetary signatures: Mars, Pluto
Zodiacal signatures: Aries, Virgo
Chakras: root, heart, third eye
Magickal uses: protection, purification, healing, curse breaking
Therapeutic indications: guilt, blame, shame, lack of trust in yourself, feelings of inadequacy, high standards for yourself, self-criticism, low self-esteem, feeling unworthy, feeling trapped by others

THE GENUS *PINUS* CONSISTS of more than a hundred individual species of evergreen, coniferous trees. Pines are widely appreciated for their wood, and their name derives from a proto-Indo-European root meaning "resin," on account of the abundance of resin borne by the trees. Pine inflorescences are exhibited in separate male and female cones, the former being much smaller and shorter lived. The female cones are wind pollinated, and male cones fall away once their pollen has dropped. Fertilization and maturation of female cones can take several years, depending on the species.

Pine trees are beloved throughout the world, and humankind has attributed a fair amount of lore to them. Pine is considered sacred to the gods Pan, Bacchus, Osiris, and Poseidon (as well as his Roman counterpart, Neptune), among others, and it is also attributed to the goddesses Cybele and Rhea. Most magickal traditions around pine are centered on protection and purification. It has been used by people across the Northern Hemisphere to avert harm and cleanse the home. Pine flower essence is similarly cleansing and protective, although it directs these actions inward more than outward. This essence clears energy and releases blockages from the energy field, while repairing boundaries, both energetic and social.[181]

Pine is one of the classic flower essences prepared by Dr. Bach; his essence is made from *Pinus sylvestrus,* the Scotch pine. He recommended the essence for people who blame themselves and are always discontent with their efforts and results. Bach described people who need pine as hardworking, but suffering much from the faults they perceive in themselves.[182] Use this essence anytime it feels as though your work falls short or when you hold shame and guilt over past actions and experiences.

Pine flower essence is a helpful remedy when you feel as though your magick and spiritual practice miss the mark or aren't up to the standards you hold yourself to. I like to use pine to help me remember that being human includes being imperfect, even with my spiritual practice. Pine lends strength and resilience to the psyche, both of which are important qualities to cultivate when pursuing a magickal path. It is a tree of insight and wisdom that helps you overcome insecurities so you can, in turn, trust your inner knowing and have faith in your ability to discern truth. This is essential to boosting your magickal prowess, as doubt in your ability to find that inner sense of truth can muddle your results in spellcraft and ritual.

Many cultures consider pine to be a masculine tree. From the deities listed above, you can see that it is associated with more gods than goddesses, and the shape of pine's cones at the end of a branch could be seen as symbolic of the phallus. For this reason, small pine cones are sometimes attached to wands to represent the divine masculine. Pine flower essence understandably contends with several themes that are viewed as stereotypically masculine. Daniel Tigner, author of *Canadian Forest Tree Essences,* writes that ponderosa pine in particular honors and nourishes the masculine side of all people, and that it further draws out the virtues of courage, honor, and chivalry.[183] While these qualities have no gender themselves, they can be warped by condemnation, guilt, and shame when certain masculine stereotypes are foisted upon anyone. Pine can help bring resolution to imbalances with the inner masculine self, even so far as to ease aggression and erase feelings of emasculation. Pine flower essence is also excellent for attuning to the masculine currents of energy in nature, particularly as embodied in the Horned God and Green Man.

Try adding the essence to offerings on the altar, or spray or diffuse it in your sacred space to prepare for rites honoring the wild god. Pine can also be diffused through the home for protection and cleansing, and it is an appropriate essence to use to celebrate the winter solstice. This essence helps you ease your inner critic and develop greater empathy, insight, and forgiveness.

Pokeweed
Phytolacca americana ♦ Bane

Elemental signatures: fire, air
Planetary signatures: Mars, Saturn, Uranus
Zodiacal signature: Aquarius
Chakras: sacral, solar plexus
Magickal uses: protection, hex breaking, cleansing, overcoming obstacles, driving away enemies, astral travel or shamanic journey
Therapeutic indications: feeling stuck or stagnant, toxic thoughts,

behaviors that do not support movement or growth, unproductive or uncreative use of the mind, feeling as though you are under attack, alienation

POKEWEED, ALSO CALLED poke, pokeberry, inkberry, and rouge-berry, is an interesting plant in the American landscape. It is a poisonous perennial with hollow, magenta stalks that die back each winter and renew each spring. It is fast-growing, and the hearty root is used for making medicine. Although all parts of the plant are poisonous, the tender young leaves may be eaten if carefully prepared by boiling twice and disposing of the water each time, as this removes the harmful compounds. The five-petaled flowers are a waxy shade of white or cream and are borne on spikes of densely packed buds. After pollination, the young fruits start green and darken to a purplish magenta, sometimes nearing black. It is not uncommon to see flower buds, open flowers, young fruit, and ripe fruit on the same spike.

Pokeweed was among the first essences I made in my exploration of native wildflowers. It seemed somehow both mysterious and perhaps forbidden. I knew that the plant could be a nutritious medicine or a poison depending on how it was prepared, and this perplexing dichotomy held my fascination with the plant and its essence. I studied the traditional magickal uses for the plant, which mostly centered around protection, hex breaking, and removing enemies and obstacles. The berries are also used to make a potent magickal ink. At that point in my life, pokeweed's medicine was a perfect fit; I was experiencing psychic attack and my life had been too stagnant for too long.

The first time I took the essence, I felt and saw its effects at work in my aura: pokeweed began to knit together the holes in my energy field and to bolster its defenses against outside energies. That aligned with pokeweed's traditional uses for protection, cleansing, and hex-breaking. I soon found that internal use of the essence can be supplemented by spraying it in the aura, especially if the energy field is severely depleted or damaged.

Pokeweed essence is protective, cleansing, and restorative. It can release outside forces and attachments while also promoting healing. I also learned in a webinar from David Dalton, founder of Delta Gardens, that pokeweed essence helps clear away subconscious patterns related to irregular cell growth; in this way, pokeweed mirrors its effect on irregularities in the aura.

Pokeweed flower essence is transformational. Christopher Penczak shares that it creates swift and sudden changes, both within and without. Take the essence when your mind is fraught with toxic thoughts and beliefs; use it whenever your mind is weighed down and cannot shift to more creative, productive patterns. Pokeweed flower essence brings a sense of inner strength and resiliency, especially when situations are dire. The essence is purgative—forcefully so—and brings with its cleansing action a sense of renewal.

Pokeweed flower essence can be used when you feel trapped by your circumstances, especially when you feel alienated, unwanted, or unloved by family, close friends, or even the world at large. Pokeweed offers a gentle nudge to encourage you to lower your guard and permit yourself to be vulnerable. When people are recovering from trauma or abuse, sometimes they can feel too toxic to allow other people to get close; pokeweed helps you feel safe when crossing into unfamiliar territory. The essence is also useful if you respond to feelings of isolation by lashing out, as it reminds you not to confuse fear for respect. If you tend to respond to the feeling of being cut off with despair or anger, pokeweed teaches you to be self-sufficient and to use those periods of quietude to heal and build yourself anew. This plant spirit reminds you that it is okay to let some things fade away or die back. Pokeweed itself appears to die off each winter as it withdraws its life force to its root. In the spring, though, new growth appears, and pokeweed is reborn. In the same fashion, the essence helps you grow back totally renewed after letting go of whatever no longer serves you.

Pokeweed's fruit are benign to birds, even though they are poison to virtually every other creature. As a result, pokeweed is associated with flight and bird spirit allies. The hollow stalks are also a signature for soul flight or astral travel, and the flower essence can clear your mind and offer more vivid journey experiences. Taking pokeweed flower essence also invites deeper communion with the elementals of fire and air as well as helping you establish relationships with bird totems or allies and other airborne spirits.

Use pokeweed in magick for protection, courage, banishing, cleansing, and removing obstacles. Add pokeweed and agrimony flower essences and a handful of salt to the bath for a rejuvenating and deeply cleansing experience. You can also mix pokeweed essence with a handful of dirt from an opponent's tracks, or you can spray or diffuse it somewhere they will step, to help them move on and stop subjecting you to harm. Pokeweed flower essence is excellent for any sort of uncrossing, hex breaking, or banishing ritual, as it helps you reclaim your power.

Pomegranate
Punica granatum ◆ Tree

Elemental signature: fire

Planetary signatures: sun, Mercury, Jupiter, Pluto

Zodiacal signatures: Virgo, Scorpio

Chakras: root, sacral

Magickal uses: fertility, luck, protection, wish granting, wealth, death and rebirth, attunement to the seasons, underworld magick, connecting to the divine feminine, ancestral healing, love and sex, strength

Therapeutic indications: difficulty accepting femininity, inability or unwillingness to nurture or be nurtured, trauma stemming from womanhood and maternal figures, lack of creative impulse, misuse or confused application of creative impulse, being forced to choose between home life and career, commitment issues

THE POMEGRANATE TREE is deciduous and long-lived, bearing fruit on its spiny branches. Pomegranate flowers are a unique shade of coral, a reddish orange. They generally have five petals but may have as few as three or as many as seven. Once fertilized, the flowers transform into large, reddish fruits containing hundreds of seeds within a thick, protective rind. Pomegranates are native to India and the Middle East, and they have been cultivated for nearly seven millennia. Today, they are grown around the world.

Pomegranates are holy in many cultures, ancient and modern. The list of deities to whom the fruit are sacred is long, and it includes Adonis, Aphrodite, Ceres, Hariti, Hekate, Hera, Persephone, and Saturn. Some people posit that pomegranate was the forbidden fruit in the Garden of Eden. In other mythic cycles, the first pomegranate tree is said to have sprung from the blood of Adonis. Persephone famously ate of the pomegranate in the underworld, thereby tying her to Hades and the world below. The compromise struck between Persephone's mother, Demeter, and Hades resulted in the maiden spending the year split between Earth and the underworld—an allegory for the changing of the seasons. Naturally, the trees bear their fruit in the dark half the year when Persephone is underground with her husband.

In light of all the mythic connections of the pomegranate, it has been used in many kinds of magick. Many traditions hold that the fruit is best used for spells of protection and fertility. Carrying the rind was thought to bring luck and love while thwarting malefic magick. The shape of the fruit has been likened to that of the womb, hence its association with fertility, creativity, and the divine feminine. Since they contain so many seeds, the fruits are also used in magick for abundance and prosperity. The essence relates to each of these themes in different ways.

The earliest references to pomegranate flower essence in modern literature suggest that it is an invaluable remedy for women and for tapping in to feminine energies.[184] All the subsequent literature agrees, and many essence producers recommend pomegranate essence for the unique troubles that women and feminine people face. Pomegranate flower essence is indicated when your self-image is negatively impacted by the portrayal of women and femininity. It is helpful when your inner maternal impulses (whether you are male, female, or beyond) are scarce, blocked, or somehow misdirected. Pomegranate invites you to nurture yourself first, and it restores and revitalizes your creative energy in every way. Use pomegranate essence to enhance the energy of the divine feminine within you and help you birth new projects in any avenue of life. Pomegranate essence is also useful if you overnurture; if you give and give without taking care of yourself, this essence teaches you the value of self-care. It is also protective of those who find themselves sensitive to environmental toxicity, whether physical or energetic in nature.

Pomegranate essence brings strength, courage, and wisdom that is rooted in the heart of the Great Mother. The jewel-like seeds glimmer with the color of blood, and thus pomegranate has a profound link to the force of life flowing through you. It helps detoxify the body, mind, and spirit so that your life force can flow freely. The connection to blood also suggests that pomegranate essence works toward ancestral healing. It is a profound ally in the quest for forgiveness, especially by opening your heart to better see and appreciate the efforts of your mothers and feminine ancestors. Pomegranate flower essence is helpful in responding to the societal and cultural pressure still placed on women to choose between careers and family life. The essence helps reconcile the false dichotomy, imparting a sense of understanding of how to navigate the use of creative and procreative potential in all areas of your life.

Pomegranate is used by many practitioners to support the health and well-being of the female reproductive system. While flower essences work primarily on emotional and spiritual levels, their effects often result in physiological balance, too. Pomegranate is helpful for irregular and painful menses and for supporting healthy pregnancy and childbirth.[185] The essence can be sensual, and it brings discernment to the expression of sexuality. The connection to temptation and the forbidden fruit underscores pomegranate flower essence's invitation to take an empowered and responsible approach to sexuality, no matter your gender or sexual orientation.

Because this essence is so deeply creative and restorative, it is a wonderful ally in magick for abundance and prosperity. Use it to help you find creative solutions to money problems and for advancing your career without having to sacrifice your personal life. Pomegranate flower essence offers a direct link to the underworld and can be used as an offering to the deities and deceased who reside there. It is a wonderful essence for rituals related to the dark moon, as well as for the sabbats celebrated in the darker half of the year, especially Samhain. The essence is useful for attuning to the tides of darkness and death that rule in this part of the year, and it may help with grieving endings of all sorts, from the loss of a loved one to the loss of a job or creative outlet.

Poppy
Papaver somniferum, Papaver spp. ♦ Bane

Elemental signature: fire

Astrological signatures: sun, moon, Saturn

Zodiacal signatures: Taurus, Leo, Virgo

Chakras: root, third eye

Magickal uses: sleep, divination, conjuring spirits, invisibility, honoring the dead, lunar magick, countermagick, causing confusion

Therapeutic indications: workaholic behavior, feeling like your worth is defined by productivity, daydreams that you can't seem to materialize, lack of imagination, difficulty sleeping, laziness, apathy, addiction, reliance on stress or fear for motivation

POPPIES HAVE BEEN CULTIVATED for thousands of years. They have been so widely cultivated and for so long, in fact, that their native range is left to conjecture, though many suspect it to be along the eastern Mediterranean. The most common species, *Papaver somniferum,* is an annual plant that is grown for its seeds, as well as for the psychoactive alkaloids found in the latex of some cultivars. Its leaves and stems are pubescent (i.e., covered in fine hairs), and the flowers are generally four-petaled. The blossoms are generally red, white, or mauve, though many other colors are available.

Poppy is a sacred plant whose use dates to the Neolithic era. It has been hailed as medicine in both the mundane and magickal sense, and the poppy is found in the art of the Sumerians, Minoans, Greeks, Romans, and many other ancient cultures. Among the Greeks and Romans, poppy was connected to deities associated with the night, including Hypnos (and his Roman counterpart, Somnus), the god of sleep; Thanatos, god of death; and Morpheus, god of dreams. Additionally, poppies were held sacred to Demeter and factored into some of the rites and symbols of the Eleusinian mysteries celebrating the descent and return of Persephone. Poppy's white latex and round, almost spherical seedpod evoke the image of the moon, and thus it has been connected to lunar and nighttime goddesses, like Nix, Hekate, and Lilith.

Poppy seeds are a common ingredient in magickal workings. They are often used in countermagick, such as reversal spells, causing confusion, and all manner of magick for dreams and divination. Lore holds that poppy seeds are used in spells for invisibility, and the smoke of the burning seeds can conjure spirits and render them visible. Poppies have long been used as offerings, and their seeds are appropriate for making cakes to feed the dead, while the smoke from burning them offers a path for the newly dead to travel to the underworld. As a flower essence, poppy makes a perfect offering on ancestral altars and can be added to the chalice for funerary workings to commemorate the deceased. Consider adding poppy to the chalice for Samhain when honoring the dead, or take the essence for dreamtime journeys to commune with spirits and invite prophetic dreams.

Poppy flower essence also helps attune the witch or magician to the tides of light and dark and life and death. Taking the essence invites communion with the infinite and helps align your thoughts and actions with your spiritual principles. Poppy offers a boost of vitality, infusing your energy field with light and clearing away blockages from the chakras; it may even awaken the coiled kundalini energy residing at the root chakra.[186]

Poppy essence is helpful in bringing balance between cycles of work and rest. Steve Johnson, the late founder of Alaskan Essences, writes that poppy essence "helps us establish a point of balance between doing and being."[187] It is one of the prime essences for workaholics and anyone obsessed with or addicted to expansion, conquest, and achievement. Many times these patterns can result from living in the future or from not accepting or integrating your past achievements. This kind of overwork easily leads to exhaustion. The dreamy, languid nature of poppy asks you to stop your work periodically so you can rest and recharge.

Poppy essence reminds you that all expansion is limited unless you have periods of rest or contraction. Imagine overfilling your lungs, never stopping to exhale—before long they'd burst. Poppy flower essence helps you find the exhale and pause your activity as needed. It finds the equilibrium between action and inaction, granting permission to simply unwind. I find poppy essence to be extremely helpful for people whose worth is defined by their productivity. I see this echoed in the dual astrological symbolism of the plant, as it exhibits both solar and lunar qualities.

Poppy flower essence is helpful for releasing worry, stress, and fear-based motivations, which are all drains on our natural reserves of energy. People who find themselves motivated by stress, often feeling simultaneously tense and drained, can use poppy to shift to a better source of motivation. However, it is worth noting that doing so may result in a couple of weeks of feeling run-down as old motivators fall away and new ones are built up.[188]

This essence helps you connect your dreams to your actions. Taking poppy essence gives an unimaginative mind permission to daydream, while also asking the ungrounded daydreamer to take steps to actualize their dreams. It helps you look at the idealized, perfected dreams you hold and fit them into your reality, while simultaneously helping you accept and forgive the imperfections and deviations from those dreams that often take place as you strive to bring them to life in the real world. It gives you the space you need to pause and assess whether you are still aligned with those dreams, and whether or not you want to be striving toward those same ideals. Poppy flower essence can help you have a more realistic means of taking steps toward your goals.

Potato
Solanum tuberosum ♦ Bane

Elemental signature: earth
Planetary signatures: moon, Saturn, Pluto
Zodiacal signature: Virgo
Chakra: root

Magickal uses: grounding, stability, protection, healing, connecting to the Earth Mother

Therapeutic indications: ungroundedness, impracticality, daydreams, escapism, inhibition, shyness, feeling weighed down, frustration, emotional avoidance, spiritual bypassing

POTATO IS AN IMPORTANT FOOD CROP belonging to the nightshade family (Solanaceae). Although it produces edible tubers, all other parts of the plant contain toxic alkaloids in concentrations that can harm human health. Potato flowers have the familiar five-petaled shape of most nightshades and are white with a yellow center; some wild relatives of the potato exhibit flowers of other colors. Potatoes were first domesticated in Peru between seven thousand and ten thousand years ago.

The key words to associate with potato flower essence are *calm* and *present*. It is a powerfully grounding essence, helping you become more anchored in the present moment. Working with potato flower essence after shock and trauma or after expansive and intense spiritual experiences helps you integrate your consciousness into your body.

Potato flower essence is a vital ally for bridging the spiritual with the mundane. For those people who constantly seek euphoric spiritual highs and bliss, potato offers a reminder to come back to Earth. This flower essence is helpful for anyone who uses spirituality as a form of escapism as well as for anyone who defaults to daydreams or delusions in lieu of ordinary life. Potato flower essence reminds you to take pleasure in the everyday, even going so far as enabling you to see the mundane as inherently magickal. It gives you a practical outlet for spiritual inspiration and creative ideas, helping you put them into motion in the material world. It also stabilizes spiritual development so that it can continue steadily without interruption.

Magickally speaking, potatoes are largely associated with healing. Potato flower essence feeds and grounds you to help provide the right setting for healing magick. Potatoes were once carried all winter long to protect against illness, and the essence can offer a similar effect: being fully present means that when your body alerts you that it's in need of care, you can stave off disease before it settles in.

Potato's nutritious tubers grow underground, where they are nurtured and fed in the dark by the Great Mother. Naturally, potato flower essence has a certain receptive, yin quality, one that receives both darkness and light to help you balance stillness and action. Because of their relationship with Earth and with soil, potatoes are often linked to Mother Earth in several cultures. Potato flower essence can help you tap in to the currents of life and light that course through the Earth so you can be better nourished and guided by the Great Mother. Potato flower essence is good-natured and loving, and it inspires you to show the benevolence of the Great Mother.

Queen Anne's Lace (Wild Carrot)
Daucus carota ♦ Balm

Elemental signatures: air, water, fire

Planetary signatures: Mercury, Neptune

Zodiacal signature: Gemini

Chakras: third eye, crown

Magickal uses: psychic development, spirit communication, lust, fertility

Therapeutic indications: scattered mind, myopic worldview, inability to be objective, ungrounded approach to spirituality, projection, isolation

QUEEN ANNE'S LACE IS THE predecessor of the cultivated carrot (*Daucus carota sativa*), and it is characterized by feathery leaves of dark green, with a multitude of white flowers arranged in umbels. The central bloom in each umbel is purplish red. The lacy appearance of the inflorescence yields the plant's common name, and the single red flower is said to have obtained its color when Queen Anne of England pricked her finger while weaving lace.

There seems to be little magickal lore regarding carrots, whether wild or cultivated, and most of what exists points toward protection, fertility, and lust. Later sources credit Queen Anne's lace for being an aid for psychic development and clairvoyance, which seems to be rooted in the plant's uses in flower essence therapy, rather than the other way around. An infusion of carrot seed added to a bath is believed to enhance communication with and connection to the spiritual world, and the flower essence derived from Queen Anne's lace addresses the same concerns.[189]

This essence is primarily focused on perception and vision. It opens the crown and third-eye chakras to support psychic development, clairvoyance, and telepathy and boost mental powers. The essence offers a calm focus that can pull together scattered or diffuse mental states, thereby facilitating meditation and other spiritual endeavors. Queen Anne's lace flower essence imparts objectivity by clearing away emotional debris from the psychic lens.[190] The essence also balances mental projections with authentic psychic perception by rooting the conscious and superconscious mind in a more objective state. In turn, this helps ease your attachment to the outcome and other factors so you can receive psychic information with greater ease and impartiality.

In addition to enhancing psychic vision, the essence of Queen Anne's lace is an ally for breaking down myopic worldviews, such as religious zeal or staunch atheism. Instead, this flower essence gently broadens your perspective so that you can be more inclusive and less rigid. Use this essence for individuals who are nearsighted, those who cannot "see the forest through the trees," for it offers a glimpse of the bigger picture and invites better insight and foresight.

Queen Anne's lace is also used to break down illusions held by the ego, such as projections of fragility, separation, or hopelessness.[191] Like all members of the family Apiaceae, Queen Anne's lace supports a sense of connection, thereby breaking down illusions of separation and division and replacing these patterns with a sense of integrated wholeness. It is a wonderful essence to take when you are separated from your community or family or otherwise isolated in some way. It reminds you that your soul is inseparable from Source and from others.

Red Clover
Trifolium pratense ◆ Balm

Elemental signatures: earth, air

Planetary signatures: Mercury, Venus

Zodiacal signatures: Taurus, Libra

Chakra: root

Magickal uses: luck, love, faithfulness, safe travel, fairy magick, beauty, prosperity, healing

Therapeutic indications: stress and anxiety, feelings of lack, emotional weakness, fear, panic, mass hysteria, group trauma, nightmares, trauma, shutting off emotional expression, cold and calculating behavior

RED CLOVER IS A MEMBER of the pea, or legume, family, and it grows as a dense groundcover with a deep taproot, leaflets arranged in groups of three, and pinkish or magenta flowers. The inflorescence is densely packed with many individual flowers together in globe-shaped clusters, and they are favored by bees and other pollinators. Red clover is widely naturalized around the world, though its native range extends through parts of Europe, Asia, and northern Africa.

As a magickal herb, red clover is most famous for its luck and wish-granting virtues, especially if you are lucky enough to find a four-leafed clover. Red clover is also used in magick associated with love and beauty, thanks to its Venusian character, and it may also be added to spells for health and healing. Clover can be carried for safety when traveling, and it is exchanged as a representation of faithfulness between lovers.

Red clover flower essence is an important ally for promoting beauty, health, and abundance. One of its primary functions is to help you detach from fear and to inspire trust in the cosmos. The essence encourages radiant health in body, mind, and spirit. It starts by cleansing, clearing, and repairing the emotional body and inviting greater connection between the linear, rational, logical self and the intuitive, emotional, spiritual self. It overcomes the tendency toward utilitarianism and softens the appearance of being cold and calculating by reminding you of the infinite abundance of energy and resources available to you. Take the essence each morning during the waxing moon to cultivate prosperity consciousness and invite material abundance.[192] You can also add the essence to the bath for beauty magick or use it in the consecration of charms for healing.

Medicinally speaking, red clover heals the blood and circulatory system. Blood itself, spiritually speaking, is the carrier of life force and personal identity. If your selfhood flows without being centered in who you are at the most core level, it predisposes you to states of panic and anxiety. If you lose touch with your inner divinity or higher self— that is, when the ego feels threatened or disrupted by what's going on around you—red clover restores a fundamental awareness of this inner self. The ego's job is to watch out for itself, not for the real you. When you misidentify with the ego, it is easy to become panicked, fearful, or otherwise unsettled. Taking red clover flower essence redirects the flow of consciousness to be centered in the true self. It is a wonderful essence to take during times of crisis, being particularly well suited to contending with group trauma and mass hysteria.

Red clover flower essence assuages fear and combats acute trauma. These states can result in being emotionally blocked or repressed because you might fear what damage your unbridled emotions can bring to the situation; red clover essence fosters a sense of reassurance and trust in the universe. It helps you understand that you are supported by an invisible ecosystem of spirits, guides, and helpers. It helps you tap in to their guidance and wisdom, as it promotes receiving psychic information through a variety of methods, including mediumship, channeling, automatic writing, dowsing, and other psychic pursuits. As a result, red clover essence supports you in forging deeper relationships with all manner of nonphysical beings, such as spirit guides, angels, nature spirits, and the fairy folk. Traditionally, red clover has been used in fairy magick, and its essence makes a lovely addition to offerings to them.

Red clover is deeply connected to the divine feminine, and the flower essence helps you commune more deeply with the Goddess in her myriad forms. The individual flowers, when viewed up close, resemble the vulva, while the crescent- or chevron-shaped markings on the leaflets resemble the womb and ovaries—all being signals of the plant's connection to the Goddess. Work with the flower essence for a complete lunar cycle, from one new moon until the next, to more deeply attune to the tides of the Great Mother. This inspires a gentle strength that enables you to speak your truth lovingly, as well as inviting deep healing through forgiveness and a greater ability to radiate unconditional love.

Rose
Rosa spp. ♦ Balm

Elemental signatures: water, spirit

Planetary signature: Venus

Zodiacal signature: Libra

Chakra: heart

Magickal uses: love, beauty, healing, protection, consecration, luck, psychic development

Therapeutic indications: apathy, resignation, feeling consigned to fate, joylessness, monotonous routine, lack of purpose, sexual insecurity, stress and anxiety, grief, emotional pain and suffering, low vitality

ROSES ARE FOUND THROUGHOUT the world's temperate regions, and more than a hundred species comprise the genus *Rosa*. The wild rose typically shows five petals, often pink in color, and five green sepals. The flowers themselves are rather like a shallow cup, and they are filled with a spiraling whorl of stamen. Roses are almost as famous for their thorns as their flowers; they are actually prickles that form as outgrowths of the epidermis. Wild roses, which often have a rambling or climbing habit, use these thorns to latch onto one another and other surfaces for support. More than ten thousand cultivars of rose are grown today, exhibiting large variations in the size, color, and shape of the flowers, as well as differences in the number of petals, scents, and habits of the plant. All roses may be made into flower essences, and there are dozens of commercial lines of essences made from different roses.

Of all plants, rose may have the largest body of lore, and a deep dive into the myths and stories about it might require an entire book. It is universally regarded as an herb of Venus, and it invites love, romance, beauty, and sensual pleasure. Rose is used in protective magick, thanks to its thorns; the stems and thorns can be hung as an apotropaic measure or added to witch's bottles or charm bags meant to tangle up harmful energies. Rose is said to represent the apex of spirituality; it is often called "the queen of flowers" or sometimes the "lotus of the West." Rose petals, infusion, tincture, hydrosol, and oil are used for consecration, for healing, and to confer luck and blessings.

Dr. Bach included wild rose (*Rosa canina,* better known as dog rose) among the later remedies in his system of flower essences. He prescribed it for cases of apathy, resignation, and joylessness. He described people in the rose state as accepting their fate without making any effort to seek joy or improve circumstances.[193] They often seem monotone, gray, and even sad, with low vitality and lack of ambition, particularly if they remain in that state for too long. Wild rose flower essence sparks the will to live and opens the heart to experience joy. It helps you feel lively and purposeful and take interest in life.

Rose flower essences display many properties depending on the species and varieties used. Generally speaking, roses are thought to be spiritually evolved flowers, and their essences bestow grace, beauty, and love. Their essences are also often deeply practical, and they generally address issues of change and evolution, including initiating the processes of inner development and healing that lead you closer to the state of perfection. They engender a sense of tenderness and a tangible link to unconditional love. This enables rose essences of all varieties to transform old emotional wounds and release deeply held trauma. Rose petals and rosewater are often used for rituals of cleansing, and the essence similarly clears away the debris of your emotional experiences so you can be clear and pure vessels of unconditional love.

Rose has a long-standing connection to love and sex; the essence can help you take pleasure in worldly activities and see the beauty and love that lies within and around you. Rose is perfect for connecting to the archetypes of Venus as both Great Mother and the goddess of love and beauty. Roses are similarly connected to Mary, the mother of Jesus, and to Hekate, who was known by the epithet of "the Fiery Rose" according to some translations of the Chaldean Oracles, a series of spiritual texts known to Neoplatonist philosophers of the thrid to sixth century CE.[194] Rose flower essence helps you commune with the heavenly forces of love and the divine feminine to empower your healing and magick no matter what you are working on.

Rose flower essence is a welcome addition to the chalice on Midsummer, when the blooms are traditionally at their height in England. It can also be used in workings associated with boundaries, not just in a protective sense but also for traversing into other worlds. Wild roses often grow as hedges, and their thorns were once said to have been used by the devil as he attempted to climb back to heaven. Rose flower essence helps you cultivate a deeper connection to what lies beyond the here and now, and it invites you to expand your heart and mind to see beyond the drudgery of everyday life. One variety of wild rose, called the Nootka rose, is used to make an essence that author and founder of Pacific Essences Sabina Pettitt describes as "a reminder that the life of the soul does not begin with physical birth, nor end with physical death."[195] Rose symbolizes the perfection at the end of the soul's journey and the alchemical transformation that leads you there.

Take rose flower essence before meditation, ritual, or journeying to open your heart and promote a sense of purpose in your spiritual practice. Add it to the bath to promote love and beauty. Conversely, add a few drops to a spray bottle and mist your face to develop an appreciation for yourself and cultivate inner and outer beauty; I use a flower essence spagyric on my face each day to the same end. You can also diffuse or spray rose essence in any space to raise the vibrations and invite love, peace, and healing.

Rosemary

Salvia rosmarinus ✦ Balm

Elemental signature: fire

Planetary signature: sun

Zodiacal signature: Leo

Chakra: crown

Magickal uses: protection, purification, exorcism, love, fidelity, sovereignty, psychic powers, sleep, creativity

Therapeutic indications: absentmindedness, forgetfulness, insecurity, sadness, feeling overwhelmed, sense of disconnection from self or community as a result of past trauma

UNTIL RECENTLY, ROSEMARY WAS PLACED in the genus *Rosmarinus,* but the few extant species in this genus, along with rosemary, have now all been moved into the sage genus, *Salvia.* Rosemary belongs to the mint family, and it is characteristically aromatic, like many mints. The leaves are shaped like needles and have a pinelike scent; the deeply invaginated flowers have bilateral symmetry and are a lovely shade of blue to lavender. Rosemary is native to the Mediterranean region, where it is commonly found near the shore, often growing in rocky conditions. It has adapted to thrive in dry soil by conserving water.

Rosemary is a versatile magickal herb, with a strong propensity for cleansing and protection. It is often burned as an incense to drive away spirits and avert harmful magick; this also uplifts the energy of your space and wards against future intrusions. Rosemary is a fiery, solar herb that brings sovereignty, success, power, and creativity. Some traditions maintain that rosemary is useful in magick for love and romance and that it ensures fidelity between lovers. Placed under the pillow or beneath the bed, it drives away nightmares and offers peaceful sleep.

This herb is best known for its relationship to the mind and memory. I remember reading Shakespeare's *Hamlet* in school, and Ophelia says, "There's rosemary, that's for remembrance. Pray you, love, remember." The playwright surely knew the herbal lore surrounding this herb, for carrying a sprig of rosemary or drinking a tea made from it was a common remedy for poor memory. As a flower essence, rosemary also helps with memory. It has a strong awakening and incarnating effect, thereby counteracting absentmindedness, forgetfulness, insecurity, and introversion. Rosemary brings warmth and clarity to the mind, offering renewed states of creativity, even going so far as to ignite inner peace and ecstatic states. It helps those who feel withdrawn or surly to become happier, more sensitive, and sentimental.[196]

Part of rosemary's gift of remembrance isn't merely jogging your personal memory or sharpening your intellect; rosemary relates to the remembrance of what has come before us. The essence is helpful for awakening ancestral and cellular memory. It helps you recall the soul's journey, thus making it useful for past-life recall and karmic healing. It is useful for experiencing the cyclical nature of time, rather than its linear progression, and it can lead you to awareness of the past, present, and future existing simultaneously.

Rosemary has a long shelf life, which, coupled with its pungent aroma, led to the herb's inclusion among the embalming methods of Egypt. In the same vein, rosemary signals the remembrance of those who have crossed over, and it celebrates and honors endings of all varieties. It is sometimes used magickally to seal the door to the spirit world, such as in exorcism and purification rites. This same property lends it well to helping you move on after suffering loss. The essence helps you remember the good while closing the door to being sucked back into old patterns, wounds, or grief. It can be used to maintain an open heart during loss, and it is helpful for those who are readying themselves to cross the threshold between life and death. Anoint the brow and wrists with rosemary flower essence to facilitate their transition.

Rosemary's name comes from the Latin words *ros,* meaning "dew," and *mar,* for "sea," an allusion to its native habitat near the seashore. It is associated with the foam-born goddess Aphrodite (or Venus), and she is sometimes depicted wearing a cloak of rosemary's blooms. The particular shade of blue that its flowers bear also connects rosemary to the Virgin Mary, and the flower was said to have brought her courage to face her challenges. A bit of herbal lore tells us that rosemary flourishes wherever the woman of the house rules. The flower essence is deeply empowering to women who carry leadership roles and otherwise act as authority figures. The essence works to overcome the patriarchal impetus to dominate and instead invites cooperation, trust, community, and friendship as tools for leadership.

Use rosemary flower essence in magick for protection and purification and for magick related to reclaiming your power and identity. It can be helpful for remembering who you are and why you're here. Rosemary is the essence for discovering and living your purpose. Try taking it before bed to ensure sound and restorative sleep; it will help you feel safe and secure as you drift off to dreamland. You can use it to honor your ancestors and to facilitate communication with them, too; give it as an offering on ancestral altars or take it internally. You can also use it to connect to the divine feminine.

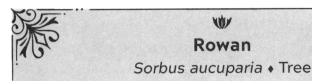

Rowan

Sorbus aucuparia ◆ Tree

Elemental signature: fire

Planetary signature: sun

Zodiacal signature: Aquarius

Chakras: heart, crown

Magickal uses: protection, fairy magick, elemental magick, healing, power, success, invocation

Therapeutic indications: being stuck in the past, reliving of old trauma, difficulty letting go, avoidance, overactive imagination, ineffective or uninspired communication, self-pity, defensiveness, resentment, disconnection from nature

ROWANS, MEMBERS OF THE ROSE FAMILY, are deciduous, small-to-medium trees with fernlike foliage, and they are famous for their bright red-orange fruits that appear in the fall. Rowan's pale yellowy-white flowers display five petals, like the flowers of most members of the rose family, and they bloom in densely packed clusters that may number as many as 250 individual blossoms. Rowan is also called mountain ash, witchwood, and quicken tree, among many other folk names, and it is common across the British Isles and other parts of western Europe.

Rowan was once widely cultivated for food, medicine, and magick, and it continues to be appreciated into the present day. The brilliantly colored berries are its most striking feature; they bear a tiny, five-pointed star that has likely connected them to magick and protection since antiquity, and in some traditions they are considered the food of the gods. Two twigs of rowan tied into an equal-armed cross with red thread is a traditional apotropaic charm; the dried berries are also strung up and hung for protection. Rowan is often connected to lightning, too, and when carried or placed in the home it is said to avert storms and defend against harmful magick, misfortune, and malefic spirits.

Rowan flower essence can be protective inasmuch that it works to release harmful, self-destructive behaviors, thereby protecting you from yourself. Try using the essence if you are faced with patterns of avoidance, judgment, self-pity, shame, and defensiveness.[197] It is an important essence for releasing the past, especially when you cling to old behaviors and beliefs or if you carry resentment over past traumas. Rowan flower essence invites you to stop perpetuating the harm caused by replaying your pain in your mind, and it helps you cultivate resilience, soulfulness, and a willingness to let go. The essence gently nudges you to stop avoiding problems and helps you take responsibility for your peace and well-being and seize opportunities for resolving long-standing problems.

Much of rowan's folklore connects it to elves, fairies, spirits, and witchery. It is thought that elves dwell among its branches and that witches can be seen meeting in its shade. All parts of the tree can be used for inviting contact with the spiritual world, from invoking the Great Goddess to summoning familiars, spirits, and elementals. The essence similarly enhances your ability to attune to the energies of nature, encouraging greater focus, discipline, and a renewed sense of clarity to better help you perceive universal and elemental consciousness.[198] While rowan essence offers a connection to the spirit world and the cosmos at large, it also supports practicality and dispels illusion.

Use it when you need better discernment and understanding along your spiritual path, especially if you are unsure whether you are experiencing genuine spirit contact or your imagination is simply running wild.

Rowan flower essence works strongly on the mind to support memory, recall, mental clarity, and clear communication. It works to balance the heart and mind and leads you toward insights that can help you solve emotional challenges. This essence is a wonderful support when you are healing from and overcoming long-held trauma. Working with the essence leads to greater levels of peace, happiness, and contentment that arise from being willing to do the inner work required to heal and grow.

Rowan flower essence can be used to celebrate Beltane as well as for any rituals related to or inspired by the fixed stars in the night sky. It carries a connection to the starry sky and may inspire you to be a better astrologer by awakening a sense of deep attunement to the cosmos. This essence can also be used in rituals to improve communication, particularly with spirits and fairies, as well as for spells for protection and healing.

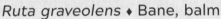

Rue
Ruta graveolens ♦ Bane, balm

Elemental signature: fire

Planetary signatures: sun, Mars

Zodiacal signature: Leo

Chakras: solar plexus, crown

Magickal uses: protection, purification, curse breaking, healing, grace, psychic development, attraction

Therapeutic indications: weak psychic senses, scattered or confused psychic forces, lack of clarity and discernment, difficulty exercising your true will, deeply hidden fears, being under psychic attack, regretfulness

RUE IS AN EVERGREEN HERB native to southeast Europe with a rich and ancient tradition of medicinal, culinary, and magickal use. It has feathery, fuzzy leaves that exhibit a bluish- or silvery-green appearance.

Rue's flowers are yellow and four-petaled, evoking the image of the solar or equal-armed cross. Although used in medicine and cuisine, rue contains compounds that are toxic in generous amounts; it also causes phototoxicity and contact dermatitis in many people and can be an abortifacient. Its nature is aggressive, as is the case for many banes, and it should be handled with reasonable care. Rue blurs the lines between banes and balms, and it may be classified as both at once.

Rue is a magickal plant long connected to witchcraft. It is among the plants most commonly mentioned in witchcraft trial records of southern England, and it has been used to protect against harmful magick for centuries, earning it the nickname *witchbane*. Rue has been used magickally to counteract poisons, boost mental powers, and facilitate healing rituals. It is considered strongly purifying, too; sprigs of rue have been used for sprinkling water for cleansing, and the dew collected from the plant in the early morning was used to make holy water by the early Catholic Church. Many practitioners use rue to strengthen their magick and bolster psychic and magickal defenses. It is a powerful ally in curse breaking and exorcism. Rue is also considered sacred to the deities Diana, Aradia, Mars, and Erzulie.

Rue flower essence is similarly protective. It offers profound protection in the psychic realm, and it helps prevention of and recovery from psychic attack and energy vampirism. The essence clears attachments from the aura and releases connections of a draining or vampiric nature. It can be used to cut energetic cords and release attached entities and thoughtforms, and it is especially helpful as a protection essence for shamanic journeys or astral travel. It is also useful for transforming unconscious energies sent to you in the form of anger, jealousy, or fear; it even works to transmute the same emotions when you project them onto yourself. The flower's fourfold symmetry signals a sense of grounding, protection, and empowerment. As a result, the essence bolsters life force and its union with the soul, thereby enabling you to manifest your true will (i.e., your higher will) in your daily life.[199] Add a few drops to some water and sprinkle it in a circle around you or your home to create a protective atmosphere—add even more power by using a sprig of fresh rue to sprinkle it.

The herb's reputation for healing the eyes has made it a useful ally for developing second sight in magickal herbalism. As a flower essence, it represents the containment and cohesion of psychic forces.[200] It strongly activates the psychic nature of the soul, promoting discernment and clarity. It opens and connects the solar plexus and the crown chakras, thereby providing you with the strength and confidence to act upon your intuition and psychic impressions. Rue essence invites you to be more aware of your emotional, mental, and spiritual patterns and helps you transform negative or harmful patterns into beneficial ones.

Rue is popularly known as the herb of grace, and it brings with it a sense of peace and holiness. Its essence draws out your inner spark of divinity so that it may truly shine. It brings mental and emotional clarity and eases feelings of self-doubt, confusion, and regret.

Sage
Salvia officinalis ♦ Balm

Elemental signature: air

Planetary signature: Jupiter

Zodiacal signature: Sagittarius

Chakra: crown

Magickal uses: cleansing, protection, healing, clarity, wisdom, longevity, love

Therapeutic indications: imbalance between material and spiritual life, lack of purpose or meaning in life events, feeling consigned to fate, blocked or stagnant communication, sluggish mind, overactive mind

SAGE, A MEMBER OF THE MINT FAMILY that is native to the Mediterranean, is much beloved for its culinary, medicinal, and spiritual qualities. Its leaves are oblong, silvery green, and dusted in fine fuzz. The flowers appear in late spring or summer and are raised into the tall spikes typical of mints; the flowers usually range from blue to purple or lavender, though they are sometimes white.

Common sage and its many relatives are most often used in rituals of healing, cleansing, and protection. Many varieties are burned to purify both people and spaces. The plant is traditionally associated with wisdom, mental clarity, and longevity, and it is occasionally used in love magick, too. The flower essence is deeply cleansing, and it works well to provide clarity to an overactive mind as well as to remove disharmonious or harmful energies from your energy field or your home. Spray, diffuse, or sprinkle the essence around your space to remove unwanted energies.

Medicinally, sage is often associated with digestion. The flower essence helps you digest your life experiences, emotional states, and mental patterns so you can distill wisdom from them. When life feels as though it lacks meaning or events appear bereft of purpose, sage flower essence invites you to reflect upon the scenario. This essence helps you process your experiences and release the weight of the past without a loss of understanding or meaning. Sage essence also offers a healthy sense of detachment so you can accept and review the ups and downs of life with better discernment, thereby leading you to a sense of peace and wisdom. It helps you rise to any occasion by integrating the wisdom of past experience. It facilitates grateful and graceful maturation in life, and it is a wonderful ally if you find yourself in a position of counseling or healing others.[201]

Part of the wisdom that sage offers comes from seeking balance in all things. Just as it balances the energy field by releasing and resolving unwanted energies, sage flower essence helps you resolve imbalances between spirituality and materiality. This flower essence ushers you toward equilibrium between belief and scepticism, thus preventing both gross materialism and religious fanaticism.[202] It offers a healthy amount of doubt but also leaves you willing to take a leap of faith. The essence also reminds you not to take yourself or life too seriously; it instills a sense of joy and surrender and helps cultivate inner silence. It is also helpful for gently opening psychic abilities and enhancing communication. It helps you find adequate means of expression, and it can lead you to find the right words for whatever audience you are addressing, no matter the medium.

Sage flower essence is helpful when you are preparing for ritual or spellcraft. Not only can you use it to cleanse yourself and your space, but it also inspires you to draw on your experience to craft better and more effective rituals. Add sage flower essence to any working to benefit from the expansive, benefic vibrations of its Jovian influence.

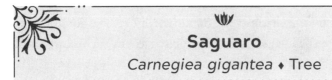

Saguaro
Carnegiea gigantea ♦ Tree

Elemental signatures: earth, spirit

Planetary signature: Saturn

Zodiacal signature: Capricorn

Chakra: throat

Magickal uses: protection, healing, psychic development, spiritual growth, connecting to the divine masculine

Therapeutic indications: power struggles with authority figures, inability to tap in to inner guidance, issues surrounding your father or father figure, inability to find your own inner authority and power, sense of disconnection from heritage or tradition

THE SAGUARO CACTUS is an enigmatic figure of the deserts in the American Southwest. It grows extremely slowly in rocky ground and foothills. Its columnar form is deeply corrugated, such that it can expand rapidly as its shallow, broad root system drinks in copious amounts of water after a rainstorm. The saguaro blooms only once it reaches about eight feet in height and thirty-five years in age. The flowers are large and white; they blossom in the evening and remain open until the following afternoon. This allows both nocturnal pollinators, like bats and moths, and diurnal pollinators, such as bees and birds, to visit the flowers. A single cactus may produce over a hundred flowers during its blooming season.

While the saguaro is not botanically classified as a tree, it serves a similar spiritual role in the landscape of the desert. Its most noticeable quality is its verticality, the way it points upward to the heavens, much like a tree trunk. Saguaro offers a sense of alignment with the higher realms. It connects with your own higher consciousness—your inner divinity—and with the realm of the heavens. It is the mystic, teacher, and wisdomkeeper of the desert.

Saguaro flower essence relates to themes of power, authority, and tradition. Cynthia Athina Kemp Scherer, founder of Desert Alchemy, likens saguaro essence to what she calls perfect father energy. She explains that energy is embodied in the father figure who helps us figure out our own problems, rather than solving them for us, all while helping us feel supported, guided, and protected along the way. She writes that saguaro essence "helps us find this relationship within ourselves. It is excellent for those of us who had troubling experiences with our fathers. It is also excellent for those whose fathers were not present physically, emotionally, or spiritually."[203]

Saguaro flower essence helps you cultivate your relationship with the divine. In a general sense, this means coming to terms with a higher power that is your Creator and the ultimate authority. It restores a deep connection to this force and invites greater understanding of your relationship to the universe at large. I find this essence ideal for connecting to the archetypes of the divine masculine—the god of the witches in his myriad forms. Saguaro flower essence also helps you during phases when you struggle with or find yourself in conflict with authority figures. It restores a sense of inner authority and helps you reclaim your power.

This essence also provides a deeper understanding of tradition and allows you to embrace and understand the past.[204] This makes it useful for times when you feel disconnected from your heritage, culture, race, family, or region. Magickally, it is a wonderful ally for rediscovering the magick of your heritage or finding the right spiritual community where you feel at home.

Overall, cacti are used in magick for protection, healing, and spiritual growth; they are also useful for learning to stand in your power and break unhealthy habits.[205] Saguaro is especially protective; its energy is like that of a wise and ancient guardian, the grandfather of the desert. Use the essence to awaken protective spirits and to maintain a connection to the spirit world during ritual, meditation, and retreat.

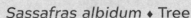

Sassafras

Sassafras albidum ♦ Tree

Elemental signature: fire

Astrological signatures: Jupiter, Sagittarius

Chakra: solar plexus

Magickal uses: healing, money, luck, protection, curse removal

Therapeutic indications: lack of self-love, feeling like a misfit, stubbornness, alienation, disconnection from heritage

SASSAFRAS, A MEMBER OF THE laurel family native to North America, is prized for its soft, pale wood and aromatic bark. It was long used as medicine by indigenous Americans and was highly sought after by European colonizers for use in medicine and for wood carving. Usually a smallish tree, sassafras is dioecious, with male and female flowers, both yellow and six-petaled, appearing on separate trees. Although the ripe fruits will bear seeds, sassafras usually reproduces clonally via its rootstock; saplings can be seen clustered around a mother tree at the forest's edge or in clearings.

The name *sassafras* is derived from the Latin *saxifraga,* meaning "stone breaker."[206] Sassafras flower essence can be used to break down patterns of obstinacy—the state of being hard and stubborn as stone. It also displaces feelings of alienation and perception of being a misfit with a sense of belonging. It connects you to ancestral healing and wisdom, helping you when you feel displaced or disconnected from your heritage. Sassafras flower essence enables you to appreciate your unique qualities and gifts, and it invites you to offer these lovingly to the world. It teaches you to better love yourself and helps you cultivate sweetness in your life.

Sassafras is traditionally used in magick related to wealth, healing, and protection. It is thought to bring good fortune in money matters and success in business and to ensure a steady increase in wealth.[207] I find that the essence helps you respect and celebrate your unique skills and talents, while learning to offer them in service and love. It helps you recognize the value of your energy, time, efforts, and other resources so that you are not giving too much of yourself at any moment. Thus, sassafras essence contributes to your overall prosperity; you can give of yourself while still anticipating equal exchange from customers, loved ones, and the universe at large.

The wood has long been believed to confer blessings and protection. Ships made from sassafras timber were renowned for making safe voyages back to Europe during the colonial era. The wood was carved into a variety of everyday goods to bring the virtues and protections embodied by the tree. Cherokee herbal wisdom regards sassafras as not only medicinal but also adept at removing curses; children bearing a particular kind of curse were said to be cured by a decoction of sassafras bark. Similarly, you can add sassafras flower essence to the bath or mist it in your space to avert harm caused by the ill intentions of others, as it bolsters your sense of worth and self-love. Diffuse it in your home to bring blessings, protection, and nurturing energies into your space.

Snowdrop
Galanthus nivalis ♦ Bane

Elemental signatures: water, fire

Astrological signatures: moon, Saturn

Chakras: sacral, heart

Magickal uses: hope, Imbolc celebration, luck, creativity, attunement to seasonal changes

Therapeutic indications: shyness, hopelessness, numbness, gloom, grief, fear of the unknown, rejection, stuck or frozen emotions, dark night of the soul, loss of innocence, long period of trauma, seasonal affective disorder

SNOWDROPS BLOOM IN LATE WINTER—hence their common name. Their petite white flowers hang downward, borne on green stalks. The downward-facing blooms have led to associations with shyness, grief, and despair; the essence of snowdrop is a potent remedy for these emotions. Snowdrop essence is deeply cleansing and initiates cycles of regeneration and renewal.

As one of the earliest flowers to bloom, rising above the snow before spring has even arrived, snowdrop brings a sense of promise and hope. Its essence embodies the proverbial light at the end of the tunnel, and it helps you trust the healing process. When you have long-standing trauma, pain, or fear, this essence helps you see the opportunity to heal through forgiveness by rekindling your personal connection to the spiritual world. It promotes self-discovery, granting lightness and innocence. The flower is itself an optimist—blooming before winter has ended— and it invites you to cultivate a hopeful heart.

Snowdrops produce their own heat, which is a rare feat in the plant kingdom. This enables them to melt the snow around them so they can push through and bloom. Their small buds hang like lanterns, lighting the way toward hope and healing. The blossoms appear around Imbolc or Candlemas (February 2) and are associated with the turning of the seasonal tides. Snowdrop flower essence is an excellent addition to an Imbolc ritual. It is also indicated for people suffering from seasonal affective disorder.

When you feel stuck in some way, snowdrop is the perfect essence to help you break through. When you are faced with trauma that has atrophied your ability to love or trust, or when you are tasked with overcoming insurmountable, paralyzing fear, snowdrop can initiate deep healing. The teardrop-shaped bulb is a signature for the water element, and it has been noted that many people who take this essence are moved to tears.[208] Any conditions characterized by dryness can be improved by this flower essence. It lightens your mood, dissolves chronic energetic blockages, and sheds new light on old situations.

Magickally, snowdrop is considered to bring luck and hope. The flower essence can help you in spells designed to turn your luck around, as it plants seeds of optimism. It is a flower of spiritual breakthrough, and working with it in ritual offers creativity and inspiration. It fosters resiliency and trust and helps you forge deeper relationships with the gods, even when you have difficulty sensing or seeing their influences in your life.

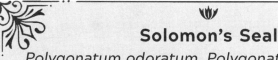
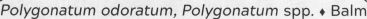

Solomon's Seal
Polygonatum odoratum, Polygonatum spp. ♦ Balm

Elemental signature: water

Planetary signature: Saturn

Zodiacal signatures: Gemini, Aquarius

Chakras: sacral, solar plexus

Magickal uses: protection, exorcism, curse breaking, wisdom, keeping promises, love

Therapeutic indications: perfectionism, overactive mind, frustration, disappointment, controlling behavior, being easily discouraged, rejection of authority, desire for leadership, procrastination, indecisiveness, lack of coordination and/or direction

SOLOMON'S SEAL IS A MEMBER of the asparagus family, like its relative lily of the valley. It has simple leaves arranged alternately on arching stems. Its tube-shaped flowers hang downward like chimes from the underside of the stems. The blooms are white with green lips. This plant is named for the hexagram-shaped scar left on the rhizome when the stalks die back in the fall. It is said that King Solomon placed his seal on the plant to indicate its value to magicians.

In magickal lore, Solomon's seal is predominantly used for apotropaic purposes, as well as for attaining wisdom. As a protective herb, the root was commonly placed in the four corners of the home to seal it from intrusion by malefic forces. The flower essence can similarly be sprayed or dropped into the four corners at the new moon to create a magickal boundary against harm. In American folk magick, Solomon's seal is frequently used to break jinxes and hexes and to avert evil. The root can be added to incense for the consecration of ritual spaces, and the essence could similarly be sprayed or diffused in a room to prepare it for magick. Try dressing altar candles with Solomon's seal essence to lend efficacy to all your magickal workings.

Solomon's seal essence is a valuable tool for developing good leadership skills and attaining wisdom. It begins by releasing unnecessary attachments to outcomes, subsequently alleviating frustration, anger, and disappointment when things do not work out.[209] This essence counteracts indecision and the urge to procrastinate by developing a sense of resolve. It hones your ability to plan, set goals, and adapt your goals as they unfold. In a sense, it is an essence of flexibility, allowing you to learn from every new experience. In magick, the plant is often used for wisdom and for boosting mental powers; as an essence, it offers clarity to a busy mind. When carried, the root garners respect and curries favor, two properties that are also cultivated by using the essence. Solomon's seal is ideal for bolstering leadership skills, helping you make wise decisions for yourself and on behalf of others. This essence also boosts communication and social skills. It promotes cooperation and coordination, and it can be diffused in a space to bring protection and harmony to any group of people gathered there.

Solomon's seal is sometimes used in love magick, and the herb is considered an aphrodisiac. The herb is used in ceremonial magick for binding magickal oaths and compacts with spirits. Use the essence to build trust and acceptance between parties, as this is a natural result from developing respect and leadership. In love magick, the essence encourages mutual respect and commitment. Consider using the essence to strengthen bonds that already exist by combining it with essences of the classic amatory herbs, such as rose.

Spiderwort
Tradescantia ohiensis, Tradescantia spp. ♦ Balm

Elemental signature: air

Planetary signature: Uranus

Zodiacal signature: Aquarius

Chakra: throat

Magickal uses: love, abundance, healing, beauty

Therapeutic indications: grief, cynicism, environmental sensitivity, low self-esteem, communication blockage, disorganization

SPIDERWORT IS A WILDFLOWER that grows abundantly in North America. Also called widow's tears, blue jacket, and spider lily, it usually sports bright blue-to-violet flowers of three petals, typically with bright yellow anthers. The flowers are arranged in clusters that hang from the stalk until they open each morning, just one or a few at a time. The blossoms close by midday, and the petals disintegrate into a sticky, mucilaginous mass, which can be spun like a web. This is one of several proposed origins for its name, although it has also been used medicinally to treat spiderbites.

The magickal lore surrounding spiderwort is relatively thin. Indigenous Americans of the Dakota carried spiderwort to attract love.[210] Modern witches also use spiderwort in love charms. The flower essence promotes inner beauty and boosts self-esteem, and it can be added to the bath for this purpose. It is also sometimes used to draw wealth and repel negativity. The three-petaled flowers are said to represent the holy trinities of the world, such as Father, Son, and Holy Ghost; Maiden, Mother, and Crone; and body, mind, and spirit. As a flower essence, spiderwort helps align the seemingly disparate elements of these trinities, thereby allowing you to tap in to your true and complete self. This integration of body, mind, and spirit yields both conviction and integrity.

Spiderwort flower essence teaches you to pay attention to the signals that are all around us. The flowers of the plant change color when exposed to contamination in the environment, such as pesticides, pollution, and harmful radiation. The flower essence can signal environmental energies that are toxic to you and nudge you to take steps to stay healthy and safe. It is a useful essence for sensitive folks, such as empaths, as well as people with medical sensitivities, such as allergies. The flowers close when the sun is too high and too hot, showing that the plant knows its own limits; the essence helps you remain in touch with your physical, psychological, and spiritual needs so you can attend to them proactively. It helps bring stagnant and toxic patterns to the surface so you can see them, much in the way that the changing color of the petals allows you to see otherwise invisible environmental factors. I know of some practitioners who use this essence to stimulate healing of the aura, building resistance to future trauma and environmental harm.

Working with spiderwort essence promotes healthy communication. It can break down resistance to using your voice, while also helping you be a more attentive listener. It teaches discernment, activating your inner lie detector and helping you sort out valuable data from background noise. It can be helpful if you feel you are sending or receiving mixed signals, too, as it clarifies and organizes the underlying message in your communication. This flower essence also overturns negative attitudes and transforms the cynic into a healthy skeptic.[211]

The folk name *widow's tears* points to the plant's ability to address issues of grief and sadness.[212] The flower essence helps you learn to use your voice to heal, as telling your story aloud or in written form is a powerful vehicle for releasing pain. Storytelling can be a potent act of magick, and this essence can strengthen community bonds by helping us discover common threads among our personal stories; try using it before a public ritual or shared magick to heighten group cohesion and boost the results of your magick.

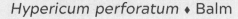

St. John's Wort
Hypericum perforatum ♦ Balm

Elemental signature: fire

Planetary signature: sun

Zodiacal signature: Leo

Chakra: solar plexus

Magickal uses: fertility, protection, abundance, purification, exorcism, psychic development, spirit communication, astral travel, inspiration, enlightenment, Luciferian magick

Therapeutic indications: depression, fear or paranoia, vulnerability, lethargy, recovery after trauma or injury, difficulty being open and honest about shortcomings, seasonal affective disorder, allergies

THE GENUS *HYPERICUM* CONSISTS of almost five hundred species with worldwide distribution. The most widely known (and most commonly available as a flower essence) is St. John's wort,

Hypericum perforatum. The plant has a yellow, five-petaled flower; its leaves are dotted with oil glands that make them appear perforated. St. John's wort is used medicinally to treat depression and to help heal wounds. In magick, itis associated with fertility, protection, purification, and exorcism. The flower essence is most potent when made in ritual at the summer solstice or St. John's Day, the celebration day of the saint for which the plant is named.

As a protective herb, St. John's wort is sublime. Its genus name is derived from a Greek expression meaning "over an image," denoting that the plant was once hung above shrines to drive away evil spirits. The plant has been used to protect the home against lighting and storms, expel the evil eye, and invite blessings. Carrying it was said to drive away harmful spirits, break curses, and banish sickness. The flower essence can be used for any of these purposes, too.

St. John's wort is primarily related to light. The tiny glands that resemble holes allow light to pass through the leaves; in a similar fashion, the flower essence allows light to penetrate even the darkest and densest areas. The essence allows you to draw in and hold more light, while simultaneously awakening and activating the inner brilliance of the soul. The herb was once used to exorcise dark forces, as its luminous presence casts out negativity. Similarly, the essence lifts the spirit by shedding light on hidden trauma and negative emotional patterns.

St. John's wort flower essence brings protection, peace, and fertility to the home. Place several drops of the essence, or spray it from a mister, in the four corners of your home or property to seal it from all harm. The flowers were once hung in windows to prevent witches and other harmful entities from peering in. Instead, consider adding a few drops of the flower essence to your window cleaner to filter the energy that comes through the windows; this will allow the light of abundance, love, and healing to enter your home while guarding against harm. Diffusing the essence in a bowl of water or on a crystal cluster fills your home with abundance, peace, and joy.

St. John's wort offers the same protection on a personal level. The yellow flowers have long been regarded as an apotropaic against malefic magick, and the flower essence is generally protective and uplifting.

Medicinally, the herb is used to promote the healing of wounds, and the essence works on a spiritual level to heal wounds in the aura and to soothe emotional wounds and past-life burdens. Christopher Penczak tells us that this plant spirit opens "psychic 'pores' in the aura and body, like opening window shades. St. John's wort doesn't destroy boundaries or create holes, but rather clears windows for light to pass through freely wherever it is needed."[213] When we are inundated with light, we shine with the radiance of a miniature sun, which effectively exorcises illness and gloom.

Working with St. John's wort flower essence alleviates trauma or injury, even when it is buried deep below the level of conscious awareness. It is often indicated for depression, fear, and paranoia, as well as anything that leaves you feeling vulnerable. The essence separates the mind from the emotions to make it easier to process old emotional patterns. It elicits joy and good cheer, expanding consciousness and boosting self-worth. It can help those who have environmental allergies and sensitivities to light or subtle energies. The essence is especially protective and strengthening for anyone in an expanded state of consciousness, such as might result from meditation, ritual, or using sacred plant medicine.

Taking this flower essence reminds you of the spiritual help that is all around you. The herb was reputedly used by witches to help them hear spirits, and the essence facilitates contact with your guides and spirit allies. It can fine-tune your psychic skills and assist you in receiving and interpreting messages from your spirits. Because the plant is so hated by evil spirits, taking the flower essence before divination or any sort of spirit contact will ensure that the messages you receive come from safe and helpful sources. During the medieval witch hunts, the herb was placed into the mouths of accused witches as it was believed to make them confess. As a flower essence, St. John's wort encourages emotional honesty, and it can make it easier to own up to your shortcomings.

The flower essence of St. John's wort also facilitates astral projection, shamanic journeys (especially to the upper world), and visionary states, and it clarifies dreams. The herb is an old remedy against nightmares and other nighttime disturbances, and the essence works equally as well. Its solar energy combats seasonal affective disorder, grants inspiration and motivation, and assuages guilt. St. John's wort flower essence is a general tonic for the nervous system, and it boosts memory and concentration. It plants seeds of optimism and cultivates laughter. It is a Luciferian essence par excellence, enabling you to bear light and hope in the most challenging of circumstances, leading you closer and closer to enlightenment.

Sunflower
Helianthus annuus ♦ Balm

Elemental signature: fire

Planetary signature: sun

Zodiacal signature: Leo

Chakra: solar plexus

Magickal uses: prosperity, healing, fertility, wishes, protection, justice

Therapeutic indications: distorted or inconsistent self-image, inflated ego, arrogance, aggression, issues with authority and authority figures, low self-esteem, self-effacement, trouble relating to your father or father figure

THE SUNFLOWER IS AMONG the most well-known flowers of the Compositae family. It has a tall, erect stem covered in rough hairs, and its leaves are generally broad, rough-margined, and usually somewhat fuzzy. Prominent flower heads grow from the top of the stem, and some varieties have smaller flowers that sprout from the stem. The classic color for the sunflower is a golden yellow, with yellow or brownish-black centers, though there are cultivars in a wide range of other colors.

As a magickal herb, sunflower is emblematic of the sun and all its connotations. It has been used in spells for success, money, fertility, wisdom, justice, and protection. The seeds were traditionally eaten by women to help them conceive. The petals can be added to charm bags and potions to draw money and increase confidence. Growing sunflowers is said to protect your home from negative energy, as if each blossom were a miniature sun that drives out darkness. The solar aspects of sunflower can be traced back to the plant's origins in the Americas. Indigenous tribes such as the Aztec and Inca, who revered the sun, held the sunflower in high regard; they surely watched the golden blooms follow the sun's path each day. Priestesses of the sun were even crowned with sunflowers, and carvings of sunflowers in pure gold adorned temples dedicated to the sun.[214]

The solar nature of the sunflower points toward its uses as a flower essence. The sun is the center of our solar system and the source of light, heat, and metabolic energy on Earth. Symbolically, the sun is the ruling authority, the central figure. Astrologically, the sun represents the self—both as ego and as personality. At one end of the spectrum, sunflower essence helps treat conditions of an overinflated or deficient ego; it balances extremes such as aggression, arrogance, pride, and self-aggrandizement. At the other end, it counteracts low self-esteem, self-effacement, lack of pride, and conditions marked by gloom, despair, and depression. The essence is like bottled sunshine: cheerful, radiant, and optimistic.

Sunflower essence is particularly helpful for instances of weak, imbalanced, or dysfunctional relationships with authority figures, especially fathers or father figures. Many practitioners use this essence to mitigate anger or hostility toward father figures. The essence solidifies personal identity and allows for healthy self-expression, thereby fostering a sense of inner authority. Young sunflowers exhibit strong heliotropism, turning their faces to follow the path of the sun. As they mature, sunflower blooms adopt a fixed position, typically facing east. This parallels the way that we follow the lead set by authority figures, often our fathers, early in life but later learn to be our own authority. Sunflower essence can help resolve lingering issues related to authority figures and the use of personal power. It fosters a sense of individuality and healthy self-expression and imparts confidence in your ability to lead. Though seemingly masculine in nature, sunflower essence does help cultivate a balance of inner masculine and feminine, or yin and yang, qualities. It is helpful for finding the inner resolve and dynamic power of the inner father while still displaying the nurturing and support of the inner mother.

Sunflower essence balances the radiant light of the spirit with the joyful presence of the body. It promotes a sense of sovereignty and boosts your ability to create, manifest, and grow here on Earth. It is excellent when used for spells related to money and abundance. It teaches you how to be discerning with your hard-earned money while still practicing generosity; accordingly, the essence neutralizes greed and inspires you to make a contribution to the world.[215] Like the manner in which the sun offers light and warmth to the planet, expecting nothing in return, sunflower essence invites you to bring more light, joy, and happiness into the world. It brings you into a place of empowerment, one in which you are confident that your actions will ripple outward to uplift others and help heal the world.

Take sunflower essence before engaging in any sort of solar magick. Consider using it for holidays that hinge around the power and light of the sun, such as the summer solstice and Lammas; try diffusing it, adding it to your chalice, or applying it to the solar plexus to boost your attunement to the sun's rays. The essence is also gently protective; since it teaches you to be your own authority, it also makes you less susceptible to others' energies. Add a few drops of sunflower essence to candles or charm bags for justice, so that the light of truth will illuminate all parties.

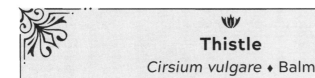

Thistle
Cirsium vulgare ♦ Balm

Elemental signature: fire

Planetary signatures: Mars, Saturn

Zodiacal signature: Capricorn

Chakra: crown

Magickal uses: protection, curse breaking, healing, exorcism, peace

Therapeutic indications: guardedness, feeling overprotective, oversensitivity to acute stress and perceived threats, difficulty maintaining or honoring boundaries, keeping others at a distance, distrust, anger, resentment, irritability, fear of or conflict with authority, feeling confined, lack of trust in spiritual connection, clinging to the past

TRUE THISTLES BELONG to the aster family (Asteraceae or Compositae) and are characterized by their spiny leaves, stems, and bracts. The sharp prickles along the leaves and other parts of the thistle are an evolutionary adaptation meant to deter herbivores from devouring the plants. The flowers of common thistle (*Cirsium vulgare*) are easily recognized by their fuzzy blooms that point skyward atop long stems. They are usually a shade of magenta or pink (sometimes yellow or white) and surrounded by thorns and spines.

Common thistle's spiny nature lends itself well to defensive magick. It can be used for breaking hexes, averting malefic magick, and defending against other forms of harm, too. When used as materia magica, thistle offers courage, strength, and peace of mind—all qualities engendered by the flower essence, too. There is a fair amount of folklore that connects various species of thistle to the devil and to witchcraft. It is even said that thistles grow near the homes of witches—and I never seem to have any shortage of them near me.

Thistle flower essence mirrors the defensive nature of the plant and its use in defensive magick. The flower essence is indicated for times when you are too guarded, defensive, or distrustful of others. Usually, this defensiveness is a result of some other trauma or fear. In Greek mythology, the thistle was created by the Earth as an expression of grief at the loss of a beautiful shepherd and poet, Daphnis.[216] The prickly defenses you might levy at those who try to get close to you may similarly result from heartache or other trauma. Thistle flower essence helps you find the strength and courage required to be vulnerable enough to lower your walls and create meaningful connections. I find thistle exceptional for treating anger and hostility used as defense mechanisms.

Thistle is a flower of courage and strength, and the essence can offer those qualities when you are faced with fear. Thistle addresses overreaction to fear, especially if you are oversensitive to perceived threats, and helps you find clarity in the midst of a fight-or-flight response. It is indicated in cases where acute stress triggers this reaction, especially when you are too quick to identify threats and feel immobilized by fear. Thistle supports you in cultivating a more reasonable and proportionate response to stress, especially by bolstering your spiritual and social boundaries. Thistle helps you identify and enforce your boundaries—as well as the boundaries of other people—with grace. Dr. Bach briefly explored the uses for yellow sow thistle (*Sonchus arvensis*) and found it helpful against gloom and joylessness.[217] Although he abandoned this essence, we can imagine that this distant cousin of the common thistle helps us set boundaries that better enable us to maintain our happiness and peace of mind.

One of thistle flower essence's gifts is the ability to trust your own inner authority. When you accept your own sovereignty, you can move on from negative experiences with outer authorities, such as parents, teachers, leaders, and law enforcement. Thistle helps you build your self-worth through honoring and trusting your inner authority, and it gradually extends this trust outward, thereby encouraging you to trust others, too. It helps when you feel confined, constrained, or restricted in any manner, as it empowers you to take the reins for your own well-being.

In a similar fashion, thistle flower essence connects you to a higher authority. The upward-pointing blooms help you see and understand your spiritual connection and gain a better understanding of spirituality and reality at large.[218] This results in an expanded view of the world, one in which you feel less constricted by the weight of past trauma or the social, cultural, or familial boundaries that you carry with you.

Thistle is helpful for witches, magicians, and other people who feel dissonance between their current spiritual path and the religious or spiritual teachings of their family. It is also useful when you feel too vulnerable or too spiritually open to engage with the world at large, especially after ritual, meditation, or other spiritual practice. Use it in potions for courage, strength, and protection, as it helps you triumph over fear and trauma. You can also use it to connect to your wild state and feel more aligned with the spiritual fabric of reality.

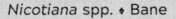

Tobacco

Nicotiana spp. ♦ Bane

Elemental signatures: earth, fire, spirit

Planetary signatures: Mars, Saturn, Uranus, Pluto

Zodiacal signature: Scorpio

Chakras: heart, crown

Magickal uses: prayer, protection, spirit contact, Earth healing, control

Therapeutic indications: spiritual disconnection, introversion, seeking happiness from social settings, rigidity, emotional numbness, cravings, addiction, lust for control, fear (especially of sleep, spiritual experiences, and death), difficulty maintaining spiritual practice, materialism, greed, guilt, anguish, sensitivity to the opinions of others

LIKE OTHER NIGHTSHADES, members of *Nicotiana* evolved to produce several alkaloid compounds, including nicotine, that deter herbivores from eating them. The most famous species in this genus, *N. tabacum,* is cultivated around the world for use in cigarettes and cigars. Wild tobacco (*N. rustica*) is the species most commonly found as a flower essence, and it is characterized by greenish, five-petaled flowers with a distinct funnel shape. Many tobacco plants are vespertines, meaning their flowers bloom in the evening. Many indigenous cultures regard tobacco as one of the holiest plants.

Of all the nightshades, tobacco is the most heart-centered, and indigenous lore often relates that tobacco is an herb for offerings and prayers. The smoke of tobacco leaves has accompanied many a prayer to the spiritual realms, and the flower essence produces an openhearted state by nourishing the heart center and providing emotional honesty and clarity. According to Patricia Kaminski and Richard Katz, founders of the Flower Essence Society, tobacco flower essence teaches "that real peace arises from being able to feel deeply with the heart, and that these deep feelings give us our true connection to the Earth and all living beings."[219] Tobacco is a willing plant spirit ally, perhaps among the friendliest and most helpful of the banes. Its essence can serve to strengthen your connections to other baneful plants, as though it is a great diplomat that makes the introduction for you. The plant is also considered a purifying agent, and it can be helpful for alleviating distress caused by working with other baneful plants.[220]

As an ingredient in folk magick, tobacco is often used to petition the spirits for favor and protection. It is often used in cases where you'd like to control the outcome, such as in court cases, winning back a lover, and jinxing/hexing.[221] Tobacco flower essence is similarly used for patterns relating to control, rigidity, and power. It is often indicated when something has control over you, such as addiction, because the essence releases anything that has power over you, empowering you to make healthy changes in your life. Many times these situations or behaviors that can control you, like addiction or cravings, result from trying to numb your emotions; since tobacco essence opens the heart, it helps you get in touch with your emotions and face the things that make you want to feel numb.

Tobacco flower essence combats rigidity, hardness, and lust for power and control. It is deeply purifying and protective, clearing the meridians and the subtle bodies. It also helps balance overly dominant masculine or yang energies by restoring a connection to the Earth. Many indigenous people use tobacco to commune with Mother Earth. Similarly, tobacco essence works to alleviate what Kaminski and Katz refer to as "hard-edged masculine forces" and promotes cooperation and community.[222] It restores the balance and flow between yin and yang energies by helping you cultivate a healthy expression of masculine energy that is in balance with the divine feminine. When aggressive, stereotypically masculine action is necessary, tobacco offers wisdom and encourages you to think through and plan your approach.

Tobacco flowers are sacred to Xochipilli, the Aztec god of art, dance, song, beauty, games, and flowers. His name means "prince of flowers," and he was frequently depicted with the tobacco flower. Tobacco flower essence evokes the jovial, pleasure-seeking nature of Xochipilli, promoting the opportunity to be social and merry. It draws out qualities of joy and happiness, and it can help you become more social and vibrant. It is a wonderful essence for people who feel awkward in social situations, as it enables vulnerability and a joyful heart. It honors all expressions of life and joy, and it helps you feel more connected to the world around you.

The flower essence of tobacco is one of deep peace. In my Patagonia Essences training with Natalia Montes, I learned that tobacco essence overcomes a sense of being trapped in feelings of guilt, anguish, fear, and doubt. Essence maker and author Cynthia Athina Kemp Scherer explains that it allows you to see "greater meaning and richness in all the events of our lives."[223] This in turn helps you release judgment, shame, and despair about your progress in life. The essence invites you to observe your personal development by staying rooted in the present and seeing the opportunity that each moment brings. It can also relieve fears about your relationship to the divine and the nature of the afterlife and help you cultivate a healthier relationship with spirituality. In this way, tobacco flower essence combats cynicism, materialism, and lack of discipline and ignites a deeper and more regular spiritual practice.

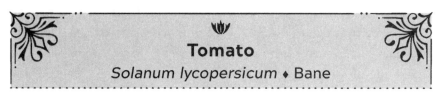

Tomato
Solanum lycopersicum ♦ Bane

Elemental signatures: water, fire

Planetary signatures: Venus, Mars

Zodiacal signature: Aries

Chakras: root, sacral, solar plexus

Magickal uses: love, lust, sex magick, divination

Therapeutic indications: fear, weakness, nightmares, shyness, blockage of any variety, procrastination, addiction

THE TOMATO ORIGINATED in Central and South America and was probably first domesticated by the indigenous peoples of Mexico. The word *tomato* ultimately derives from the Nahuatl *tomatl,* a word that referred to the round, swollen shape of the fruit. Though tomatoes are classified as *Solanum lycopersicum,* belonging to the same genus as black nightshade, potato, and eggplant, they are sometimes grouped into a genus all their own, as *Lycopersicon esculentum.* The plant is usually a vine, though bushy cultivars have been bred. It has compound leaves with serrated margins, and the stems and leaves are often covered in hairlike structures. The leaves and stems emit an odor reminiscent of other nightshades, like datura, when bruised. Tomato flowers are usually bright yellow and five-petaled, with the fused anthers common to most nightshades.

There is not a lot of spiritual and magickal lore readily available about tomatoes. The indigenous Pueblo tribes of the American Southwest record a belief that eating the seeds of the tomato results in the gift of divination. Tomato's gift for divination and psychic development isn't so surprising when you consider the spiritual effects of many of its relatives among the nightshade family. The name *lycopersicum* is taken from Greek, meaning "wolf peach," referring to a belief that tomato was once used in shape-shifting potions and other magickal brews. Wolves have a long association with witchcraft, and tomato is a close relative of many of the baneful herbs used in flying ointments, so it isn't much of a stretch to think that the spirit of this plant might lend itself to rituals of shape-shifting, astral travel, and divination. I find that the essence is rather protective and cleansing, which helps clear the way for other nightshade essences to work more effectively.

The most renowned of tomato's magickal uses is aimed at drawing love and inciting lust. Some Europeans believed tomato to be the original forbidden fruit of Eden, and it was said that a single bite of the tomato could induce uncontrollable lust. Tomato is accordingly associated with the planets Venus and Mars; its bright display of colors evokes sensual pleasure, a trait carried by its essence. Tomato flower essence is helpful when you feel guarded against love and eroticism, and it can be added to love potions to break free of shyness and promote a more assertive approach to dating and romance. Tomato flower essence is also sometimes used in the treatment of sexual dysfunction, as it can clear any baggage related to sex.

The tomato was once known as the "golden apple," or *pomo d'oro* in Italian, and it has been used in magick for prosperity and abundance, too. Magickal herbalist Scott Cunningham suggests placing a tomato on the mantle to draw prosperity.[224] Added to prosperity blends, tomato flower essence engenders a sense of self-worth that helps you feel deserving of material success.

Like other nightshades, tomatoes are sometimes used in apotropaic magick, and the flower essence can be used in similar fashion. In flower essence therapy, tomato essence is adeptly used for addressing fear, insecurity, and pessimism. It is sometimes deemed "the warrior essence," as it helps you confront fear head-on.[225] It nurtures the ability to plan and strategize, teaching you how to learn from past events rather than fear repeating them. It also supports endurance, strength, decisiveness, and courage. It is a loving essence that promotes an I-can-do-it attitude and strengthens conviction, making it easy to overcome a fear of failure. Tomato essence may be used to counteract anxiety, nightmares, procrastination, and a tendency to give up.

The essence is also a powerful and fast-acting cleanser. It is sometimes described as "shattering" blockages, infections, or other imbalances.[226] Any time you feel blocked or held back, tomato initiates a deep sense of release. I like to use this essence when I feel as though my creativity is in some way impeded. It helps me get back into the flow by releasing any blocks, real or imagined, so I can feel inspiration coursing through me once again. Tomato's ability to break down and detoxify, when coupled with its warrior-like symbolism, also predisposes it to defending against infection and illness. It can mobilize your spiritual and etheric defenses against illness, thereby improving your immune response, too. It is sometimes used topically on wounds to prevent infection—just be sure to dilute it appropriately or avoid direct contact.

When making flower essence spagyrics, tomato can substitute for the salt or soma of many of the more toxic nightshades; try using a little bit of tomato juice or an infusion made from sun-dried tomatoes in place of an infusion or tincture of belladonna, mandrake, or datura for a nontoxic, low-potency alternative to a more conventional flower essence spagyric. Alongside potato essence, tomato essence can also be used to prepare yourself for working with more potent baneful plants. Since it helps to break up harmful and unpleasant energies, tomato flower essence can help you disperse and release the intense effects sometimes experienced from working with its more potent relatives, like belladonna, henbane, and mandrake. Use it in tandem with potato essence to provide both cleansing and grounding after shamanic journey with a flying essence blend.

Trillium
Trillium erectum, Trillium spp. ♦ Balm

Elemental signature: water

Planetary signatures: Venus, Saturn, Pluto

Zodiacal signatures: Scorpio, Capricorn

Chakras: root, sacral, heart

Magickal uses: love, lust, sex magick, luck, protection

Therapeutic indications: shame, disconnection, difficulty making friends, stagnant relationships, rigid attitude about sex, self-consciousness, issues regarding sex, materialism, excessive ambition or agression, rebirthing process, ungroundedness

TRILLIUM IS A GENUS of roughly fifty species of plants that are native to parts of North America and Asia. The genus name is taken from the triune morphology of the plant, which exhibits three leaf-like bracts, three sepals, and three petals. Of all the members of the trillium genus, it seems that the red trillium (*T. erectum*), or wake robin, has been most widely used both medicinally and as a flower essence. It is also used in hoodoo, conjure, and other forms of American folk magick, where it is known by a number of folk names, including bethroot, birthroot, Dixie John root, southern John root, and rattlesnake root.

Trillium is an alchemical flower essence. Its threefold symmetry speaks of integration of the body, mind, and spirit, as well as the three alchemical primes (salt, mercury, and sulfur). All varieties of trillium help you integrate the various aspects of self into a unified whole. This unification improves communication and cooperation, as it helps coordinate seemingly separate aspects and unites them in a common cause. In a similar fashion, the essence improves communication among individuals, and it uplifts and heals relationships as a whole. One of the hidden signatures for trillium's effects on relationships comes from its unique interaction with ants. The fleshy appendages on trillium seeds are an ant delicacy; the insects carry the seeds to the nests, devour the edible bits, and discard the rest. The seeds lie protected by the ants' waste until spring, when they sprout and flourish.[227] The essence therefore is deeply tied to themes of relationship, collaboration, and interdependence.

Most of the magickal lore regarding this plant is connected to love, romance, and sex. An old charm for attracting love is to rub the root of trillium over your body. Drinking a tea made from the root was said to attract an ideal partner for marriage, and parts of the dried plant could be burned as incense for the same outcome. Trillium is also used in magick to strengthen marriages, calm lovers' quarrels, and improve sex.[228] The essence can be used for many similar functions, and it can enhance any relationship, especially when taken by both partners. Pam Montgomery writes in *Plant Spirit Healing:* "Because Trillium combines sexual energy with heart energy and grounds it into one's body, it is an excellent love remedy. Platonic love based in the heart brings compassion and sexual love brings passion. When the two are combined the ultimate union can exist. Trillium can resolve any differences between the two, eliminating separation and allowing a union of these very powerful energies, creating one dynamic force."[229] Trillium helps you understand the abundant and bountiful nature of love, and it invites you to become an overflowing vessel for love to radiate into the world.

As a general love-drawing practice, anoint or spray your body with a dosage-level mix of trillium flower essence; ideally, do this in the light of the full moon in the hour of Venus. You can also add the essence to the bath to draw love and romance or to prepare for a night of love-making. Trillim root is sometimes added to the laundry when washing bedsheets to inspire more passionate sex. The flower essence also enhances your bedroom adventures; you can spray the essence on the bed, diffuse it in the bedroom, or add a few drops to the laundry when washing your sheets. Alternatively, simply take the essence by mouth or apply topically. Trillium essence promotes deeper and more meaningful connection during intimate moments and allows for more comfort and tenderness alongside greater passion. The dried root is sometimes used to prevent a lover from wandering or to end an affair that is impacting a long-standing relationship. Trillium flower essence can be used to positively impact similar situations, as it alleviates addiction to sex and clandestine behavior; try coupling it with basil to improve the efficacy.

In folk medicine, trillium is a remedy for hemorrhaging and is often used to promote healthy childbirth, a use alluded to in red trillium's common name *birthroot*. The deep red color of the flower is a signature for blood and birth; the essence is ideal for use during transitional phases. It enables you to embrace the death of one cycle with grace and provides the stamina and flexibility you will need to flourish during a period of rebirth. In addition to assisting during cycles of death and rebirth in a spiritual sense, trillium flower essence can help you birth new projects by giving you the courage and connection to the bigger picture to see things through to the end.

Trillium is sometimes used in magick for luck and protection. The plant is often associated with boundaries and liminal spaces; magickally, it is used to avert harmful energy and to protect the home and family. As an essence, white trillium (*T. grandiflorum*) is helpful for psychic protection. It is especially suited to use during periods of psychic development and spiritual practice, as these processes can leave you feeling more open and vulnerable to outside influences. Red trillium is more protective at the physical level, and it can also offer a sense of security during intimate moments, as it allows the heart to be open and protected simultaneously.

Most varieties of trillium are supremely grounding. They work to clear and cleanse the root chakra of imbalances and blockages, thereby addressing concerns related to survival and materialism and drawing in unconditional love. This eases any fears rooted in concern for your material well-being and displaces them with altruism, compassion, and peace. Trillium can be used to address fears related to appearance, aging, money, success, and power. Taking the essence consistently can eliminate deeply seated poverty consciousness as well as greed, as both stem from the same fear of not having enough. Instead, trillium reframes the mind to look at the interconnection of life and our interdependence on one another and the Earth; simultaneously, it shifts your focus to the spiritual and transpersonal perspectives and helps you derive a sense of worth and well-being from your relationship to the divine.[230] The end result is feeling as if you always have—and *are*—enough, just as things are now.

Vervain
Verbena officinalis ◆ Balm

Elemental signatures: earth, water

Planetary signature: Mercury

Zodiacal signature: Leo

Chakras: throat, third eye, crown

Magickal uses: abundance, prosperity, protection, love, healing, mental power, divination, social justice

Therapeutic indications: overenthusiasm, obstinacy, excessive eagerness, perfectionism, proselytizing, tension, anxiety, sensitivity to injustice, being spread too thin

VERVAIN IS A PERENNIAL HERB common in gardens and wild places throughout its native range of Europe, and it is naturalized in many other parts of the world today. It is characterized by jagged leaves and magenta, five-petaled flowers borne on tall spikes. Vervain is considered a holy and highly medicinal herb and is known by many epithets, including simpler's joy, holy herb, and iron herb.

Bach described the person in need of vervain as having "fixed principles and ideas, which they are confident are right, and which they very rarely change."[231] Vervain types are prone to overenthusiasm; they are crusaders who seek to convert others to join their cause. Positive aspects of the vervain type include inspiring and teaching others, as well as having the staying power to stick with a cause when others have given up. This state often leads to tension and anxiety. Vervain flower essence is helpful for all forms of mental stress, as it eases the work of an overactive mind and helps release tension in mind and spirit alike. It is the perfect ally for the self-possessed and driven people who put all their time and energy into a particular mission. Vervain teaches them moderation, helping them discern between having sincere motivation to succeed and being an outright workaholic.

Vervain is a versatile plant spirit that has been used in magick for protection, love, exorcism, luck, success, healing, and divination. As an ingredient in love potions, vervain flower essence inspires passion and enthusiasm in a budding relationship; it also tempers overexcitement with respect for your loved one's boundaries. Vervain was also used to quench lust; the juice of the plant harvested just before sunrise could be consumed as an anaphrodisiac, thereby attesting to the essence's ability to temper overenthusiasm.[232]

As a protective herb, vervain is excellent for repelling the ill effects of harmful magick and for stopping gossip. The herb is used to protect against nightmares and promote restful sleep; the essence has helped me experience fewer restless nights plagued by dreams of work yet undone. The Welsh name for this plant, *ferfaen,* shares the meaning of "to drive away," attesting to its ability to drive out harmful forces, as well as for expelling stones in the body.[233] When strewn in the fields, vervain protected against storms and malefic magick.

The Greek and Hebrew names for vervain stem from the word meaning "flying," and vervain has been used in flying ointments and similar concoctions.[234] Added to blends for astral travel and spirit flight, vervain essence can alleviate mental tension from trying too hard, thereby permitting the experience to happen organically and easily.

The Druids reportedly gathered flowering vervain to make lustral baths and holy waters to enhance divination and promote ritual purification. The flower essence may be used in a similar manner to prepare scrying mirrors, crystal balls, or other tools for divination—or else the essence may be anointed at the brow or taken internally—to assist you in receiving an accurate reading. Not only does the flower have a natural affinity for the third-eye chakra, but its ability to curb overenthusiasm will help you maintain objectivity such that you can better receive and interpret the messages from divination with greater impartiality. Thus, vervain flower essence can help you achieve more accurate readings.

I love using vervain flower essence in magick to manifest justice and healing for the world. Bach once described the essence as for people "with big ideals and ambitions for the good of humanity."[235] Roman soldiers carried vervain into battle to protect themselves against fatal wounds, as well as to ensure victory. You can use vervain flower essence in workings designed to inspire justice, strength, and equality. Try using it to charge crystals or other talismans that can, in turn, be carried for luck and success in receiving justice.

Vervain is an excellent flower essence for celebrating the summer solstice and the power of the sun. While it displays many Mercurial qualities, the plant flowers in the summertime and has garnered a reputation for use by blacksmiths, thus connoting a fiery nature. Sacred to the smith archetype of the god of the witches, vervain helps you refine your craft in every way.

Vervain flower essence speeds up the transmission, reception, and use of higher energies through spiritual work, including creative visualization, thus making it a helpful ally for supporting manifestation and spellwork.[236] I learned early on in my magickal practice that vervain can be added to spells to increase their efficacy and expediency, and I've found that a couple drops of flower essence can produce similar results. It helps you maintain a clear focus on your desired outcome, thereby boosting your work.

Vine (Grape)
Vitis vinifera, Vitis spp. ◆ Tree

Elemental signature: water

Astrological signatures: moon, Jupiter, Neptune

Zodiacal signature: Leo

Chakras: solar plexus, heart

Magickal uses: fertility, abundance, prosperity

Therapeutic indications: issues with authority and authoritarianism, being carried away by power, being overly ambitious, lacking ambition, inability to give in, cruelty, pitilessness, savior complex, bullying, being opinionated, greed, lust, jealousy, abandonment, neediness, feeling disconnected and noncommittal, codependency

GRAPES BELONG TO THE GENUS *Vitis,* which contains nearly eighty different species and several thousand distinct cultivars. Over time, grapevine produces woody stems supported by tendrils, making them well suited to grow on trellises and along the trunks of trees. The vines produce tiny, greenish flowers that are usually inconspicuous. Though the flowers are hardly noticeable, they result in large, showy berries that attract the attention of wildlife and humankind alike. This genus of plants is most famous for the fermented juice of grape: wine (note that *wine* and *vine* derive from the same linguistic root). The woody stems and vertical orientation of grapevines make them suitable to be classed as tree spirits, though they share some qualities with balms and banes, too.

Grapevine was one of the seven additional flower essences, called "the seven helpers," explored by Dr. Bach as an adjuct to the original twelve remedies he made. He called the essence "vine" and described people who benefited from it as thus: "Very capable people, certain of their own ability, confident of success. Being so assured, they think that it would be for the benefit of others if they could be persuaded to do things as they themselves do, or as they are certain they are right. Even in illness they will direct their attendants. Great value in an emergency."[237]

We can see from Bach's description that vine (or grape) flower essence helps you contend with issues of power and authority. The essence is indicated for anyone who abuses or runs from positions of power. Vine helps you come to grips with power and transforms you into a compassionate leader. This essence works to break down deeply held beliefs about authority, often stemming from the way authority figures treated you in early childhood. It instills empathy, respect, and a genuine desire to support others. This essence is helpful for anyone in a leadership role, from people in management positions to public servants and spiritual leaders.

The flower essence of grapevine instills healthy boundaries while celebrating interdependence and healthy community. The grapevine itself requires a tree or trellis for support, as it does not have enough structure on its own. The essence helps you break the bonds of both codependency and fierce independence, instead helping you find the middle ground of healthy interdependence. Vine uses obstacles as support while growing; the essence thus teaches you to see obstacles as opportunities.[238] It is helpful for those who feel they are always right or who meddle in other people's problems.

Lila Devi, founder of Spirit-in-Nature Essences, calls grape "the rewarder." She tells us that grape flower essence leads you to a state of openheartedness wherein you are willing to take risks to let others in.[239] Grape essence transforms base passion into love and devotion through its alchemical nature. Wine, and therefore grape, has long represented the mysteries of rebirth and transmutation, thereby rendering them symbols of alchemy and magick. Grape essence opens a window to the alchemical nature of love. It removes the veils that surround the heart— illusions of emotional poverty, bitterness, and separation. This essence reveals the heart's natural ability to love unconditionally.

Grapevine has an ancient history of cultivation, stretching back at least six thousand years, and that history is replete with religious symbolism and esoteric lore. Both vine and fruit have been sacred to many cultures. The ancient Sumerians depicted the Tree of Life as a grapevine, while the people of ancient Egypt called white and red wines the right and left eyes of Horus, respectively.[240] Wine was said to be the favored libation of the gods Dionysus and Bacchus, as they were slain and reborn just as grapes are crushed and transformed into wine. Pagans and Christians alike associated the mystery of fermentation with death and rebirth, for Jesus was also connected to the mystery of the vine. Grapes are symbols of fertility, and their likeness has been painted on garden walls to ensure prolific growth and harvests.

Magickally, grapes represent bringing ideas into fruition and contribute to success in magickal working. Pieces of grapevine were once placed under the pillow to bring dreamtime visitations from a lover, and all parts of the plant were used in love potions. Grape essence is very heart-centered, and it helps you forge authentic connections with your teachers-in-spirit, such as gods, guides, and spirits of the land. I use it in offerings to the spirits and gods in my personal practice. Wine has been called the drink of the gods, and it gradually became a symbol of magick itself. Magick makes us all into leaders and authorities, for it helps us direct our lives and spirits through extraordinary means. Vine flower essence invites you to look more deeply into your role as the author of your destiny.

The flower essence of grapevine can be added to the chalice to transform any liquid into a holy sacrament. I suspect it might make ordinary grape juice feel more magickal to those who wish to abstain from alcohol. Taking the essence grants you the drive to make changes happen, as well as the ability to take hold of the resources at your disposal. Using it in magickal settings enhances your work as a magician, supporting successful results in your spellcraft. The essence can be added to blends focused on love, fertility, and blessings.

Another interesting use for this flower essence is in treating imbalances or healing crises caused by baneful plant essences. The Greeks once used wine as a remedy against the poisons borne by monkshood, hellebore, mistletoe, mushrooms, and poppy.[241] I like to combine it with potato and garlic essences to neutralize any unpleasant effects from taking other essences, particularly those of baneful plants. When taken alongside baneful plant essences, it concretizes the effects of those plant spirits, grounding their often numenous benefits by inspiring practical decisions and action.

Violet
Viola spp. ♦ Balm

Elemental signature: water

Planetary signatures: Venus, Neptune

Zodiacal signature: Pisces

Chakras: heart, crown

Magickal uses: love, luck, wish granting, peace, protection, spirit communication, psychic development

Therapeutic indications: intense shyness, aloofness, loneliness, fear of crowds, fear of being seen or noticed, feeling restrained by modesty, temptation to stray from moral or spiritual principles

VIOLETS ARE FOUND THROUGHOUT the world's temperate regions, with more than five hundred species confirmed to date. The common violet, *Viola odorata,* also known as the wood violet or English violet, prefers damp, shady environments, where its violet-to-white blooms appear close to the ground each spring. Common violet is praised for its rich scent, which is used in cuisine and perfumery.

I have fond memories of picking candied violets out of one of my favorite dried tea blends as a sweet snack. The tender, sweet violets were hidden among tea leaves and other botanicals, and finding them was a special treat. That hidden beauty exemplifies the magick and healing of violets. They are Venusian flowers, owing to their heady fragrance and five-petaled form, thus lending to their use in magick for love and romance. Violets are thought to grant wishes, instill peace, and assist in communing with the spiritual realms. Their divine color also bestows the gift of protection.

Violets also have folkloric associations with the dead and with grief. In some tellings of the myth of Persephone, she was gathering this tender wildflower when she was abducted by Hades. In other stories, the first violets are said to have sprouted from the blood of slain heroes, and violets have been planted in cemeteries to guard against the noxious vapors and harmful spirits in these liminal spaces. Modern magickal herbalists sometimes use violets to assuage the grief of lost loved ones, particularly children.[242] The grimoire tradition describes incenses and fumigations made from violet roots that induce visions, help you see and contact spirits, and confer the gift of prophecy.[243] The flower essence assuages grief and instills courage, helping you recover from loss and tragedy.

As a flower essence, violet is a deeply spiritual remedy. It helps you cultivate awareness of and trust in your spiritual path, thereby bringing you peace, resilience, and the ability to see life as sacred, finding magick amid the mundane. Violet flower essence also facilitates psychic development, particular by stimulating clairvoyance and clairaudience.[244] The essence can ease the grief of losing a loved one, and it can also help attune you to better communicate with loved ones on the other side.

Violet flower essence is often indicated for people who find themselves overwhelmed by shyness and aloofness. The environment and stature of the plant are signatures for its affinity for these qualities. Patricia Kaminski writes that these flowers "bloom in early spring, flourishing in damp, moist and shady woodland habitats. Their deep purple colour and sweet fragrance suggest a refined spirituality, which holds back from the full sun and warmth of daylight."[245] Consider the expression "shrinking violet" and you'll better understand the nature of the person who benefits from this essence. Violet offers warmth and a sense of security to those who have difficulty warming up to others or who feel as though they might lose their sense of identity or safety among crowds.

Violet flower essence—in fact, essences from all members of the violet family, Violaceae—helps multiply the amount of divine beauty in the world.[246] Add violet essence to rituals for beauty, self-love, and courage; it may offer a gentle boost of confidence without any loss of gentleness or tenderness. It also helps you elevate your spiritual perspective, act with integrity, and feel more inspired in everything you do.

Walnut
Juglans regia ♦ Tree

Elemental signature: fire
Planetary signature: sun
Zodiacal signature: Taurus
Chakra: heart
Magickal uses: protection, aura cleansing, love, fertility, happiness
Therapeutic indications: change, transition, oversensitivity to the opinions of others, past experiences that inhibit growth

THE WALNUT TREE OWES its origins to ancient Persia, but it was cultivated far and wide by the Romans, who distributed it throughout their empire. It is a deciduous tree with a relatively large stature. Walnut is harvested for food, dye, and wood. The trees bear separate male and female flowers on the same plant. Male flowers are drooping catkins, while female flowers are inconspicuous and form in small clusters at the tips of branches.

Walnut is probably the most popular of Bach's single remedies. It is the quintessential flower essence for periods of change and transition, and Bach considered it to give a sense of "constancy and protection from outside influences."[247] Walnut is indicated for any sort of change that you might be experiencing, from moving to a new home to starting a new job. Walnut even supports the efforts of other flower essences, as taking flower essences is, in itself, a means of initiating positive change.

In folklore, the walnut is an excellent ally for protective magick. The hard shell confers protection from the outside world, keeping the seed safe within, and few other plants grow in the shade of the walnut tree. Because of the nut's resemblance to the brain, walnut flower essence is linked to the mind and head; it protects the mind from beliefs, expectations, ideas, and projections that come from outside influences. Taking the essence can help you break ties to unhealthy people, places, and memories. It is an excellent ally for use in defensive magick, and I like to add some to witch's bottles for a gentle and effective protective boost.

The plant has long held a solar correspondence, and solar herbs are considered good for the heart. Thus, walnut flower essence helps the heart chakra, as it clears away outside influences and long-held experiences. This allows the inner nature of the self, with all its history and hopes, to be revealed. This self-knowledge confers a greater sense of security, for it is only in knowing yourself that you can truly recognize and combat the influence that others have over you.[248] Further, this essence seals the aura so those outside influences can no longer return. I was taught to make a powerful cleansing bath using walnuts in my witchcraft training, and I find that placing several drops of the flower essence in the tub is similarly cleansing and protective.

Walnut has been favored in magick for love and fertility. Planting a walnut tree was meant to ensure a long and happy marriage, while the nuts were given as gifts at weddings for similar purposes. The inflorescence of the plants has been likened to reproductive organs: the male catkins resemble a phallus, whereas the female flowers evoke the image of a uterus. The generative power of the sexes combined symbolizes fertility of body, mind, and spirit. Folk magick for ensuring—and preventing—conception often made use of walnuts. As an essence, walnut works to ensure that your creative power and fertile imagination can be used for their best purpose; it prevents your work from being impeded or distracted. Walnut essence could be added to spells related to all kinds of fertility and love magick, as it protects new love and strengthens established romantic bonds.

Walnut has a dual nature in legend and lore. On one hand, it is considered a sacred and regal tree. The genus, *Juglans,* is said to have taken its name from *Jovis glans,* meaning "Jupiter's nuts," for walnuts were considered the food of the gods. The wood was said to alternately attract or repel lightning in various parts of the world, further connecting the tree to Zeus and Jupiter. The tree is also sacred to Diana/Artemis. The flower essence feeds your inner divinity and clears the way for you to experience the divine within. Walnuts also have a fair amount of sinister lore, and they are sometimes connected to underworld deities, like Persephone, and to the devil himself. Witches were said to gather beneath walnut trees, and the nuts have been used as an offering for the dead. You can use the flower essence as an offering on ancestral shrines or to your patron deities.

Walnut flower essence ensures safety, health, and happiness. It thwarts harmful or misguided energies from the outside world and helps you cultivate your hopes and dreams. Add it to spells for creativity, protection, healing, and love, and take it to help you find your inner resilience and divinity.

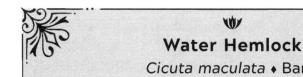

Water Hemlock
Cicuta maculata ♦ Bane

Elemental signatures: water, air

Planetary signatures: Saturn, Pluto

Zodiacal signature: Pisces

Chakras: sacral, third eye

Magickal uses: protection, astral travel, spirit communication, psychic development, banishing, cursing, social justice

Therapeutic indications: emotional dishonesty, inability to ask for help, self-deception or being deceived by others, need for emotional release, understanding and healing violent patterns, trauma, abuse

WATER HEMLOCK IS A MEMBER of the carrot family, closely resembling poison hemlock and its relatives. It has the hollow stems, pinnate leaves, and white flowers arranged in umbels on long stalks that are typical of Apiaceae. A perennial, it favors wet environments, like marshes and the banks of streams. Water hemlock is a deadly poison and should be approached with caution; **do not make an essence from this plant via direct methods unless you practice extreme care.** Consider using an additional dilution (i.e., a fine dosage, see page 101 for instructions) to ensure the overall safety of the essence. Alternatively, use a commercially prepared flower essence.

Water hemlock shares many properties with poison hemlock, both magickally and as a flower essence. It can be used for protection, like most baneful plants, and it is adept at facilitating spirit flight and astral travel. The hollow stalk and umbelliferous flowers indicate that the essence facilitates spirit communication and psychic development. Use it to aid lucid dreaming, to facilitate all varieties of journeying, and to sharpen and maintain your focus during guided meditations. Like the common hemlock, water hemlock can also treat feelings of being stuck or paralyzed by fear and change.

Since this plant has a more watery nature than poison hemlock, its essence is extremely cleansing and detoxifying. Some varieties of water hemlock grow only in uncontaminated waters, and taking their essences helps you detoxify your thoughts and emotions. Water hemlock flower essence is an excellent ally for shadow work because it promotes emotional honesty and takes you deep into the subconscious to explore the learned patterns of toxicity, prejudice, and violence. Because its appearance is so deceptive (it resembles many plants in the Apiaceae family that are cultivated for food and medicine), water hemlock helps you recognize when you are deceiving yourself or others. Take this essence to stop pushing pain down beneath a cheerful face, and it will help you communicate your emotions honestly and ask for help when you need it. Water hemlock essence catalyzes processes of release—often via tears—to help you purify your inner nature and move forward.

Magickally speaking, water hemlock has historically been used for cursing.[249] The violent and rapid effect of its toxicity has been used to target malefic influences via baneful magick. As a flower essence, it can highlight patterns of violence in the psyche and personality. Over time, taking water hemlock essence reveals how violence was seeded in your life, and it helps you take actions to overcome it. This makes water hemlock a valuable essence for recovering from abuse, oppression, and other traumas. In spellcraft, you can use the essence to banish harmful people or circumstances and also to banish your own violent or harmful habits. Add water hemlock to spells for social justice, too, for it offers solace from and inspiration to overcome violent and oppressive systems in the world.

Willow
Salix spp. ♦ Tree

Elemental signature: water

Planetary signatures: moon, Saturn

Zodiacal signatures: Taurus, Cancer

Chakras: root, solar plexus, crown

Magickal uses: love, divination, protection, healing, malefic magick

Therapeutic indications: resentment, bitterness, self-pity, blame, irritability, ungratefulness, inflexibility

THE GENUS *SALIX* IS HOME to many species of willow around the world. Most are deciduous trees with long leaves, often with serrated margins. Willows are notoriously flexible (with the notable exception of the crack willow), and they have watery sap and tenacious roots. Willow flowers are usually furry catkins, often white or tinged yellow with pollen. The trees have open crowns, and many have branches that hang or droop. Bach's willow was *Salix alba* var. *vitellina,* often called the golden willow. It is a fast-growing tree that roots readily from branches broken off the tree.

Willow has a long tradition of use in magick, in medicine, and as a weaving material in basketmaking. In many cultures it also has funereal associations. The drooping branches seem rather somber, and it grows in liminal spaces, usually near water. Willow has thus symbolized grief and sorrow; it is often used in rites of mourning and grown in cemeteries and graveyards. Willow is even attributed to goddesses connected to death and the underworld, including Hekate and Persephone. Its magickal properties include healing, protection, and certain forms of divination. The more sinister aspects of the tree lead some to use it for darker magick.

The traditional indications for willow flower essence are resentment, bitterness, and blaming others. Anyone who feels like a victim of life's vicissitudes may be in need of willow essence. It is helpful when misfortune and adversity make life too difficult to enjoy; take it when you lose interest in the small things. Willow counteracts the feeling of unfairness by inspiring optimism, faith, and a recognition that you have the power to turn things around. It is also helpful for patterns of inflexibility and refusing to take responsibility for your own actions. Willow essence removes resistance to conscious creation by dissolving your self-imposed limitations and victimhood so that you can be in greater alignment with the universe. It therefore enables you to become more flexible and resilient.

Willow essence helps you access deep levels of knowledge and balance the complementary forces of the material and mystical. Taking the essence helps you recognize and harness raw potential and lead it toward manifestation. It gradually removes the ego's filter, which is ultimately the source of bitterness and resentment. As a result, willow enables you to be a better channel for higher consciousness and universal energies. The essence promotes a sense of bliss deriving from relating to the universe as a whole.[250]

Willow essence can be used in magick for healing, protection, and love. By removing the tendency to feel embittered, attacked, or victimized, this essence helps you feel more empowered and optimistic; it is thus a helpful addition to protection magick and for recovery from psychic attack. Willow essence's ability to release tragedy, sorrow, and grief also permits you to use it for love, as it helps make space in your mind and heart for love to blossom again.

❦ Wormwood
Artemisia absinthium ♦ Bane

Elemental signature: fire

Planetary signature: Mars

Zodiacal signature: Aries

Chakras: sacral, solar plexus, crown

Magickal uses: protection, communication with the dead, spirit conjuring, psychic development, luck

Therapeutic indications: anger, resentment, dwelling in the past, disappointment, inability to forgive, inability to let go, obsessive thoughts or behaviors, inability to end relationships, exhaustion

AS A MEMBER OF THE COMPOSITAE FAMILY and the genus *Artemisia,* wormwood is a close relative of mugwort. Its feathery leaves are silvery- or blue-green in color, and its flowers are small and inconspicuous. A perennial, wormwood originated in the temperate regions of Europe, Asia, and northern Africa; it is widely naturalized across the globe today.

Wormwood is a classic witching herb. It is widely recorded as an ingredient in rituals to summon spirits, converse with the dead, and open the doorway to psychic vision. It is considered more fiery than mugwort and is typically linked to the planet Mars. As a result, wormwood is strongly protective in nature, and it has been used to banish and exorcise all manner of parasitic entities. Medicinally, this herb is considered a vermifuge, and it is used to rid the body of parasites and other infections. As a flower essence, wormwood is adept at removing foreign entities, thoughtforms, and etheric cords.

Wormwood flower essence is helpful for cleansing the energy field of other types of unwanted energy, too. The essence is often indicated for people who harbor anger or disappointment or are unable to forgive. It is able to address patterns of being stuck in the past, obsession, inability to break old habits, and similar situations rooted in your personal history. The essence helps you release the final vestiges of the past, especially when these conditions have been returning time and time again. David Dalton tells us that wormwood "clears out the psychic 'debris' that remains in the energy field, even when one has done some processing or therapeutic work."[251] Wormwood essence carries the change in thought or behavior to the root cause of a situation, thereby helping you heal from the inside out. Perhaps the ghosts it conjures are really the attachments to the past that we harbor, and the essence offers us an opportunity to heal and transform the burdens of the past once and for all.

In spite of its fiery, combative magickal associations, wormwood has a softer side, too. The essence is particularly well suited to bringing closure through forgiveness. It helps heal emotional scars caused by disappointment, loss, and trauma. Wormwood works to dissolve judgment and allow you to cultivate compassion for yourself and for others. It is helpful for people who have endured difficult lives.

Wormwood is associated with Hekate, death, and Samhain. Add a drop or two of the essence to an incense blend to be burned at Samhain or use it as an offering to the deceased. Spray the essence in your aura or around your home to expel entities and other energies that may be residing there uninvited. Wormwood can also help enforce stronger energetic boundaries around parasitic or vampiric people and places. When blended with other essences that support psychic development, wormwood ensures that lower entities cannot take advantage of your more vulnerable and open state.

Yarrow
Achillea millefolium ♦ Balm

Elemental signatures: air, fire
Planetary signatures: Venus, Mars
Zodiacal signature: Libra
Chakras: solar plexus, third eye

Magickal uses: protection, bravery, curse breaking, recovery from
   psychic attack, love, divination, spirit communication
Therapeutic indications: feeling vulnerable, depletion, distraction,
   psychic toxicity, environmental pollution

YARROW HAS BEEN EMPLOYED as a medicinal and magickal herb
for millennia. It is a member of the aster family, with several species found worldwide. Its genus, *Achillea,* is named for the Greek
hero Achilles, a renowned warrior who used the herb to treat battle
wounds. It is perhaps most famous for its apotropaic qualities; yarrow
spirit medicine is described by Christopher Penczak as "the gift of the
warrior" that "establishes and defends boundaries."[252] As a magickal
herb, it is frequently used for general protection and warding, breaking curses, and averting psychic attack. American folk magick traditions use yarrow to confer protection and bravery.

Flower essence literature largely focuses on the protective nature of
this flower. Yarrow helps establish and enforce boundaries of all sorts.
Medicinally, the plant is associated with healing wounds, thus healing the boundary of our physical bodies. The herb often grows along
hedges, ditches, and other geographical boundaries, too. As an essence,
it cleanses, heals, and strengthens the aura, particularly its outer layers. Spraying the essence in the aura enables it to most effectively comb
through the layers of the subtle bodies to clear away foreign energies.
The essence can heal tears and holes in the aura, such as those created
by psychic attack and environmental factors.

This flower essence is invaluable if you are subjected to electromagnetic pollution from electronics, radiation, or other artificial sources.
Taking yarrow can also help lessen your sensitivity to allergens and
other people's emotions. It is the very best essence for protection against
any sort of harmful influence, including negative thoughtforms (internal or external), psychic attack, extreme emotions, negative magick, geo-
pathic stress, and electromagnetic pollution.

Yarrow is indicated for anyone who is easily depleted or oversensitive to energy. It is my favorite flower essence to recommend
to empaths and other sensitive people. As the plant grows, it gives

strength to neighboring plants, making them more disease resistant; the essence similarly confers protection to whoever takes it.[253] This flower essence expands your awareness to encompass your entire energy field, making you more mindful of the health and integrity of your energy field. It can alert you to psychic vampires in your surroundings. Use this essence when traveling to mitigate the effects of jet lag and fatigue.

Yarrow's flowers are sacred to the Horned God, and several of its folk names attribute it to the devil. Taking this essence can help you attune to the god of the witches, especially if you seek to call upon him for guidance and protection. Because of its liminal nature, yarrow can help you engage in meditations and shamanic journeys to the crossroads to meet with the Horned One. Yarrow shares the role of gatekeeper with the Horned God, and the essence can be helpful in opening the doors to deeper meditation, spirit communication, and astral travel.

Yarrow has a long history of divinatory use. The stalks feature into the art of reading the I Ching, wherein the patterns they make when thrown provide divinatory meanings. Infusions of this herb are used to consecrate scrying mirrors, and the essence can be used similarly. Folk magick also recounts that yarrow was used for communicating with the deceased; try anointing your eyes, ears, and brow with the flower essence to facilitate communication with spirits.

Yarrow is a common ingredient in love spells, too. It brings hope, especially in matters of the heart. Pink-flowered yarrow is best suited to this, but any variety will work. Yarrow is sometimes used magickally to unburden troubled emotions, thus clearing the heart and emotional body so you can more effectively receive love.[254] Since it is so protective and nurturing, this flower essence helps you feel secure enough to let your guard down and fall in love.

Yew
Taxus baccata ♦ Tree, bane

Elemental signature: earth

Planetary signatures: Mercury, Saturn, Pluto

Zodiacal signatures: Virgo, Capricorn

Chakras: root, third eye

Magickal uses: protection, prophecy, hex breaking, binding, longevity, spirit communication, ancestral healing, shamanic journey, banishing, rebirth, wisdom

Therapeutic indications: ungroundedness, feeling emotionally weak or brittle, lack of follow-through, losing sight of purpose, directionless, rigidity, codependency, living in the past, emotional burdens preventing growth, karmic cycles that repeat endlessly

THE GENUS *TAXUS* CONSISTS of only eight species, all evergreen and all toxic. The yew (*T. baccata*) has inconspicuous green flowers that produce red berries. All parts of the plant are toxic, though there is some history of medicinal use. Yews are among the oldest living organisms on Earth, with some specimens estimated to be upward of three thousand years old. They are frequently found in churchyards and cemeteries, having a long history of funerary associations.

Yew is one of the best essences for protection. The bark, needles, berries, and wood of the tree are often carried or burned in protective magick. Given the toxicity of the plant, though, the flower essence is a much safer option. Taking the essence strengthens the root chakra and initiates the instinct to survive. It is grounding and energizing, helping to maintain the integrity of your entire energy field. Yew's connection to death and dying may contribute to its protective nature, as it stands at the threshold (the boundary) between this world and the next. The essence can be employed in magick for binding, banishing, and breaking curses.

Yew's funereal character can be traced to the ancient world. It is considered a tree of mourning, and the essence can help you process grief.

Yew's trunk tends to become hollow as it ages, making the tree resemble an uncanny doorway that leads to the underworld. Accordingly, yew is traditionally associated with underworld deities such as Hekate and Persephone. It is said to be one of the plants in Hekate's garden.[255] As an essence, it facilitates all sorts of journeying, especially psychic travel and dreamtime journeys that lead to the underworld.

Yew is a tree of wisdom and transformation. This plant spirit ally guards the gateway to inner wisdom, and it helps you venture to your interior world to discover the wisdom held within. Yew is sometimes burned to permit communication with the spirits of the deceased, and as a flower essence it helps you tap in to currents of ancestral energy for deep healing. This ancestral energy allows yew to reach deep into the karmic patterning you carry to undo the burden of the past, making it an essence that lends itself well to karmic and ancestral healing. It offers spiritual insights into past, present, and future and connects you to your ancestors. The essence offers guidance and direction on the spiritual path, thereby helping you reconnect with your sense of purpose.

Yew trees survive for thousands of years. Their branches are able to bear the immense weight of their boughs thanks to the flexibility of yew wood. This sense of flexibility is a vital aspect of yew's essence. Arthur Bailey, creator of the Bailey Flower Essences, describes yew essence as promoting resilience and combatting rigidity in thought and behavior; he writes that yew is "a very useful essence for people who have become trapped by their own beliefs and opinions."[256] The essence of this tree imparts a sense of being deeply rooted and flexible, so that you can weather any challenges the universe may send your way. The essence helps regulate your energy levels, while also imparting practicality, strength, and a focus on the present moment.[257]

APPENDIX

Flower Essence Suppliers

During my years of working with flower essences, I've explored dozens of lines of vibrational essences. Some of my favorite and most trusted suppliers are listed below. While making your own essences is ideal, it's not always possible, and there are some plants that many of us simply don't have access to. Check out the essences offered by these providers to broaden your stock of flower essences.

ALASKAN ESSENCES

https://alaskanessences.com

The Alaskan Essence project began in 1984 when founder Steve Johnson started to explore the healing qualities of wildflowers in Alaska. The company was the first to produce a line of environmental essences, and it carries a wonderful array of gem elixirs, too.

BACH FLOWER REMEDIES

www.bachremedies.com

www.healingherbs.co.uk

The two makers found at the websites listed above provide the original thirty-eight remedies pioneered by Dr. Edward Bach. The Bach remedies are frequently available at health food stores (Rescue Remedy in particular is stocked at many pharmacies and grocery stores), and several other makers also offer the complete collection of essences made from

457

the same plants as Dr. Bach, but these two producers are among the most trusted and make the highest-quality remedies.

BANE FOLK
https://banefolk.com

Sarah Anne Lawless offers a range of flower essences produced from poisonous plants through her online store, Bane Folk. It is a small operation, and the quality of each essence is superb—although order processing times are rather long because of the high demand for Bane Folk's many offerings. Many baneful plants that are hard to find as flower essences are available here, and you can even find the Witch Flight Flower Essence blend made in the tradition of flying ointments.

CHALICE WELL ESSENCES
https://chalicewell.org.uk

This is the line that helped me fall in love with flower essences all over again. These essences are some of my favorites, and they contain a magick unique to Chalice Well and the sacred land in Glastonbury. Each one is bottled with love by the community of volunteers, and they are available directly from the Chalice Well Trust online shop. In addition to flower essences, their collections include vibrational essences made from astrological transits and other spiritual energies.

DELTA GARDENS
https://deltagardens.com

Delta Gardens produces a large variety of flower essences and other vibrational elixirs. Two collections are particularly relevant to this book: the medicinal herb and power plant sets. The latter consists mostly of baneful herbs, and I used this set as part of my research for this book.

DESERT ALCHEMY
. . . .
www.desert-alchemy.com

I've had the pleasure of attending an online workshop led by the founder of this company, Cynthia Athina Kemp Scherer, and her wisdom and dedication are an inspiration. The Desert Alchemy essences are made from plants found in the Sonoran Desert, and together they form an incredible and unique collection of plant spirit medicines. Desert Alchemy also offers one of the most extensive collections of combination essences of any essence maker on the market.

FLORACOPEIA
. . . .
www.floracopeia.com

My dear friend Elena Rosa first introduced me to Floracopeia, and I've fallen in love with their Flower Essence Tinctures. These remedies blend flower essences, plant tinctures, and minute amounts of essential oils to unite the body, soul, and spirit of the plant into a powerful healing tool, not unlike the flower essence spagyrics described in chapter 10.

FLORA CORONA
. . . .
www.floracorona.com

The Flora Corona essences are a collection of flower, gem, light, and vibrational elixirs handcrafted by Deborah Craydon, coauthor of *Floral Acupuncture.* These are some of the most incredible essences I've used, and the bottle designs are visually and vibrationally exquisite. You'll love the energy and efficacy of these essences.

FLOWER ESSENCE SERVICES
. . . .
www.fesflowers.com

Flower Essence Services (FES) is the most trusted essence producer in North America with an extensive lineup of essences made from wildflowers found in California. Patricia Kaminski and Richard Katz, the founders of FES, have pioneered new developments in flower essence therapy and continue to maintain the gold standards for the practice. The quality of the essences is excellent, and there is a wide selection. FES also distributes the HealingHerbs line of Bach flower essences made by Julian Barnard.

GREEN MAN ESSENCES

www.greenmanshop.co.uk

Green Man Essences are crafted by Sue and Simon Lilly, and they are some of the most beloved tools in my essence toolkit. The Lillys have been using and making essences for decades, offer several lines of essences, and provide high-quality training as correspondence courses. I've had the pleasure of enrolling in the Green Man Essence Practitioner Diploma course with Sue as my tutor, and I cannot recommend the training and books highly enough. While Green Man Essences cover a range of plants, places, stones, and other energies, their tree essences are my favorite.

PEGASUS ESSENCES

www.pegasusproducts.com

With easily the largest selection available from any single maker, Pegasus has essences made from flowers, gemstones, starlight, and more.

THE POISONER'S APOTHECARY

www.thepoisonersapothecary.com

My friend and fellow author Coby Michael provides a variety of essences made from baneful plants in his online shop, in addition to other hand-crafted botanical tools and formulas.

POWER OF FLOWERS
· ·
www.powerfloweressences.com

This line of flower essences is produced by Isha Lerner, an accomplished astrologer, author, and flower essence therapist. You'll find a beautiful selection of single essences, blends, books, and oracle cards themed around the wisdom of the flowers.

TEMPLE GARDEN ESSENCES
· ·
www.templeofwitchcraft.org

The Temple of Witchcraft is a not-for-profit organization cofounded by Steve Kenson, Adam Sartwell, and my teacher and mentor Christopher Penczak. The organization occasionally offers powerful, handmade flower essences crafted from the gardens on-site; they are potent and magickal essences that have become staples in my toolbox. Sartwell offers flower essence consultations and Penczak also teaches classes on baneful flower essences, both online and in person. Flower essence training is included as part of the third degree of the Temple of Witchcraft's Mystery School. When essences are available, they are listed in the online shop.

WHISPERING WINDS VIBRATIONAL ESSENCES
· ·
https://divinearchetypes.org

My friend and fellow author Candice Covington has an amazing line of vibrational essences made with flowers, fungi, and more. Her Whispering Winds essences taste amazing (like elderflower!) and are potent tools for healing and magick. She also handcrafts flower essence cordials, wherein the essences are preserved and stabilized in a liqueur of the same flower. The flower essence cordials are a treat for the palate and the soul alike, and they offer a deep and swift link to the spirits of the green.

WOODLAND ESSENCE

https://woodlandessence.com

Woodland Essence offers a selection of well-made essences from the forests of the northeastern United States. They are crafted from a selection of trees, shrubs, and plants that grow on the forest floor. Woodland Essence offers essences from several otherwise hard-to-find plants found in chapter 11.

Notes

CHAPTER 1. WHAT ARE FLOWER ESSENCES?

1. Wright, *Perelandra Essences,* 11.
2. Bach, *Collected Writings,* 117.
3. Kaminski, *Flowers That Heal,* 37.
4. Wright, *Perelandra Essences,* 11.
5. Dennis, *Orchid Essence Healing,* 10.
6. Lilly, *Essence Practitioner,* 25.
7. Lilly, *Essence Practitioner,* 28–29.

CHAPTER 2. A HISTORY OF FLOWER ESSENCES

1. Lilly, *Essence Practitioner,* 32.
2. Wood, *Vitalism,* 5.
3. Lilly, *Essence Practitioner,* 32.
4. White, *Australian Bush Flower Essences,* 1; Leigh, *Findhorn Flower Essences Handbook,* 13.
5. Dennis, *Orchid Essence Healing,* 5.
6. Dennis, *Orchid Essence Healing,* 5.
7. Wood, *Vitalism,* 193.
8. Vlamis, *Bach Flower Remedies,* 12.
9. Bach, *Collected Writings,* 111.
10. From an article called "Twelve Healers" that likely appeared in *The Homeopathic Journal,* in Bach, *Collected Writings,* 77.
11. Bach, *Collected Writings,* 171.

CHAPTER 3. DEVAS, PLANT SPIRITS, AND GREEN FAMILIARS

1. Lilly, *Tree: Essence, Spirit and Teacher,* 84.
2. Bailey in Leigh, *Findhorn Flower Essences,* 18.
3. Pogačnik, *Nature Spirits & Elemental Beings,* 67–68.
4. Lupa, *Plant and Fungus Totems,* 11.
5. Penczak, *Plant Spirit Familiar,* 18.
6. Penczak, *Plant Spirit Familiar,* 18.

CHAPTER 4. BALMS, BANES, AND TREE SPIRITS

1. Barnard, *Bach Flower Remedies,* 86.
2. Draco, *By Wolfsbane and Mandrake Root,* 53.
3. Weeks, *Medical Discoveries,* 48.
4. Penczak, *Plant Spirit Familiar,* 116.
5. Penczak, *Plant Spirit Familiar,* 79.
6. Weeks, *Medical Discoveries,* 48.
7. Weeks, *Medical Discoveries,* 49.
8. Bach, *Collected Writings,* 99.
9. Bach, *Collected Writings,* 117.
10. Penczak, *Plant Spirit Familiar,* 80.
11. Schulke, *Veneficium,* 9.
12. Ravenwolf, *To Stir a Magick Cauldron,* 224–25.
13. Barnard, *Bach Flower Remedies,* 86.
14. Lilly, *Tree: Essence, Spirit and Teacher,* 41.
15. Lilly, *Tree: Essence, Spirit and Teacher,* 42.
16. Heaven, *Plant Spirit Wisdom,* 15–24.
17. Penczak, *Plant Spirit Familiar,* 127.
18. Tigner, *Canadian Forest Tree Essences,* 1.

CHAPTER 5. MAKING FLOWER ESSENCES

1. Simon Lilly in Titchiner, *New Vibrational Flower Essences of Britain and Ireland,* 83.
2. Dennis, *Orchid Essence Healing,* 10.
3. Tigner, *Canadian Forest Tree Essences,* 19.
4. Singleton, *Wild and Sacred Medicine,* 94.

5. Riparetti, *Bliss and Blessings*, 96.

6. Singleton, *Wild and Sacred Medicine*, 95.

7. Tigner, *Canadian Forest Tree Essences*, 39.

8. Lambert, *Falling Leaf Essences*, 36.

9. Rogers, *Mushroom Essences*, xix.

10. Johnson, *Essence of Healing*, 10.

CHAPTER 6. DECIPHERING THE LANGUAGE OF FLOWERS

1. Barnard, *Bach Flower Remedies*, 315.

2. Chiazzari, *Flower Readings*, 72.

3. Chiazzari, *Flower Readings*, 72.

4. Kaminski, *Flowers That Heal*, 81.

5. Graves, *Language of Plants*, 84.

6. Kaminski, *Flowers That Heal*, 82.

7. Kaminski, *Flowers That Heal*, 81.

8. Kaminski, *Flowers That Heal*, 81.

9. Kaminski, *Flowers That Heal*, 81.

10. Graves, *Language of Plants*, 79.

11. Barnard, *Bach Flower Remedies*, 49.

12. Barnard, *Bach Flower Remedies*, 87.

13. Barnard, *Bach Flower Remedies*, 311.

14. Graves, *Language of Plants*, 112.

15. Kaminski, *Flowers That Heal*, 83.

16. Kaminski, "Extending the Legacy," 24.

17. Graves, *Language of Plants*, 119.

CHAPTER 7. CHOOSING AND USING FLOWER ESSENCES

1. Lilly, *Essence Practitioner*, 43–44.

2. Lilly, *Essence Practitioner*, 49.

3. Lilly, *Essence Practitioner*, 69.

4. Dalton, *Stars of the Meadow*, 16.

5. Lilly, *Essence Practitioner*, 70.

6. Lilly, *Essence Practitioner*, 70.

7. Lilly, *Essence Practitioner*, 71.

8. Gurudas, *Gem Elixirs and Vibrational Healing*, 109.

9. Kaminski, *Flowers That Heal*, 72–73.

10. Kaminski, *Flowers That Heal*, 74.

CHAPTER 8. FLOWER ESSENCES IN MAGICK

1. Penczak, *Plant Spirit Familiar*, 208.

2. Penczak, *Plant Spirit Familiar*, 209.

3. Beyerl, *Compendium of Herbal Magick*, 84.

4. Mankey, *Transformative Witchcraft*, 314–15.

CHAPTER 9. FLOWER ESSENCE FORMULARY

1. Penczak, *Plant Spirit Familiar*, 172.

2. Rätsch, *Dictionary of Sacred and Magical Plants*, 188.

3. Penczak, *Plant Spirit Familiar*, 172.

CHAPTER 10. PLANT SPIRIT ALCHEMY

1. Hughes, *Druid's Handbook*, 25.

2. Graves, *Language of Plants*, 245.

CHAPTER 11. DIRECTORY OF ONE HUNDRED FLOWER ESSENCES

1. Montgomery, *Plant Spirit Healing*, 204.

2. Noriega, *Bach Flower Essences*, 111.

3. Lilly, *Tree: Essence of Healing*, 69.

4. Lilly, *Tree: Essence of Healing*, 71.

5. Montgomery, *Plant Spirit Healing*, 203.

6. Schultes, Hoffman, and Rätsch, *Plants of the Gods*, 64.

7. Schultes, Hoffman, and Rätsch, *Plants of the Gods*, 67.

8. Kaminski and Katz, *Flower Essence Repertory*, 168.

9. Hess, *Flowerevolution*, 167.

10. Stein, *Healing Flowers A–Z*, 35.

11. Stone, *Essential Flower Essence Handbook*, 192.

12. Tigner, *Canadian Forest Tree Essences*, 139.

13. Lilly, *Tree: Essence of Healing*, 77.

14. Boyer, *Under the Witching Tree*, 211.

15. yronwode, *Hoodoo Herb and Root Magic*, 37.

16. Müller-Ebeling, Rätsch, and Storl, *Witchcraft Medicine*, 108.

17. Müller-Ebeling, Rätsch, and Storl, *Witchcraft Medicine*, 109.

18. Chase and Pawlik, *Trees for Healing,* 222.

19. Lilly, *Healing Energies of Trees,* 181.

20. Johnson, *Essence of Healing,* 127.

21. Boyer, *Under the Bramble Arch,* 32.

22. Boyer, *Under the Bramble Arch,* 34.

23. Boyer, *Under the Bramble Arch,* 26.

24. Boyer, *Under the Bramble Arch,* 27.

25. Lilly, *Tree: Essence of Healing,* 93.

26. Lilly, *Tree: Essence of Healing,* 94.

27. Oakley Harrington, *Treadwell's Book of Plant Magic,* 30.

28. Dalton, *Stars of the Meadow,* 13.

29. Harvey, *Practitioner's Encyclopedia,* 134.

30. Riparetti, *Bliss and Blessings,* 187.

31. Albertus Magnus in Beyerl, *Compendium of Herbal Magick,* 239.

32. Oakley Harrington, *Treadwell's Book of Plant Magic,* 81.

33. Kaminski, *Flowers That Heal,* 85.

34. Marquis in Penczak, *Green Lovers,* 120.

35. Schultes, Hoffman, and Rätsch, *Plants of the Gods,* 92.

36. Marquis in Penczak, *Green Lovers,* 119.

37. Müller-Ebeling, Rätsch, and Storl, *Witchcraft Medicine,* 74.

38. Müller-Ebeling, Rätsch, and Storl, *Witchcraft Medicine,* 74.

39. Schultes, Hoffman, and Rätsch, *Plants of the Gods,* 97.

40. Harvey, *Practitioner's Encyclopedia,* 188.

41. Whitehurst, *Magic of Flowers,* 81–82.

42. Beyerl, *Compendium of Herbal Magick,* 129.

43. Oakley Harrington, *Treadwell's Book of Plant Magic,* 41.

44. Johnson, *Essence of Healing,* 161.

45. Gurudas, *Spiritual Properties of Herbs,* 109.

46. Bach, *Collected Writings,* 39.

47. Bach, *Collected Writings,* 64.

48. Kyd, *Plants of Dr Bach,* 105.

49. Mack, *Igniting Soul Fire,* 92.

50. Stein, *Healing Flowers A–Z,* 65–66.

51. Beyerl, *Compendium of Herbal Magick,* 269.

52. Beyerl, *Compendium of Herbal Magick,* 270.

53. Gurudas, *Flower Essences and Vibrational Healing,* 152.

54. yronwode, *Hoodoo Herb and Root Magic,* 80–81.

55. Scherer, *Alchemy of the Desert,* 120.

56. Brannen, *Entering Hekate's Garden,* 120.

57. Scherer, *Alchemy of the Desert,* 251.

58. Stein, *Healing Flowers A–Z,* 36.

59. Penczak, *Plant Spirit Familiar,* 139.

60. Summer Deer, *Wisdom of the Plant Devas,* 72.

61. Scherer, *Alchemy of the Desert,* 251–52.

62. Beyerl, *Compendium of Herbal Magick,* 152.

63. yronwode, *Hoodoo Herb and Root Magic,* 85.

64. Penczak, *Plant Spirit Familiar,* 120.

65. Wright, *Flower Essences,* 33.

66. Cunningham, *Cunningham's Encyclopedia,* 107.

67. Kaminski and Katz, *Flower Essence Repertory,* 204.

68. Altamirano Antenucci, *Essences of Nature,* 15.

69. Guyett, *Sacred Plant Initiations,* 162.

70. Sheehan, *Guide to Green Hope Farm,* 162.

71. Diaz, *Plant Witchery,* 158.

72. Johnson, *Essence of Healing,* 280.

73. Beyerl, *Compendium of Herbal Magick,* 172.

74. Lilly, *Healing Energies of Trees,* 183.

75. Penczak, *Plant Spirit Familiar,* 193.

76. Rogers, *Mushroom Essences,* 136.

77. Rogers, *Mushroom Essences,* 138.

78. Penczak, *Plant Spirit Familiar,* 127.

79. Cunningham, *Cunningham's Encyclopedia,* 119.

80. Gurudas, *Flower Essences and Vibrational Healing,* 158.

81. Kaminski and Katz, *Flower Essence Repertory,* 213.

82. Bach, *Collected Writings,* 38.

83. Barnard, *Bach Flower Remedies,* 146.

84. Barnard, *Bach Flower Remedies,* 146–47.

85. Barnard, *Bach Flower Remedies,* 148.

86. Leigh, *Findhorn Flower Essences,* 62.

87. Lilly, *Tree: Essence of Healing,* 143.

88. Barnard, *Bach Flower Remedies,* 160.

89. Kaminski and Katz, *Flower Essence Repertory,* 219.

90. Cunningham, *Cunningham's Encyclopedia,* 134.

91. Whitehurst, *Magic of Flowers,* 161.

92. Whitehurst, *Magic of Flowers,* 163.

93. Beyerl, *Compendium of Herbal Magic,* 190.

94. Olive, *Flower Essences for Well-Being,* 46.

95. Olive, *Flower Essences for Well-Being,* 64.

96. Draco, *By Wolfsbane & Mandrake Root,* 45.

97. Pettitt, *Energy Medicine,* 112.

98. Rätsch, *Dictionary of Sacred and Magical Plants,* 99.

99. Roth, *Witching Herbs,* 199.

100. Kaminski and Katz, *Flower Essence Repertory,* 220.

101. Hess, *Flowerevolution,* 313.

102. Whitehurst, *Magic of Flowers,* 167.

103. Bach, *Collected Writings,* 42.

104. Bach in Scheffer, *Encyclopedia of Bach Flower Therapy,* 109.

105. Lilly, *Tree: Essence of Healing,* 147.

106. Dalton, *Stars of the Meadow,* 39.

107. Roth, *Witching Herbs,* 117.

108. Kaminski and Katz, *Flower Essence Repertory,* 228.

109. Beyerl, *Compendium of Herbal Magick,* 205.

110. Kaminski and Katz, *Flower Essence Repertory,* 228.

111. Cunningham, *Cunningham's Encyclopedia,* 147.

112. Whitehurst, *Magic of Flowers,* 204.

113. Lilly, *Healing Energies of Trees,* 109.

114. Lilly, *Healing Energies of Trees,* 109.

115. Tigner, *Canadian Forest Tree Essences,* 108.

116. Tigner, *Canadian Forest Tree Essences,* 136.

117. Tigner, *Canadian Forest Tree Essences,* 108.

118. Penczak, *Plant Spirit Familiar,* 118.

119. Kaminski, "Extending the Legacy," 29.

120. Dalton, *Stars of the Meadow,* 50.

121. Leigh, *Findhorn Flower Essences,* 74.

122. Kaminski, "Extending the Legacy," 29.

123. Brannen, *Entering Hekate's Garden,* 144.

124. Gurudas, *Flower Essences and Vibrational Healing,* 165.

125. Olive, *Flower Essences for Well-Being,* 41.

126. yronwode, *Hoodoo Herb and Root Magic,* 121.

127. Harvey, *Practitioner's Encyclopedia,* 262.

128. Whitehurst, *The Magic of Flowers,* 102.

129. Olive, *Flower Essences for Well-Being,* 41.

130. Penczak, *Green Lovers,* 51.

131. Penczak, *Green Lovers,* 52.

132. Dalton, *Stars of the Meadow,* 52.

133. Summer Deer, *Wisdom of the Plant Devas,* 106.

134. Penczak, *Green Lovers,* 55.

135. Cunningham, *Cunningham's Encyclopedia,* 157.

136. Olive, *Flower Essences for Well-Being,* 45.

137. Scherer, *Alchemy of the Desert,* 188.

138. Stein, *Healing Flowers A–Z,* 127.

139. Pettitt, *Energy Medicine,* 94.

140. Sarah Anne Lawless, www.facebook.com/banefolkbotanicals, June 2, 2020, 10:02 a.m.

141. Gurudas, *Flower Essences and Vibrational Healing,* 171.

142. Graves, *Language of Plants,* 76.

143. Kaminski and Katz, *Flower Essence Repertory,* 233

144. Penczak, *Plant Spirit Familiar,* 125.

145. Harvey, *Practitioner's Encyclopedia,* 257.

146. Olive, *Flower Essences for Well-Being,* 43.

147. Grimassi in Penczak, *Green Lovers,* 166.

148. Rätsch, *Dictionary of Sacred and Magical Plants,* 126.

149. Rätsch, *Dictionary of Sacred and Magical Plants,* 126.

150. Müller-Ebeling, Rätsch, and Storl, *Witchcraft Medicine,* 156.

151. Stein, *Healing Flowers A–Z,* 132.

152. Kaminski and Katz, *Flower Essence Repertory,* 241.

153. Roth, *Witching Herbs,* 144–45.

154. Montgomery, *Plant Spirit Healing,* 183.

155. Montgomery, *Plant Spirit Healing,* 184.

156. Scherer, *Alchemy of the Desert,* 210.

157. Kaminski and Katz, *Flower Essence Repertory,* 245.

158. Stein, *Healing Flowers A–Z,* 133.

159. Scherer, *Alchemy of the Desert,* 210.

160. Dalton, *Stars of the Meadow,* 86.

161. Johnson, *Essence of Healing,* 283.

162. Bach, *Collected Writings,* 44.

163. Barnard, *Bach Flower Remedies,* 157.

164. Lilly, *Tree: Essence, Spirit and Teacher,* 316.

165. Lilly, *Tree: Essence, Spirit and Teacher,* 317.
166. Whitehurst, *Magic of Flowers,* 267.
167. Brannen, *Entering Hekate's Garden,* 157.
168. Bach, *Collected Writings,* 39.
169. Weeks, *Medical Discoveries,* 102
170. Lilly, *Healing Energies of Trees,* 151.
171. Harvey, *Practitioner's Encyclopedia,* 216, 247.
172. yronwode, *Hoodoo Herb and Root Magic,* 142.
173. Gurudas, *Flower Essences and Vibrational Healing,* 187.
174. Kaminski and Katz, *Flower Essence Repertory,* 253.
175. Gurudas, *Spiritual Properties of Herbs,* 195.
176. Harvey, *Practitioner's Encyclopedia,* 257.
177. yronwode, *Hoodoo Herb and Root Magic,* 145.
178. Harvey, *Practitioner's Encyclopedia,* 142.
179. Pettitt, *Energy Medicine,* 106.
180. Scherer, *Alchemy of the Desert,* 222.
181. Lilly, *Healing Energies of Trees,* 175
182. Bach, *Collected Writings,* 42.
183. Tigner, *Canadian Forest Tree Essences,* 125.
184. Gurudas, *Flower Essences and Vibrational Healing,* 196.
185. Hess, *Flowerevolution,* 304, and Gurudas, *Flower Essences and Vibrational Healing,* 196.
186. Stein, *Healing Flowers A–Z,* 150.
187. Johnson, *Essence of Healing,* 125.
188. Whitehurst, *Magic of Flowers,* 298.
189. Gregg, *Complete Illustrated Encyclopedia,* 278.
190. Kaminski and Katz, *Flower Essence Repertory,* 262.
191. Sheehan, *Guide to the Green Hope Farm,* 320.
192. Whitehurst, *Magic of Flowers,* 107.
193. Bach, *Collected Writings,* 39.
194. Brannen, *Entering Hekate's Garden,* 175.
195. Pettitt, *Energy Medicine,* 98.
196. Gurudas, *Flower Essences and Vibrational Healing,* 202.
197. Titchiner et al, *New Vibrational Flower Essences of Britain and Ireland,* 206.
198. Lilly, *Healing Energies of Trees,* 173.
199. Penczak, *Plant Spirit Familiar,* 121.

200. Harvey, *Practitioner's Encyclopedia,* 357.
201. Kaminski and Katz, *Flower Essence Repertory,* 270.
202. Gurudas, *Flower Essences and Vibrational Healing,* 203.
203. Scherer, *Alchemy of the Desert,* 255.
204. Kaminski and Katz, *Flower Essence Repertory,* 272.
205. Diaz, *Plant Witchery,* 102.
206. Graves, *Language of Plants,* 225.
207. yronwode, *Hoodoo Herb and Root Magic,* 179.
208. Graves, *Language of Plants,* 173.
209. Dalton, *Stars of the Meadow,* 82.
210. Cunningham, *Cunningham's Encyclopedia,* 234.
211. Gurudas, *Flower Essences and Vibrational Healing,* 126.
212. Penczak, *Temple of Shamanic Witchcraft,* 324.
213. Penczak, *Plant Spirit Familiar,* 137.
214. Kaminski, *Flowers That Heal,* 17.
215. Stein, *Healing Flowers A–Z,* 185.
216. Boyer, *Under the Bramble Arch,* 37.
217. Barnard, *Bach Flower Remedies,* 89.
218. Scherer, *Alchemy of the Desert,* 299.
219. Kaminski and Katz, *Flower Essence Repertory,* 248.
220. Pendell, *Pharmako/Poeia,* 32.
221. yronwode, *Hoodoo Herb and Root Magic,* 199.
222. Kaminski and Katz, *Flower Essence Repertory,* 248.
223. Scherer, *Alchemy of the Desert,* 174.
224. Cunningham, *Cunningham's Encyclopedia,* 246.
225. Stone, *Essential Flower Essence Handbook,* 124.
226. Wright, *Flower Essences,* 46.
227. Graves, *Language of Plants,* 306.
228. yronwode, *Hoodoo Herb and Root Magic,* 189.
229. Montgomery, *Plant Spirit Healing,* 196.
230. Kaminski and Katz, *Flower Essence Repertory,* 290.
231. Bach, *Collected Writings,* 45.
232. Roth, *Witching Herbs,* 127.
233. Kyd, *Plants of Dr Bach,* 85.
234. Roth, *Witching Herbs,* 132.
235. Bach, *Collected Writings,* 66.
236. Gurudas, *Spiritual Properties of Herbs,* 226.

237. Bach, *Collected Writings,* 45.

238. Scherer, *Alchemy of the Desert,* 96–97.

239. Stone, *Essential Flower Essence Handbook,* 248.

240. Pendell, *Pharmak/Poeia,* 58.

241. Rätsch, *Dictionary of Sacred and Magical Plants,* 188.

242. Beyerl, *Compendium of Herbal Magick,* 352.

243. Boyer, *Under the Bramble Arch,* 123.

244. Stein, *Healing Flowers A–Z,* 190.

245. Kaminski, *Flowers That Heal,* 42–44.

246. Whitehurst, *Magic of Flowers,* 280.

247. Bach, *Collected Writings,* 49.

248. Lilly, *Healing Energies of Trees,* 207.

249. Draco, *By Wolfsbane & Mandrake Root,* 61.

250. Lilly, *Healing Energies of Trees,* 221.

251. Dalton, *Stars of the Meadow,* 97.

252. Penczak, *Temple of Shamanic Witchcraft,* 325.

253. Johnson, *Essence of Healing,* 179.

254. Beyerl, *Compendium of Herbal Magick,* 363.

255. Boyer, *Under the Witching Tree,* 81.

256. Bailey, *Handbook of Bailey Flower Essences,* 162.

257. Lily, *Tree: Essence of Healing,* 312.

Bibliography

Altamirano Antenucci, Mary Ann. *Essences of Nature: Botanical Remedies for Growth and Empowerment.* Flagstaff, Ariz.: Light Technology Publishing, 2013.

Bach, Edward. *The Collected Writings of Edward Bach.* Edited by Julian Barnard. London: Ashgrove Publishing, 1999.

Bailey, Arthur. *The Handbook of Bailey Flower Essences.* West Yorkshire, England: Yorkshire Flower Essences Limited, 2020.

Barnard, Julian. *Bach Flower Remedies: Form & Function.* Great Barrington, Mass.: Lindisfarne Books, 2002.

Beyerl, Paul. *A Compendium of Herbal Magick.* Blaine, Wash.: Phoenix Publishing, Inc., 1998.

Boyer, Corinne. *Under the Bramble Arch.* London: Troy Books, 2019.

Boyer, Corinne. *Under the Witching Tree.* London: Troy Books, 2017.

Brannen, Cyndi. *Entering Hekate's Garden: the Magick, Medicine & Mystery of Plant Spirit Witchcraft.* Newburyport, Mass.: Weiser Books, 2020.

Brewer, Gregory Michael. *The Ancient Magick of Trees: Identify & Use Trees in Your Spiritual & Magickal Practice.* Woodbury, Minn.: Llewellyn Publications, 2019.

Chase, Pamela Louise, and Jonathan Pawlik. *Trees for Healing: Harmonizing with Nature for Personal Growth and Planetary Balance.* North Hollywood, Calif.: Newcastle Publishing, 1991.

Chiazzari, Suzy. *Flower Readings.* Saffron Walden, U.K.: C. W. Daniel Company Limited, 2000.

Critchlow, Keith. *The Hidden Geometry of Flowers: Living Rhythms, Form and Number.* Edinburgh, Scotland: Floris Books, 2011.

Cunningham, Donna. *Flower Remedies Workbook: Emotional Healing & Growth with Bach & Other Flower Essences.* New York: Sterling Publishing, 1992.

Cunningham, Scott. *Cunningham's Encyclopedia of Magical Herbs.* St. Paul, Minn.: Llewellyn Publications, 2000.

Dalton, David. *Stars of the Meadow: Exploring Medicinal Herbs as Flower Essences.* Great Barrington, Mass.: Lindisfarne Books, 2013.

Darcey, Cheralyn. *Flowerpaedia: 1000 Flowers and Their Meanings.* Summer Hill, NSW, Australia: Rockpool Publishing, 2017.

Dennis, Don. *Orchid Essence Healing: A Guide to the Living Tree Orchid Essences.* Isle of Gigha, Scotland: International Flower Essence Repertoire, 2010.

Diaz, Juliet. *Plant Witchery.* Carlsbad, Calif.: HayHouse, Inc., 2020.

Draco, Mélusine. *By Wolfsbane & Mandrake Root: The Shadow World of Plants and Their Poisons.* Winchester, U.K.: Moon Books, 2017.

Graves, Julia. *The Language of Plants: A Guide to the Doctrine of Signatures.* Great Barrington, Mass.: Lindisfarne Books, 2012.

Graves, Julia. *The Lily Circle: Practical Guide & Repertory.* Montpelier, Vt.: Green Tara Flower Essences, 2013.

Gregg, Susan. *The Complete Illustrated Encyclopedia of Magical Plants.* Revised edition. Beverly, Mass.: Fair Winds Press, 2014.

Gurudas. *Flower Essences and Vibrational Healing.* San Rafael, Calif.: Cassandra Press, 1989.

Gurudas. *Gem Elixirs and Vibrational Healing.* Vol. 2. San Rafael, Calif.: Cassandra Press, 1986.

Gurudas. *The Spiritual Properties of Herbs.* San Rafael, Calif.: Cassandra Press, 1988.

Guyett, Carole. *Sacred Plant Initiations: Communicating with Plants for Healing and Higher Consciousness.* Rochester, Vt.: Bear & Co., 2015.

Harvey, Clare G. *The Practitioner's Encyclopedia of Flower Remedies.* London: Singing Dragon, 2015.

Heaven, Ross. *Plant Spirit Wisdom: Celtic Healing and the Power of Nature.* Winchester, U.K.: Moon Books, 2008.

Hess, Katie. *Flowerevolution: Blooming into Your Full Potential with the Transformative Power of Flowers.* Carlsbad, Calif.: HayHouse, Inc., 2016.

Hughes, Jon G. *A Druid's Handbook to the Spiritual Power of Plants: Spagyrics in Magical and Sexual Rituals.* Rochester, Vt.: Destiny Books, 2014.

Johnson, Steve. *The Essence of Healing: A Guide to the Alaskan Essences.* Second edition. Homer, Alaska: Alaskan Flower Essence Project, 2000.

Kaminski, Patricia. "Extending the Legacy of Dr. Edward Bach: Flower Essence Therapy in the Twenty-First Century." *Calix: International Journal of Flower Essence Therapy* 2004: 6–31.

Kaminski, Patricia. *Flowers That Heal: How to Use Flower Essences.* Dublin, Ireland: Newleaf, 1998.

Kaminski, Patricia, and Richard Katz. *Flower Essence Repertory: A Comprehensive Guide to the Flower Essences Researched by Dr. Edward Bach and by the Flower Essence Society.* Revised edition. Nevada City, Calif.: Flower Essence Society, 2015.

Kyd, Gwenda. *The Plants of Dr Bach: Molecules, Remedies and Lore.* Cambridge, U.K.: Vervain Publishing, 2018.

Lambert, Grant. *Falling Leaf Essences: Vibrational Remedies Using Autumn Leaves.* Rochester, Vt.: Healing Arts Press, 2002.

Leigh, Marion. *Findhorn Flower Essences Handbook.* Findhorn, Scotland: Nature Spirits Publishing, 2012.

Lilly, Sue. *The Essence Practitioner: Choosing and Using Flower and Other Essences.* London: Singing Dragon, 2015.

Lilly, Sue and Simon. *The Healing Energies of Trees and Their Flower Essences.* Llangammarch Wells, Wales: Tree Seer Publications, 2020.

Lilly, Sue and Simon. *Tree: Essence of Healing.* Berkshire, U.K.: Capall Bann, 1999.

Lilly, Sue and Simon. *Tree: Essence, Spirit and Teacher.* Berkshire, U.K.: Capall Bann, 1999.

Lilly, Sue and Simon. *Tree Seer.* Berkshire, U.K.: Capall Bann, 1999.

Lupa. *Plant and Fungus Totems: Connect with the Spirits of Field, Forest, and Garden.* Woodbury, Minn.: Llewellyn Publications, 2014.

Mack, Gaye. *Igniting Soul Fire: Spiritual Dimensions of the Bach Flower Remedies.* London: Polair Publishing, 2004.

Mankey, Jason. *Transformative Witchcraft: The Greater Mysteries.* Woodbury, Minn.: Llewellyn Publications, 2019.

Montgomery, Pam. *Plant Spirit Healing: A Guide to Working with Plant Consciousness.* Rochester, Vt.: Bear & Company, 2008.

Müller-Ebeling, Claudia, Christian Rätsch, and Wolf-Dieter Storl. *Witchcraft Medicine: Healing Arts, Shamanic Practices, and Forbidden Plants.* Rochester, Vt.: Inner Traditions, 2003.

Noriega, Pablo. *Bach Flower Essences and Chinese Medicine.* Trans. Loey Colebeck. Rochester, Vt.: Healing Arts Press, 2016.

Oakley Harrington, Christina. *The Treadwell's Book of Plant Magic.* London: Treadwells' Books, 2020.

Olive, Barbara. *Flower Essences for Well-Being: Energetic Healing for Health and Harmony.* London: CICO Books, 2018.

Pearson, Nicholas. *Crystal Basics: The Energetic, Healing & Spiritual Powers of 200 Gemstones*. Rochester, Vt.: Destiny Books, 2020.

Penczak, Christopher, ed. *The Green Lovers: A Compilation of Plant Spirit Magic*. Salem, N.H.: Copper Cauldron Publishing, 2012.

Penczak, Christopher. *The Plant Spirit Familiar: Green Totems, Teachers & Healers on the Path of the Witch*. Salem, N.H.: Copper Cauldron Publishing, 2011.

Penczak, Christopher. *The Temple of Shamanic Witchcraft: Shadows, Spirits and the Healing Journey*. Woodbury, Minn.: Llewellyn Publications, 2005.

Pendell, Dale. *Pharmako/Poeia: Plant Powers, Poisons & Herbcraft*. Berkeley, Calif.: North Atlantic Books, 2010.

Pettitt, Sabina. *Energy Medicine: Healing from the Kingdoms of Nature*. Victoria, B.C., Canada: Pacific Essences, 1999.

Pogačnik, Marko. *Nature Spirits & Elemental Beings: Working with the Intelligence in Nature*. Rochester, Vt.: Findhorn Press, 2009.

Rätsch, Christian. *The Dictionary of Sacred and Magical Plants*. Trans. John Baker. Dorset, U.K.: Prism Press, 1992.

Ravenwolf, Silver. *To Stir a Magick Cauldron: A Witch's Guide to Casting and Conjuring*. St. Paul, Minn.: Llewellyn Publications, 1995.

Riparetti, Star. *Bliss and Blessings: The Divine Alchemy of the Star Flower and Gemstone Essences*. Santa Barbara, Calif.: Laughing Star Press, 2003.

Rogers, Robert. *Mushroom Essences: Vibrational Healing from the Kingdom Fungi*. Berkeley, Calif.: North Atlantic Books, 2016.

Roth, Harold. *The Witching Herbs: 13 Essential Plants and Herbs for Your Magical Garden*. Newburyport, Mass.: Weiser Books, 2017.

Scheffer, Mechthild. *The Encyclopedia of Bach Flower Therapy*. Rochester, Vt.: Healing Arts Press, 2001.

Scherer, Cynthia Athina Kemp. *The Alchemy of the Desert: A Comprehensive Guide to Desert Flower Essences for Professional and Self-Help Use*. 4th ed. Tucson, Ariz.: Desert Alchemy Editions, 2020.

Schulke, Daniel. *Veneficium: Magic, Witchcraft and the Poison Path*. Three Hands Press, 2018.

Schultes, Richard Evans, Albert Hoffman, and Christian Rätsch. *Plants of the Gods: Their Sacred, Healing, and Hallucinogenic Powers*. Rochester, Vt.: Healing Arts Press, 2001.

Sheehan, Molly. *A Guide to Green Hope Farm Flower Essences*. Meriden, N.H.: Green Hope Farm, 2012.

Singleton, Rachel. *Wild and Sacred Medicine: The New Lightbringer Essences*

Handbook. Little Langdale, U.K.: Ash Keys Publishing, 2020.

Smith, Heidi. *The Bloom Book: A Flower Essence Guide to Cosmic Balance.* Boulder, Colo.: Sounds True, 2020.

Stein, Diane. *Healing Flowers A–Z.* Twin Lakes, Wisc.: Lotus Press, 2012.

Stone, Lila Devi. *The Essential Flower Essence Handbook.* Nevada City, Calif.: Crystal Clarity Publishers, 2007.

Summer Deer, Thea. *Wisdom of the Plant Devas: Herbal Medicine for a New Earth.* Rochester, Vt.: Bear & Co., 2011.

Szott-Rogers, Laurie, and Robert Rogers. *Prairie Deva Flower Essences.* Edmonton, Alberta, Canada: Prairie Deva Press, 2017.

Thomas, Jamie Lynn. *Cannabis Energy Medicine.* Lakewood, Colo.: CanaEssence, 2016.

Tigner, David. *Canadian Forest Tree Essences: Vibrational Healing through the Natural Resonance of Trees.* Ottawa, Ontario, Canada: Canadian Forest Tree Essences, Inc., 1998.

Titchiner, Rose, et al. *New Vibrational Flower Essences of Britain and Ireland.* Suffolk, U.K.: Waterlily Books, 1997.

Vlamis, Gregory. *Bach Flower Remedies to the Rescue.* Rochester, Vt.: Healing Arts Press, 1990.

Weeks, Nora. *The Medical Discoveries of Edward Bach, Physician.* Saffron Walden, U.K.: C. W. Daniel Company Limited, 1973.

Weeks, Nora, and Victor Bullen. *The Bach Flower Remedies: Illustrations and Preparations.* Saffron Walden, U.K.: C. W. Daniel Company Limited, 1990.

White, Ian. *Australian Bush Flower Essences.* Findhorn, Scotland: Findhorn Press, 1991.

Whitehurst, Tess. *The Magic of Flowers: A Guide to their Metaphysical Uses & Properties.* Woodbury, Minn.: Llewellyn Publications, 2013.

Wood, Matthew. *Vitalism: The History of Herbalism, Homeopathy, and Flower Essences.* Berkeley, Calif.: North Atlantic Books, 2005.

Wright, Machaelle Small. *Flower Essences: Reordering Our Understanding and Approach to Illness and Health.* Jeffersonton, Va.: Perelandra, Ltd., 1988.

Wright, Machaelle Small. *The Perelandra Essences: A Revolution in Our Understanding and Approach to Illness and Health.* Jeffersonton, Va.: Perelandra, Ltd., 2011.

yronwode, catherine. *Hoodoo Herb and Root Magic: A Materia Magica of African-American Conjure.* Forestville, Calif.: Lucky Mojo Curio Company, 2002.

Index of
Flower Essences

Index